THE HELLER COMMITTEE FOR RESEARCH IN SOCIAL ECONOMICS OF THE UNIVERSITY OF CALIFORNIA

Membership in 1938:

EMILY H. HUNTINGTON, *Chairman*
BARBARA NACHTRIEB ARMSTRONG
CHARLES A. GULICK, JR.
ALBERT H. MOWBRAY
JESSICA B. PEIXOTTO
ERNEST F. PENROSE
PAUL S. TAYLOR
MARY GORRINGE LUCK, *Research Associate*

Membership in 1942:

EMILY H. HUNTINGTON, *Chairman*
BARBARA NACHTRIEB ARMSTRONG
MILTON A. CHERNIN
CHARLES A. GULICK, JR.
ALBERT H. MOWBRAY
RUTH OKEY
DOROTHY S. THOMAS
MARY GORRINGE LUCK, *Research Associate*

DOORS TO JOBS

DOORS TO JOBS

A Study of the Organization of the Labor Market in California

By EMILY H. HUNTINGTON

ASSOCIATE PROFESSOR OF ECONOMICS IN
THE UNIVERSITY OF CALIFORNIA

Issued under the Auspices of the Heller Committee for Research in Social Economics of the University of California

UNIVERSITY OF CALIFORNIA PRESS
BERKELEY AND LOS ANGELES · 1942

UNIVERSITY OF CALIFORNIA PRESS
BERKELEY, CALIFORNIA

CAMBRIDGE UNIVERSITY PRESS
LONDON, ENGLAND

Preface

ALTHOUGH the United States has taken pride in its application of scientific principles to the organization of industry, one of the most important and difficult problems—that of bringing together jobs and workers—has been, if not entirely neglected, at least not attacked with the same vigor and determination which have been applied to other problems. This study of the organization of the labor market in California was undertaken for the purpose of determining in how far there are centers for the exchange of jobs and workers, how effectively these agencies function, and what are the hopes for the future. Although the data are geographically limited to California, and thus the analysis applies specifically to that state, it is believed that with certain variations the general picture of the types of agencies now in existence and of the disorganization of the labor market would be true for most other states.

This study was undertaken in 1938, a year in which the problem of unemployment was uppermost in the minds of everyone. There were literally dozens of workers for every job. Employers reported over and over again that "workers come in droves," and workers realized that the first man in line at the factory or farm gate was most likely to get the job. The existence of many agencies through which labor might be marketed showed that there was a need for these organizations, but the fact that in practically no instance had a labor exchange been able to exercise control over a large proportion of the labor market indicated that there was little recognition of the enormous benefits which would result from a well-organized labor market.

The organization of a state-wide system of public employment offices in the period 1935–38 was at least a sign that the government recognized the need for a central marketing place for labor. A variety of factors, however, varying all the way from the state of the labor market to lacks in efficiency and prejudices against the use of any labor exchange, prevented the California State Employment Service from becoming a real factor in the organization of the labor market. Before this study was published, war had changed the condition of the labor market to one in which, in many occupations, jobs were plentiful and workers scarce, and this will undoubtedly be a strong incentive to employers to use the State Employment Service and probably other agencies as well. In March 1941 the State Employment Service reported nearly 30,000 placements, approximately 10,000 more than in the same month of 1940. The State Department of Employment reported that this increase was traceable to greater defense activity and to the general improvement in business conditions. Since the State Employment Service is the logical agency to coördinate, although not to monopolize, activities in the organization of the labor market, it is hoped that it can do a creditable job in the present emergency and that this may be of use in educating employers and workers to recognize the assistance which a public labor exchange can offer in bringing together employers and workers. If it becomes customary to use the State Employment Service when workers are scarce, a new attitude may be carried over into the future and the State Employment Service given an opportunity to act as a coördinating agency in the organization of the market for labor.

The author wishes to express her appreciation to those who assisted in the writing of this book. Special gratitude is due Mrs. Mary Gorringe Luck, Research Associate of the Heller Committee for Research in Social Economics. Mrs. Luck assisted in the planning of the book, in the field work, in editing the manuscript, and is the author of the chapter on labor contractors. Norman Corse, Irving Don Elberson, Hilda Kessler, Robert Muir, and Jessie Schilling interviewed dozens of people from whom the original information was obtained and also assisted in the first organization of some of the materials gathered in the field. Miss Bernice Luckenbaugh, secretary of the Heller Committee for Research in Social Economics, was of great assistance in preparing the final manuscript for publication. It would be impractical and also would not preserve anonymity to list all of the people who coöperated in giving the information on which this study is based. Officials and staff of the California State Employment Service were most generous in their coöperation, as were also other state officials, managers of fee-charging and other types of employment agencies, trade union officials, managers of factories, and farmers.

This study was financed in part by the Rockefeller Foundation, to whom the author wishes to express sincere thanks. Without this grant the study could not have been made. The Heller Committee appropriated an equal sum from funds donated by Mrs. E. S. Heller and by the University.

E. H. H.

Contents

Tables

PAGE

PAGE

I. Introduction

THE PROBLEM

How SHALL I find a job? is a question which occurs again and again during the lives of most of our working population. In spite of the possession of all the virtues of a good employee, vast numbers of our workers frequently find themselves in the position of a job seeker. This is due in part to the nature of our industrial system and in part to the lack of organization of the labor market. In many instances the employer, if he is to make profits, cannot give his employees steady employment. If he is engaged in agriculture, he cannot employ the large number of people required to pick the crop when the seed is germinating, and likewise in many industries the demand for labor is highly seasonal. And again, if a new machine is invented, certain jobs will be outmoded and fewer workers employed. The problem of unemployment rises to its height when a general business depression brings wholesale shutdowns. It is not, however, the purpose of this study to discuss what can and should be done to relieve distress which results from mass unemployment, when obviously the problem is one of relief and not one of bringing the job and the worker together.

Because of a lack of organization of the labor market, when workers are laid off for any one or a combination of the reasons mentioned above, how, where, and when they can find employment is left almost entirely to chance. Thus it is scarcely to be expected that the number of workers of a given skill who turn up at a given time and place will approach the number needed. The hit-and-miss process of job hunting is illustrated by the fact that large pools of labor congregate where they have heard, usually via the grapevine, that jobs are available. News travels fast, and the spectacle is often seen of a thousand workers arriving at a factory gate or in an agricultural community when only a hundred are needed. These people tramp the streets or drive their cars over many miles of highway in search of work, and all but the first comers find a "no help wanted" sign at every gate. Some of these job seekers could find work elsewhere; for others there may be no jobs available; but, whichever is the case, this kind of job hunting is destructive. It results not only in economic loss of shoe leather and gasoline but in human suffering, in competition for jobs and consequent lowering of wage rates and earnings, and in disintegration of work habits. The employer is likewise faced with the problem of getting a given number of workers when and where he needs them. He not unnaturally wants to be certain of an adequate supply of labor. If the supply of labor is undirected, he may not be able to get qualified workers when he needs them; as a result he may lose an order, his crop may spoil, or he may be forced to employ inefficient labor. The employer, under the present condition of disorganization in the labor market, is often confronted with the dilemma of either encouraging a reserve of labor available for occasional employment or of suffering losses due to intermittent labor shortages at a given time and place. It is also frequently to the advantage of the employer to have an excess supply of labor in that it puts him in a better bargaining position. If there are, as has sometimes been said, "two workers for every potato," it will almost certainly be possible to reduce wages; and, if there is a surplus of labor and the workers strike for higher wages, it is probable that there will be plenty of workers who have had scarcely any work for months and who will be willing to take the jobs left vacant by the strikers.

Society as a whole, as well as employers and workers, is concerned with the fact that, in general, mere chance determines whether the worker and the job are brought together. If employers cannot get workers properly qualified for their jobs, costs and prices rise and the whole community suffers. Furthermore, if there are jobs in one place and workers in another, unemployment compensation funds will be depleted and relief costs will rise.

There has never been any real organization of the labor market, that is, a central place or "exchange," such as is found in most commodity markets, where buyers and sellers come together for the mutual advantage of both. Within the network of disorganization in the labor market there have, however, developed certain customs and institutions through which the man in search of a job and the employer in need of workers are brought together. It is the purpose of this study to examine in some detail these customs and institutions with a view to determining their relative importance in the various fields of activity, their interrelationships, wherein there are deficiencies in the placement resources of the community, and the prospects for better organization of the labor market in the near future.

This study was geographically limited to certain areas of California which represented California's most important industries and crops, diversities in the make-up of its population, and many different types of intermediaries between jobs and workers. Although the facts and conclusions specifically apply only to California, some light will be shed on situations and problems which are inherent in our industrial system and therefore are not restricted to the state in which the investigation was made.

The general plan of the study was to visit for a month or longer certain representative areas of California in order to determine what placement resources were available in each of these communities, and to investigate an adequate sample of the more important of these agencies to discover what type of jobs they were filling, how they operated, and how much placement they were actually doing. In addition, a sample of employers was visited in each area as a check on the agencies' report of the extent of their operations and, more important, to determine how the employer and job seeker got together in the very large proportion of placements where no intermediate agency operated. Time and funds did not permit visiting a sample of workers to determine how they set about job hunting. Only problems related to placement in commercial employment were considered to come within the scope of this study; thus any discussion of placement of workers on relief projects, W.P.A., N.Y.A., etc., was omitted from the analysis. The civil service, a source of placement for large numbers of governmental workers, was also excluded, since this would have required an extension of the study beyond the limits set by the funds available. It cannot be claimed that this study is all inclusive. Limitations of time and of funds made it impossible to list every possible type of placement agency in the areas visited; furthermore, it was necessary to limit the number to be studied and the amount of information which could be gathered concerning their activities. It is, however, believed that all of the more important types of intermediaries between job and worker were included in this study and that sufficient evidence was gathered to give a fairly complete picture of the extent to which the labor market in California was organized.

CALIFORNIA—ITS POPULATION, INDUSTRIES, AND CROPS

Since this is a California study, it is important to characterize the state briefly in terms of its population, industries, and crops, that is to say, in terms of who are the job seekers and what jobs they may expect to find. In general, California resembles the major part of the United States in offering employment in both industry and agriculture; and, as in many parts of the country, there is a large seasonal variation in the demand for labor. California also resembles other parts of the United States in that it has a considerable foreign-born white population; but, in addition, there is a large nonwhite population, and in recent years there have been migrations of drought refugees from the Middle West and South.

California's Population.—In 1940 California was the fifth largest state in the union, with a population of 6,907,000. Approximately 60 per cent of this population lived in the two large cities of San Francisco and Los Angeles or in the metropolitan areas surrounding them. Of the population outside the two metropolitan areas, about 60 per cent lived in towns of less than 5,000 or in unincorporated rural areas.[1] The smaller towns and cities of the state are usually centers of agricultural areas.

The population of California is composed to a considerable extent of people who were born in many different countries and who are of a variety of races. Migrations to California have been somewhat different from those to the East and Middle West. Although California has been the final destination for considerable numbers of people of the white races from European countries, it has been the port of entry for large numbers of the nonwhite races from the Orient and from Mexico. In recent years the principal migrations have been of native-born whites from the drought-stricken Middle West.

In 1930[2] nearly 15 per cent of the population of California were foreign-born whites, chiefly from England, Italy, Germany, Russia, and Sweden. Many, before arriving in California, have had work experience elsewhere in the United States, have become partially assimilated, and thus have created no serious social or economic problems. California, like the other states, has had no large additions to its European-born population since the Immigration Law of 1924.

Very important in the economic and social life of California

[1] Because in California there are large numbers of migratory laborers who are never found by the census enumerators, it is probable that the proportion of the population which lived in small towns and rural areas was considerably underestimated.

[2] These data for the 1940 Census had not been published at the time of writing.

is that part of the population which is of the nonwhite races. In 1930, 11 per cent of California's population were classified as nonwhite. Although about half of these were born in the United States, they nevertheless continue to remain groups apart. The largest group of nonwhites in 1930 were the Mexicans, 368,000. There were also considerable numbers of five other races, Japanese, Negroes, Chinese, Filipinos, American Indians, and about 3,000 of various minor races. To a large extent these groups represent a series of labor migrations to California, stimulated first by the needs of gold mining, then by the railroads, and finally by the needs of intensified agriculture.[3] The Chinese came with the gold rush in '49 and were later used extensively in railroad construction and agriculture, but immigration was cut off by the exclusion act in 1882, and today most of the Chinese are found in the cities, particularly San Francisco and Sacramento. They were followed at the end of the 19th century by the Japanese, who completely displaced Chinese labor in agriculture and white labor to a large extent. The importance of the Japanese in California agriculture was greatly decreased by immigration restrictions, by the 1913 law which prohibited selling or leasing land to them, and by the tendency of second-generation Japanese to prefer city to farm labor. By 1930 nearly 30 per cent of the Japanese in California were living in the cities of Los Angeles, San Francisco, and Oakland. From about 1915 the Mexicans began to fill the gap left by the Japanese in the agricultural labor supply, but the great influx of Mexicans occurred between 1920 and 1929, when they became the principal source of farm labor in the state and gained a strong foothold in California industries.[4]

[3] For more complete details on California immigrants see State Relief Administration of California, *Migratory Labor in California*, prepared under the direction of Alma Holzschuh (San Francisco, 1936), from which much of the following information has been taken.

[4] *Mexicans in California*, Report of Governor C. C. Young's Mexican Fact-Finding Committee (San Francisco: California State Printing Office, Oct. 1930), pp. 28, 94, and 171; State Relief Administration of California, *op. cit.*

In 1930, 45 per cent of the Mexicans enumerated in California gave Los Angeles County as their permanent residence. Since 1930 the number of Mexicans admitted has been reduced by stricter administration of the "likely to become a public charge" clause in the immigration law,[5] and the repatriation policy of the Mexican Government has started many Mexicans on their homeward journey, so that the number of Mexicans now in California is probably considerably smaller than in 1930. At about the same time that the stream of Mexican immigration began there was also an influx from the Philippines. In 1922 only 545 Filipinos entered through the ports of San Francisco and Los Angeles, whereas in 1929, 5,795 were admitted. These workers have competed with white labor in the cities in hotel and domestic employments and with Mexicans and other nonwhite races in agriculture in the Sacramento and San Joaquin valleys and in the northern and central coast counties.[6] The number of Filipinos now in California is probably smaller than in 1930 because of immigration quotas established by the Philippine Independence Act of 1935 and because of free repatriation by the Philippine Government. The number of Negroes in California, on the other hand, has probably increased since 1930, because within the last few years considerable numbers have migrated to California from the cotton districts of the South. According to Professor Taylor, "it is possible that Negroes may play an increasingly important role in the future."[7] Until recently about 60 per cent of the Negroes of the state lived in San Francisco, Oakland, and Los Angeles and were employed almost exclusively in various types of restaurant and domestic service and by the Pullman Company.

---

[5] U. S. Bureau of Labor Statistics, *Handbook of Labor Statistics: 1931 Edition*, Bulletin No. 541 (Washington: Government Printing Office, Sept. 1931), p. 281.

[6] For additional information on Filipinos in California see State of California Department of Industrial Relations, *Facts about Filipino Immigration into California*, Special Bulletin No. 3 (San Francisco: California State Printing Office, Apr. 1930).

[7] Paul S. Taylor and Edward J. Rowell, "Refugee Labor Migration to California, 1937," *Monthly Labor Review*, 47 (Aug. 1938), p. 245.

The most recent influx into California has been that of the "dust bowlers," who, in the main, are native whites migrating from the southwestern part of our own country. Hardly had the Mexicans turned their faces towards Mexico when the droughts and dust storms of 1933 to 1936 struck the Great Plains. From 1933 to 1938 streams of stricken people have sought refuge by migrating to other regions. Many of these were truly "drought refugees," but others came because of "the accumulated forces of years of agricultural depression, and now the beginning of mechanization in the Cotton Belt."[8] One of the most important movements in this flight has been to California, where nearly continuous crops of one kind or another offer opportunity to earn something, however little that may be.[9]

Accurate figures as to the magnitude of this most recent migration are not available, but through the efforts of Dr. Paul Taylor a count of "persons in need of manual employment" has been taken at the Plant Quarantine Stations since 1935. Between July 1935 and March 1938, roughly a quarter of a million persons (241,930), usually in family groups, entered California. It is impossible to determine the extent to which this migration has been a net increase in our working or in our total population, but it has probably been of considerable magnitude.[10] Eighty-five per cent of the migrants who where counted at the border came from the so-called "drought states." The largest number, nearly a quarter, gave Oklahoma as their state of origin, 10 per cent gave Texas, 10 per cent Arizona, and 8 per cent Arkansas.[11] Information was not available as to the occupational status of these refugees, but a study of the heads of transient families on relief in Imperial County between 1935 and 1937 revealed in broad outlines the occupational char-

[8] *Ibid.*, p. 240.

[9] Paul S. Taylor and Tom Vasey, "Drought Refugee and Labor Migration to California, June–December 1935," *Monthly Labor Review*, 42 (Feb. 1936), p. 312.

[10] Taylor and Rowell, *op. cit.*, pp. 240–241.

[11] *Ibid.*, p. 242.

acteristics of the migration. Approximately half of those included in this study reported former experience in agriculture, and the remaining 50 per cent had worked in miscellaneous business and industrial activities. It should, however, be pointed out that these figures must be interpreted with caution since the material was drawn from relief families and from only one county.[12]

No statistical data were available to indicate the extent to which the new migrants had sought employment in the cities and on the farms of California. Several months spent in interviewing employers in industry and agriculture in California, however, furnished evidence that the vast majority were seeking employment in agriculture, whatever may have been their past work experience. While city employers occasionally mentioned the "Arkies" and the "Okies" (by which names they characterized all of the new migrants) as having applied for jobs, farmers almost without exception said, "The 'Arkies' and the 'Okies' are arriving in droves; they camp in the ditch banks or on our property in hope of work."

California's Industries.—From 1849 through the 1850's California was chiefly known as a gold-mining state. The growth in population, however, and the availability of land in the fertile valleys soon brought an expansion of agriculture, at first extensive and later, with the development of irrigation, intensive farming. For many decades California was thought of primarily as an agricultural state. This is not surprising in view of the quality of the land available for cultivation and also because, in general, industries move more slowly than does population. Manufacturing in California first developed in those goods necessary to supply consumer needs and in commodities for which raw materials were available locally, such as the canning of fruit, fish, and vegetables. As the population increased there was an expansion of manufacturing into other fields.

[12] *Ibid.*, p. 246.

Transportation costs have, however, been a deterrent to the development of manufacturing in California, and to some degree there has been specialization in products with a high ratio of value to weight which can be transported at a cost which is not so high as to be prohibitive.[13] Certain natural advantages have led to the development of some of California's industries. The discovery of oil has stimulated the growth of plants to construct machinery to be used in oil wells and refineries, and the moving picture and the airplane industries have developed here largely because of the climate.[14]

In 1935 products manufactured in California were valued at 2 billion dollars, and the manufacturing industries employed an average of nearly 250,000 wage earners. The following were the most important manufacturing industries in 1935:[15]

Aircraft	Motion pictures
Bread and bakeries	Motor vehicles
Canning (fish)	Petroleum refining
Canning (fruits and vegetables)	Printing and publishing
Furniture	Railroad repair shops
Lumber	Steel works and rolling mills
Machinery	Tires
Meat packing	Women's clothing

The manufacturing industries of the state are, in the main, concentrated in the San Francisco-Oakland and the Los Angeles industrial areas. However, the centers of several manufacturing industries are found elsewhere. Sacramento has the largest railroad repair shops; fruit and vegetable canning is widely distributed throughout the agricultural districts; and lumbering is concentrated in the northern counties. In general, California's manufacturing is urban in character, not scattered through the rural districts.

The extractive industries have always been important in

[13] G. E. McLaughlin, *Growth of American Manufacturing Areas* (Pittsburgh: University of Pittsburgh, 1938), pp. 211–214.

[14] *Ibid.*, pp. 224–225.

[15] California State Chamber of Commerce, *Economic Survey Report*, Nos. 8 and 10, Series 1937–1938. Mimeographed.

certain areas of California. Petroleum has become the most important of the extractive industries. Los Angeles and Kern Counties are the chief centers for the output of crude oil. Gold is the only metal which is mined in considerable quantities. It is mined chiefly in the northern counties.

Wholesale and retail trade play an important role in California's economic system. Combined sales amounted to 5 billion dollars in 1935, and these establishments employed an average of about 350,000 wage earners. Although wholesale and retail trade is carried on in every district of the state, San Francisco and Los Angeles are the most important centers.

Another industry of importance in California is the transportation industry. For many years this state has been the terminal point for several transcontinental railroads, and a number of railroads have shops at various points which employ considerable groups of workers. Since California is a seacoast state, many of its products are transported by water; thus a large group of workers are employed in the maritime trades.

California's Crops.—Although the value of manufactured products fabricated in California in 1935 was approximately four times the value of its farm products, the fact that 538 million dollars was yielded by farms indicates that agriculture is of enormous importance to the state. In 1936 California's most important farm products in order of their value were livestock, field crops, fruits and nuts, and truck crops.[16]

Field crops	*Fruits and nuts*	*Truck crops*
Hay	Citrus	Lettuce
Cotton	Grapes	Tomatoes
Beans	Peaches	Asparagus
Barley	Prunes	Cantaloupes
Potatoes	Apricots	Peas
Wheat	Walnuts	Celery
Sugar beets	Pears	
Rice		

[16] *Ibid.*, No. 4.

The development of transportation, refrigeration, and irrigation facilities since about 1885 has made California agriculture what it is today.[17] Field crops such as hay and grain, which require little labor, are being displaced by such field crops as cotton, beets, and potatoes and by fruits and vegetables, all of which have a highly seasonal demand for large amounts of hand labor. This is especially noticeable in truck crops, which increased from 3 per cent of the state's total income from crops in 1889 to 20 per cent in 1936.[18]

The crops which in the twentieth century have taken precedence in California agriculture demand large amounts of labor, much of which is highly seasonal and thus must be mobile. There is no reliable count or even estimate of the number of farm laborers in California. In the Census of 1930 about 195,000 farm laborers were enumerated, but this figure is, for reasons already indicated, undoubtedly a serious underestimate for 1938, and there is no way to determine by what amount it should be increased. Various attempts have been made to estimate the demand for "efficient seasonal workers."[19] Professor Taylor and Mr. Rowell have quoted these estimates, which run from about 47,000 in March to 198,000 in September.[20] One estimate has been made of the need for migratory workers, excluding those resident within the county where employed. These figures are 13,000 in January and 49,500 in October.[21] There are no figures available to indicate with exactitude the size of our migratory labor population. Professor Taylor and Mr. Rowell, however, came to the conclusion that from

[17] State Relief Administration of California, *Migratory Labor in California*, pp. 4–8.

[18] *Ibid.*, p. 7. California State Chamber of Commerce, *Economic Survey Report*, No. 4, p. 1.

[19] See especially R. L. Adams, *Seasonal Labor Requirements for California Crops*, Giannini Foundation Bulletin 623 (Berkeley: University of California, July 1938), pp. 22–23.

[20] Paul S. Taylor and Edward J. Rowell, "Patterns of Agricultural Labor Migration within California," *Monthly Labor Review*, 47 (Nov. 1938), p. 980.

[21] State Relief Administration of California, *Migratory Labor in California*, pp. 4–8.

the limited data available there would appear to be no ground for lowering the prevailing estimate of 150,000 men, women, and children who at some time during the year leave their residence, if any, in order to work in the crops. They suggested that the influx of dust-bowl migrants warrants an increase in the estimates but made no attempt to indicate a figure by which the 150,000 should be raised.[22]

[22] Taylor and Rowell, *op. cit.*, p. 981.

II. Method

THE AREAS SELECTED FOR STUDY

IN ORDER TO bring this study within reasonable limits, it was necessary to make a choice as to the areas to be included. In a state as large as California it is difficult to choose a relatively small number of districts which will represent diversities of population, industries, and crops. With these problems in mind the areas chosen were San Francisco; Los Angeles city, with its adjacent urban areas in which certain important industries are located,[1] the citrus belt to the east, and the diversified agricultural region of the San Fernando Valley; Sacramento city, the delta region and Yolo County to the south and west, and Eldorado, Sutter, Yuba, Placer, and Nevada counties, which are adjacent to Sacramento County on the north and east; Bakersfield city, the centers of oil production in the vicinity of Bakersfield and to the west, and the cotton, potato, and grape areas about 30 miles north, south, and west of Bakersfield, all within Kern County; and a grape district in the vicinity of Fresno.[2] Although the study was centered in the districts mentioned above, a few days were spent in Santa Maria and its vicinity, which represents one of the large pea-producing areas of the state, and one day in the Santa Clara Valley to secure some additional information on labor contractors.

It should be pointed out that, although the geographic area of this study may be described in a general way in the above terms, it was not possible to include all the placement resources in each of the areas. In the four chief cities visited all aspects

[1] Huntington Park, Vernon, South Gate, Torrance, Long Beach, El Segundo, Inglewood, Santa Monica, Burbank, Glendale.

[2] In the subsequent discussion the terms Los Angeles, Sacramento, Bakersfield, and Fresno areas will be used when reference is made to these cities and the districts contiguous to them which were visited in the course of the study.

of the problem were studied. The investigation in the smaller cities, towns, and agricultural areas, on the other hand, was concentrated on problems peculiar to them. For instance, Taft in Kern County was visited to secure information regarding employment methods in oil refineries; Inglewood and Santa Monica, only to ascertain employment methods in the aircraft factories.

San Francisco and Los Angeles represent the large metropolitan centers of the state; Sacramento, with a population of 106,000 in 1940, represents the fairly large cities of the state; and Bakersfield, with a population of 29,000, the smaller cities. The areas surrounding the above cities included, for certain aspects of the study, some fairly large population centers; but, with the exception of Los Angeles County, the towns in these districts were either small incorporated places of two to three thousand or smaller and unincorporated, and the major portion of the outlying districts was purely rural.

Since nativity and race are important factors in the labor market of California, it was necessary that the areas chosen represent these population characteristics. All of the important countries of origin of California's foreign-born white population are represented by considerable numbers in San Francisco and in Los Angeles. Both these cities contain a large proportion of the foreign born, whereas in Kern County the proportion is small. The nonwhite races are also adequately represented. The discussion of California as a whole showed that the Chinese, Japanese, and Negroes were largely resident in the metropolitan areas, which were included in the sample visited, and that nearly half the Mexicans of the state reported Los Angeles County as their permanent residence. No information was available on the residence of the Filipino population of the state, but it is a well-known fact that considerable numbers live in Los Angeles, San Francisco, and Sacramento, where they are engaged in domestic and restaurant pursuits. The Mexicans and Filipinos engaged in migratory agricultural labor were well represented in the rural districts visited. The newer group of Negroes engaged in agriculture were found in Kern County. The dust-bowl migrants came into the state chiefly in the extreme south and spread north. Because the sample included rural areas in both the northern and southern portions of the state, a broad view was obtained of the infiltration of this latest wave of migrants.

The sample districts were likewise representative of the major industries of California. Three-quarters of the manufacturing in California was concentrated in the Los Angeles and San Francisco metropolitan areas, and, with the exception of railroad repair shops and lumbering, all of the important manufacturing industries of the state (see p. 10) were represented here. The Sacramento area contained large railroad shops and fruit and vegetable canneries that produced one-third of California's canned goods output.[3] Bakersfield was not a manufacturing center, but it was one of the chief centers for petroleum manufacturing and refining. Over half of the wholesale and retail trade of the state was concentrated in the two metropolitan areas. San Francisco, Los Angeles, and Sacramento were all important railroad centers, and San Francisco and the harbor towns of Los Angeles were the only important commercial shipping ports of the state. The only two important industries inadequately represented in the sample were lumbering and mining. The lumber industry was, in the main, concentrated in northern counties which were excluded from the study, but there were several lumber mills in the vicinity of Placerville which were included as a small sample of the industry. Gold mining was important in only one of the counties (Nevada County) which were included in the sample, and the extent to which it was covered there cannot be considered representative of the whole industry in the state.

[3] Sacramento Chamber of Commerce, *Sacramento Business Barometer* (Feb. 1938), pp. 9–10.

On the whole, the sample districts also represented California's most important crops (see p. 11). The field crops were represented by large acreages of cotton and potatoes in Kern County, sugar beets around Sacramento, and beans in the San Fernando Valley outside Los Angeles. Hay and grains and livestock were produced in each of the agricultural areas visited. The citrus belt east of Los Angeles was included; peaches, pears, prunes, apricots, and almonds were grown in the area around Sacramento; walnuts, around Los Angeles. Truck crops, with the exception of asparagus, were less adequately represented. The Imperial Valley and the coast counties north of Los Angeles, the two most important areas of production of commercial vegetable crops, were omitted from the study because of lack of time and funds. However, almost all of the asparagus acreage of the state lay in the Sacramento delta, some peas and tomatoes were grown around Sacramento and Los Angeles, and Santa Maria was one of the large centers for peas. Three of California's important truck crops—lettuce, cantaloupes, and celery—except for insignificant acreages were not grown in the areas chosen for study.

It is apparent therefore that the sample districts chosen for study represented California with fair adequacy in regard to rural districts and urban centers, type of population, industries, and crops. Since this study is concerned with the mechanics of bringing the job and the worker together, it seems reasonable to assume that areas which included most of the types of workers and of jobs to be found in the state will be representative for our purposes, that is to say, that they will contain examples of all the important placement agencies operating in California. No doubt there were local peculiarities in the type of placement resources available and in their use in some of the areas which were not visited. But the sample studied should give at least the main outlines of the organization of the labor market throughout California.

TECHNIQUES OF INVESTIGATION

Within a labor market characterized by disorganization there are innumerable avenues along which the job hunter and the employer in need of workers may travel in search of a meeting place. Some of these are well-established routes, and others are like a maze in which the meeting of the two is almost entirely a matter of chance. Furthermore, it should be pointed out that the routes between job and worker may be well defined for certain industries, occupations, or groups and ill defined and haphazard for others. A study of placement resources is complicated not only by the fact that the worker may seek a job or the job may seek a worker in many different ways but also by the fact that organization, custom, and prejudice have resulted in the development and more or less habitual use of different methods of bringing the job and the worker together in various spheres of activity.

The first step in this study was to list all known placement resources. The next step was to consult various sources of information in each of the communities included in the study for general information which might bear on the subject under discussion in order to make the list of placement resources as exhaustive as possible and to decide which of these should be included in the sample. Since complete information was not available from any one source, it was necessary to consult a wide variety of agencies and persons, all the way from such organized groups as Chambers of Commerce to a Mexican pool hall and a Filipino grocery store. The following is a list of the chief sources of information, but it should be pointed out that it is not complete, since every person seen in the course of the study was a source of information not only as to his own activities but also as to others within his community.

Government agencies

United States Agricultural Adjustment Administration
United States Bureau of Foreign and Domestic Commerce
Federal-State Crop Reporting Service

State Department of Industrial Relations
Deputy Labor Commissioners
State Department of Immigration and Housing
State Relief Administration
State Employment Service
United States Farm Placement Supervisors attached to State Employment Service

County Agricultural Commissioners
County Farm Advisors

Municipal tax collectors' offices
Municipal police departments

Central social service agencies

Community Chests
Social Service Exchanges
Council of Social Agencies
International Institutes
Travellers' Aid

Organizations of employers

Chambers of Commerce—city and state
Industrial Association
Merchants and Manufacturers' Association
Personnel Managers' Association
Central offices of trade associations in specific industries and crops

Organizations of workers

State Federation of Labor
C.I.O. headquarters
Central Labor Councils
Central union councils within specific trades and industries
Pacific Coast Labor Bureau
Specific unions
California State Nurses' Association
California State Teachers Association

Key men within foreign and racial groups

Heads of associations
Heads of social service agencies
Officials of Chambers of Commerce
Consuls
Managers of foreign language newspapers
Lawyers
Owners of stores

Miscellaneous

Employers with special knowledge of the placement field
University professors with special knowledge in the general field
Better Business Bureau
Newspapers
Classified telephone directory
Academy of Motion Picture Arts and Sciences
Heads of college placement bureaus
Municipal League

From these sources lists were compiled of all the possible placement resources in each community, and a sample was selected for visiting which would include all the important types and the largest and most active agencies, as well as a representation of those smaller ones which served particular groups or occupations.[4] At the same time a list was compiled, based on the same sources of information, of the largest or otherwise most important employers in the principal industries or crops of the area, with a certain representation of the smaller employers also, from which those to be interviewed were selected.

This is not a statistical study, but rather a description, as complete as possible within the financial limits, of the channels from job to worker. Every effort was made not to overlook any important type of placement resource, but it was impossible to get a complete count of the total number of agencies or individuals through whom jobs may be obtained. Furthermore,

[4] For complete details of the agencies included in the sample, see the succeeding chapter.

although an attempt was made to visit only those agencies which functioned in this field, some of those included on the theory that they might do placement work proved to engage in no activity of this kind. These obviously do not represent the total number of such agencies outside the placement field.

With the exception of certain materials from government departments and agencies, this study is based entirely on interviews, and it is important to emphasize the fact that, although the interviews were voluntary, rarely did anyone refuse to give information as to methods of placement. Insofar as governmental agencies were concerned, there was wholehearted coöperation in facilitating the study, and the nongovernmental associations and organizations in most cases were willing to give the necessary information. In one instance the interviewer was catechized for an hour as to his political and economic views. Occasionally an employer from whom an interview was requested was somewhat suspicious of the purposes of the study, but in most cases he could be convinced that no harm could come from a presentation of the facts concerning the methods of bringing together employers and workers. In some instances the task of the interviewer was made easier by letters of introduction, but in most cases coöperation depended on the ability of the interviewer to convince the informant of the merits of the study. It is believed that assurance of anonymity elicited responses which were frank and reliable to the extent of the knowledge of the person interviewed.

The staff consisted of a director and five assistants. There was some division of work in accordance with subject matter. One person did a large part of the research on the California State Employment Service, and two people gathered most of the information on placement by trade unions. No strict lines were drawn, however, and the entire staff in conference and from interviews became familiar with all of the aspects of the study.

Preliminary to the field work, schedules were drawn up. These schedules were tried out and altered in the light of experience, and in certain instances topical outlines were substituted for the more rigid schedules. The schedules and outlines which were used in the study of placement agencies were designed to determine whether placement was the sole or primary function or one of many activities, the number and types of people placed, the kinds of jobs filled, whether or not a fee was charged, and relations with and attitudes towards other placement resources. The employers were asked to list the resources used when a job was to be filled, their attitudes towards various placement resources, and certain supplementary information in regard to types and number of workers.

Since this is not a statistical study, it appeared more important to get side lights and supplementary information when it was available and to make changes in the schedules which were suggested by experience rather than to adopt a hard and fast list of questions. There were certain disadvantages in this method, the chief one being that the same information was not always available for all of those interviewed. Furthermore, it should be mentioned that in many instances check lists of possible answers to questions were not used. The reasons for this were that, in the first place, it was difficult to predetermine all possible answers to certain questions, and, in the second place, it was feared that such lists would put words into the mouth of the person interviewed. For example, although every person interviewed was asked his attitude towards the State Employment Service, the interviewer merely reported the response as given and did not suggest reasons to which the informant might have acquiesced. As a consequence, although this study undoubtedly presents the chief reasons for commendation or criticism of the State Employment Service, it does not represent a complete count of those who might have checked a list of reasons which could have been suggested to them.

In the course of six months, two months of which were spent in San Francisco, two months in Los Angeles, one month in Sacramento, and one month in Bakersfield, approximately 1,100 people were interviewed.[5] Included in this number are those who gave information of a general character, those who assisted in making up lists of placement resources, and all of the agencies and individual employers who were visited. Between 350 and 400 were interviewed in both San Francisco and Los Angeles, about 150 in Sacramento and Bakersfield, nearly 40 in the vicinity of Fresno, and 15 in other districts which were visited for the purpose of securing certain special information. Some of those interviewed, of course, gave more complete data than others, but only 10 refused to give any information. In most cases the interviews were given willingly, and there seldom appeared any desire consciously to misstate facts. Discrepancies in information were checked wherever possible, but it must be recognized that any study based on interviews is subject to certain inaccuracies of memory or of careless statement.

[5] These interviews cannot be distributed among the types of placement resources because in a number of cases one person gave information in regard to several different types of resources, and in some cases agencies themselves fell into several categories. The following chapters, in which the various types of placement resources will be discussed in detail, will indicate the number in each category, the total of which will be larger than the number of interviews.

III. The Placement Resources of the Communities Visited

TYPES OF PLACEMENT RESOURCES

THE WORKER in search of a job and the employer in need of workers are confronted with literally hundreds of placement resources. A preliminary survey of the field yielded a long list of places where labor may be marketed, and from this list a rough classification according to types was made. The classification is as follows:

- I. Governmental Agencies
  - A. Placement primarily
    - (1) California State Employment Service
    - (2) Other
  - B. Relief primarily
  - C. Educational institutions and other types
- II. Nongovernmental Free Agencies
  - A. Social service agencies
  - B. Private trade schools
  - C. Businesses giving service to customers
  - D. Occupational associations
  - E. Fraternal orders and other associations
  - F. Other free agencies
- III. Fee-Charging Employment Agencies
- IV. Labor Contractors
- V. Trade Unions
- VI. Employers' Associations

From the list of placement resources in each community samples were chosen for study. It was impossible in the time available to sample every type of placement service in each of the communities visited. An attempt was made, however, to sample all possible methods of bringing together jobs and workers in

San Francisco, Los Angeles, and Bakersfield. In Sacramento only a few of the most important types were covered; in the districts surrounding Los Angeles, Sacramento, and Bakersfield attention was concentrated on the routes between job and worker in particular industries and crops, and no organized placement services except the California State Employment Service were studied. Because the lists varied in their completeness and the sampling procedure differed with the type of placement resource and with the area, it will be necessary to discuss the sampling method for each type of placement resource.

Governmental Agencies

Placement primarily.—The California State Employment Service is the one state agency whose function is primarily that of placement. At the time this study was initiated in February, and until July 1938, the California State Employment Service was organized on a district basis. There were 15 district offices, 48 branch offices, and several "operating" offices which were set up primarily to take unemployment compensation claims. In July the district organization was abandoned, and each of the district and branch offices became independent offices. In addition, plans had been set up for an itinerant service in 15 of the less heavily populated counties. The administration of the employment service and of unemployment compensation was centralized in the Department of Employment located in Sacramento, the state capital.

It was not within the scope of this study to visit all of the offices of the California State Employment Service, but rather to select a sample within the geographic areas which were centered in San Francisco, Los Angeles, Sacramento, and Bakersfield and to obtain as complete a picture as possible of their activities. Included in the sample were the four offices in the above-named cities; and, because for certain purposes visits were made to Marysville, Santa Barbara, and Santa Maria, these three offices were included, although the analysis of their activities was less complete. In addition, 10 of the 16 offices in Los Angeles County were visited, 3 in the Sacramento area, and 1 itinerant service in Kern County. It is believed that the offices excluded were relatively unimportant from the point of view of placement work in these areas. Certain information was also obtained from the central administrative office in Sacramento. Since, however, this is not a study of the mechanics of administration, the central administrative office was called upon only for information which was related to the placement work of the district and the branch offices.

Los Angeles was the only area in which there was found to be a governmental agency other than the State Employment Service engaged exclusively in placement work. The Los Angeles Board of Supervisors has organized and administers the Labor Coördinating Bureau of Los Angeles County. Since there was only one such agency, it was included in the study, and there was no problem of sampling.

Relief primarily.—In the course of the preliminary investigations comments were frequently heard that various of the governmental relief organizations were engaged in placement of workers in commercial employment. These agencies included the S.R.A., W.P.A., N.Y.A., state camps for single men, and the F.S.A. grant offices. The county relief organizations were excluded from this study because in California they were concerned with granting aid to the unemployable and categorical aid to the aged, the blind, and children, so that their case loads did not represent a placement problem. C.C.C. camps were also excluded on the theory that these camps, located outside the centers of employment, would not be called upon to function as a placement service.[1]

The S.R.A., W.P.A., and N.Y.A. were operating in all of the

[1] Subsequent correspondence suggests that this theory was erroneous. The statement of the Regional Director's office in this respect is included in a later section of this report.

areas visited; the state camps for single men, only in the Sacramento and Los Angeles areas; and the F.S.A. grant program, in the Sacramento and Bakersfield districts. Although it was not possible to visit all of the relief agencies in each of the areas visited, it is believed that a sufficient number were visited to give a fairly complete picture of the activities of these agencies in the placement field.

Educational institutions and other types.—Research indicated that certain governmental agencies which fell outside the categories already discussed had organized some placement work for special groups. The schools, junior colleges, and universities had developed placement services for young people. The Bureau of Vocational Rehabilitation limited its services to the handicapped; the F.S.A. camps, to migratory farm families; and the Indian Bureau, to Indians. It is possible that among the innumerable governmental agencies there may also have been others which did a little informal placement work for special groups. Since, in the course of a careful survey, no others than those mentioned above turned up, it is not likely that any which were omitted were of great importance as regards numbers placed.

In order to secure information concerning the activities of the schools in the placement field, the central school departments were visited in San Francisco, Los Angeles, and Bakersfield and the public vocational training schools in San Francisco and Los Angeles. Junior colleges were included in the San Francisco, Los Angeles, and Bakersfield areas. Two employment departments of universities were included, one in Los Angeles and one at the state university in Berkeley.[2] Although it was impossible to investigate the placement work of all the schools and universities, the sample is probably representative of the way in which educational institutions function in the

[2] Although Berkeley is outside the geographic limits of the study, the employment department of the state university was included because a large number of placements are made in San Francisco and in other areas visited.

placement sphere within the districts visited. A general view of the work of the Bureau of Vocational Rehabilitation was obtained by interviews with an official of this agency in San Francisco and by interviews with officials of affiliated organizations in Los Angeles and Bakersfield. Three of the four F.S.A. camps within the geographic limits of the study were visited. The Indian Bureau was included in Los Angeles, the only place within the geographic areas covered in which this bureau maintained a placement service.

Nongovernmental Free Agencies

Social service agencies.—Many private social service agencies have in the past included job finding for their clients as one of their functions. It might be expected that with the inauguration of the State Employment Service these agencies would refer all of their clients to the state service and thus be relieved of this responsibility. At the time this study was made, however, there were no indications that this transfer had been complete; consequently it was necessary to attempt to determine which of the social service agencies were maintaining placement services. The chief sources of information for lists of these agencies were officials of the Community Chest in San Francisco, Bakersfield, and Sacramento and the Council of Social Agencies in Los Angeles. Other people familiar with the social service agencies in the communities were also consulted, particularly in regard to foreign and nonwhite groups. Although time did not permit an attempt to secure an exhaustive list of all social agencies that might do some placement work, it is probable that there were no important omissions, since the officials of the Community Chests and of the Council of Social Agencies and others who were consulted were familiar with their communities. The Los Angeles list was the most nearly complete, because only here was there available, through the Council of Social Agencies, a complete list of member agencies that did placement work.

In San Francisco 16 social service agencies were visited. From all available information these appeared to be the agencies most likely to do placement work, but it is probable that some of those omitted also functioned in this field. In Los Angeles the 19 social service agencies visited included all of those listed as doing placement work by the Council of Social Agencies and several others suggested by people interviewed in the course of the investigation. In Sacramento the Community Chest stated that all member agencies referred job seekers and employers to the State Employment Service. In Bakersfield two social service agencies were included. The Community Chest suggested only one of its member agencies which might do placement work, and to this was added a Mexican church.

Private trade schools.—There are in many fields of activity private schools which prepare people for vocations and presumably most of them make efforts to place their graduates. Such schools prepare for business and secretarial occupations, for the stage, for hotel service, for barber and beauty shops, for mechanical trades, and for various other types of vocations.[8] These schools were studied only in San Francisco and in Los Angeles, both of which cities are large centers for their activities.

The chief source of information for the lists of schools of the type within the scope of the study was the telephone directory, but this was supplemented by a cursory examination of newspaper advertisements. Nearly 90 such schools were found in San Francisco and more than 150 in Los Angeles.

Within the limitations of this study it was impossible to visit a large number of each type of school. One or two of each of the chief types were selected for study. In the main, the larger schools were included, but where small schools represented a particular problem they also were sampled. An illustration of this was the small, rather select, secretarial school. In

[8] Private schools giving general academic training and those training the self-employed, such as art schools, are excluded from this study.

San Francisco 18 schools,[4] representing all of the important types, were visited. Since time was limited, and since there was a great similarity in the way these schools function in the placement field, a sample of only 10[5] was taken in Los Angeles. Three of these were schools for aircraft mechanics, chosen because of the importance of the airplane industry in Los Angeles, two were large business colleges, four were schools run by business equipment companies, and one was a school for practical nurses.

Businesses giving service to customers.—A considerable number of business organizations have entered the placement field as a service to their customers. In the course of this investigation the most common type of service of this sort was found in typewriter and business machine companies. These companies frequently operate a placement service in order to assist those who have purchased machines in finding competent operators. A variety of other types of businesses have entered this field in order to encourage the use of their commodity by offering an unusual type of service to their customers. Examples of businesses giving this service were a wholesale druggist, a manufacturer of cosmetics, an ambulance company, rooming houses, and retail stores in certain small towns. The chief sources of information as to the placement services described above were the telephone directory and people interviewed who were familiar with their communities. From the telephone directory a list of typewriter and business machine companies was made, including 13 in San Francisco and 11 in Los Angeles.[6] All of these were either visited or called by telephone to request information concerning their placement activities. The list of other types of businesses which have entered the placement field as a service to their customers was not exhaustive. There are undoubtedly many businesses which give this

[4] Seven of these are included in other categories and discussed there.
[5] Five of these are included in other categories and discussed there.
[6] One of each of these totals was a licensed employment agency.

sort of service to their customers which were not found. The subject was not, however, considered of sufficient importance to warrant the expenditure of a great deal of time in an effort to make the list exhaustive. Those studied were therefore merely examples of this type of service: five in San Francisco, three in Los Angeles, four in the Sacramento area, and three in Bakersfield.

Occupational associations.—There were a number of occupational groups, particularly in the professional and clerical fields, in which trade union organization had not developed to any considerable extent. A number of these groups have, however, organized occupational associations. Some are purely social organizations, others serve as a meeting place for exchange of ideas among people engaged in the same occupation, and some have assumed a placement function. It was impossible in the time available to secure an exhaustive list of these associations, because in many instances their organization was so informal that they were not listed in any of the usual sources. The number visited was limited to a small group, five in San Francisco and four in Los Angeles, because it did not appear that their work was of sufficient importance to warrant the time necessary to find the secretaries of large numbers of small associations. Those visited included two state-wide organizations of teachers and nurses and a few local associations merely as examples of the type of placement services they offered.

Fraternal orders and other associations.—In the early stages of this study it was suggested that various nonoccupational associations, such as fraternal orders and associations of veterans and of foreign groups, might engage in placement work. The chief sources of information for lists of these associations were the telephone directory and people interviewed in the course of the investigation, and it was impossible to compile an exhaustive list.

In San Francisco 15 and in Los Angeles 12 fraternal orders

were called on the telephone to determine whether placement of their members or of others was one of their functions. The American Legion was included in San Francisco, Los Angeles, and Bakersfield; and certain associations of the largest foreign groups in the community were included in San Francisco, Sacramento, and Bakersfield. No foreign associations were visited in Los Angeles because an agency familiar with these associations stated that placement was not one of their functions.

Other free agencies.—In the course of interviews with organizations and individuals familiar with the communities visited, it was suggested that there were certain places where employers might go for workers or workers go for free placement other than those already mentioned. In San Francisco three foreign newspapers and one foreign consul were visited. In Los Angeles a street corner used as a meeting place for jobs and workers and in Sacramento a Filipino newspaper and a representative of a foreign consulate were visited.

Fee-charging Employment Agencies.—Perhaps the best-known type of organized employment agency, and certainly the one with the longest history, is the private agency conducted for profit and commonly known as a fee-charging agency. The basic information on these agencies was obtained from the State Department of Industrial Relations, Division of Labor Statistics and Law Enforcement, the department which was responsible for licensing and for securing records of certain of their activities from employment agencies which charge a fee to the person seeking employment. From this office a complete list of employment agencies licensed by the state in San Francisco, Los Angeles, and Sacramento was obtained, and the Deputy Labor Commissioners were interviewed in the two latter cities to secure any additional information which might be available. There were no licensed fee-charging agencies in Bakersfield. There were also some employment agencies which required a fee from the employer instead of from the worker placed, although such agencies are not required to have a state license. In San Francisco and in Los Angeles employment agencies were required to have a city as well as a state license. The departments issuing these licenses were visited and their lists checked against the state list. Every effort was made to find any fee-charging agencies which might be operating without a license. Various sources of information were consulted for this purpose, such as the telephone directory, newspaper advertisements, philanthropic agencies, public employment services, and employers who might use such fee-charging agencies. Only one non-theatrical fee-charging agency which did not have a license was found in the course of this investigation. Although there may have been others, it is almost certain that they would have turned up if they had been doing any considerable amount of business. It is possible that there are a good many theatrical agencies which charge fees and which are not licensed by the state. An indication of this was found in the list of bookers licensed by the American Federation of Musicians. Of 20 appearing in this list in San Francisco, only 9 were identified as having state licenses, and in Los Angeles there were 20 such agencies apparently not licensed by the state. Time did not permit an investigation of these unlicensed agencies.

In San Francisco there were, so far as this investigation was able to determine, 56 fee-charging agencies. Of these, 54 were licensed by the state and 2 were licensed by the city alone. In Los Angeles 301 fee-charging agencies licensed by the state were listed in the course of the study. In addition, 1 Los Angeles agency was visited which charged a fee to applicants but which was not licensed. There were also 6 agencies licensed by the city and not by the state.[7] In Sacramento there were 9 employment agencies licensed by the state; in Bakersfield, none.

[7] These agencies were not included in the total of Los Angeles licensed agencies because they were not visited and it was therefore uncertain as to whether the lack of a state license was a violation of the law or was because they did not charge fees to applicants.

There were certain differences in the types of licensed employment agencies in the three areas included in this study. In San Francisco approximately 25 per cent were classified as commercial and about 15 per cent in each of the three categories of general, oriental, and theatrical. Of the remainder, one specialized in placing in the engineering trades, and the rest operated in several fields. In Los Angeles approximately two-thirds were theatrical agencies, about 6 per cent were commercial, and almost the same number were general agencies. About 2 per cent were in the categories of domestic, nurses, and oriental; the remainder, with the exception of two teachers agencies, made placements in several fields. Of the nine employment agencies in Sacramento, seven were classified as general, one was a theatrical agency, and one was a nurses agency.

The sample of licensed agencies in San Francisco and in Los Angeles, except for theatrical agencies which it was impossible to sample adequately in the latter city, was based on information from the State Department of Industrial Relations. The sampling took into account the type of agency, number of placements, amount of fees collected, number of complaints, and fees refunded. The agencies visited included both large and small offices, with some concentration on those making a considerable number of placements. The sample included those against which applicants had filed complaints and those against which no complaints had been filed, and a representation of agencies in which refunds of fees were respectively small and large proportions of the total fees collected.

Two things precluded the possibility of adequately sampling theatrical agencies in Los Angeles. In the first place, time did not permit sampling a representative group of the very large number of these agencies; in the second place, it was practically impossible to secure a complete list from which to choose a sample because so many of these businesses are fly-by-night affairs. The theatrical agencies visited in Los Angeles were chosen on the advice of people in the community who were familiar with the motion-picture, radio, and theatrical world. Attention was focused on agencies placing considerable numbers rather than on the actors' agent, who perhaps did a very lucrative business but who handled only a small number of clients. The most important agencies in the above-mentionel fields were visited, but it should be pointed out that those visited do not represent the work of theatrical agencies a a whole.

In Sacramento attention was concentrated on general labor agencies, and the two agencies which fell into other categories were omitted.

A total of 66[8] fee-charging agencies were visited in the course of this investigation—19 in San Francisco, 41 in Los Angeles, and 6 in Sacramento. With the exception of the fugitive theatrical agencies in Los Angeles, it is undoubtedly fair to assume that the sample is representative of fee-charging agencies for the state as a whole. San Francisco and Los Angeles are centers of concentration for many different types of fee-charging agencies; Sacramento represents a center in which unskilled labor congregates, and thus the general labor agency flourishes.

Labor Contractors.—Another type of employment agent is the labor contractor, who operates principally in agriculture. He relieves the grower of the responsibility of securing his labor supply. In some instances his only function is to supply labor, but in others he takes over the entire responsibility for harvesting a crop. Frequently the labor contractor has a nucleus of workers who follow him from place to place, but he may supplement his gang from workers in the community.

There are so many gradations within the labor contracting system that it is frequently difficult to determine who really is a labor contractor. A permanent foreman may be the grower's employment agent, but the labor contractor is more commonly thought of as a man seeking an agreement whereby he will fur-

[8] Sixty-four state licensed, one city licensed, one not licensed.

nish labor for a given crop or operation, after which he moves elsewhere. The functions and responsibilities of a labor contractor vary all the way from the temporary boss or foreman, who merely agrees to get a crew together, to the man who contracts to harvest a crop for one or several growers at a given price. In this case he decides the number of workers to be employed, the wages to be paid, and supervises the work, and the workers are his employees rather than the employees of the farmer. Some labor contractors charge a fee to the workers for getting them jobs, some are paid for this work by the employer, and others report that they are paid the same wage as their crew. It is probable that most of these men in some way or other make something in addition to wages. They may get a percentage on provisions purchased from the local store, or they may run a boarding house or commissary on which they make a considerable profit.

If a labor contractor charges a fee to the workers for getting them jobs, he comes within the jurisdiction of the Private Employment Agency Law, and according to this law he must be licensed. The records of the Department of Industrial Relations showed that there were approximately 65 licensed labor contractors in California. Although 11 of these had taken out their licenses in the areas included in this study, it immediately became clear that their addresses were of little use, because contractors move with the crops and frequently have no permanent residence. Therefore the chief source of information as to names of contractors was of necessity employers who used this type of labor agent. Often even these contractors had moved elsewhere and could not be found, although they had been in the community only a few days prior to the visit. Twenty-two labor contractors were interviewed, ranging all the way from the independent entrepreneur to every variety of gang boss. Among those interviewed there were a few with whom, because of language difficulties, the interview was unsatisfactory. In addition, a good deal of secondary information was obtained, from which it will be possible to describe in general terms the position of this type of labor agent in the placement of agricultural workers.

Trade Unions.—From their earliest history trade unions have been a source for the dissemination of information concerning employment opportunities for their members. In some instances there is no formal organization of the placement work, and information is merely spread by word of mouth at meetings; in some, a union secretary devotes all or part of his time to securing jobs for members; in others, there is an organized labor exchange which is usually characterized as a hiring hall.

The first step in this study of the place which has been taken by trade unions in the organization of the labor market was to secure as complete as possible a list of trade unions in the areas visited and then to select a sample of unions which would represent the most important industries and diversities in types of hiring systems. The sample was heavily weighted by unions with large memberships, but smaller organizations were also included if they represented peculiar types of hiring systems or industries of particular importance. The chief sources of information in making up the lists and choosing the sample were the central and local offices of the A.F.L. and the C.I.O., publications of these two organizations, and the offices of the Pacific Coast Labor Bureau.

The offices of 201 trade unions were visited, of which 94 were in San Francisco, 78 in Los Angeles, 21 in Sacramento, 7 in Bakersfield, and 1 in Santa Maria.[9]

The sample of San Francisco unions included the skilled building trades—carpenters, bricklayers, plumbers, etc.,—a large group of unions of maritime workers, such as longshoremen, marine engineers, and seamen, and a number of organiza-

[9] It should be pointed out that these totals include in some cases whole trades or even an entire industry; in others, one local within a trade. Furthermore, some of the unions visited claimed jurisdiction over broad geographic areas.

tions of workers in the food industries, such as bakers, butchers, brewers, and cannery workers. Other industries and trades important in the sample were retail trade, the metal trades, printing and publishing, clothing manufacture, hotels and restaurants, and laundry and dry cleaning. Also represented were building service and hospital employees, teamsters, warehousemen, street-car workers, communications, public utilities, garage men, newspaper and office workers, musicians and other employees in the recreational field, barbers and hairdressers, miscellaneous manufacturing trades, and two unions of specialized workers in agriculture.

In Los Angeles some of the same unions visited in San Francisco were included in the sample for the purpose of determining differences in hiring systems in the two areas, but particular attention was given to securing a sample of unions in industries of special importance in the Los Angeles area. The Los Angeles sample therefore included some representation of most of the general categories of unions which were visited in San Francisco, but emphasis was placed on securing information from unions in the motion-picture and amusement industries and from unions of automobile, tire, aircraft, oil, and furniture workers.

In the Sacramento area the unions visited included a representation of those industries and occupations in which considerable numbers were organized, with particular emphasis on trades and industries of special importance in Sacramento and the surrounding district. Included in the group studied were several unions in the building trades, hotel and restaurant workers, cannery workers, railroad workers, teamsters organizations, and several unions of agricultural workers.

In Bakersfield seven unions were visited which included one building trade and a few other miscellaneous craft unions, one agricultural workers local, and two locals of an oil workers union, which is important because this is the center of the oil industry. Outside the primary areas included in this investigation only one union was studied; this was an organization of agricultural workers in Santa Maria.

The sample of trade unions was not representative of every trade or occupation which was organized, nor can it be claimed that the unions studied represented every conceivable type of placement system. Great care was taken, however, to consult all available sources of information, and it appears safe to assume that the sample was representative of all of the important industries in which trade unions had assumed some responsibility for securing jobs for their members.

Employers' Associations.—Associations of industrial employers have at various times entered the placement field. Some of these organizations have maintained actual employment bureaus, and others have done placement on a more informal scale. There was no one source of information from which a complete list of employers' associations operating in this field could be made, so that it was necessary to consult many community resources and individuals familiar with the work of these associations. The chief sources of information were Chambers of Commerce, the Industrial Asociation, the State Employment Service, and employers who were interviewed with regard to their own hiring methods.

At the outset of the study in San Francisco those who were consulted for general information indicated that employers' associations were not important in the placement field, and these statements were apparently correct. Officials of the State, City, Junior, and Italian Chambers of Commerce, the Industrial Association, and the Master Painters were interviewed; but it was found that the Industrial Association was the only one of these which operated a placement department, and that there was one other, the Italian Chamber of Commerce, which did a little informal placement work. There were, of course, innumerable employers' associations in San Francisco which were not visited. While it is probable that some of these did placement work, it is unlikely that any of those omitted operated on a large scale in this field.

In Los Angeles it appeared that employers' associations were active in employment work. In this city the Chamber of Commerce was visited for general information and to determine whether this organization considered placement to be one of its functions. In addition, 17 other employers' associations were visited. These were chosen on the basis of suggestions from various people that they might have placement departments, but interviews brought to light the fact that approximately half of those visited did no employment work of any sort. In Sacramento and in Bakersfield several employers' associations were visited, but none was found which did placement work.

In the course of this investigation it was found that associations of employers in agriculture sometimes act as an intermediary between the worker seeking employment and the farmer in need of workers. A considerable number of such associations were visited in an attempt to find those which did placement work. Among those included were the Associated Farmers, the Southern California Farm Federation, the Chambers of Commerce in the agricultural areas, the Agricultural Labor Bureau of the San Joaquin Valley, the California Fruit Growers Exchange, the California Fruit Exchange, and many local associations of fruit, nut, vegetable, and cotton growers. Only one of the these, the Labor Bureau of the San Joaquin Valley, had an organized employment department. With this exception, those doing placement work were the local growers associations, acting in an informal way as a source of labor supply for their members, and one Chamber of Commerce in a small town.

Nineteen associations of farmers were visited in the Los Angeles area, 14 in the vicinity of Sacramento, 7 in the Bakersfield district, and 7 in Fresno and the surrounding grape district. These included all of the large central organizations and many small local associations in the crops covered by the study. Although it was not possible to cover all of the local associations, a sufficient number were visited to represent adequately the work of these associations in the placement of agricultural labor.

Secondary Data.—It should be pointed out that in the course of this study a great deal of supplementary information was obtained from secondary sources, and thus certain fields were covered more adequately than the number of interviews would indicate. This secondary information was obtained from people who had special knowledge of a particular type of placement resource or of a certain group of associations or organizations. It was of assistance in supplementing information obtained from primary sources and in ruling out the necessity of interviews with certain agencies which had been suggested as possible placement resources. An example of the former was employers who gave information on the employment methods of the labor contractor; of the latter, a member of a foreign community who stated definitely that none of the organizations within his group was engaged in placement work.

Summary.—In each of the areas there were found to exist numerous placement resources varying all the way from the formal employment agency to the organization which was in no sense an organized placement service, but which occasionally in an informal way acted as an intermediary between job and worker. The State Employment Service was operating in each of the cities visited, and, except in the Bakersfield area, there were branch offices in the surrounding territory. The public schools offered some sort of placement service to their graduates in each of the areas, but this service had been developed much more completely in Los Angeles than in the other cities.

One or another of the governmental relief agencies occasionally did some placement work in each of the districts, but it was only in Los Angeles that a governmental relief agency had set up a formal placement service. Licensed fee-charging agencies were operating in San Francisco, Los Angeles, and Sacramento. In San Francisco and in Los Angeles these agencies were serving many different occupational groups, whereas in Sacramento they were, in the main, general labor agencies. In some instances social service agencies and fraternal orders had entered the placement field. Such organizations were, however, most likely to perform a placement function in the metropolitan centers. Trade schools frequently assisted their graduates in obtaining employment. Although such schools undoubtedly existed in Sacramento and in Bakersfield, they were studied only in San Francisco and in Los Angeles. Another type of placement service was the business which, as a special service to its customers, offered assistance in securing workers or employment. Businesses giving this type of service were found in each of the areas, but a large majority of those studied were in the two metropolitan centers. Industrial employers' associations had quite frequently taken some responsibility for assisting their members in securing workers. Such associations were, of course, concentrated in San Francisco and in Los Angeles, and this study indicates that those in Los Angeles were more active in the placement field. In the agricultural areas the labor contractor frequently acted as an intermediary between job and worker, and it was found that growers associations, packing houses, and cotton gins had become sources of information for workers and for farmers. In addition to the placement resources already mentioned, organizations of workers performed a placement service for their members. The largest group was, of course, the trade unions, whose activities varied all the way from an occasional placement made by a trade union secretary to a highly organized placement service. There were also certain nonunion occupational associations which assisted their members in securing employment. A few of these were studied in San Francisco and in Los Angeles, but undoubtedly such associations existed in the other areas.

The problem of choice among the various placement resources described above may be illustrated by an example of a young person recently graduated from high school with training in one of the clerical occupations. Leaving out of account the possibility of securing a job by direct application, this young person may select one or many of a long list of placement services. He may register at the State Employment Service, at a large number of private fee-charging agencies, at the public school from which he has graduated, at a business school, at several typewriter or business machine companies. His father may be a member of a fraternal order or of some other association which will assist him in his search for work, or, if his family has been on relief, the relief agency may be one which has an employment service. The employer, of course, is also confronted with this network of possibilities, and there is certainly no assurance that his and the boy's choices will be the same. This is the inevitable result of the fact that there is no one central labor market or exchange which is commonly accepted as the place where jobs and workers are brought together.

CLASSIFICATION OF PLACEMENT RESOURCES

Since the purpose of this study was not only to determine the types of placement resources but also to examine their place in the organization of the labor market, it was important to attempt to classify these agencies and associations in accordance with their activity in this field. The best basis for such a classification would have been the number of placements in relation to the demand for each type of worker, but the data necessary for such a classification were not available, and in many instances exact reports as to the number placed could not be obtained. Because of this lack of statistics which could be used to measure activity, other criteria, which were not always satisfactory, had to be used. Furthermore, the same system of classification could not be used for all types of agencies. For this reason trade unions and labor contractors will be discussed in a later section.

Four categories have been used for the purpose of roughly classifying the placement agencies, exclusive of trade unions and labor contractors, in a descending order of their activity. In category I have been placed all of those agencies whose function was solely that of placement work or in which a department was set up definitely for placement work with a full-time person in charge. The next two categories had no full-time person in charge of placement work but registered applicants and jobs. There appeared, however, to be two groups of agencies with this sort of administrative setup—those which solicited business and those which remained passive in respect to bringing together jobs and workers. Category II includes those in this group which solicited business; and category III, those which merely accepted registrations or requests for workers that came to them voluntarily. Category IV includes those organizations and places which served in an informal way for exchange of information in regard to unemployed workers and job openings. These were in no sense organized placement resources, and there was no formal registration of workers or soliciting of business. Examples of those in this category were organizations, such as fraternal orders, which did a little informal placement work and boarding houses for foreign workers.

It was not difficult to determine which were the formal organized placement services to be classified in category I, although not all of these placed considerable numbers of people. The greatest difficulty came in drawing the line between agencies which fell in categories II and III. The distinction was based on solicitation of business, and sometimes it was difficult to determine whether the agency did not solicit business because it was not necessary or because placement work was considered to be only a very minor activity. Undoubtedly some of those in category III which had been in business for years did a considerable business in spite of the fact that they did no soliciting. Category IV was not difficult to distinguish, since these were clearly not in any sense organized placement agencies. The classification must be considered merely as a rough approximation of varying degrees of activity, and too much emphasis must not be placed on the lines of demarcation.

The following table indicates that the placement resources studied included the formal placement agencies and a considerable group of organizations which performed some function in the field of employment, but which varied all the way from those with some sort of definite plan for bringing together employers and workers to informal centers where information was exchanged as to jobs available and workers seeking employment. It should perhaps be reiterated that, with the exception of government agencies engaged primarily in placement work, it was necessary to resort to some sort of sampling procedure, and therefore the agencies visited did not equal the total number in existence.

In the course of this study 236[10] organizations were visited which in some fashion or other assisted in the process of bringing together jobs and workers. Since emphasis was naturally placed on the formal organized placement services, 116, nearly half of those visited, are in category I. In this group are found all of the licensed agencies, the two[11] governmental agencies engaged primarily in placement work, 8 of the 10 employment

[10] Eighteen of these appear under more than one type of employment service. (See footnote § to table 1 for duplications.) In the following analysis the totals quoted include these duplications, amounting in sum, therefore, to more than 236. Labor unions and labor contractors are excluded from this total.

[11] In table 1 each district of the State Employment Service is counted separately.

TABLE 1

PLACEMENT RESOURCES VISITED IN EACH AREA, CLASSIFIED BY TYPE OF AGENCY AND EXTENT OF PLACEMENT WORK*

Type of agency	Extent of placement work†														
	Total—all cities					San Francisco					Los Angeles				
	Total‡	I	II	III	IV	Total‡	I	II	III	IV	Total‡	I	II	III	IV
Total, unduplicated§	236	110	28	49	49	89‖	30	18	24	17	112	70	7	19	16
Total, including duplicates	255	116	31	54	54	96	33	21	25	17	118	73	7	22	16
Government—placement	5	5	..	..	..	1	1	..	..	..	2	2	..	..	..
Government—relief	6	1	1	..	4	2	..	..	..	2	2	1	..	..	1
Government—other	15	8	2	2	3	5	3	2	..	..	5	4	..	1	..
Social service agencies	34	10	4	16	4	14	1	2	10	1	18	9	2	5	2
Fraternal and associations	26	3	..	1	22	13	1	..	..	12	12	2	..	1	9
Trade schools, private	28	7	16	5	..	18	3	13	2	..	10	4	3	3	..
Businesses giving service to customers	34	4	6	21	3	16	2	4	10	..	13	2	..	9	2
Other nongovernmental, free	3	..	..	..	3	2	..	..	..	2	1	..	..	..	1
Fee-charging, licensed	65	65	..	..	..	19	19	..	..	..	40	40	..	..	..
Fee-charging, nonlicensed	1	1	..	..	..	..	..	..	..	..	1	1	..	..	..
Occupational associations	8	4	2	2	..	4	2	..	2	..	4	2	2	..	..
Employers' associations—industry	12	7	..	4	1	2	1	..	1	..	10	6	..	3	1
Employers' associations—agriculture	9	1	..	2	6	..	..	..	..	..	..	..	..	..	..
Employers—industry**	4	..	..	..	4	..	..	..	..	..	..	..	..	..	..
Employers—agriculture**	5	..	..	1	4	..	..	..	..	..	..	..	..	..	..

Type of agency	Extent of placement work†														
	Sacramento					Bakersfield					Fresno				
	Total‡	I	II	III	IV	Total‡	I	II	III	IV	Total‡	I	II	III	IV
Total, unduplicated§	16	7	2	3	4	16	2	1	2	11	3¶	1	..	1	1
Total, including duplicates	19	7	2	4	6	18	2	1	2	13	4	1	..	1	2
Government—placement	1	1	..	..	..	1	1	..	..	..	..	..	..	..	..
Government—relief	1	..	..	..	1	1	..	1	..	..	..	..	..	..	..
Government—other	1	..	..	..	1	4	1	..	1	2	..	..	..	..	..
Social service agencies	1	..	..	1	..	1	..	..	..	1	..	..	..	..	..
Fraternal and associations	..	..	..	..	..	1	..	..	..	1	..	..	..	..	..
Trade schools, private	..	..	..	..	..	..	..	..	..	..	..	..	..	..	..
Businesses giving service to customers	3	..	2	1	..	2	..	..	1	1	..	..	..	..	..
Other nongovernmental, free	..	..	..	..	..	..	..	..	..	..	..	..	..	..	..
Fee-charging, licensed	6	6	..	..	..	..	..	..	..	..	..	..	..	..	..
Fee-charging, nonlicensed	..	..	..	..	..	..	..	..	..	..	..	..	..	..	..
Occupational associations	..	..	..	..	..	..	..	..	..	..	..	..	..	..	..
Employers' associations—industry	..	..	..	..	..	..	..	..	..	..	..	..	..	..	..
Employers' associations—agriculture	3	..	..	1	2	3	..	..	..	3	3	1	..	1	1
Employers—industry**	..	..	..	..	..	4	..	..	..	4	..	..	..	..	..
Employers—agriculture**	3	..	..	1	2	1	..	..	..	1	1	..	..	..	1

* Excludes agencies visited which proved to do no placement work and labor contractors. Unions are also not included in this table. See table 24.

† The categories of degree of placement activity are defined as follows: I. Agencies either solely engaged in placement work or with a separate department for placement work with a full-time person in charge. II. Agencies which may or may not have separate employment departments, but which do not have a full-time person engaged solely in placement work. These agencies take registrations of applicants and vacancies and solicit vacancies when necessary. III. Agencies which may or may not have separate employment departments, have no full-time person engaged solely in employment work, and do no soliciting of business. They take registrations of applicants and vacancies. IV. Not an organized placement agency in any sense but a place where information in regard to unemployed workers and jobs available is passed around or where labor congregates for another purpose and employers can come to hire directly. No formal registration, no soliciting, other than announcement, e.g., at meeting, that workers are available.

‡ Duplications between types of agencies included in all but the first item of this column.

§ 17 agencies appeared as two types and one as three types. These duplications were businesses giving service to customers which also ran a trade school, businesses and trade schools which were licensed as fee-charging agencies, and employers' associations which also operated as employers of labor. There were no duplications between classifications of the extent of placement work.

‖ One trade school counted twice because two separate divisions of placement work.

¶ Does not purport to represent the total of placement agencies in Fresno which might have been visited. Interviews in this area were limited to employers and their associations dealing with grapes.

** These were employers engaged in processing of agricultural products and who also acted as a placement source for agricultural labor.

departments of the schools and colleges visited, a majority of the industrial employers' associations, and half of the nonunion occupational associations. Category II includes agencies which, although they did not have a full-time person in charge of employment work, were definitely organized to perform all of the functions necessary to bring jobs and workers together. In this category there are 31 agencies, which include nearly 60 per cent of the trade schools. Category III is distinguished by the fact that, although applicants and vacancies are registered, there is no solicitation of business. In this group there are 54 agencies, which include a great majority of the social service agencies—except in Los Angeles, where half of these agencies fell in category I. Also in category III are about 60 per cent of the businesses which offered a placement service to their customers. In category IV there are 54 very informal placement resources. Included in this group are all of the F.S.A. camps, all but two of the governmental relief organizations, most of the fraternal orders, most of the agricultural employers' associations, all but one of the individual employers in industry and in agriculture who served as a source of labor supply, and all of the miscellaneous group, such as foreign newspapers.

In summary, it should again be emphasized that the placement resources which have been described, varying all the way from the organized employment agency to the most informal channels of information which guide those seeking employment or workers, do not complete the picture of the alternates available to the job-hunting worker. Almost always he has the option of hawking his own labor at offices or workshops. The following chapters will discuss in more detail the various methods by which labor is bought and sold, the extent to which there are organized centers for the exchange of labor, and in how far the meeting of manpower and job is left wholly, or almost wholly, to chance.

USERS OF PLACEMENT RESOURCES[12]

The employer, whether he is engaged in industry or in agriculture, is the final arbiter as to the methods that will be used in adding to his labor force. It was therefore of importance to interview employers of labor in order to determine just what the employer does when he is in need of workers. Does he use any of the more or less organized placement services? Does he depend on the chance application of the worker who hawks his labor from door to door, or has he developed some system by which he secures direct application by a more or less selected group?

There are many hundreds of individual employers in both industry and agriculture, and it was clearly beyond the scope of this study to secure a list of all employers or even to use any strict sampling procedure in choosing those to be visited. In each of the areas visited an attempt was made to represent the important industries and crops and their processing,[13] that is, those employing large numbers of workers. Emphasis was placed not only on industries and crops employing large numbers of workers but also on large operating units within these categories. Some small firms and farmers with small acreages were also interviewed because of special problems which might be found in their relations with the labor market.

[12] Limitations of time and funds made it impossible to interview a sample of workers to determine the extent to which they made use of the placement resources of the community. The various agencies' claims concerning the extent and type of their activities were therefore checked only against the statements of the sample of employers described here.

[13] The term *processor* will be used to include only those individuals and firms who were not themselves growers. If individuals or firms were engaged in both growing and packing, they were classified as growers. This was necessary because of the difficulties in determining which of a grower's activities are processing and which are agricultural in the more strict sense. Almost all growers do some secondary handling of their crops on the ranch, such as packing cherries or washing potatoes, although this is less true in citrus and in walnuts than in other crops. Therefore any discussion of the way packing-shed labor is employed must include growers as well as firms which do only processing.

In San Francisco 76 employers in industry[14] were visited. Forty-two were engaged in trade, of which 26 were retail establishments—clothing, department, furniture, and variety stores, various types of food stores, and service stations. Nine firms engaged in wholesale trade were visited. Included in this group were drug, drygoods, grocery, liquor, and hardware firms. Banks, insurance companies, and automobile agencies were also represented in the sample of those engaged in trade. Twenty-eight employers engaged in manufacturing and mechanical industries were interviewed, representing principally the clothing, food, paper and printing, and petroleum industries.[15] Other important industries included in the sample were transportation companies, hotels and restaurants, public utilities, fishing and radio broadcasting. The sample of San Francisco firms was heavily weighted by those engaged in trade. An attempt was made to visit one or two firms in the most important manufacturing industries, but it should be pointed out that only one firm in the metal trades was visited.

In the Los Angeles area 74 industrial employers were visited. Fifty-five, nearly three-quarters, were in the manufacturing and mechanical industries representing aircraft, oil machinery, steel fabrication, petroleum, clothing, food, furniture, tires, automobiles, printing and publishing, and building. Thirteen firms engaged in trade were visited, of which two were banks and the remainder were retail establishments—department and variety stores, food stores, mail order houses, and service stations. Also represented in the sample were motion-picture companies, broadcasting companies, restaurants, laundries, and

[14] The term *industry* will be used to include manufacturing, trade, transportation, motion pictures, radio, restaurants, public utilities, extraction of minerals, and forestry; the term *agriculture* will include all operations connected with crop production and certain types of processing which are, in general, sometimes done by the farmer and sometimes by a person who is not a grower. In certain instances the distinction between industry and agriculture is somewhat arbitrary; for instance, fruit and vegetable canning is classified as industry and fruit drying as agriculture.

[15] The petroleum industry in San Francisco is represented by the office staffs of companies engaged in refining.

public utilities. The Los Angeles sample was heavily weighted by manufacturing industries. This was done for two reasons. In the first place, Los Angeles manufactures certain products, such as airplanes, furniture, women's clothing, and refined petroleum, which were produced not at all or only to a limited extent in San Francisco. In the second place, since manufacturing had been slighted in San Francisco, it was important to try to cover this field more adequately in Los Angeles.

In the Sacramento area attention was concentrated on industries of particular importance in that district. Fifteen industrial employers were interviewed, of whom six were canners and two were sugar refiners. One trip was made to a lumbering and one to a gold mining center, but in the time available it was possible to obtain only a very sketchy picture of employment methods in these industries. The remaining industrial employers were manufacturers in the city of Sacramento.

In the Bakersfield area attention was focused primarily on the oil and cotton industries. Thirty-five industrial employers were visited, of which 20 were in some way concerned with the oil industry and 9 were cotton processors. The remaining six included two railroads, a gold mine, a borax company, a cement company, and a winery.[16]

Employers in agriculture were chosen with a view to securing a representation of crops employing a considerable number of workers at certain seasons of the year. For this reason growers of some of the field crops—such as hay, grain, and rice—in which relatively small numbers of workers are employed were excluded, and for the same reason the livestock industry was omitted from the study. With these exceptions, and insofar as was possible within the limits of time and money, an attempt was made to investigate the hiring methods in most of the important crops of California.[17]

[16] Two additional wineries were visited in the Fresno area.

[17] Lettuce, cantaloupes, and celery were not grown in significant amounts in the areas visited; hence, hiring methods in these crops are not covered. (See p. 17.)

In the area surrounding Los Angeles growers of citrus, walnuts, tomatoes, and beans, and processors[18] of citrus and walnuts were interviewed. Ten walnut growers, three tomato, three bean, and two oranges growers were interviewed.[19] In spite of the importance of the citrus crop only a very small number of growers were interviewed, because it was found that all of the harvesting, the only process in which there was a heavy labor requirement, was done by the packing houses; and the grower himself, with the assistance of perhaps a man or two, performed only the tasks necessary to keep the groves in condition. As one packing-house man expressed it, "The less the grower does the better—the trees are better if not given too much attention." Ten citrus-packing houses were visited which handled navel and Valencia oranges, lemons, and grapefruit, and four walnut coöperatives engaged in sorting, grading, shelling, and packing.

In the Sacramento area 29 growers were interviewed, many of whom grew more than one crop. Information was obtained from several growers in each crop as to methods of employment in almonds, apricots, asparagus, beets, cherries, hops, peaches, pears, plums, and prunes. Many of these growers also packed and processed their own and others' crops; but, in addition, seven firms or associations were visited which were engaged in packing asparagus and fruit or in processing dried fruits and nuts.

In the Bakersfield district 64 growers were interviewed; and again, many grew more than one crop. Information was obtained from approximately 50 people who grew cotton, 18 vineyardists, and 13 potato growers. Many of these farmers also did some processing of their crops. Only one processor who was not a grower was visited; this was the manager of a coöperative potato shed.[20]

[18] See footnote 13, p. 49.

[19] One man grew two crops.

[20] Processing of cotton is included in industry.

Three days were spent in Fresno and the surrounding grape area. Twenty-seven grape growers were interviewed to supplement the information in regard to the grape industry in the Kern County area. Three associations were also visited which processed raisins or packed fresh grapes, but which did not grow any fruit.

The sample of employers in industry and in agriculture who were interviewed could not be chosen on the basis of a statistical sampling procedure which would make it possible to state conclusively that those selected were representative of employers as a whole. Furthermore, for certain industries and for some crops it was possible to interview a relatively large number of employers, whereas in others limitations of geography, of time, and of money restricted the interviews to a small number. In spite of the limitations of the sampling procedure, and although there are undoubtedly deviations from the general pattern drawn from the interviews, it is believed that from the 202 industrial employers and the 165 growers and processors of agricultural crops in California it will be possible to describe fairly accurately the general rules which govern the action of the employer in search of workers and his attitudes towards the organized placement services.

IV. California State Employment Service

HISTORY

AMONG THE multiplicity of placement resources which exist in every community there is one, the free public employment service, which by common consent should be the cornerstone for the development of organized methods of bringing workers and jobs together. Although Sir William Beveridge is undoubtedly correct when he says that perfect organization of the labor market is a Utopian dream, it is possible to take steps to establish centers or exchanges which will serve as a common meeting ground for jobs and workers. Only recently, however, have we in the United States become even vaguely aware of the need for orderly machinery for the marketing of labor. We have started to erect the groundwork upon which a superstructure for the organization of the labor market may be built, but it remains for the future to determine the extent and the effectiveness of this organization.

Prior to 1933.—California has at various times, usually in order to meet the exigencies of a particular situation, made sporadic attempts to set up public employment exchanges.[1] In 1868 the city of San Francisco established the California Labor Exchange, which from 1870 to 1872 received some state funds, but which was returned to private support in 1872. For about the next 20 years there were no public employment offices in

[1] For the period prior to 1910 see Lucile Eaves, *A History of California Labor Legislation* (Berkeley: University of California Press, Aug. 1910). For information up to 1924 see Shelby M. Harrison and Associates, *Public Employment Offices* (New York: Russell Sage Foundation, 1924). For later years see Frances Cahn and Valeska Bary, *Welfare Activities of Federal, State, and Local Governments in California, 1850–1934* (Berkeley: University of California Press, 1936).

California. From 1895 to 1913 several bills were introduced in the California Legislature to establish public employment offices. These bills, however, were either not passed or not signed by the Governor because adequate funds were not provided, and the only state support for an employment office came for one year from the regular contingent fund of the California State Bureau of Labor Statistics for an office in San Francisco. Several municipal offices were established in this period, but they were all, with the exception of Los Angeles, discontinued after a short life because of lack of interest and of funds. Labor unions took some part in the establishment of public employment offices in this period; in some instances the trade unions actually organized an employment service which was subsequently taken over by a municipality, and in others the unions contributed to the support of an agency organized by the city.

In 1915 the California Legislature passed a law authorizing the establishment of free employment bureaus. Offices were opened in San Francisco, Sacramento, and Oakland, and a co-operative arrangement was made with a municipal office in Los Angeles. In 1918 the United States Employment Service was created as an independent unit of the Department of Labor, and funds were allocated to the public employment offices in California. In 1919 the state assumed responsibility for the public employment offices but in return for the privilege of franking mail agreed to furnish certain information to the U.S.E.S. Between 1915 and 1931 the public employment offices in California grew very slowly, and by the latter date there were offices in only 11 cities, the four mentioned above and Bakersfield, Berkeley, Fresno, San Bernardino, San Diego, San Jose, and Stockton; and, in addition, temporary employment offices were established each year to place seasonal farm labor. In the period 1916–17 to 1932–33 the offices of the California free employment agencies spent annually sums varying between $34,000 and $105,000, averaging about $81,000. During this period placements averaged about 166,000 a year, but it is significant that during the later years there was a considerable decline in the number of placements. In the year 1931–32 only 80,000 placements were made, whereas in the period from 1918 to 1926 frequently as many as 180,000 placements were made in a year.[2]

In 1931 under the "Doak plan" six federal employment offices were opened in California. These offices were located in cities in which there already existed state employment offices and therefore merely provided a duplicating service. Except for the veterans office in San Francisco and the farm labor office in Los Angeles, these federal offices were discontinued in 1932.

The Wagner-Peyser Act and the National Reëmployment Service.—It is only since 1933 that California has developed a state-wide system of public employment offices. In that year Congress passed the Wagner-Peyser Act, the purpose of which was to promote the establishment of a system of public employment offices by means of grants-in-aid to state employment services which met certain standards set by a reorganized U.S.E.S. The California Legislature did not accept the provisions of the Wagner-Peyser Act until June 1935. In the period from 1933 to 1935 the U.S.E.S. set up 53 federal (N.R.S.) employment bureaus in districts of California not served by existing state employment offices; and, in addition, nearly 300 N.R.S. employees were placed in the state employment offices.[3] These offices were organized by the U.S.E.S. in order to meet its responsibility for recruiting labor for the public works program under the National Industrial Recovery Act and later for the C.W.A. and the W.P.A. The N.R.S. functioned in California from 1933 to 1937 either through independent offices or through contribu-

[2] *Report and Recommendations of the California State Unemployment Commission, November 1932* (Sacramento: California State Printing Office, 1933), p. 790; and typed material furnished by the California State Employment Service.

[3] California State Employment Service, *Manual of Operations* (Nov. 1937), p. xviii. Mimeographed.

tions to state employment offices. Funds were provided by the U.S.E.S., and in some instances cities and counties made additional contributions. By the time this study was undertaken in 1938 the California State Employment Service had taken over the work of the N.R.S., which had closed its offices in California.

The California Unemployment Reserves Act and the C.S.E.S.[4]—In June 1935 the California Unemployment Reserves Act was signed by the Governor. The Unemployment Reserves Commission, the governing body of the newly created Department of Employment, was charged with the responsibility for administering unemployment compensation and for establishing and maintaining a system of public employment agencies, and these agencies were designated as the place where workers applying for unemployment compensation would be required to file their claims when benefits became payable in January 1938. In June 1935 the California public employment service became affiliated with the U.S.E.S., and in June 1936 the Division of State Employment Agencies in the Department of Industrial Relations was transferred to the Department of Employment. Since the transfer the public employment service has been called the California State Employment Service.

Following the affiliation agreement with the U.S.E.S., the C.S.E.S. was organized on a state-wide basis. The state was divided into 15 districts, each with a district office, and by January 1938, 47 branch offices had been opened which served areas contiguous to those in which district offices were located. There were 15 counties in which there was neither a district nor a branch office, and these counties were to be served by means of "itinerant services" which were open on certain days each week. These offices were under the jurisdiction of the district or branch offices. In July 1938 the district organization was abandoned; instead, three administrative regions were set up,

[4] In 1939 the title of the Act was changed to the California Unemployment Insurance Act and the governing head to the California Employment Commission.

and each district and branch office became an independent unit. As of January 1, 1939, there were 70 independent offices of the C.S.E.S. located in 47 of the 58 counties.[5]

Recent Financial History.—The period from 1933–34 to 1937–38 was one of expanding expenditures for the public employment service in California. In 1933–34 a total of about $137,000 was spent, of which $92,000 was received from state funds and about $10,000 from cities and counties, and nearly $36,000 was granted by the U.S.E.S. from N.R.S. funds. In the year 1934–35 expenditures increased to $415,000; and in the two following years, to over $900,000. In each of these three years the state contributed about $90,000. There was some increase in the sums granted by cities and counties, but in the latter two years the major portion of the increased expenditures was borne by the U.S.E.S. In 1937–38 a new source of revenue became available to the C.S.E.S. Plans were inaugurated for the payment of unemployment compensation benefits, and the Social Security Board contributed large sums from funds available for the administration of unemployment compensation. In this year a total of $1,692,000 was spent by the public employment offices in California, of which $842,000 was contributed by the Social Security Board, $541,000 by the U.S.E.S. from Wagner-Peyser and from N.R.S. funds, $300,000 by the state, and only a few thousand dollars by cities and counties.

THE 1938 SAMPLE DATA

Localities and Offices Visited.—In the course of this study 21 offices of the C.S.E.S. were visited, and about 100 people were

[5] On January 1, 1942, after this study was in press, all personnel and facilities of the California State Employment Service were transferred to the United States Employment Service. President Roosevelt and the Governor of California requested this transference because of the importance of a nation-wide unified employment service in a country at war. A coöperative arrangement was established so that unemployment insurance claims will be taken at the offices of the Employment Service, but all determinations as to the validity of claims will continue to be made by the California Department of Employment.

TABLE 2

SOURCE OF FUNDS EXPENDED FOR THE PUBLIC EMPLOYMENT SERVICE IN CALIFORNIA, 1932–33 TO 1937–38

Source of funds	Total	1932–33	1933–34	1934–35	1935–36	1936–37	1937–38
Total public employment service funds	$4,199,726.52	$100,908.00	$137,483.95	$415,109.96	$938,245.94	$916,131.56	$1,691,847.11
Total California State Employment Service funds	3,241,907.01	100,908.00	101,638.00	154,660.00	648,032.77	640,035.23	1,596,633.01
State funds	761,526.00	100,908.00	91,638.00	89,660.00	89,660.00	89,660.00	300,000.00
City and county funds	116,342.84	Not known	10,000.00*	20,000.00	43,493.25	34,027.86	8,821.73
Wagner-Peyser funds	664,772.88	None	None	45,000.00	175,724.04	133,143.25	310,905.59
N.R.S. funds in C.S.E.S. offices	857,328.79	None	None	None	339,155.48	383,204.12	134,969.19
Social Security Board funds	841,936.50	None	None	None	None	None	841,936.50
Total National Reëmployment Service funds	957,819.51	None	35,845.95	260,449.96	290,213.17	276,096.33	95,214.10
N.R.S. funds	621,225.62	None	13,738.94	135,879.03	182,670.71	193,722.84	95,214.10
City and county funds	336,593.89	None	22,107.01	124,570.93	107,542.46	82,373.49	None

SOURCE: Unpublished data from the California State Department of Employment.

* Estimated.

interviewed for the purpose of getting as complete a view as possible of the way in which the Employment Service was functioning as a market for labor. Four of the offices visited, San Francisco, Los Angeles, Sacramento, and Bakersfield, had been in existence before 1933 and until 1936 were affiliated with the Division of State Employment Agencies in the State Department of Industrial Relations; five had been operated as N.R.S. offices from 1933 until 1937 when they became offices of the C.S.E.S. in the State Department of Employment; and 11 were established between 1935 and 1938.

The offices visited included the administrative office in Sacramento, 6 district offices, and 14 branch offices.[6] The district offices were responsible for the work of the branch offices located in contiguous territory.[7] The San Francisco district office was responsible for only the relatively compact territory of San Francisco City and County. The jurisdiction of the Los Angeles office included all of Los Angeles County, in which there were 15 branch offices for whose work the Los Angeles district office was responsible. The Sacramento office was responsible for the work in five counties in which there were three or four branch offices. The Bakersfield office was the only office in Kern County; the Santa Barbara office had jurisdiction over three counties, in each of which there was a branch office; and the Marysville district included seven northern counties, in which there were three branch offices.

[6] List of Offices Visited.

- San Francisco
- Los Angeles area
  - Los Angeles
  - Covina
  - Culver City
  - Hollywood
  - Huntington Park
  - Long Beach
  - Pomona
  - San Fernando
  - San Pedro
  - Van Nuys
  - Whittier
- Sacramento area
  - Sacramento
    - district office
    - administrative office
  - Grass Valley
  - Marysville
  - Placerville
  - Woodland
- Bakersfield
- Other offices
  - Santa Barbara
  - Santa Maria

[7] All of the offices, with the exception of the one in Bakersfield, were visited before the reorganization (described on pp. 57–58) had taken place. Before this reorganization the Bakersfield district office was responsible for Inyo as well as for Kern County.

State-wide Data.—A considerable amount of data concerning the work of the C.S.E.S. throughout the state was obtained from the administrative office in Sacramento. This office was the source of information as to broad principles underlying the work of the C.S.E.S. and was of great assistance in securing statistical data. Members of the staff conferred with the writer, and published as well as unpublished statistics were made available. Much of the material as to procedures, rules, and regulations under which the offices operated was obtained from the *Manual of Operations*. The statistical data were obtained from unpublished sources and from the following publications of the California State Department of Employment: *Operations of Offices, Classified Reports of Applications and Placements, Analysis of Placements by Occupation and Industry, Employment Service Placements by Age Groups, Field Office Activities*. In addition, certain unpublished statistics were obtained from the office of the U.S.E.S. in Washington.

Basis of Appraisal of the Work of the C.S.E.S.—Sufficient data were available to form a basis for an appraisal of the work of the C.S.E.S. throughout the state, although it must be recognized that the analysis is, in the main, based on a sample of offices. It is, however, probably fair to assume that the problems and procedures in the offices visited were, on the whole, similar to those found in offices in other parts of the state.

ADMINISTRATIVE PROBLEMS OF REORGANIZATION AND EXPANSION

Conflicts of Authority.—Although this is not an administrative study, something must be said concerning the administrative setup of the State Department of Employment within which the State Employment Service is a division, because difficulties of an administrative character have affected the work of the Employment Service. The C.S.E.S. offices had certain functions to perform in relation to unemployment compensation in addition to their placement work, and it was obvious that these functions were not independent of one another. Under the administrative setup which existed from 1936, when the Division of State Employment Agencies was transferred to the State Department of Employment, to July 1938, the chief of the Division of Employment Agencies had a direct line of authority over the offices insofar as their placement functions were concerned, and the chief of the Unemployment Compensation Division of the Department of Employment had authority over the work in connection with unemployment compensation. The chief of the Division of Employment Agencies was given power "to coöperate with all the authorities of the United States having powers and duties under said [Wagner-Peyser] act of Congress, and with the approval of the commission, to do and perform all things necessary to secure to this State the benefits of that act of Congress in the promotion and maintenance of a system of public employment offices."[8] This was interpreted to mean that the chief of the Division of State Employment Agencies had the power to sign the agreements with the U.S.E.S., and that he was not directly responsible to the executive direction of the State Department of Employment insofar as his relations with the U.S.E.S. were concerned. The chiefs of the two divisions gave independent orders in regard to personnel, policies, and procedures, and sometimes these orders were in conflict. Obviously this seriously interfered with the over-all job to be done—registration of workers, taking of claims, and placement. In the words of a person thoroughly familiar with the organization, "The present situation [June 1938] is impossible. . . . the executive has been unable to control the situation and they are all at each other's throats."

It became clear to the Unemployment Reserves Commission that there was need for unified control, and that all orders to

[8] California Unemployment Reserves Act, As Amended, 1937 (Sacramento: California State Printing Office, 1938), Art. 7, Sec. 93.

the offices of the C.S.E.S. should be issued by one administrator who should be held responsible for efficient administration of both the employment service and unemployment compensation. In March 1938 the Commission proposed a plan which it hoped would accomplish this purpose, and the new plan was put into effect in July. Under this plan, although the Divisions of Employment Agencies and of Unemployment Compensation were retained, the chiefs of these divisions were no longer permitted to give orders directly to the offices of the C.S.E.S.[9] All orders were required to pass through the hands of the executive director of the State Department of Employment.

Serious objections to this new form of organization were raised at that time by the director of the U.S.E.S., in whose hands rested the decision as to whether federal grants would be made to the C.S.E.S. Early in 1938 he sent a telegram to the Governor of California stating that the Unemployment Reserves Commission was "blocking the employment service," and as late as November 1938 he made the following statements:

> The U.S.E.S. holds that this [the new California plan] is not an employment service plan. . . . The chief of the Division of Employment Agencies cannot go into the local offices. . . . The line of authority is from the executive director [of the Department of Employment] to the manager, all on the payroll of unemployment compensation. . . . The U.S.E.S. has insisted that the managers of these offices must be employment service people, responsible to the objectives, ideals, and purposes of the employment service; and therefore the managers must not be wholly responsible to unemployment compensation administrators nor on unemployment compensation payrolls.[10]

[9] Because the personnel of the administrative staff remained the same, a mere change in administrative procedures apparently did not bring about the desired results. Subsequent to the time this study was made, a new director of the Department of Employment was appointed. The position of chief of the Division of Employment Agencies was abolished, and the responsibility for the duties of this position was taken over by the director. It is not within the scope of this study to discuss the advisability of this procedure. It should, however, be pointed out that the purpose was to coördinate and unify the over-all job to be done by the Department of Employment.

[10] Comments made by F. W. Persons (then Director of the U.S.E.S.) at a meeting to discuss problems of the C.S.E.S., San Francisco, Nov. 26, 1938.

Obviously the director of the U.S.E.S. was concerned with maintaining an employment service, and apparently he did not think that this was possible without giving direct administrative authority to the chief of the Division of Employment Agencies. The Commission, on the other hand, believed that there should be one authority through which the two coördinate functions should be administered. It would appear that the opinion of the Commission was consistent with sound administrative practice.

Relations with Federal Agencies.—Another difficulty of an administrative character should also be mentioned. At the federal level there were two agencies which allocated funds, and which therefore issued orders to the State Department of Employment—the U.S.E.S. in the Department of Labor and the Bureau of Unemployment Compensation in the Social Security Board. The Social Security Board granted funds not only for the central office administration of unemployment compensation but also some funds for local office administration of the Employment Service. The funds granted to the latter were to cover the cost of taking benefit claims and to cover part of the cost of placement activities for workers covered by unemployment compensation, which is, of course, essential to the proper functioning of an unemployment insurance system. Frequent lack of coöperation between the two federal agencies—"part of an old fight between the employment service and the Social Security Board"[11]—naturally translated itself into antagonism within the state.

Farm and Veterans Placement Representatives.—Another complication was the presence of special representatives of the U.S.E.S. within the state office. The U.S.E.S. maintained a representative of its division of Veterans Placement Service in every state, and a representative of its division of Farm Placement Service in states where the agricultural labor problem

[11] Quotation from a person familiar with the situation.

made such a service necessary. California had representatives of both of these divisions. The salaries of these men and of their clerical staff were paid by the U.S.E.S., and they were responsible to the U.S.E.S. and to the chief of the Division of State Employment Agencies. They were attached to the administrative staff of the State Employment Service, and their function was to act as special supervisors of placement of veterans and of agricultural workers in the local offices. The fact that they were responsible to both the federal and the state agencies resulted in difficulties. Orders from the two agencies sometimes were in conflict, and it was not unnatural for these men to consider that their major responsibility was to the U.S.E.S. since they were employed by that office. Another point of view regarding the conflict of authority is illustrated by a quotation from a speech by F. W. Persons (then Director of the U.S.E.S.) on September 24, 1938: "I can give an order to my farm placement representatives, but they are not endowed with the authority to pass the order along. They can't make placements. . . . local personnel do or do not as they choose." Another problem arose out of the fact that the state agency did not have the power to appoint or remove these men, and thus the state administrator did not feel that he had the same authority over the farm placement and veterans' representatives as over other staff members, and there was always a fear of federal interference in the local offices. This California study leads to the same general conclusion as was found in a recent survey in 25 states—that these conditions do not make for the proper integration of veterans and farm placement work with the regular activities of the State Employment Service.[12]

[12] Raymond C. Atkinson, Louise C. Odencrantz, and Ben Deming, *Public Employment Service in the United States* (Chicago: Public Administration Service, 1938), pp. 415–416, 425–426.

Subsequent to the time that this study was made, the California State Department of Employment appointed its own farm placement and veterans' placement supervisors to be responsible for activities throughout the entire state. The appointees of the U.S.E.S. were removed from California, and it has been reported that the difficulties mentioned above have been overcome.

Office Location.—An employment office, like other businesses, must be accessible to its customers. If there is one public employment office for an entire city, it should be located within the main business district. If, on the other hand, there is decentralization based on occupational groups, such as factory, clerical, and agricultural workers, the offices should be located with reference to the requirements of each group. The offices of the C.S.E.S. in urban areas were, in general, in accessible locations, although the need for economy in rental sometimes resulted in an office somewhat distant from the industrial centers of cities. The San Francisco office which included all departments except the commercial was located some distance from the center of the industrial district. Transportation to and from this office was, however, not difficult. In San Francisco and in Los Angeles, where there were separate offices for the clerical department, these offices were housed in office buildings near the commercial center of the city, and in Sacramento there was a separate agricultural office located on a street where it was customary for workers to congregate and for farmers to send trucks to pick up men. In the rural areas the offices of the C.S.E.S. were often located in towns many miles distant from the population they hoped to serve. Except in Los Angeles County there was seldom more than one office in a county, and it was obviously impossible in the large counties of the state for one office to make many agricultural placements. Apparently this problem was not as serious in Sacramento County as in some other areas, since it was customary for both farmers and workers to make Sacramento a meeting place. A quite different situation, however, existed in Kern County, where the Bakersfield office was able to do little in the placement of laborers on farms in the outlying areas. It would certainly not be economical to set up permanent employment offices in large numbers of small communities; but, if the C.S.E.S. is to serve rural areas, it will be necessary to open temporary offices at various points throughout the state at the time when they are needed.

Personnel.—The period between 1935 and 1938, the date when this study began, can be characterized as one of expansion and reorganization of the California State Employment Service involving all of the difficulties of any new organization in a field in which little past experience was available. Many new offices were opened between 1935 and 1938, and it was necessary to employ additional personnel to administer these offices. In October 1937 there was a staff of approximately 350 in the field offices of the free employment service, including the C.S.E.S. and the N.R.S. By January 1938 the number had expanded to nearly 1,100, almost a threefold increase, and in May and December of 1938 there were between 925 and 950 employed in the field offices of the C.S.E.S. throughout the state. Although a considerable group of workers had had some experience in the N.R.S., many were of necessity appointed from the ranks of the untrained.

It was not within the scope of this study to make a thorough and comprehensive study of personnel administration in the State Department of Employment, and no attempt was made to investigate civil service job specifications or examinations. Since, however, the success of an employment service depends so largely on the people responsible for its operation, an effort was made to secure as much information as possible as to personnel practices and problems in the offices visited.

Personnel problems inevitably accompany the rapid expansion of any organization, and the C.S.E.S. was not an exception to this rule. The problems in this field most frequently mentioned by the staff of the Employment Service were the following: the offices were understaffed, the workers were untrained and overworked, the method of efficiency rating was unsatisfactory, the staff was shifted arbitrarily from department to department and even from one city to another, and politics played a considerable part in appointments and in shifts between offices. While it was not possible to check the validity of many of these statements, the fact that they occurred over and over again is probably significant.

The need of a training program was frequently mentioned; but, although the affiliation agreement with the U.S.E.S. specified that a training program should be in operation before April 15, 1936,[18] the development of such a program was hampered by the pressure of work. It was evident in the offices visited that little was being done to instruct new employees in their duties or responsibilities or in the techniques of employment service procedures. A quotation from a person qualified to speak on this subject will serve to summarize the situation: "So far as is known, no field office has carried on a continuous, progressive, and well-coördinated program of training. . . . Such training meetings as are held are usually confined to a rehash of the history of social insurance and theoretical discussions of personnel problems which do not apply to the business of filling jobs. . . . The personnel is not instructed in the technique of straightening out a claim that has become snarled or in taking a job order that is sufficiently clear for intelligent handling."

Observance of the standard 38-hour week was almost unknown in the offices of the C.S.E.S. during the early months of 1938. In some offices overtime was rotated, while in others the entire staff worked until 11 o'clock almost every night for the three months during which unemployment compensation claims procedure was getting under way.

Another personnel practice which caused discontent was related to the method of efficiency rating. The central administrative office required that all employees should be given an efficiency rating based on attendance and on quality and quantity of work. An employee with an efficiency rating lower than

[18] For a discussion of the subject of training see Atkinson, Odencrantz, and Deming, *Public Employment Service in the United States,* pp. 176–196.

85 per cent was not permitted to take promotional examinations; and, if the rating was below 70 per cent, a charge of inefficiency could be filed and the employee could be demoted or removed from civil service.[14] The statement was frequently made that supervisors were instructed to give only a few ratings as high as 85 per cent, and that in some instances supervisors' ratings were arbitrarily lowered by higher authorities. Obviously such an arbitrary ruling was not designed to stimulate efficiency.

Another criticism which frequently occurred was that there were many shifts in staff which were not related to the needs of a department or of an office. As a long-range policy it may be advisable for certain members of the staff to be familiar with all aspects of the work. When, however, an office is in the process of being organized, and when no one is thoroughly familiar with any phase of the work, confusion and dissatisfaction are bound to result if the manager makes arbitrary shifts, if the head of a department does not know from day to day who is on his staff, and if employers must explain their needs to a different person every time they call. In one of the larger offices in which the manager definitely held the theory that employees must be shifted so that they would have a comprehensive picture of the way the service operated, it was reported that there was a 500 per cent turnover in the staff of one department between October 1937 and March 1938.

While many of the shifts in personnel were probably unavoidable, they did not make for smooth administration, and there was a general feeling that some of the shifts both within and between offices were not for the good of the service. It was fairly frequently stated that "politics," sometimes internal and sometimes state-wide, played a part in appointments and in transfers or attempted transfers, particularly from the larger

[14] California State Personnel Board, *Laws and Rules Governing the California State Civil Service* (rev. ed.; Sacramento: California State Printing Office, July 1, 1940), pp. 43, 49, and 50.

cities to more remote communities. The following statements made by a staff member are illustrative of this problem:

> The administration is out to get me. They have tried to transfer me to El Centro and to several other places, but I know my rights and so far they have not been successful.
>
> There are many cases of the appointment of relatives of those on the administrative staff, persons who have been appointed not because of their qualifications but because of "influence."

In spite of the existence of many problems of personnel administration which caused dissatisfaction and discouragement and in some instances resignation, the general impression gained from the offices visited was of a staff interested in their work and loyal to the service, but sometimes baffled by the complexities of the situation and impatient with the inefficiencies of the administration.

With time and sufficient finances it should be possible to staff the offices with competent and adequately trained personnel. If the morale of the staff is to be maintained, there must be developed a less arbitrary system of efficiency rating, shifts within or between offices must be based on the needs of the jobs to be done and on the efficiency of the worker to perform the task, and there must be established a consistent policy of appointments and promotions free from political influence.

Statistical Reporting.—The offices of a public employment service should be the source of statistics which are essential for efficient administration and which would be useful for an analysis of the labor market. As long as all workers are not registered at the public employment offices, the data for the analysis of the labor market will be incomplete. Since the inauguration of unemployment compensation, however, large numbers of workers have been required to register at the C.S.E.S., and thus an analysis of the conditions of the labor market based on registrants at the C.S.E.S. would at least be applicable to a large cross section of the unemployed. An analysis of the Employment

Service statistics available at the time this study was made will be found in the Appendix. Both the California and the United States Employment Services have published vast quantities of statistical data. There appeared to be a number of deficiencies in these employment service statistics. There were in several instances inaccuracies in reporting; there was no attempt to analyze or interpret the material to make it usable for the busy administrator or for the labor market analyst, and certain important tabulations were not always currently available—for instance, such breakdowns as industry and occupation of workers who registered at the C.S.E.S. and statistics as to employers' orders. Statistical reporting was looked upon as mere paper work, and there was almost no recognition of its importance in the operation of employment offices or of the fact that employment service statistics, while not furnishing a complete picture of the labor market, could provide valuable data as to employment and unemployment, at least insofar as workers covered by unemployment compensation were concerned.

Effect of Registration for Unemployment Compensation.—During 1938 the most serious problems which confronted the C.S.E.S. were related to its responsibility for registering claimants for unemployment compensation benefits. A test of availability for work is essential to the protection of the unemployment compensation funds, and it is universally agreed that the public employment office is the place where this test should be applied, so that if work is available it can be offered to the claimant. From January 1938 the C.S.E.S. was faced with the responsibility of taking thousands of claims and of registering the claimants for placements. Adequate preparations had not been made to handle this burden. The offices were short of personnel, the available staff was overworked and untrained, procedures were complicated, and in every office there were long lines of people waiting hour after hour to register for jobs and to file their claims. The pressure of work in the offices was terrific, and even with long hours of overtime it was impossible to take registrations and claims with sufficient care to insure accuracy. It was impossible to conduct careful interviews on the basis of which proper selection of workers to be placed could be made; and, since the entire force was required to devote much of its time to registration of claimants for unemployment compensation benefits, other activities were neglected. There was no time for contacts with employers, for proper classification of workers, for accurate statistical reporting, for gathering information concerning the industries and occupations of importance in the various communities, or for proper selection of applicants to be referred to jobs, and employers who tried to use the C.S.E.S. were discouraged by what they saw or heard of the confusion in the offices. Although in 1938 the Employment Service was swamped with work connected with unemployment compensation, and placement activities were to a large extent neglected, it should be pointed out that in this year there was a business recession and jobs were necessarily scarce. This will, however, inevitably be the situation whenever the number of unemployment compensation claims is large, and it is important that in the future plans be laid to carry changing loads of work in various departments, for an orderly transfer of employees from placement to claims taking and vice versa, without the disruption of the placement function which occurred during the early months of 1938.

APPLICANTS FOR JOBS

If an employment service is to perform the function of a market place where labor and jobs are to be exchanged, it must have available both sellers and buyers. The quantity and quality of workers and of job orders are the limiting factors in placements. This section will be limited to a discussion of registration of applicants for jobs. Several questions will be raised. How are the applicants registered? How many? What types of persons are registered?

Procedures.—An applicant who comes to an office of the C.S.E.S. should be quickly and courteously directed to the department which can serve him best. It has already been pointed out that, at the time this study was made, in the larger and more congested offices the facilities for routing of applicants were inadequate. Thus in many instances by the time the worker finally reached an interviewer he was discouraged, if not disgusted. By the end of 1938 the congestion in the offices had to a large extent been overcome, and it is at least possible that the facilities for reception and for routing were more adequate. In one office which was revisited early in 1939 it was, however, still necessary for an applicant to depend upon signs which directed him up long flights of stairs and down dreary halls.

When the applicant reached an interviewer, a registration card was made out for the purpose of obtaining the facts which would be useful in placement. These forms, if filled out properly, were considered fairly adequate for the purpose, although they have been the subject of some criticisms. Some interviewers expressed the opinion that sufficient space was not allowed for previous work history. Only three previous employers could be entered on the card, and it was pointed out that, particularly in the case of a person who had had irregular employment for some time, the information might not be adequate for placement purposes. It would appear, however, that, if the interviewer followed instructions to enter those jobs which represented the most significant work experience of the applicant, and if the occupational and industrial classifications were properly entered, the space was adequate. The card used in the technical and professional departments met with some disapproval. The head of a commercial department was of the opinion that sufficient space was not allowed for the special skills of applicants for commercial employment, and that the card should contain a check list of machines which the applicant could operate. In one of the offices visited an interviewer in charge of registration of agricultural workers believed that the card used for these workers was more elaborate than was necessary. He reported that in many instances workers were placed out of his office on jobs which had to be filled immediately, and no registration cards were made out for them. It was suggested in the handbook for farm placement supervisors that the registration blank be made out in skeleton form, filling in only those items which were important for this group of workers. It was also suggested that there was nothing to be gained from registering migratory workers who stopped at an office to inquire about work, but who would be gone from the vicinity by the end of the day, and frequently had no permanent address. If these workers were registered, the result would be an active file which would be largely useless from the point of view of placement. A special card in use in the Junior Department was also subject to criticism in that it contained irrelevant information, such as number of brothers and sisters, and because it was a double card, which was awkward to handle and to file.

Secondary cards were provided for the purpose of giving workers skilled in several occupations and juniors with previous work experience opportunities for consideration by placement officers in more than one occupation. Actually, during 1938, because of the pressure of work, secondary cards were seldom used except in the case of juniors in those offices which had separate junior departments and in cases where a worker was registered in a branch office and wished to be placed in the area covered by the district office. This lack of secondary classification might seriously interfere with the quality of service to both worker and employer, particularly in the large offices where it would be quite impossible to look through large numbers of cards for possible secondary occupations.

It should be remembered that the registration card is merely a tool for the interviewer, and that the real test is the skill of the interviewer, not only in securing standardized information which should be available for every applicant, but also in getting other relevant information which will assist in determining the applicant's special qualifications or disabilities.

After an applicant was registered at the C.S.E.S., his card went to the statistical department or clerk and then was placed in the active file. In the larger offices it was reported that this processing took several days, during which time the applicant could not be considered for placement. In some departments the interviewer made out a 3 by 5 card for the more promising applicants and thus overcame delay for this group. This was, however, not an established practice, and whether or not it was done was determined by department heads or individual placement officers.

When the cards were placed in the active file they were classified by sex and by occupation according to a classification set up by the U.S.E.S. The occupational classification is the cornerstone on which placement rests. The comment was frequently made that untrained and overworked interviewers frequently entered wrong classifications, which seriously interfered with the usefulness of the files for placement purposes as well as for any statistical analysis of the occupations represented by those registered.

Until March 1938 S.R.A. and W.P.A. registrants were separated from nonrelief applicants. In February 1938 a bulletin was issued by the U.S.E.S. instructing the C.S.E.S. to abolish the separation of relief from nonrelief registrants, and in March a bulletin to this effect was issued by the Sacramento administrative office of the C.S.E.S. In the summer of 1938 most of the offices visited no longer filed relief and nonrelief applicants separately. There were, however, certain exceptions to this. In one of the departments of a large office this separation was still maintained, and in another department, although the cards were not filed separately, they were marked with an "R." The reason for these separations, in the words of the persons interviewed, was that "relief clients are hard to place."

The active file is the source material for placement officers. It should also serve as a basis for administrative policy and planning; and, in addition, it should yield valuable information as to the unemployed population. This latter function can, however, be served only in a very rough way. Since registration is not compulsory for all unemployed workers, the active file will not give the total number of persons unemployed nor an accurate picture of the characteristics of the unemployed population as a whole. Compulsory registration of those applying for unemployment compensation will, however, result in an active file which is representative of fluctuations in the amount of unemployment and of the characteristics of a large group of the unemployed.[15]

The usefulness of the active file depends on the extent to which it is kept up to date. If it is full of "deadwood"—people who for one reason or another are no longer seeking work—it will be of little use to the placement officer or as a source of information as to the unemployed population. The *Manual of Operations* in California at the time this study was made required that the files of nonrelief registrants be cleared monthly, and that all cards not renewed within 30 days should be removed to the inactive file. Since the files were cleared at a given date, the cards of those who registered immediately after that date remained in the files almost 60 days. This obviously could not be avoided unless the files were cleared at frequent

[15] A comparison of the active file of the public employment services of the country as a whole as of November 1937 with the Unemployment Census of November 1937 indicated even at that time that there were many striking similarities in the characteristics of the unemployed in the two studies. See E. D. Hollander and J. F. Wellemeyer, Jr., "Can Employment Service Reports Be Used to Measure Unemployment?" *Monthly Labor Review,* 46 (June 1938), pp. 1456–1464, and 47 (July 1938), pp. 156–163.

intervals, and such an additional cost would probably not have been justified. In the offices visited it appeared to be the general rule to clear the files monthly. Whether during times of great pressure this was always done could only have been determined by a careful examination of the files.

Until March of 1938 the registration cards of relief registrants were renewed automatically and thus remained in the active file until such time as notification was received that the person was no longer available for employment. After this date the offices were instructed to clear the files of relief registrants unless they had renewed their cards within a month. This was necessary because there were no longer separate files for those with relief status. Actual physical appearance of those with relief status in an office of the C.S.E.S. each month was not always possible; therefore in some instances arrangements were made whereby lists were submitted by S.R.A. and W.P.A. to be checked against those cleared from the files. No very satisfactory method of keeping relief registrants' cards active was worked out by the end of 1938. It is probable that in most offices these cards were kept active, but it is possible that in cases where the lists were not regularly supplied by S.R.A. and W.P.A., and where there was no distinguishing mark on the cards of those with relief status, some may have been placed in the inactive file while still unemployed.

Numbers of Registrants.—The active file is the source of information as to the labor supply available at the offices of the public employment service. As has been already pointed out, the active file of the C.S.E.S. may at times have included people who were no longer seeking work. It is impossible to determine the effect that failures to clear the active file may have had on the reliability of active file statistics, but they probably are a fairly good indication of the labor supply available at this source.

TABLE 3

ACTIVE FILE OF ALL OFFICES OF THE CALIFORNIA STATE EMPLOYMENT SERVICE AND THE NATIONAL REËMPLOYMENT SERVICE, 1935–1938

Date	All offices	Date	All offices
1935		1937	
January	*	January	221,837
February	*	February	215,551
March	*	March	218,458
April	*	April	231,264
May	110,304	May	218,769
June	141,684	June	204,629
July	182,279	July	202,687
August	234,494	August	204,864
September	291,321	September	198,761
October	309,118	October	202,813
November	331,101	November	198,938
December	367,375	December	244,598
Average	245,960†	Average	213,597
1936		1938	
January	392,312	January	320,399
February	400,950	February	370,261
March	401,367	March	361,162
April	367,289	April	397,820
May	353,630	May	379,516
June	241,628	June	376,108
July	230,027	July	325,360
August	226,654	August	315,102
September	225,230	September	292,102
October	229,939	October	298,812
November	232,017	November	305,322
December	215,378	December	319,732
Average	293,035	Average	338,475

SOURCE: California State Department of Employment, *Operations of Offices*.

* Figures for these months not available.

† Average for 8 months.

The active file of the free employment service in California from 1935 through 1938 showed large variations, some of which were related to changing business conditions, some to the availability of offices, and some to changing attitudes towards the service; but the large fluctuations were, in the main, the result of special inducements to the unemployed to register. From the latter part of 1935 all relief applicants under S.R.A. and W.P.A. were required to register, and since the beginning of 1938 registration has been compulsory for claimants for unemployment compensation benefits.

In May of 1935 the active file of the N.R.S. and the C.S.E.S. combined was 110,000. The numbers began to increase rapidly after the middle of the year and by December had reached 367,000, remaining at about this figure until nearly the middle of the next year. This phenomenal rise in the number of registrants at the free employment service was primarily due to registration of those seeking W.P.A. assignments. It is probable that for several months in 1936 the active file contained considerable numbers of people who were not actually available for employment. In June of 1936 a special survey was made to determine the availability for employment of active registrants. As a result of this survey those found not to be available for prompt referral were removed from the active file.[16] This undoubtedly accounted for the decrease of the active file from about 350,000 in May 1936 to 242,000 in June. During the remainder of 1936 and 1937 the active file remained at approximately 200,000 for about a year and a half. In 1938, under the stimulus of unemployment compensation, the active file again rose to a high point of nearly 400,000 in April, and during the last six months of 1938 it was less than 300,000 in only two months.

The active files in the offices in the areas visited reflected fluctuations similar to those found in the state figures, that is, large increases in the latter months of 1935 lasting through the early months of 1936, followed by decreases to the end of 1937 and rapid expansion in the early months of 1938. Certain features regarding the active files in these offices are, however,

[16] United States Employment Service, Division of Standards and Research, *Who Are the Job Seekers?* (Washington: Government Printing Office, 1937), p. 10.

TABLE 4

ACTIVE FILE OF THE SAN FRANCISCO, LOS ANGELES, SACRAMENTO, AND KERN COUNTY OFFICES OF THE CALIFORNIA STATE EMPLOYMENT SERVICE, 1935–1938

Date	San Francisco	Los Angeles	Sacramento	Kern
1935				
January	*	*	*	*
February	*	*	*	*
March	*	*	*	*
April	*	*	*	*
May	10,682	10,375	3,520	2,775
June	12,836	25,597	2,423	3,035
July	21,547	29,643	3,848	4,410
August	27,050	59,719	5,798	4,589
September	30,091	116,580	4,968	3,948
October	33,340	140,549	3,401	3,782
November	42,405	157,205	6,952	4,871
December	46,439	168,172	7,668	5,492
Average†	28,049	88,480	4,822	4,113
1936				
January	48,801	177,104	8,479	4,588
February	44,614	182,530	9,305	4,751
March	47,450	179,045	9,569	4,591
April	50,522	154,823	8,478	4,537
May	49,125	150,060	7,643	4,006
June	27,793	97,011	2,376	3,699
July	20,998	92,632	1,924	2,389
August	21,592	98,895	2,598	2,485
September	22,954	95,805	2,033	2,619
October	23,605	99,593	1,585	2,508
November	24,516	101,564	1,142	2,305
December	25,466	80,869	4,530	2,738
Average	33,953	125,828	4,972	3,435
1937				
January	26,865	84,015	3,949	2,986
February	26,779	78,798	3,386	3,139
March	29,158	85,424	4,047	3,527
April	30,413	93,762	4,565	2,863
May	31,246	88,032	3,500	2,283
June	25,711	81,978	4,409	2,160

* Figures for these months not available.

† Average for 8 months.

TABLE 4 (*Continued*)

Date	San Francisco	Los Angeles	Sacramento	Kern
1937 (*Continued*)				
July	21,983	89,444	4,272	2,266
August	24,617	90,756	4,095	2,228
September	22,787	92,729	2,560	1,829
October	26,211	90,478	3,417	1,587
November	29,297	71,747	5,793	1,865
December	33,021	89,802	8,103	3,318
Average	27,341	86,414	4,341	2,504
1938				
January	43,873	114,717	10,502	5,209
February	46,853	141,903	12,998	6,238
March	39,608	149,910	14,855	4,401
April	45,797	169,487	11,653	5,590
May	46,754	171,936	10,044	4,343
June	46,891	172,192	9,668	4,344
July	40,184	131,506	10,354	4,555
August	27,803	140,639	9,275	4,641
September	31,867	129,571	7,315	4,636
October	35,291	126,625	5,939	4,992
November	32,631	121,107	7,382	5,846
December	29,884	116,507	6,830	8,572
Average	38,953	140,508	9,735	5,281

SOURCE: Figures for January 1935 through June 1938 from California State Department of Employment, *Operations of Offices;* figures for July 1938 through December 1938 from California State Department of Employment, *Comparison of Field Office Activities.*

worthy of comment. In Los Angeles in 1935 the active file increased nearly sixteenfold, whereas for the state there was not quite a fourfold increase. San Francisco showed a fourfold increase, and the Sacramento and Bakersfield active files about doubled. In the later months of 1936 the active files in these offices declined, as did the state-wide figures. The greatest decline, however, was in the Sacramento office where the active file in November was only a little more than one-tenth of its high point in March. As was true for the state as a whole, the average numbers in the active files in the offices under discussion were lower in 1937 than in 1936. The advent of unemployment insurance payments in 1938 brought additional registrants to the C.S.E.S., and thus the average active file was also larger in those offices in 1938 than for the other years included in this study.

The above figures throw little light on the question as to the proportion of the unemployed in California who were registered at the C.S.E.S., and data for such an analysis are available only for November 1937 when the Census of Unemployment was taken.[17] In November 1937 it was reported that 350,000 persons were unemployed in California. At the same date nearly 200,000, or 57 per cent, were registered at the free employment service. Since the Unemployment Census was voluntary, the number reported as unemployed was undoubtedly an understatement of the total number of unemployed, and therefore it cannot be stated that 57 per cent of the unemployed in the state were registered at the free employment service. Furthermore, it should be pointed out that in November 1937 registration at the C.S.E.S. was heavily weighted by those certified to relief projects. The noncertified registrants of the C.S.E.S. were only about one-third of the noncertified unemployed enumerated in the Unemployment Census, whereas the number of relief registrants was slightly larger than the number enumerated by the Unemployment Census as certified for relief work.[18]

In San Francisco, Sacramento, and Kern counties the active file was between 65 and 70 per cent of those registered as unemployed in the Census of 1937; and in Los Angeles, 45 per cent. It is not possible to give a definite explanation for the lower figure in Los Angeles, but it may be related in part to the fact that at this date there were few offices in Los Angeles

[17] Census of Partial Employment, Unemployment, and Occupations: 1937, *Final Report on Total and Partial Unemployment for California* (Washington: Government Printing Office, 1938).

[18] United States Employment Service, Division of Standards and Research, *Survey of Employment Service Information* (Washington: Government Printing Office, Feb. 1938), p. 11.

County, a county with a large and scattered population, and in part to possible differences in coverage of the Unemployment Census.[19] It should again be emphasized that the Unemployment Census was voluntary, and therefore in no case did the number reported as unemployed equal the total number of unemployed.

Characteristics of Registrants.—In addition to the number of persons registered at the C.S.E.S., it is important to know something of the characteristics of the people who were available for placement by this agency. At intervals analyses have been made from which it is possible to describe the registrants in the active file in terms of occupation, industry, and age.

Occupation.—The active file of all the offices of the C.S.E.S. at the time of five inventories from July 1936 to April 1938[20] contained persons in a wide variety of occupations.[21] Professional, sales, and clerical workers, which together may be characterized as white-collar occupations, made up about a quarter of the registrants at the earlier and a fifth at the last inventory; domestic and personal service workers made up about 20 per cent at the earlier and 15 per cent at the last inventory; and manual workers about 55 per cent at the earlier inventories and nearly two-thirds at the last inventory. The change in representation of the various occupational groups at the last inventory may have been related to a number of factors, such as differences in the amount of unemployment within various occupational groups. In the case of manual workers, how-

[19] It is possible that in some areas those registered with the Employment Service were more likely to report their employment status than were those who were not so registered. In any areas where this was true, the active file of the Employment Service would represent a large proportion of the unemployed counted in the Census.

[20] There were six inventories. Unpublished data concerning the characteristics of the active file for the state and for certain counties were, however, supplied by the U.S.E.S. for five inventories.

[21] The occupational classification was assigned by the interviewer, and it was the occupation for which, in the interviewer's judgment, the individual was best qualified and his prospects for placement were best. United States Employment Service, Division of Standards and Research, *Survey of Employment Service Information* (Washington: Government Printing Office, 1937), p. 42.

TABLE 5

OCCUPATIONS OF REGISTRANTS IN THE ACTIVE FILE OF THE CALIFORNIA STATE EMPLOYMENT SERVICE, AT THE TIME OF FIVE INVENTORIES, JULY 1936–APRIL 1938

Occupation	July 1936		April 1937		July 1937		November 1937		April 1938	
	Number	Per cent	Number	Per cent	Number	Per cent	Number	Per cent	Number	Per cent
Total	241,875		219,609		214,080		181,323		359,322	
Total unclassified	13,144		7,031		8,272		6,493		8,626	
Total classified	228,731	100.0	212,578	100.0	205,808	100.0	174,830	100.0	350,696	100.0
White-collar workers	53,566	23.4	49,133	23.1	50,431	24.5	45,447	26.0	71,463	20.4
Domestic and service workers	42,425	18.6	40,268	18.9	41,364	20.1	35,895	20.5	50,301	14.3
Manual workers	132,740	58.0	123,177	58.0	114,013	55.4	93,488	53.5	228,932	65.3

SOURCE: Unpublished data from the United States Employment Service.

TABLE 5A

CLASSIFICATION OF REGISTRANTS WITHIN OCCUPATIONAL GROUPS AT THE TIME OF FIVE INVENTORIES OF THE ACTIVE FILE OF THE CALIFORNIA STATE EMPLOYMENT SERVICE, JULY 1936–APRIL 1938

Occupation	July 1936		April 1937		July 1937		November 1937		April 1938	
	Number	Per cent	Number	Per cent	Number	Per cent	Number	Per cent	Number	Per cent
White-collar workers	53,566	100.0	49,133	100.0	50,431	100.0	45,447	100.0	71,463	100.0
Professional	10,757	20.1	9,031	18.4	9,057	18.0	7,066	15.6	9,190	12.9
Semiprofessional*	10,053	18.8	8,550	17.4	8,330	16.5	7,287	16.0	11,449	16.0
Sales	11,274	21.0	11,588	23.6	11,132	22.1	10,803	23.8	20,733	29.0
Clerical	21,482	40.1	19,964	40.6	21,912	43.4	20,291	44.6	30,091	42.1
Domestic and service workers	42,425	100.0	40,268	100.0	41,364	100.0	35,895	100.0	50,301	100.0
Domestic	15,550	36.7	14,665	36.4	15,598	37.7	13,228	36.9	16,153	32.1
Other	26,875	63.3	25,603	63.6	25,766	62.3	22,667	63.1	34,148	67.9
Manual workers	132,740	100.0	123,177	100.0	114,013	100.0	93,488	100.0	223,932	100.0
Skilled	40,056	30.2	32,852	26.7	31,129	27.3	27,298	29.2	65,321	28.5
Semiskilled	48,724	36.7	44,445	36.1	38,131	33.4	32,167	34.4	83,088	38.5
Unskilled	43,960	33.1	45,880	37.2	44,753	39.3	34,023	36.4	75,523	33.0

SOURCE: Unpublished data from the United States Employment Service.

* Includes technicians and administrative and supervisory workers.

TABLE 6

OCCUPATIONS OF REGISTRANTS IN THE ACTIVE FILE OF THE SAN FRANCISCO, LOS ANGELES, SACRAMENTO, AND KERN COUNTY OFFICES OF THE CALIFORNIA STATE EMPLOYMENT SERVICE AT THE TIME OF FIVE INVENTORIES, JULY 1936–APRIL 1938

Occupation	July 1936	April 1937	July 1937	November 1937	April 1938
NUMBER					
Total					
San Francisco	26,430	27,964	21,252	24,884	38,027
Los Angeles	92,624	82,448	85,483	66,306	144,922
Sacramento	2,335	4,566	5,076	4,290	15,139
Kern	3,624	3,332	2,525	1,454	4,243
White-collar workers					
San Francisco	8,097	9,624	7,725	8,664	11,636
Los Angeles	26,677	21,920	24,002	20,171	34,389
Sacramento	596	927	1,296	1,130	1,734
Kern	353	279	309	251	281
Domestic and service workers					
San Francisco	5,680	6,217	4,798	5,935	7,588
Los Angeles	18,474	16,900	18,945	14,310	22,620
Sacramento	397	678	918	720	1,624
Kern	841	568	474	319	421
Manual workers					
San Francisco	12,653	12,123	8,729	10,285	18,803
Los Angeles	47,473	43,628	42,536	31,825	87,913
Sacramento	1,342	2,961	2,862	2,440	11,781
Kern	2,430	2,485	1,742	884	3,541
PER CENT OF TOTAL					
White-collar workers					
San Francisco	30.6	34.4	36.3	34.8	30.6
Los Angeles	28.8	26.6	28.1	30.4	23.7
Sacramento	25.5	20.3	25.5	26.3	11.5
Kern	9.7	8.4	12.2	17.3	6.6
Domestic and service workers					
San Francisco	21.5	22.2	22.6	23.9	20.0
Los Angeles	19.9	20.5	22.1	21.6	15.6
Sacramento	17.0	14.8	18.1	16.8	10.7
Kern	23.2	17.0	18.8	21.9	9.9
Manual workers					
San Francisco	47.9	43.4	41.1	41.3	49.4
Los Angeles	51.3	52.9	49.8	48.0	60.7
Sacramento	57.5	64.9	56.4	56.9	77.8
Kern	67.1	74.6	69.0	60.8	83.5

SOURCE: Unpublished data from the United States Employment Service.

ever, the larger representation at the last inventory was probably in part related to compulsory registration for unemployment compensation.

As was true for the C.S.E.S. as a whole, the registrants in the active files of the offices in San Francisco, Los Angeles, Sacramento, and Kern counties represented a wide variety of occupations. Until the last inventory of April 1938 the so-called white-collar workers—professional, sales, and clerical workers—constituted from one-fourth to one-third of the registrants in San Francisco, Los Angeles, and Sacramento counties but only between 10 and 15 per cent in Kern County. The proportions of white-collar workers declined in each of these offices at the time of the last inventory but to a much greater degree in Sacramento and in Kern than in the other two counties. Manual workers, including skilled, semiskilled, and unskilled workers, were always the largest group. In the earlier inventories they made up over 40 per cent of the active file in San Francisco, about 50 per cent in Los Angeles, from one-half to nearly two-thirds in Sacramento, and from 60 to 75 per cent in Kern County. In every instance there was an increase in the proportion in this classification of workers at the last inventory, but Sacramento and Kern counties still had larger proportions in this group than did San Francisco and Los Angeles. The most significant change within the group of manual workers was the increase in semiskilled workers in Sacramento and Kern counties. Their proportion of the total nearly doubled between the last two inventories. Probably this change was primarily the result of unemployment compensation, which brought large numbers of semiskilled workers to the employment offices, although it may also have been related to differences in the incidence of unemployment in the various groups. Service and domestic workers in the first four inventories made up about a fifth to a quarter of the total in San Francisco and in Los Angeles and a slightly smaller proportion in Sacramento and Kern counties. At the time of the last inventory this group of workers made up a smaller proportion of the total in each of these areas, but the decline was greatest in Sacramento and Kern counties. It is evident from the above analysis that there were considerable differences in the occupations of the registrants in the four

TABLE 7

COMPARISON OF OCCUPATIONS OF REGISTRANTS IN THE ACTIVE FILE OF THE CALIFORNIA STATE EMPLOYMENT SERVICE IN NOVEMBER 1937 WITH THE OCCUPATIONS OF THOSE REGISTERED AS UNEMPLOYED IN THE UNEMPLOYMENT CENSUS OF 1937

Occupational classification	United States Unemployment Census, 1937		Active file of the California State Employment Service, November 1937	
	Number*	Per cent	Number	Per cent
Total classifiable	319,891	100.0	174,830	100.0
White-collar workers	100,098	31.3	45,447	26.0
Domestic and service workers	26,704	8.3	35,895	20.5
Manual workers	193,089	60.4	93,488	53.5

SOURCE: United States Unemployment Census 1937 and unpublished data from the California State Department of Employment.

* Totally unemployed plus emergency workers. Partly unemployed and new workers excluded.

offices. These differences were in part due to differences in occupations represented in the various communities, but they were probably also related to variations in the degree to which persons in certain occupations registered at these offices of the C.S.E.S.

The question is often raised as to whether the occupations of the Employment Service registrants are representative of the unemployed population. The only information available as to the occupation of the unemployed population was that from the Unemployment Census of 1937. A comparison of these figures with the active file at the time of the November 1937 inventory will indicate similarities and differences between the two groups.[22] The largest group in both series was that of manual workers; the second, white-collar; and the third, domestic and service workers. There were, however, differences in the proportions in these categories. There was a somewhat smaller proportion of manual and of white-collar workers and more than double the proportion of domestic[23] and service workers in the active file than in the group enumerated as unemployed in the Census of 1937. The counties visited showed the same differences between the active file and the Unemployment Census as did the entire state.

Caution must be exercised in drawing conclusions from the above comparison, but it is probable that the large representation of domestic and service workers in the active files of the C.S.E.S. offices is related to the fact that domestic workers have for many years been more accustomed to using free employment services than have those in other occupational groups. It is probable that the overweighting of this group will become less under the influence of unemployment compensation. An indication of this is found in the smaller proportion of domestic and service workers in the active files in the inventory of April 1938 than in the earlier inventories. Apparently the state employment offices attract certain types of workers more than others; and if the employment offices are to serve as a place where workers of all skills may be found by prospective employers, it will be necessary to overcome the reluctance to register of those groups now underweighted in the active file. Unemployment compensation will undoubtedly increase the registration of these groups,[24] but in how far the Employment

[22] There was some difficulty in matching the classifications of the two studies, and therefore comparisons are made only between very broad groups.

[23] It is probable that part of this difference is due to the fact that unemployed domestic workers were not fully enumerated in the Census; but, allowing for this, domestic service heavily weighted the active file.

[24] It is not possible to compare the occupations of the unemployed in April 1938, three months after unemployment compensation payments began, with the Unemployment Census, since the degree of unemployment in the various occupational groups may not have been the same in 1938 as in 1937.

TABLE 8

INDUSTRIAL GROUPS OF REGISTRANTS IN THE ACTIVE FILE OF THE CALIFORNIA STATE EMPLOYMENT SERVICE AT THE TIME OF FIVE INVENTORIES, JULY 1936–APRIL 1938

Industry	July 1936	April 1937	July 1937	November 1937	April 1938
NUMBER					
Total	241,875	219,609	214,080	181,323	359,322
Total unclassified	72,522	57,396	59,053	46,058	48,129
Total classified	169,353	162,213	155,027	135,265	311,193
Agriculture, forestry, and fishing	26,535	28,091	26,458	18,561	38,725
Extraction of minerals	4,093	3,340	2,662	2,575	6,533
Building and construction	26,221	23,318	19,585	17,262	37,000
Private	*17,309*	*15,157*	*12,925*	*11,406*	*26,431*
Public	*8,912*	*8,161*	*6,660*	*5,856*	*10,569*
Manufacturing	30,912	28,364	28,387	25,196	98,423
Commercial and mechanical services	245	3,082	6,028	6,195	13,453
Distribution	25,708	22,296	20,109	18,264	38,637
Domestic and personal service, hotels, restaurants, amusements	25,627	22,059	28,835	25,832	40,663
Finance, banks, etc.	2,095	6,041	—	—	—
Government service	8,032	7,531	7,665	7,191	9,943
Professional service	8,211	7,294	6,214	5,516	6,864
Transportation and communication	9,764	9,175	7,662	7,342	18,352
Other public utilities	1,910	1,622	1,422	1,331	2,600
PER CENT					
Total classified	100.0	100.0	100.0	100.0	100.0
Agriculture, forestry, and fishing	15.7	17.3	17.1	13.7	12.5
Extraction of minerals	2.4	2.1	1.7	1.9	2.1
Building and construction	15.5	14.4	12.6	12.8	11.9
Private	*10.2*	*9.3*	*8.3*	*8.4*	*8.5*
Public	*5.3*	*5.0*	*4.3*	*4.3*	*3.4*
Manufacturing	18.3	17.5	18.3	18.6	31.6
Commercial and mechanical services	0.1	1.9	3.9	4.6	4.3
Distribution	15.2	13.7	13.0	13.5	12.4

TABLE 8 (*Continued*)

Industry	July 1936	April 1937	July 1937	November 1937	April 1938
PER CENT (*Continued*)					
Domestic and personal service, hotels, restaurants, amusements	15.1	13.6	18.6	19.1	13.1
Finance, banks, etc.	1.2	3.7	——	——	——
Government service	4.7	4.6	5.0	5.3	3.2
Professional service	4.9	4.5	4.0	4.1	2.2
Transportation and communication	5.8	5.7	4.9	5.4	5.9
Other public utilities	1.1	1.0	0.9	1.0	0.8

SOURCE: Unpublished data from the United States Employment Service.

Service will serve as a placement agency for all groups depends on a variety of factors, including not only registration but also attitudes of employers, workers, and their organizations.

Many industries[25] as well as occupations were represented in the active file of the State Employment Service. If the industries are grouped, it will be seen that at each inventory over 80 per cent of the registrants were in five industrial categories—agriculture, building, manufacturing, distribution, and domestic and personal service—and until the last inventory there were no large differences in the numbers in each of these categories. At the last inventory, however, over 30 per cent were in manufacturing, nearly twice the proportion in any of the other industrial groups. At all of the inventories there was a considerable concentration of registrants within the manufacturing group. The food industries always included from 30 to 40 per cent of the total in manufacturing. The only other industries which at

[25] The industrial classification is determined on the basis of the last regular nonrelief job in which the applicant had been working. In most cases this indicated the usual occupation of that individual. However, since the term "regular job" includes any job of more than one month's duration, the last regular job is not always the usual field of employment. See United States Employment Service, Division of Standards and Research, *Filling Nine Million Jobs* (Washington: Government Printing Office, 1937), p. 27.

TABLE 9

INDUSTRIAL GROUPS OF REGISTRANTS IN THE ACTIVE FILES OF THE SAN FRANCISCO, LOS ANGELES, SACRAMENTO, AND KERN COUNTY OFFICES OF THE CALIFORNIA STATE EMPLOYMENT SERVICE AT THE TIME OF FIVE INVENTORIES, JULY 1936–APRIL 1938

Industry	July 1936	April 1937	July 1937	November 1937	April 1938
	NUMBER				
San Francisco					
Total classifiable	18,662	20,989	15,845	18,859	31,423
Agriculture, forestry, and fishing	328	501	498	624	775
Extraction of minerals	123	129	105	123	181
Building and construction	3,011	2,614	1,841	2,002	3,338
Manufacturing	3,929	4,313	3,115	3,900	8,893
Commercial and mechanical services	33	378	809	1,036	1,589
Distribution	3,144	3,518	2,558	2,923	4,938
Domestic and personal service, hotels, restaurants, amusements	3,620	3,907	3,654	4,394	5,923
Finance, banks, etc.	429	1,166	——	——	——
Government service	747	961	857	1,014	1,145
Professional service	1,310	1,380	1,073	1,186	1,301
Transportation and communication	1,840	2,000	1,229	1,547	3,195
Other public utilities	148	122	106	110	145
Los Angeles					
Total classifiable	61,516	54,917	56,452	46,984	124,130
Agriculture, forestry, and fishing	3,090	3,526	3,735	2,504	4,910
Extraction of minerals	1,232	879	802	727	2,009
Building and construction	9,269	7,841	7,142	5,637	16,606
Manufacturing	12,883	11,024	10,918	9,460	39,772
Commercial and mechanical services	66	1,443	2,843	2,778	6,871
Distribution	11,693	9,273	8,912	7,560	19,022
Domestic and personal service, hotels, restaurants, amusements	11,079	8,461	12,813	10,481	18,997
Finance, banks, etc.	907	2,617	——	——	——
Government service	3,214	2,785	2,901	2,574	3,948
Professional service	3,808	3,106	2,861	2,315	3,255
Transportation and communication	3,587	3,311	2,937	2,450	7,471
Other public utilities	688	651	588	498	1,269

TABLE 9 (*Continued*)

Industry	July 1936	April 1937	July 1937	November 1937	April 1938
(NUMBER—*Continued*)					
Sacramento					
Total classifiable	1,925	4,172	4,436	3,728	14,412
Agriculture, forestry, and fishing	375	1,320	1,491	927	3,648
Extraction of minerals	55	96	87	97	344
Building and construction	223	480	367	332	1,175
Manufacturing	389	630	581	691	4,760
Commercial and mechanical services	5	80	142	139	368
Distribution	310	450	503	459	1,334
Domestic and personal service, hotels, restaurants, amusements	238	415	724	534	1,328
Finance, banks, etc.	22	181	—	—	—
Government service	136	205	247	230	423
Professional service	67	100	104	93	138
Transportation and communication	91	189	158	201	802
Other public utilities	14	26	32	25	92
Kern					
Total classifiable	3,126	3,210	2,366	1,352	4,160
Agriculture, forestry, and fishing	1,282	1,693	1,033	494	2,300
Extraction of minerals	118	109	84	54	409
Building and construction	338	302	260	136	340
Manufacturing	310	188	148	98	173
Commercial and mechanical services	—	42	59	40	133
Distribution	232	168	168	120	208
Domestic and personal service, hotels, restaurants, amusements	504	409	400	277	319
Finance, banks, etc.	9	75	—	—	—
Government service	74	65	65	45	55
Professional service	56	40	43	30	25
Transportation and communication	170	95	90	48	170
Other public utilities	33	24	16	10	28

TABLE 9 (*Continued*)

Industry	July 1936	April 1937	July 1937	November 1937	April 1938
	PER CENT				
San Francisco					
Total classifiable	100.0	100.0	100.0	100.0	100.0
Agriculture, forestry, and fishing	1.7	2.4	3.1	3.3	2.5
Extraction of minerals	0.7	0.6	0.7	0.6	0.6
Building and construction	16.1	12.4	11.6	10.6	10.6
Manufacturing	21.1	20.5	19.7	20.7	28.3
Commercial and mechanical services	0.2	1.8	5.1	5.5	5.1
Distribution	16.8	16.8	16.1	15.5	15.7
Domestic and personal service, hotels, restaurants, amusements	19.4	18.6	23.1	23.3	18.8
Finance, banks, etc.	2.3	5.6	—	—	—
Government service	4.0	4.6	5.4	5.4	3.6
Professional service	7.0	6.6	6.8	6.3	4.1
Transportation and communication	9.9	9.5	7.7	8.2	10.2
Other public utilities	0.8	0.6	0.7	0.6	0.5
Los Angeles					
Total classifiable	100.0	100.0	100.0	100.0	100.0
Agriculture, forestry, and fishing	5.0	6.4	6.6	5.3	4.0
Extraction of minerals	2.0	1.6	1.4	1.6	1.6
Building and construction	15.1	14.3	12.7	12.0	13.4
Manufacturing	21.0	20.1	19.3	20.1	32.1
Commercial and mechanical services	0.1	2.6	5.0	5.9	5.5
Distribution	19.0	16.9	15.8	16.1	15.3
Domestic and personal service, hotels, restaurants, amusements	18.0	15.4	22.7	22.3	15.3
Finance, banks, etc.	1.5	4.8	—	—	—
Government service	5.2	5.1	5.1	5.5	3.2
Professional service	6.2	5.6	5.1	4.9	2.6
Transportation and communication	5.8	6.0	5.2	5.2	6.0
Other public utilities	1.1	1.2	1.1	1.1	1.0

TABLE 9 (*Concluded*)

Industry	July 1936	April 1937	July 1937	November 1937	April 1938
PER CENT—(*Continued*)					
Sacramento					
Total classifiable	100.0	100.0	100.0	100.0	100.0
Agriculture, forestry, and fishing	19.5	31.7	33.6	24.9	25.3
Extraction of minerals	2.8	2.3	2.0	2.6	2.4
Building and construction	11.6	11.5	8.3	8.9	8.1
Manufacturing	20.2	15.1	13.1	18.5	33.0
Commercial and mechanical services	0.3	1.9	3.2	3.7	2.6
Distribution	16.1	10.8	11.3	12.3	9.3
Domestic and personal service, hotels, restaurants, amusements	12.4	10.0	16.3	14.3	9.2
Finance, banks, etc.	1.1	4.3	—	—	—
Government service	7.1	4.9	5.6	6.2	2.9
Professional service	3.5	2.4	2.3	2.5	1.0
Transportation and communication	4.7	4.5	3.6	5.4	5.6
Other public utilities	0.7	0.6	0.7	0.7	0.6
Kern					
Total classifiable	100.0	100.0	100.0	100.0	100.0
Agriculture, forestry, and fishing	41.0	52.7	43.7	36.5	55.3
Extraction of minerals	3.8	3.4	3.6	4.0	9.8
Building and construction	10.8	9.4	11.0	10.1	8.2
Manufacturing	9.9	5.9	6.2	7.2	4.1
Commercial and mechanical services	—	1.3	2.5	3.0	3.2
Distribution	7.4	5.2	7.1	8.9	5.0
Domestic and personal service, hotels, restaurants, amusements	16.1	12.7	16.9	20.5	7.7
Finance, banks, etc.	0.3	2.3	—	—	—
Government service	2.4	2.0	2.7	3.3	1.3
Professional service	1.8	1.3	1.8	2.2	0.6
Transportation and communication	5.4	3.0	3.8	3.6	4.1
Other public utilities	1.1	0.8	0.7	0.7	0.7

SOURCE: Unpublished data from the United States Employment Service.

any of the inventories included as many as 10 per cent of those in manufacturing were lumber and transportation equipment.

Since California is a state with a considerable diversity of industry, it was not surprising to find that the proportions of the

TABLE 10

COMPARISON OF INDUSTRIES REPRESENTED IN THE ACTIVE FILE OF THE CALIFORNIA STATE EMPLOYMENT SERVICE IN NOVEMBER 1937 WITH THE INDUSTRIES REPORTED BY THOSE WHO REGISTERED AS UNEMPLOYED IN THE UNEMPLOYMENT CENSUS OF 1937

Industry	U. S. Unemployment Census, 1937		Active file of the California State Employment Service, November 1937	
	Number*	Per cent	Number	Per cent
Total classifiable	288,684	100.0	135,265	100.0
Agriculture, forestry, and fishing	25,874	9.0	18,561	13.7
Extraction of minerals	7,220	2.5	2,575	1.9
Building and construction	41,999	14.5	17,262	12.8
Manufacturing	66,925	23.2	25,196	18.6
Commercial and mechanical services and distribution	47,228	16.3	24,459	18.1
Transportation, communication, and public utilities	28,010	9.7	8,673	6.4
Government and professional service	23,284	8.1	12,707	9.4
Hotels, restaurants, and amusements	28,198	9.8	13,376	9.9
Domestic and personal service	19,946	6.9	12,456	9.2

SOURCE: United States Unemployment Census 1937 and unpublished data from the United States Employment Service.

* Totally unemployed plus emergency workers. Partly unemployed and new workers excluded.

registrants in the various industrial groups in the San Francisco, Los Angeles, Sacramento, and Kern County offices were somewhat different from those for the State Employment Service as a whole. San Francisco and Los Angeles, in general, had larger proportions in manufacturing, distribution, and domestic and personal service and a very much smaller proportion of agricultural workers. Sacramento and Kern counties, on the other hand, had a large representation of agricultural workers and usually relatively smaller proportions in the other groups.

A comparison of the industries represented in the active file in November 1937 and in the Census of Unemployment of 1937 will again give some evidence as to whether the C.S.E.S. registrants were representative of the unemployed of the state.[26] In both series, agriculture, building, manufacturing, distribution, domestic and personal service, and hotels, restaurants, and amusements made up about 80 per cent of the total. Manufacturing and building were, however, less heavily represented and the other four groups more heavily represented in the active file than in the Census of Unemployment. Another point of difference should also be mentioned. In the Census of Unemployment about 10 per cent of those enumerated had been employed in transportation and communication, whereas only about 6 per cent of the Employment Service registrants had been employed in this industry.

Age.—Since age is an important factor in determining employability, it was of interest to examine the age distribution of the C.S.E.S registrants. At the time of the five inventories from July 1936 to April 1938, between 16 and 20 per cent of the registrants in the active file in the state-wide organization were under 25 years of age, from 45 to 50 per cent were between 25 and 44, about a third were from 45 to 64, and 2 or 3 per cent were 65 and over. There were no very striking differences in the age distribution in the last as compared with the earlier inventories, although there was a slightly larger per cent in the age group 25 to 44 and a somewhat smaller proportion from 45 to 64. It is impossible to determine whether this is a chance variation or whether it bears some relation to unemployment

[26] The industries represented by those enumerated in the Census of Unemployment of 1937 are not available for counties; thus it is impossible to determine even roughly whether the Employment Service registrants in San Francisco, Los Angeles, Sacramento, and Kern counties are a good sample of the unemployed from the point of view of industries represented.

compensation. If the latter is the case, the younger age groups may be represented in larger proportions in the future.

The age distribution of those registered at the C.S.E.S. offices in San Francisco, Los Angeles, Sacramento, and Kern counties

TABLE 11

AGE GROUPS OF REGISTRANTS IN THE ACTIVE FILE OF THE CALIFORNIA STATE EMPLOYMENT SERVICE AT THE TIME OF FIVE INVENTORIES, JULY 1936–APRIL 1938

Age	July 1936	April 1937	July 1937	November 1937	April 1938
NUMBER					
Total unspecified	7,925	48	37	77	69
Total specified	233,950	219,561	214,043	181,246	359,253
19 years and under	9,952	7,263	12,490	9,183	9,432
20 to 24 years	27,806	29,287	31,556	25,234	54,443
25 to 34 years	51,179	51,187	47,770	41,460	98,347
35 to 44 years	55,239	50,884	47,342	40,537	82,588
45 to 54 years	49,436	45,920	42,497	37,079	66,662
55 to 64 years	31,681	30,069	28,236	24,549	40,686
65 years and over	8,657	4,951	4,152	3,204	7,095
PER CENT					
Total specified	100.0	100.0	100.0	100.0	100.0
19 years and under	4.3	3.3	5.8	5.1	2.6
20 to 24 years	11.9	13.3	14.8	13.9	15.2
25 to 34 years	21.9	23.3	22.3	22.9	27.4
35 to 44 years	23.6	23.2	22.1	22.4	23.0
45 to 54 years	21.1	20.9	19.9	20.4	18.5
55 to 64 years	13.5	13.7	13.2	13.5	11.3
65 years and over	3.7	2.3	1.9	1.8	2.0

SOURCE: Unpublished data from the United States Employment Service.

at the time of the inventories was in most respects similar to that of registrants throughout California. There are, however, one or two points of difference upon which comment should be made. The proportion of registrants under 25 was lower in the San Francisco County active file and higher in Kern County than in the other two county offices for which data are presented, and the same contrast is apparent when a comparison is made with the active file for the state-wide organization. This is somewhat surprising in view of the fact that in San Francisco there was a junior department which presumably should have attracted this group of registrants, and that in Bakersfield, on the other hand, there appeared to be little interest in registering young people. It is possible that these differences may in part be related to differences in age distribution of the unemployed population. The only evidence on this point is the age distribution of those enumerated as unemployed in the Census of Unemployment of 1937.

The age distribution of C.S.E.S. registrants for the state as a whole and of those who registered as unemployed in the Census of 1937 were in most respects similar. Approximately the same proportions were under and over 45, although the active file contained slightly larger proportions from 25 to 44 and a somewhat smaller proportion under 25 and over 65.

In San Francisco, Los Angeles, Sacramento, and Kern counties the age distribution of those who reported themselves as unemployed was in most respects similar. In Kern County, however, a somewhat larger proportion of the unemployed were under 25 and a smaller per cent between 45 and 64. A comparison of the active files in these offices with the Census of Unemployment shows that the active files were somewhat more heavily weighted with people from 25 to 44, and in San Francisco and Kern counties a considerably smaller proportion of those in the active files were under 25. Thus it does not appear that the differences in the per cent of people under 25 in the active files of San Francisco and Kern counties mentioned above is accounted for by differences in the age distribution of the unemployed in these counties.

Relief status.—It has already been pointed out that applicants for relief have been required to register at the offices of the

TABLE 12

AGE GROUPS OF REGISTRANTS IN THE ACTIVE FILES OF THE SAN FRANCISCO, LOS ANGELES, SACRAMENTO, AND KERN COUNTY OFFICES OF THE CALIFORNIA STATE EMPLOYMENT SERVICE AT THE TIME OF FIVE INVENTORIES, JULY 1936–APRIL 1938

Age	July 1936	April 1937	July 1937	November 1937	April 1938
NUMBER					
San Francisco					
Total unspecified	873	6	1	3	8
Total specified	26,920	29,612	22,429	26,321	39,425
19 years and under	774	742	867	1,032	899
20 to 24 years	2,676	2,951	2,171	2,718	4,239
25 to 34 years	5,532	6,505	4,982	5,905	9,397
35 to 44 years	6,837	7,686	5,789	6,516	9,843
45 to 54 years	6,094	6,716	4,936	5,852	8,656
55 to 64 years	3,769	4,245	3,218	3,780	5,456
65 years and over	1,238	767	466	518	935
Los Angeles					
Total unspecified	3,218	13	8	37	15
Total specified	93,793	84,274	88,708	68,567	148,323
19 years and under	2,849	2,754	4,459	3,733	3,153
20 to 24 years	9,716	10,495	13,075	9,758	21,507
25 to 34 years	21,447	19,362	19,414	16,163	40,598
35 to 44 years	24,013	20,280	20,220	15,723	34,797
45 to 54 years	20,452	17,829	17,936	13,432	27,639
55 to 64 years	12,832	11,863	11,990	8,752	17,671
65 years and over	2,484	1,691	1,614	1,006	2,958
Sacramento					
Total unspecified	2	—	—	1	4
Total specified	2,374	4,672	5,184	4,329	15,194
19 years and under	132	112	306	244	343
20 to 24 years	296	537	637	530	2,044
25 to 34 years	495	1,130	1,058	943	4,077
35 to 44 years	494	1,108	1,254	953	4,014
45 to 54 years	485	1,033	1,109	936	2,874
55 to 64 years	327	631	694	660	1,577
65 years and over	145	121	126	63	265
Kern					
Total unspecified	71	—	—	—	2
Total specified	3,628	3,570	2,732	1,599	4,399
19 years and under	179	124	201	115	165
20 to 24 years	480	550	482	270	802
25 to 34 years	831	1,033	735	389	1,410
35 to 44 years	848	777	595	341	967
45 to 54 years	723	648	424	300	651
55 to 64 years	455	378	262	170	358
65 years and over	112	60	33	14	46

TABLE 12 (*Continued*)

Age	July 1936	April 1937	July 1937	November 1937	April 1938
	PER CENT				
San Francisco					
Total specified	100.0	100.0	100.0	100.0	100.0
19 years and under	2.9	2.5	3.9	3.9	2.3
20 to 24 years	9.9	10.0	9.7	10.3	10.8
25 to 34 years	20.6	21.9	22.2	22.4	23.8
35 to 44 years	25.4	26.0	25.8	24.8	25.0
45 to 54 years	22.6	22.7	22.0	22.2	21.9
55 to 64 years	14.0	14.3	14.3	14.4	13.8
65 years and over	4.6	2.6	2.1	2.0	2.4
Los Angeles					
Total specified	100.0	100.0	100.0	100.0	100.0
19 years and under	3.0	3.3	5.0	5.4	2.1
20 to 24 years	10.4	12.4	14.8	14.2	14.5
25 to 34 years	22.9	23.0	21.9	23.6	27.4
35 to 44 years	25.6	24.1	22.8	22.9	23.5
45 to 54 years	21.8	21.1	20.2	19.6	18.6
55 to 64 years	13.7	14.1	13.5	12.8	11.9
65 years and over	2.6	2.0	1.8	1.5	2.0
Sacramento					
Total specified	100.0	100.0	100.0	100.0	100.0
19 years and under	5.6	2.4	5.9	5.6	2.3
20 to 24 years	12.5	11.5	12.3	12.2	13.5
25 to 34 years	20.8	24.2	20.4	21.8	26.8
35 to 44 years	20.8	23.7	24.2	22.0	26.4
45 to 54 years	20.4	22.1	21.4	21.6	18.9
55 to 64 years	13.8	13.5	13.4	15.3	10.4
65 years and over	6.1	2.6	2.4	1.5	1.7
Kern					
Total specified	100.0	100.0	100.0	100.0	100.0
19 years and under	5.0	3.5	7.4	7.2	3.8
20 to 24 years	13.2	15.4	17.6	16.9	18.2
25 to 34 years	22.9	28.9	26.9	24.3	32.1
35 to 44 years	23.4	21.7	21.8	21.3	22.0
45 to 54 years	19.9	18.2	15.5	18.8	14.8
55 to 64 years	12.5	10.6	9.6	10.6	8.1
65 years and over	3.1	1.7	1.2	0.9	1.0

SOURCE: Unpublished data from the United States Employment Service.

State Employment Service, and that at times these registrations assumed mass proportions. Until 1938 the registration cards of this group were maintained in a separate file and were renewed automatically until notification was received that the person was no longer available for employment. Since a large proportion of the unemployed have been on relief, and since registration was not compulsory for the unemployed not on relief, it would be expected that those certified for relief would make up a large proportion of the active files of the employment offices.

TABLE 13

COMPARISON OF AGES OF REGISTRANTS IN THE ACTIVE FILE OF THE CALIFORNIA STATE EMPLOYMENT SERVICE IN NOVEMBER 1937 WITH THE AGES OF THOSE REGISTERED AS UNEMPLOYED IN THE UNEMPLOYMENT CENSUS OF 1937

Age	U. S. Unemployment Census, 1937		Active file of the California State Employment Service, November 1937	
	Number*	Per cent	Number	Per cent
Total classifiable	347,656	100.0	181,246	100.0
19 years and under	25,989	7.5	9,183	5.1
20 to 24 years	45,131	13.0	25,234	13.9
25 to 34 years	67,688	19.5	41,460	22.9
35 to 44 years	70,359	20.2	40,537	22.4
45 to 54 years	70,807	20.3	37,079	20.4
55 to 64 years	54,524	15.7	24,549	13.5
65 years and over	13,158	3.8	3,204	1.8

SOURCE: United States Unemployment Census 1937 and unpublished data from the United States Employment Service.

* Totally unemployed plus emergency workers, including new workers. Partly unemployed workers excluded.

From December 1935 to November 1937[27] about one-half to two-thirds of those registered in the public free employment offices in California were people receiving relief. In the San Francisco and Los Angeles County offices, those on relief made up from about one-half to three-quarters of the active file. There were much greater variations in the proportions in this category in Sacramento and Kern counties. In the two earlier and in the last inventory in these counties the numbers in this group ranged from over one-half to three-quarters of the active file, in con-

[27] Information on this subject is available for inventories which differ somewhat from those for which the discussion on the preceding pages is based.

TABLE 14

Comparison of Ages of Registrants in the Active Files of the San Francisco, Los Angeles, Sacramento, and Kern County Offices of the California State Employment Service with the Ages of Those Who Registered as Unemployed in Those Counties in the Unemployment Census of 1937

Age	U. S. Unemployment Census, 1937		Active file of the California State Employment Service, November 1937	
	Number*	Per cent	Number	Per cent
San Francisco				
Total	43,632	100.0	26,321	100.0
19 years and under	2,703	6.2	1,032	3.9
20 to 24 years	4,630	10.6	2,718	10.3
25 to 34 years	8,150	18.7	5,905	22.4
35 to 44 years	9,616	22.0	6,516	24.8
45 to 54 years	9,763	22.4	5,852	22.2
55 to 64 years	7,287	16.7	3,780	14.4
65 years and over	1,483	3.4	518	2.0
Los Angeles				
Total	159,465	100.0	68,567	100.0
19 years and under	10,258	6.4	3,733	5.4
20 to 24 years	19,920	12.5	9,758	14.2
25 to 34 years	32,006	20.1	16,163	23.6
35 to 44 years	33,548	21.1	15,723	22.9
45 to 54 years	32,541	20.4	13,432	19.6
55 to 64 years	24,745	15.5	8,752	12.8
65 years and over	6,447	4.0	1,006	1.5
Sacramento				
Total	8,098	100.0	4,329	100.0
19 years and under	608	7.5	244	5.6
20 to 24 years	1,018	12.6	530	12.2
25 to 34 years	1,483	18.3	943	21.8
35 to 44 years	1,672	20.7	953	22.0
45 to 54 years	1,765	21.8	936	21.6
55 to 64 years	1,281	15.8	660	15.3
65 years and over	271	3.3	63	1.5
Kern				
Total	2,824	100.0	1,599	100.0
19 years and under	269	9.5	115	7.2
20 to 24 years	487	17.2	270	16.9
25 to 34 years	536	19.0	389	24.3
35 to 44 years	527	18.7	341	21.3
45 to 54 years	528	18.7	300	18.8
55 to 64 years	378	13.4	170	10.6
65 years and over	99	3.5	14	0.9

Source: United States Unemployment Census 1937 and unpublished data from the United States Employment Service.

* Totally unemployed plus emergency workers, including new workers. Partly unemployed workers excluded.

trast with only about a third in the three inventories from December 1936 to July 1937. Without making a more thorough investigation than time permitted, it was impossible to account for the wide variations in Sacramento and Kern counties. They may be due to differences in numbers on relief or to the fact that at certain times compulsory registration of applicants for relief work was not fully enforced.

TABLE 15

PER CENT OF REGISTRANTS IN THE ACTIVE FILE OF THE CALIFORNIA STATE EMPLOYMENT SERVICE WHO WERE CERTIFIED FOR RELIEF AT THE TIME OF SIX INVENTORIES, DECEMBER 1935–NOVEMBER 1937

Office	December 1935	July 1936	December 1936	April 1937	July 1937	November 1937
State	59.5	64.8	46.9	62.8	64.1	53.7
San Francisco	47.0	77.8	57.0	58.9	71.5	58.2
Los Angeles	60.6	77.2	58.2	69.8	68.4	54.3
Sacramento	76.7	69.3	33.0	37.1	40.7	68.3
Kern	61.1	73.5	32.5	38.8	37.9	54.4

SOURCE: Typed material from the California State Department of Employment.

Employees of the C.S.E.S. in the offices visited were particularly concerned with the quality of relief registrants, and they were quite generally of the opinion that those who registered for relief certification were the "difficult-to-place." While the difficulties were most frequently described in terms of personal appearance or personality problems, the staff of the Employment Service also seemed to feel that these people were, in general, on the margin of employability from the point of view of skills as well as from that of appearance and personality. In some instances it was also stated that the situation was further complicated by errors in classification as to employability by the S.R.A., and thus some obvious unemployables were registered and placed in the active file.

Whatever the facts may have been as to the employability of

this group of Employment Service registrants, the Employment Service staff was frequently convinced that they were on the margin of employability. Thus it could not be expected that this group would be given much consideration during a time when job orders were scarce.

Several studies in other areas will throw some light on this problem, and it is probably fair to assume that the conclusions of these studies would be at least roughly true of California. A Philadelphia study of applicants at the state employment office, who were certified for relief in the years 1934-36, showed a higher proportion of unskilled workers, a higher average age, and a higher proportion of the long-time unemployed than was found for applicants not on the relief rolls.[28] Special emphasis on the importance of length of unemployment is found in a study of urban workers on relief.[29] "... length of time out of work is the best available measure of the employability or re-employment prospects of the relief population.... The longer persons are out of work, the worse their chances are for re-employment at their customary occupation or, in fact, at any type of job." This group will have special difficulties in finding opportunities for reëmployment, in some instances because their previous employment has been in a decaying industry, or in an occupation which has become obsolete; in others, increasing age will be a barrier, and to this may be added loss of occupational skills and personality difficulties which may increase not only with age but also with the discouragement and poverty of unemployment.[30] A recent Philadelphia study empha-

[28] Gladys L. Palmer, *Recent Trends in Employment and Unemployment in Philadelphia*, Works Progress Administration, National Research Project, and Industrial Research Department, University of Pennsylvania, Philadelphia Labor Market Studies, Report No. P-1 (Dec. 1937), p. 37. For additional evidence on this point see Gladys L. Palmer and Katherine D. Wood, *Urban Workers on Relief*, Works Progress Administration, Division of Social Research, Research Monograph IV, Part 1 (Washington: 1936).

[29] Palmer and Wood, *op. cit.*, pp. xxvi and xxvii.

[30] *Ibid.*, p. 100. Also see Joseph C. Bevis and Stanley L. Payne, *Former Relief Cases in Private Employment*, Works Progress Administration, Division of Re-

sizes the fact that specialized requirements as to experience and personality are frequent barriers to employment in depression years. "The persons who could meet the specialized requirements secured temporary jobs and then permanent jobs, or a series of temporary jobs. The unemployed who could not meet these requirements stayed unemployed, many of them for relatively long periods of time."[31]

A New York study also discusses some phases of the problem of the employment service registrant with relief status.[32] The author of this study raises the question as to whether this group of registrants is likely to be at a disadvantage in obtaining jobs in private industry. He points out that, although adequate information is not available for a conclusive answer to this, some evidence of difficulties is found in the fact that state employment service records of those with relief status are in many instances not as active as they should be to facilitate the service to them. He also mentions the fact that there is a tendency to consider the unemployed receiving relief as a special and, to some extent, as a substandard or even unemployable group. This obviously results in discrimination against this group in competition for such jobs as are available. Mr. Lurie concludes that the attitude described above is not well founded, and that in the relief group, "as in every group of applicants, there are variations in skill, ability, work experience, and vocational ratings."

It is undoubtedly true that in California, and elsewhere, con-

search, Special Report 1939 (Washington: Government Printing Office, 1939), p. 11. This is a study of 1,108 families in 13 cities which left the relief rolls during the summer of 1935 because a member of the family had obtained employment in private industry.

[31] Gladys L. Palmer, *The Search for Work in Philadelphia, 1932–36,* Works Progress Administration, National Research Project, and Industrial Research Department, University of Pennsylvania, Philadelphia Labor Market Studies, Report No. P-7 (May 1939), p. 35.

[32] H. L. Lurie, *Relief and Reëmployment,* a report of a brief study of the placement of employables from relief to work projects and private jobs in New York City. Prepared for the State Advisory Council of the New York State Employment Service (1936), pp. 26–31. Mimeographed.

siderable numbers of employment service registrants with relief status are fully as employable as are the unemployed who are not on relief. Nevertheless there are certain special difficulties which must be overcome in placing relief applicants, not the least of which is the widespread opinion that these people are on the margin of employability.

Registration of Union Members.—Prior to January 1938, when registration was required for unemployment compensation, few union members registered at the Employment Service except those seeking employment on P.W.A. projects for which registration was required. In such cases, however, the Employment Service did only the paper work, and the enforcement of regulations concerning eligibility for employment and the actual selections were frequently made by the unions. Although union as well as nonunion members must register for unemployment compensation, whether the registration of union members is for the purpose of securing jobs depends largely on coöperative arrangements between the unions and the C.S.E.S.

During the early days of unemployment compensation a number of the offices of the C.S.E.S. which were visited had attempted to work out a coöperative arrangement with certain trade unions which would facilitate the registration of unemployed trade union members, with the hope that later it would be possible to work out coöperative arrangements in regard to placement. In some instances representatives of the Employment Service were assigned to union headquarters to take unemployment compensation claims and registration cards. This arrangement lasted only a month because a rule was made that it was mandatory for union members to register at the office of the C.S.E.S. The reason given for this ruling was that signatures must be obtained on unemployment compensation folders, which were confidential and could not be removed from the employment office. It was, however, suggested that this ruling was not necessarily correct, since in some of the northern counties certification by mail was permitted, and certification out of a union office is not fundamentally different. Another difficulty which was mentioned in regard to placing Employment Service representatives in the offices of trade unions was that the expense of keeping a man in every union office would be prohibitive. However, it was suggested that for the smaller unions it would be possible to carry out the work at centrally located headquarters of groups of unions. Although union as well as nonunion men applying for unemployment compensation were required to register at the offices of the C.S.E.S., it was the general opinion of the Employment Service personnel that union members registered solely for the purpose of unemployment compensation and that, in the main, they would not accept jobs offered by the C.S.E.S because of union rules regarding rotation of jobs or because the jobs were at a wage below the union scale.

The union officials interviewed in the vast majority of cases stated definitely that they were unwilling to share their placement functions with the C.S.E.S., and thus it was clear that from the unions' point of view registration was, in the main, to secure relief or unemployment compensation. While registration of union members undoubtedly improves the quality of the active file, if these registrations are merely a matter of formality, the quality of those available for placement will not in fact be affected.

EMPLOYERS' ORDERS

Employers are not required to use the State Employment Service in recruiting their labor,[38] and therefore this agency has a responsibility similar to that of a business concern in maintaining a demand for its goods and services. Although public employment offices have existed for many years in certain parts

[38] An exception to this is employment in public works, where it is required that workers be secured through the State Employment Service.

of California, it has only been since 1935 that these offices have existed on a state-wide basis and have therefore been in a position to fill a really important place in the organization of the labor market. Its task has not been easy. Employers were accustomed to depending on direct applications at the gate, on private fee-charging agencies, or on other established channels, and in many instances they had a strong prejudice against any organization operated by the government. Furthermore, the new C.S.E.S. came into being in a depression period when jobs were scarce and labor plentiful. The effort to convince employers on any large scale of the need for an agency to dovetail jobs and workers therefore met with rigid obstructions. They preferred the old way, and it was difficult to convince them of a need for the new.

Methods of Securing Employers' Orders.—The *Manual of Operations* sets up a fairly elaborate series of instructions for a field visiting and public relations program. The following quotation indicates the purpose of the field visiting program: "Although the employer visit is a business-getting device, the securing of actual openings is necesarily the ultimate rather than the immediate objective. In general . . . 'the object of every employer visit is to establish or strengthen a continuing relationship with the employer.'" Even broader is the purpose of the public relations program: "To gain the goodwill of the public for our Service and to attain the widest possible acceptance for our Service." The methods recommended are letters, bulletins, news articles, radio broadcasts, participation in civic and club affairs, and advisory councils. The *Manual* further emphasizes that these are major functions of an employment office and not to be regarded as incidental spare-time duties.

Some attention had been given to the problem of employer visits in all of the offices visited, and in San Francisco and Los Angeles there was a fairly elaborate administrative setup for field visiting. In both of these offices an attempt had been made to make up lists of employers and to organize the work on an industrial basis. In the words of the head of one of these departments: "This makes it possible for the field men to become educated in the terminology and needs of the industry and to establish friendly relations with those in charge of hiring."

In the offices in both the large and small communities, at the time this study was made, the field visiting program appeared, in the main, to be a "paper plan." Statements in the following or similar words were made over and over again by members of the staff of the C.S.E.S.: "From the beginning of 1938 the field visiting program has been seriously curtailed. Every member of the staff has worked in the compensation department, and practically no field visits have been made." Further evidence from one of the offices is found in the statement: "Since January 1938 there have been only 2 men in this department, in contrast with 10 the preceding year." To statements such as those above were sometimes added the following remarks: "The field visiting program has ceased because of the disruption and turnover in personnel." "Cuts in travel allowances have made it impossible to do any field visiting." "We cannot go into the field with confidence until the files are in shape and the office force trained to handle the volume of orders which will result from an intensive field visiting program."

Closely allied to the field visiting program are the activities aimed toward creating good public relations. It is important to recognize the fact that the Employment Service is not permitted to pay for publicity or advertising, although such material as letters and bulletins may be printed or mimeographed and distributed by the offices. Copy for all such publicity, as well as for news releases and radio and other addresses, must be submitted to the Sacramento administrative office. A staff member stated that this rule seriously interfered with publicity work since timeliness is of such great importance. It is obvious that there must be some control as to the type of publicity which will be of advantage to the Service, but, if too strictly applied, it may prevent timely publicity and discourage initiative on the part of office managers. A recent study[34] has suggested that the state office might lay down a few basic rules and permit managers to release stories subject to these general limitations. If a manager failed to handle publicity properly, this privilege could be suspended.

All of the offices visited had made some attempt to bring the C.S.E.S. before the public by means of form letters to employers and occasional articles in the newspapers and in trade journals. Most of the offices had secured some time on the radio for spot news announcements to inform the public of the work of the Employment Service or to announce unusual job openings, and in many instances the managers had made efforts to establish contacts with various clubs of business men and civic organizations, but the following comment was sometimes made: "We cannot afford to belong to these organizations, and, after all, such memberships are a part of the public relations program of the C.S.E.S. and the expense should not be borne by the employees."

Los Angeles was the only office with a public relations department separate and distinct from the field visiting program, and therefore it warrants special comment. The personnel of this department included a manager and two assistants, one of whom was a trained radio speaker and writer of copy. The material sent out by this department included a weekly bulletin to employers, occasional special bulletins, blotters, material for speeches, and "human interest" stories in the newspapers. A quotation or two from the weekly bulletin *Employ* and from one of the special bulletins will serve to illustrate something of their purpose and character: "The purpose of 'Employ' will be

[34] Atkinson, Odencrantz, and Deming, *Public Employment Service in the United States*, p. 322.

to pass on to those who hire, new information (not propaganda merely!) that will perhaps be helpful to them in choosing the most fit employees."[35] "You will find the California State Employment Service helpful to you when you discharge, as well as when you employ."[36] "Applicants have been carefully interviewed, registered, classified, and indexed by occupation and also by name—they are 'on tap' at your call. You are saved the time, trouble, and expense of making the preliminary choice."[37]

It was not possible to judge the effectiveness of the rather elaborate publicity program in Los Angeles, but it appeared significant that between 1936 and 1938 placements in Los Angeles declined slightly more than in San Francisco where no such elaborate program had been developed.[38]

The *Manual* recommends, but does not require, that local advisory councils be set up for the purpose of interpreting the service to the community and the needs of the community to the employment office administration. If such councils are set up, the membership must consist of at least nine persons, representing employers, employees, and the public, with the manager of the local employment office as an ex officio member.

Advisory councils had been set up in most of the areas visited. When none had been appointed, the reasons given were usually either that the manager had been too busy to make the necessary contacts or that labor disturbances in the community made it inadvisable for the time being to try to establish a council which would include employers and members of unions.

Where there were advisory councils, it was reported in a good many instances that they had not been very effective. Statements

[35] California State Employment Service, *Employ*, a weekly bulletin to Los Angeles employers, No. 1, June 4, 1938.

[36] *Ibid.*, No. 2, June 11, 1938.

[37] A message to Los Angeles employers, personnel directors, and employment managers, undated.

[38] The decline in placements in both counties was, of course, due to a multiplicity of causes, and therefore the above statement must not be taken as conclusive evidence of the ineffectiveness of the publicity program in Los Angeles.

such as the following were frequently made by members of the staff of the C.S.E.S.: "The advisory council is merely a nominal organization—it has been practically worthless." "The advisory council met only three times in the past year. The members knew little of the work of the C.S.E.S, and frequently we could not transact business because a quorum was not present." That advisory councils have, in general, been ineffective throughout the national system of public employment services is shown in a recent study in which the following statements appear:[39] "... their existence is often more nominal than real." "The council was interested and active during the first year. . . . Then it became increasingly difficult to obtain a quorum at meetings, and the council disappeared from the scene." This study concludes that it does not appear that offices with advisory councils have been more successful than those without.

Effectiveness of the Program.—All of the available evidence leads to the conclusion that since 1935 the activities of the C.S.E.S. in connection with securing employers' orders and with establishing good public relations have been a minor rather than a major function. The reasons for this have been both internal and external: the organization was in its infancy and had to meet all the problems of personnel and of new administrative procedures; it was made responsible for the registration of vast numbers of relief applicants and, from 1938, for registering and taking claims for applicants for unemployment compensation. Managers simply did not have time for anything but the routine administration of their offices and for making whatever placements they could in jobs which were listed without solicitation. Perhaps the greatest hindrance to this, as well as to other parts of employment service activity, has been the business depression. When the manager of an employment office knows that most employers are laying off workers and that the occasional job will be filled by an old employee, in which case

[39] Atkinson, Odencrantz, and Deming, *op. cit.*, p. 149.

there is no reason for application to an employment service, it can hardly be expected that an already overworked staff will do much field visiting or publicity work. Furthermore, the staff was pretty well convinced that if they did secure orders they could not be promptly or efficiently filled because of the lack of trained personnel and because the filing system was in such poor shape.

At the time this study was made, statistics on employers' orders were almost completely lacking. The only information which related to this subject were the statistics of placement. These statistics were, of course, proof that some employers were using the public employment offices, but they provided no information as to the type of employer using the service or as to the success with which orders were being filled. Information should be available as to employers' orders received, canceled, and still open, as well as to those which have been filled; these subjects should be broken down by industry, occupation, sex, and duration of the job; and the reasons for cancellation of orders should be analyzed.[40] Statistics of this sort are essential for any judgment of the efficiency of the staff of the Employment Service. Furthermore, this type of information will yield valuable data as to the types of employers and jobs which are being listed with the Employment Service and will indicate wherein there may be a shortage of workers with particular skills registered with the Employment Service. These facts will serve as a guide to the manager of the employment agency in directing his staff as to the points of special emphasis. For instance, even in a time of a general surplus of labor and dearth of jobs, there may be orders for workers with certain skills which cannot be filled. An analysis of statistics of job orders

[40] There are many problems connected with statistics of employers' orders. For instance, a time limit must be established after which an order is no longer considered open. For a discussion of this problem see A. M. Stewart and B. M. Stewart, *Statistical Procedure of Public Employment Offices* (New York: Russell Sage Foundation, 1933).

would bring this to light and might indicate the necessity of special recruiting methods for workers with the necessary skills. Again, employers' orders, if analyzed in relation to the important economic activities in the community, might indicate that certain industries or employers are making little or no use of the State Employment Service, and thus that special effort should be made to determine the reasons for this and to convince employers who are doing any hiring as to the advantages of using a centralized employment service.

PLACEMENTS

Placement is the primary function of an employment office. It is the test of service to workers and to employers and of the place an employment service has taken in the organization of the labor market. It is unlikely that hiring will ever be completely centralized at any marketing place, since the marketing of labor involves a complexity of human problems, preferences, and prejudices, and some employers and workers will always prefer a direct rather than an indirect method of contact. Nevertheless there are wide areas in which hit-and-miss personal contacts between employer and worker are clearly to the disadvantage of both, and where there is an obvious need for an intervening agency in order to bring the two together expeditiously and economically. The extent to which the C.S.E.S. fills this need is the test of its successful operation, and the measure of its work is the number and type of placements made through its services.

If placements are to be made, there must be jobs to be filled; and it must be possible within reasonable limits to refer to the employer a worker who meets his specifications. The work of the C.S.E.S. in getting employers' orders and in maintaining a file of job seekers has already been described. The present section is concerned with its success in fitting together the job and the applicant.

Procedures

Selecting qualified applicants.—A few general rules have been set up regarding the selection of applicants for referral. The primary consideration must be the qualification of the applicant for the job, but it is important to recognize that skill alone does not determine a worker's qualification for a particular job. Other factors, such as idiosyncracies of the employer and personality of the worker, must be taken into account. Certain regulations have been set up to prevent preferences to special groups. For instance, the placement officers are expected to consider, on an equal basis, relief and nonrelief applicants and veterans and nonveterans. It is also recommended that those present in an office should not be given first consideration when job orders come in, although it is recognized that spot placements of workers present in an office may sometimes be necessary if there is a shortage of applicants for a particular type of job or if an employer sends in a rush order.

Placement officers.—No rules are set up as to whether placements shall be the responsibility of specialists whose functions shall be solely in this field or of staff members who both interview applicants and make placements. The *Manual of Operations,* however, points out that there is considerable to be said for special placement officers. In large offices where there is a constant flow of applicants through the office, employers' orders may be given secondary consideration unless there are special placement officers who have time to consider every job order carefully. If there is to be this type of specialization, however, there must be sufficient coöperation between interviewers and placement officers, so that the official in charge of placement will have more information as to the qualifications of applicants than is usually found on a registration card.

In the offices in the metropolitan centers of Los Angeles and San Francisco certain members of the staff of the various departments were usually designated as placement officers, although exceptions to this were found in the junior departments in both cities, in the Chinese department in San Francisco, and in the department for the handicapped in Los Angeles where the same persons both registered and placed. In the Bakersfield and Sacramento offices the person in charge of each department was responsible for placements; but this work did not require his entire time, so he registered workers as well. In the smaller offices the managers were primarily responsible for the placement work, but strict lines were not drawn, and everyone in the office probably at times did some placement work.

The files.—When a job order is received, the placement officer is expected to search the active file of primary and secondary occupations. If a suitable person is not found, the inactive file should be consulted. Finally, other community resources should be used, such as employers of workers with similar skills; other free employment agencies, such as trade unions, social agencies, educational institutions, and professional organizations; and newspaper advertisements and other types of publicity, such as the radio. If all local resources fail, and if the employer is willing, there should be recourse to clearance, through which the job order is communicated to other C.S.E.S. offices in the state or even to offices of the U.S.E.S. in other states. There is no general rule that applicants must be reinterviewed before referral to a job, although it is stated in the *Manual of Operations* that careful consideration of the qualifications of an individual necessitates that he be reinterviewed before being referred. The matter of the number of persons to be referred to a job is left to the placement officer, and his decision must, in considerable measure, depend upon the desires of the employer.

It appeared evident that the staff members in the offices visited were making an effort to search the files for qualified people to fill jobs in the skilled trades and in the clerical and professional fields.[41] In many instances, however, it was reported that the files did not easily and correctly yield the necessary information. In the larger offices the files were so large as to be unwieldy, and in all of the offices it was reported that the files were frequently useless because the registration cards had been made out sketchily or incorrectly. As a consequence, workers who could not meet the specifications set up by the employer were frequently referred to jobs. This was particularly true when referrals were made without reinterview, which was necessary if the job had to be filled immediately. A case in point was a man with one arm and a wooden leg who was sent out to do farm labor. The staff member who told this story said, "The man was removed and the farmer soothed, but he probably won't call the C.S.E.S. the next time he needs workers." While this is an exaggerated case of misfit of worker to job, it was undoubtedly true that the registration cards frequently did not divulge the qualifications of an applicant.

Mistakes of the sort described above were avoided in certain departments which were staffed by people who had been in the public employment service for 10 or 15 years, who knew many of their applicants by name, and who were thoroughly familiar with the job specifications in their department. In other cases special files of qualified workers facilitated the job of referring qualified workers. Some of the offices reported plans for visits of the staff to various manufacturing plants in order that they might become more familiar with the processes and jobs in which workers might be placed. Such plans, however, had not been carried very far in the early months of 1938.

If a job order is received which cannot be filled by applicants with primary occupations which meet the specifications, the secondary occupational cards become a source from which referrals may be made. At the time that the offices of the C.S.E.S.

[41] The use of "spot placements" of persons who happened to be present when the order was received is discussed on pages 122–124.

were visited, the supply of labor in most occupations was so much greater than the demand that little attention was given to secondary occupations. The staff seemed to feel that the condition of the labor market did not warrant the time necessary to make out many secondary cards;[42] and, furthermore, frequently the burden of work was so heavy that there was not time for the extra clerical work. It was reported that there were practically always applicants available under the primary classifications, and some of the managers were of the opinion that secondary occupations were frequently merely "second choices" for which the worker had no real qualifications. For instance, those in charge of placing domestic and hotel workers said that office workers were sometimes given secondary cards for domestic and hotel employment but that these were almost always useless, since office workers seldom had experience in these occupations and the Employment Service found it difficult to check on the workers' statements. It seems evident that any considerable use of secondary occupations is a refinement which will have to be developed as the need becomes more apparent and when the staff is not working under such pressure.

The inactive file is another source which may be used in filling difficult jobs. Here again, the condition of the labor market usually made it unnecessary to use this resource. Even in occupations such as domestic service, where there was a scarcity of applicants, it was felt that to review the inactive file would produce no results. Certain departments, most frequently the commercial, made some use of the inactive files for jobs which were out of the ordinary or which demanded unusual skills. A manager of a commercial department said, "People in these occupations often become discouraged and fail to renew their registrations even though they are unemployed."

Use of other local agencies.—At the time the offices were visited, little had been done to establish coöperative arrange-

[42] There was no statistical evidence available as to the number of secondary cards.

ments with other community placement agencies. The overworked staff did not have time to make such contacts; and, furthermore, it was generally considered unnecessary when the files of the Employment Service were so large. Occasionally, however, an office did use outside resources. A men's industrial department reported that sometimes trade unions and employers of similar workers were called; commercial departments sometimes called personnel managers, business machine companies, and trade schools; the manager of a Chinese department visited stores in Chinatown or called the Chinese Y.M.C.A. and left word that applicants were needed at the Employment Service "for good jobs"; and an agricultural department occasionally called a supply company for Mexicans with special qualifications. In a few instances social service agencies reported that the C.S.E.S. sometimes called them if there was a shortage of applicants with a particular qualification. In one or two instances employers' associations were called to secure highly skilled workers.

Since each year vast numbers of young people come forth from the schools and colleges seeking employment, some sort of coöperative relationship between the schools and colleges and the C.S.E.S. might have been expected. All of the offices, with one exception where the manager said, "We don't want to handle placements for the schools," reported that efforts were being made to establish coöperative arrangements with the schools. It appeared, however, that plans for coöperation had not developed into anything tangible except in Los Angeles where the Central Employment Service of the school system is affiliated with the C.S.E.S. and is, in fact, the Junior Department of the C.S.E.S. The Central Employment Service is supported by the Los Angeles school department, with the exception of a statistical clerk and a typist whose salaries are paid by the C.S.E.S. It is responsible for the registration and placement not only of students of Los Angeles high schools but also of all young people under the age of 21, and up to 25 if without work experience, who make application either at the office of the C.S.E.S. or at the Central Employment Service. Placements made by this agency are included in the C.S.E.S. statistics.

Clearance.—If workers with a particular skill which is necessary to fill a job order cannot be found within a community, the Employment Service is expected to make use of the clearance system. At the time the offices were visited, it seemed to be quite generally agreed that clearance was not a very important factor in making placements. Frequently managers of various departments said, "Jobs which cannot be filled locally pay such low wages that clearance is seldom worth while," or, "If we cannot fill the job, there is little possibility that other offices have qualified applicants," or, "Usually clearance is of no use because employers want workers immediately."

In certain instances, however, clearance was used. In Los Angeles and in San Francisco, for instance, there was some interchange of information between offices in nearby localities in regard to jobs which were difficult to fill. In Los Angeles jobs in the industrial field were sometimes filled by calling the Huntington Park office, which had a large file of men in those occupations; and, similarly, San Francisco sometimes called the Oakland office. It would be expected that clearance would be most frequently used for jobs in agriculture, which demands a fluctuating and mobile labor supply. One manager of an agricultural department commented, "There is too much red tape in clearance." This same official, however, claimed considerable success in transferring workers from one part of the state to another. He said, "Last year I brought in 10,000 workers for hop picking by broadcasting over the radio, by newspaper write-ups, and by bulletins to other offices, but only a fraction of these passed through the office of the C.S.E.S." As far as could be determined, this was an independent activity of this manager with no tie-up with the central clearance system. There was no evidence in any of the agricultural offices visited that clearance orders were filled by routing specific agricultural laborers from one place to another in the state. The system seemed to be to issue bulletins from the Sacramento central office that 100 or 200, or an unspecified number, of pickers were needed in a given area and to leave it pretty much to chance as to whether 100 or 1,000 arrived.

An examination of the clearance bulletins, issued by the Sacramento headquarters at frequent intervals from February 1937 to May 1938, yielded some interesting data on the subject of the use of clearance for agricultural labor. Bulletins were issued in the following terms for workers in hops, beets, grapes, tree fruits, cotton, peas, and lettuce: "We expect a demand for beet thinners in the Sacramento area." "600 grape and fig pickers are needed in Fresno." "700 cotton pickers can find employment in Bakersfield and 2,000 pea pickers in El Centro." At other times bulletins were issued advising the offices of the C.S.E.S. of surpluses of agricultural labor. For instance, during April and May 1937 a series of bulletins was released to the effect that migration of labor to Monterey County should be discouraged. In September all offices were notified of a surplus of workers in hops in Santa Rosa. In February 1938 the following statement was issued: "Do not refer any agricultural laborers to Imperial Valley. It is estimated that there is a surplus of labor double the number that can be placed within 60 to 90 days. Remove all signs, if such exist, urging workers to go to Imperial Valley."

Special Problems

Spot placements.—In general, the managers of the offices visited subscribed to the theory that spot placements—preferential treatment to those in the office at the time a job order came in—are not in accordance with the best employment office procedure, but they also stated that this type of placement had not been eliminated. The reason for this appeared to be that a large proportion of the placements were rush orders for temporary employment in relatively unskilled work. There were considerable differences between the various offices in their use of spot placements.[43] All of the departments in the San Francisco office reported that spot placements were discouraged and resorted to only if an employer needed someone immediately and it was not possible to take the time to check the files and telephone applicants. This occurred most frequently in the men's industrial and the women's domestic departments. In Los Angeles a member of the staff of the men's industrial department stated, "When orders come in they are typed on small slips of paper and placed on a board by the 'job opening' window. These slips are left at the window for an hour for spot placements before the placement officer starts to telephone for applicants. We figure that a man who is really interested will come down to the office and see what opportunities are available." In other departments of the Los Angeles office it appeared that spot placements were resorted to only for rush orders or during periods when the files were in such a bad shape that they could not be used for filling orders. In Sacramento spot placements were pretty much the rule in both the men's industrial department and in the agricultural office. The manager of the men's industrial department said, "When an employer wants a man for a job, he wants him immediately, and as a result placements are made from those who hang around the office regularly." The comment was also made that the files were cluttered up with transients whose addresses were useless. The manager of the agricultural office explained that practically all of his placements were from those who walk up and down the "Skidway" looking for work. He said, "I haven't time to hunt up specific men because employers usually want their orders filled within an hour, and in any case

[43] There were no statistics available as to the number of spot placements. The following statements are based on a discussion of this subject with the managers of the offices and of departments.

the men move so much that their addresses are no good." The Bakersfield office estimated that 50 per cent of the placements in the men's department were spot placements. The jobs filled in this way were usually relatively unskilled and temporary work. A staff member said, "When an employer calls, he wants a worker immediately, and the man in the office is the one who gets the job."

It was quite obvious in most of the offices visited that, when an unskilled or temporary job order was listed or a rush order came in, there was a tendency to refer the man in the office rather than to use the file of registrants as a source of referral. Spot placements were also frequent in highly skilled domestic work because of a shortage of skilled workers in this occupational group, and thus applicants could frequently be referred immediately on registration.

Preferential treatment of certain groups.—In general it was stated that there was conformity to the rule that the best-qualified person available should be referred to the job. However, in some instances, if several equally competent men registered, those on relief were given the first referrals. One manager said, "I have had some trouble with my placement officers adopting a social-service attitude. The placement officer must learn not to feel sorry for the applicant's economic or family difficulties but to concentrate on his qualifications." More frequently, however, the placement officers were of the opinion that those who were certified for relief were, in general, the less well-qualified. It is impossible to estimate how widespread was this feeling, but undoubtedly in some instances it resulted in discrimination against qualified workers who were on relief.

The problem of preferential treatment has also been raised in relation to veterans. In accordance with the affiliation agreement with the U.S.E.S., there was in each of the offices visited some person designated to give special attention to veterans, with particular reference to their legal rights to preferences in certain jobs, such as public works. For other types of jobs veterans must compete on an equal basis with nonveterans. Apparently in some offices certain special efforts were being made to place veterans. For instance, when an order came in for several men, an assistant manager—himself a veteran—suggested to the placement officer that at least one veteran be sent out among the various referrals for the job. This was probably not a violation of the principle of sending the man best qualified for the job, because these orders were for unskilled workers. In a number of offices veterans were "given a break" when jobs came in for older men to act as janitors or watchmen, but frequently the opinion was expressed that veterans as a group were not able to compete with the younger applicants for the better jobs.

This study was made too early in the history of unemployment compensation to determine the effect of this legislation on the problem of preference in referrals. Prior consideration to those receiving unemployment compensation would violate the rule that the best-qualified person must be referred, and, furthermore, it would discriminate against the noncovered worker who has an equal right to expect service from the employment office. In general, the offices visited maintained that preference was not given to claimants for unemployment benefits. Some of the managers pointed out, however, that these workers may, in fact, find themselves on a preferred list as far as employment is concerned if employers call for former employees by name. The manager of an office in the citrus district recommended that an agreement might be drawn up with employers in this industry whereby all referrals would be limited to those who had been employed in the citrus industry within a year. Another member of the staff of the C.S.E.S. reported that he attended a meeting of the citrus packers at which he said: "I assured these people that the C.S.E.S. will give preferential treatment to those who have worked for a packer before. Furthermore, the C.S.E.S. will make every effort to place those laid off in some other packing plant before their waiting period has expired. I emphasized, however, that this will only be possible if jobs as well as workers are registered." It is possible that there will be pressure from various industries for arrangements of this sort. Whether this will be considered to be an unwarranted preference to a special group is a matter of speculation, but it certainly would limit the employment opportunities of those who might wish to transfer from uncovered to covered employments.

It may appear in some instances that the employment office is giving preference to certain groups. Further analysis, however, may indicate that the preference is related to the right of the employer to set up job specifications. For instance, an employer may request veterans, and in such a case a worker possessing this qualification will have a better chance of placement than will a nonveteran.

Labor disputes.—An important general rule in regard to placements is related to situations in which a strike or lockout exists. If there is a strike or lockout in a plant which has applied for workers, the employment office may not solicit workers for these jobs. It may, however, refer workers who call at the office after they have signed an acknowledgment of a notice that the condition exists.[44] It appeared that the offices visited were acting in conformity with the regulation that workers should not be solicited for jobs in establishments in which there was a strike or lockout. A labor coördinator in one of the offices

[44] This was in accordance with the United States Employment Service Bulletin No. II in force at the time this study was made. (See California State Employment Service, *Manual of Operations*, p. 144). Subsequently the Social Security Board issued a new rule on this subject as follows: "The State service shall require that each employment office under its supervision refrain from referring any person or persons to any positions left vacant by reason of a labor dispute at any place of employment by a person belonging to a grade or class of workers participating in, or directly interested in such labor dispute, at such place of employment." Letter from Ralph G. Wadsworth, Acting Director, California Department of Employment, August 30, 1941.

pointed out, however, that the C.S.E.S. sometimes referred workers to a plant where there was a strike or lockout of which the worker had not been notified because it was not known that a labor dispute existed. He said, "When this happens, the unions accuse the C.S.E.S. of breaking the law. However, the C.S.E.S. has in such cases acted in good faith. I point out to the union that the people in the C.S.E.S. are not crystal gazers and that it is, in part, the responsibility of the union to notify the C.S.E.S. that a labor dispute exists." In order to protect the Employment Service from violating the provisions of the Wagner-Peyser Act, it is essential that a system should be worked out whereby there will be immediate notification of the existence of a labor dispute.

The Employment Service in California has met with considerable opposition in administering the rule in regard to strike jobs. In September 1938 an official of the Associated Farmers in Kern County made the following statement: "A few days ago we called the office of the C.S.E.S. and asked for workers to replace workers on strike. We were told that this office could not solicit workers for strike jobs. From this moment on we will have nothing to do with the C.S.E.S. It has refused to perform its function of serving workers and farmers."[45] It should be emphasized that the action of the local manager of the C.S.E.S., described above, was in accordance with the rules and regulations of his office. If the attitude expressed by the official of the Associated Farmers in Kern County is typical of

[45] A quotation from a statement made by the Associated Farmers to the Tolan Committee in September 1940 further verifies the above-mentioned attitude of the Associated Farmers: "Under these regulations [regulations regarding referral of persons to jobs vacant because of a labor dispute] the farmers find they cannot work with or use with dependability or efficiency the California Department of Employment. . . . As long as this regulation is in effect, the systems now in existence for aiding these migrants to find jobs cannot be utilized by agriculture." *Hearings before the Select Committee to Investigate the Interstate Migration of Destitute Citizens, House of Representatives,* 76th Cong., 3d sess., Part 6, San Francisco Hearings, Sept. 24 and 25, 1940 (Washington: Government Printing Office, 1941), p. 2753. See also Resolution number 18 passed at a meeting of the Associated Farmers, Dec. 1941.

other parts of the state, it will seriously hinder the activity of the Employment Service in agriculture.

Substandard jobs.—Another problem which the Employment Service has had to face is the procedure to be followed when substandard jobs are listed. It is the general policy of the offices to list all job orders, to obtain information as to wages and conditions of employment, and to leave it to the worker to decide whether or not he will apply for the job. If, however, the job is too undesirable, no effort may be made to refer applicants. Clearly the Employment Service cannot attempt to raise prevailing wage rates; but, at the same time, it should not become an agency through which the exploitation of labor is facilitated. It cannot dictate wages to employers, but it should offer reasonable protection to the workers, particularly to those groups for whom there are legal standards, and to young people and newcomers to the community who may be ignorant of prevailing wage rates. The offices of the C.S.E.S. that were visited, in general, listed all jobs, informed workers of the conditions of employment, and allowed them to make their own choice. Some, however, took more definite action in regard to women and young people for whom maximum hours and minimum wages have been established by law and refused to make placements in jobs offering conditions which did not conform to legal requirements. That this policy had not been uniformly adopted is indicated by a statement of a manager of a women's industrial department. She said, "If an employer requests a woman at less than the minimum wage, women who need work very badly are sent out because they will get more than they can get on relief. The C.S.E.S. is not a spy organization, and therefore we do not report violations to the State Department of Industrial Relations."

The women's domestic departments in San Francisco and in Los Angeles had attempted to adopt standards set up by local committees. In both of these departments employers requesting workers at less than from $25 to $30 a month and room and board were told that it would be difficult to fill the position. It is probable that in a good many instances these standards were not maintained, but it has perhaps been of some value in indicating to employers and to workers that the State Employment Service is not merely a market for cheap jobs and cheap labor.

The industrial departments were sometimes confronted with the fact that the only jobs listed were at rates of pay less than the union rate, and the fact that in unorganized trades it was frequently impossible to determine what was the prevailing rate. In these cases, the worker was informed and allowed to make his own choice. The commercial departments in most instances also followed this practice; but little effort was made to fill jobs which were entirely on a commission basis, because such jobs often cost the worker more in carfare and shoe leather than he could possibly earn.

It would seem reasonable to assume that the Employment Service can best fulfill its function as a place where workers and jobs are brought together if, in the main, it continues its policy of leaving the decision as to acceptance or rejection of jobs to the individual employee; however, the Employment Service should refuse to fill jobs in which legal requirements are not met and should inform workers and employers when jobs are offered under conditions definitely less good than those prevailing in the community.

Numbers and Kinds of Placements.—The real test of the success of an employment agency is the record of placements. If this record is to be an index of the service being rendered, it should not be merely in terms of numbers of placements but also in terms of duration of the job and industries and occupations in which placements are made, and information should be available regarding the age and sex of those placed. Mere numbers alone may impress or discourage either an interested

TABLE 16

PLACEMENTS BY THE CALIFORNIA STATE EMPLOYMENT SERVICE AND THE NATIONAL REËMPLOYMENT SERVICE, 1935–1938

Date	Total	Private	Public excluding relief	Relief
1935				
Total	233,694*	‡	‡	‡
January	†	‡	‡	‡
February	†	‡	‡	‡
March	†	‡	‡	‡
April	†	‡	‡	‡
May	18,703	‡	‡	‡
June	19,716	‡	‡	‡
July	18,677	‡	‡	‡
August	23,532	‡	‡	‡
September	27,843	‡	‡	‡
October	36,034	‡	‡	‡
November	48,538	‡	‡	‡
December	40,651	‡	‡	‡
1936				
Total	442,517	175,973	169,876	96,668
January	43,643	5,607	7,426	30,610
February	32,938	5,536	8,665	18,737
March	38,784	9,811	10,586	18,387
April	29,576	11,755	11,048	6,773
May	31,942	14,341	13,567	4,034
June	39,522	14,976	13,935	10,611
July	40,906	15,732	18,381	6,793
August	41,575	21,209	19,901	465
September	42,154	24,365	17,700	89
October	42,663	24,036	18,556	71
November	31,774	15,076	16,639	59
December	27,040	13,529	13,472	39
1937				
Total	275,441	202,357	72,872	212
January	18,025	11,338	6,632	55
February	19,865	11,359	8,494	12

SOURCE: Unpublished data from the California State Department of Employment, Division of Research and Statistics.

* Total for 8 months.

† The California State Department of Employment did not publish placement figures in these months, and those published by the California State Department of Industrial Relations did not include N.R.S. placements.

‡ Figures not available.

TABLE 16 (*Continued*)

Date	Total	Private	Public excluding relief	Relief
1937 (*Continued*)				
March	22,123	15,028	7,054	41
April	23,843	16,111	7,709	23
May	27,658	19,685	7,960	13
June	25,721	18,449	7,231	41
July	24,964	18,629	6,328	7
August	24,827	19,068	5,756	3
September	28,775	23,947	4,828	—
October	26,836	22,346	4,488	2
November	18,740	15,163	3,568	9
December	14,064	11,234	2,824	6
1938				
Total	223,303	169,563	53,620	120
January	10,443	7,803	2,640	—
February	10,474	8,018	2,456	—
March	16,788	13,194	3,594	—
April	18,346	15,392	2,954	—
May	22,124	13,576	8,504	44
June	20,649	14,617	6,012	20
July	18,099	14,442	3,601	56
August	21,023	16,956	4,067	§
September	21,488	17,263	4,225	§
October	23,339	18,410	4,929	§
November	20,979	16,156	4,823	§
December	19,551	13,736	5,815	§

§ Record discontinued.

member of the public or an administrator. They do not tell the whole story, and in some instances comparisons of total placements may create an impression so erroneous as to interfere with the smooth functioning of an employment office. For instance, an office may find itself under fire of criticism because its total placements are few in comparison with other offices. It is possible, however, that the small number of placements were, in the main, permanent, and that they were in occupations which demanded time and special care in selection. The efficiency of an employment office cannot be judged unless a good deal more than the number of total placements is known.

At the time that this study was made, the statistical data in regard to placements were in a number of respects incomplete.[46] For the state as a whole, from January 1936 it was possible to obtain total placements broken down by private, public, and relief, by industries and occupations, and by age. For the offices visited the only breakdown for the period 1936–38 was by public, private, and relief; placements classified by industry and occupation were available only for 1938. No information was available as to duration of placements or as to sex of those placed.

Total number placed.—In the period under discussion (1935–38) annual placements by all of the offices in California public employment service were at their highest point in 1936. In that year about 443,000 placements were made. In 1937 about 275,000 were placed, and in 1938 there was a further drop to about 200,000. Placements by the San Francisco, Los Angeles, Sacramento, and Kern County offices of the C.S.E.S. likewise declined between 1936 and 1938. All, however, did not fall to a like degree. Placements in San Francisco and Los Angeles counties dropped about 55 per cent; in Sacramento and Kern, 61 and 42 per cent, respectively.

From 1936 to 1938 the fluctuations in total placements made by the C.S.E.S. were primarily the result of changes in the numbers of relief and public works placements. During 1935 and 1936 the C.S.E.S. was responsible not only for registering applicants for relief work but also for placing this group of people on relief work projects.[47] A few placements of this type were made in 1937 and in 1938, but the numbers were so small

[46] A placement is defined as a position filled for which a verification has been received.

[47] The 1935 placements are not broken down by relief and nonrelief. Certain scattered evidence, however, points to the conclusion that a large proportion of placements in 1935 were on relief projects. See *Monthly Labor Review*, 42 (Mar. 1936), p. 729.

TABLE 17

PLACEMENTS BY THE SAN FRANCISCO, LOS ANGELES, SACRAMENTO, AND KERN COUNTY OFFICES OF THE CALIFORNIA STATE EMPLOYMENT SERVICE, 1936–1938

Year	Total	Private	Public	Relief
NUMBER				
San Francisco				
1936	35,247	13,980	8,338	12,929
1937	20,049	13,445	6,604	—
1938	16,085	15,070	1,015	—
Los Angeles				
1936	166,747	46,356	73,914	46,477
1937	86,109	60,914	25,194	1
1938	71,621	54,702	16,919	—
Sacramento				
1936	20,520	14,540	3,945	2,035
1937	14,549	13,466	1,083	—
1938	7,941	6,664	1,277	—
Kern				
1936	13,684	9,315	2,993	1,376
1937	12,389	10,854	1,534	1
1938	7,958	6,253	1,705	—
PER CENT				
San Francisco				
1936	100.0	39.7	23.6	36.7
1937	100.0	67.1	32.9	—
1938	100.0	93.7	6.3	—
Los Angeles				
1936	100.0	27.8	44.3	27.9
1937	100.0	70.7	29.3	—
1938	100.0	76.4	23.6	—
Sacramento				
1936	100.0	70.9	19.2	9.9
1937	100.0	92.6	7.4	—
1938	100.0	83.9	16.1	—
Kern				
1936	100.0	68.1	21.9	10.0
1937	100.0	87.6	12.4	—
1938	100.0	78.6	21.4	—

SOURCE: Unpublished data from the California State Department of Employment, Division of Research and Statistics.

as to be negligible, and the record was discontinued about the middle of 1938. In 1936 nearly 97,000, about 20 per cent of the total, were relief placements, whereas in 1937 only 212 and in 1938 only 120 placements in this category were made. In San Francisco County in 1936 relief placements were about 40 per cent of total placements, in Los Angeles 28 per cent, and in Sacramento and Kern counties about 10 per cent. The decline in total placements between 1936 and 1938 may be explained in part in terms of the removal of the responsibility for relief work placements. If these placements were excluded in each year, the net total for the state was about one-third lower in 1938 than in 1936. There was also a considerable decline in the field of public placements, from about 170,000, nearly 40 per cent of the total, in 1936, to 73,000 in 1937 and 54,000 in 1938. In the two later years public placements were about one-fourth of the total placements. The proportion of public to total placements was smaller in 1938 than in 1936 in all the counties visited except in Kern County. There were, however, large variations in the importance of public placements between these four counties. In 1936, 44 per cent of the placements in Los Angeles were classified as public, in contrast with 24 per cent in San Francisco and about 20 per cent in Sacramento and Kern counties, and in 1938 public placements in Los Angeles had declined to less than 25 per cent, Sacramento to 16 per cent, and San Francisco to 6 per cent. The state-wide figures for this period show a decline in public placements from 38 to 24 per cent.

The total number of placements in private employment did not vary greatly in the three years 1936, 1937, and 1938. Although between 170,000 and 200,000 private placements were made in each of these years, because of the decline in other types of placements mentioned above, the proportion of private to total placements increased from 40 per cent in 1936 to about 75 per cent in the two following years. Private placements in-

TABLE 18

INDUSTRIAL GROUPING OF PLACEMENTS BY THE CALIFORNIA STATE EMPLOYMENT SERVICE AND THE NATIONAL REËMPLOYMENT SERVICE IN CALIFORNIA, 1936–1938

Industry	1936		1937		1938	
	Number	Per cent	Number	Per cent	Number	Per cent
Total*	216,916	100.0	264,655	100.0	219,931	100.0
Agriculture, forestry, and fishing	57,508	26.5	65,131	24.6	32,178	14.6
Extraction of minerals	813	0.4	712	0.3	909	0.4
Building and construction	52,143	24.0	71,249	26.9	53,241	24.2
Private	*14,628*	*6.7*	*13,636*	*5.1*	*10,977*	*5.0*
Public	*37,515*	*17.3*	*57,613*	*21.8*	*42,264*	*19.2*
Manufacturing	26,724	12.3	27,439	10.4	31,274	14.2
Commercial and mechanical services and finance	125	0.1	6,743	2.5	7,202	3.3
Distribution	15,439	7.1	16,330	6.2	17,680	8.0
Domestic and personal service, hotels, restaurants, amusements	51,560	23.8	64,536	24.4	61,932	28.2
Government service	3,754	1.7	4,630	1.7	8,139	3.7
Professional service	4,730	2.2	3,845	1.5	3,567	1.6
Transportation and communication	3,545	1.6	3,308	1.2	3,403	1.6
Other public utilities	575	0.3	732	0.3	406	0.2

SOURCE: Unpublished data from the California State Department of Employment, Division of Research and Statistics.

* Totals do not include placements on relief work projects and also exclude a few cases in each year in which the industry was not specified.

creased slightly in this period in San Francisco and in Los Angeles and decreased in Sacramento and Kern counties. In San Francisco the proportion of private to total placements increased from 40 to 94 per cent, in Los Angeles from 28 to 76 per cent, and in Sacramento and Kern counties the rise in the proportion of private to total placements was much smaller.

The complicating factors are so great that it is not possible to determine whether the C.S.E.S. might have been expected to have increased its private placements by appreciable numbers in the period 1936 to 1938. General employment conditions in California improved throughout 1936 and to the middle of 1937 and then declined to the end of 1938. Employment Service placements in private employment increased considerably throughout the spring and fall of 1936, but declined sharply at the end of the year. During the spring and summer of 1937 placements increased, but this was followed by a sharp decline at the end of the year, and total private placements for 1938 were considerably less than in the preceding year. With the exception of the decline in late 1936 and early 1937, the movements of private placements conformed in a general way to those of general employment conditions in California. It is, however, not possible to draw any conclusions as to whether the amount of these changes was more or less than might have been expected in view of the general employment situation.

Placements by industry.—An analysis of the placement activities of the C.S.E.S. becomes more complete if the industries[48] which were served by these offices are examined. In each of the three years, 1936, 1937, and 1938, the largest number of placements were made in agriculture, domestic and personal service, and public employment, including public construction and other governmental employment. From about 60 to 70 per cent of the placements were in these three categories. Manufacturing was the only other industrial category that included as many as 10 per cent of the placements. The relative order of importance of placements in these three industry groups changed

[48] Relief placements have been excluded from total placements classified by industry, since "relief work projects" is not an industrial classification. It should be noted that total relief placements as given in table 16 do not equal the total excluded from the industrial classification as placed on relief work projects. Apparently the State Department of Employment has used two definitions of relief placements. In the industrial breakdown all public placements except public building construction and government service were included as relief work projects, whereas in the breakdown by private, public, and relief placements the category "public excluding relief" included not only public building and government service but also large numbers who were subsequently, in the industrial breakdown, classified as employed on relief work projects.

somewhat during the period under discussion. For instance, agriculture dropped from first to third place (from 27 to 15 per cent), and domestic and personal service rose from second to first place (from 24 to 28 per cent). The decline in agricultural placements was probably in part because farmers did not feel the need of any employment service, but there was considerable evidence to the effect that, at the time this study was made, the Employment Service did not have the facilities to serve the farmers even when they might need it. Only in Sacramento was there an agricultural office, and it was reported that this office did not have an adequate staff for field visiting or for publicity. In some instances growers who were interviewed did not even know of the existence of the C.S.E.S. In Kern County the only office of the C.S.E.S. was in Bakersfield, which in many instances was a long distance from the source of employment. It could hardly be expected that any considerable number of either employers or workers would spend the time or money necessary to travel to Bakersfield to register at the office of the C.S.E.S. Another fact of importance is revealed by the agricultural placement figures for 1938. In that year agricultural placements in Los Angeles County were a negligible proportion of the total. The number of agricultural wage earners in Los Angeles County is over five times as large as in Kern County, yet the total number of agricultural placements in Los Angeles was slightly less than in Kern County, despite the inconvenient disposition of offices in the latter area. There is no simple explanation of this fact. It is probably, at least in part, due to the differences in the type of labor used in the two areas. Farmers in Kern County depend to a large extent upon migratory laborers who move from one part of the state to another; thus the Employment Service can, at least at times, be of service in bringing the two together. The citrus growers in Los Angeles County, on the other hand, depend to a large extent on residents of their own district who work for the same employer year after year and who, because they live nearby, have full knowledge as to when the season is about to open. It is probable that under such arrangements an intermediate agency is not necessary except at such times as there may be a shortage of local labor. It is suggested, however, that the Employment Service in Los Angeles County could perform a very useful service for employers and workers in other crops, particularly walnuts, which to a much larger extent than citrus depend on nonresident labor. If this field of activity were developed, the Employment Service could prevent much of the wasteful door-to-door application for jobs.

The large number of placements in domestic and personal service can probably be explained by reference to the history of the Employment Service, which has always been looked upon as a source for relatively unskilled domestic workers. The importance of placements in public construction can be accounted for by the requirement that employers must secure their workers through the public employment service.

A comparison of the industrial distribution of placements with the industries represented by the active file registrants will give an indication as to whether the concentration of placements in certain groups is related to the industries in which the registrants had formerly been employed.[49] For the state as a whole, in 1936 and 1937 there was a much larger proportion of placements than of registrants in agriculture, in domestic service, and in public employment. In 1938 placements in agriculture had declined to about 50 per cent of the preceding year. Agricultural registrants also dropped, and thus this industry was represented by only a slightly larger proportion of placements than of registrants. As in the two preceding years, domestic service and public employment were again represented by

[49] The industrial breakdown of the active file is available only for the inventory dates, whereas placements classified by industry are available monthly. However, a comparison of these two sets of data will indicate in a general way the relationship between the industries of registrants and of those placed.

TABLE 19

INDUSTRIAL GROUPING OF PLACEMENTS BY THE SAN FRANCISCO, LOS ANGELES, SACRAMENTO, AND KERN COUNTY OFFICES OF THE CALIFORNIA STATE EMPLOYMENT SERVICE, 1938

Industry	San Francisco	Los Angeles	Sacramento	Kern
NUMBER				
Total	16,085	71,621	7,941	7,958
Agriculture	61	1,791	1,383	2,280
Forestry and fishing	8	186	186	152
Private construction	1,025	3,071	252	150
Manufacturing	3,142	16,034	294	90
Commerce and business	4,714	10,702	871	1,082
Domestic service	5,370	21,657	3,478	2,409
Professional service	750	1,259	200	90
Public and relief	1,015	16,921	1,277	1,705
PER CENT				
Total	100.0	100.0	100.0	100.0
Agriculture	0.4	2.5	17.4	28.7
Forestry and fishing	*	0.3	2.3	1.9
Private construction	6.4	4.3	3.2	1.9
Manufacturing	19.5	22.4	3.7	1.1
Commerce and business	29.3	14.9	11.0	13.6
Domestic service	33.4	30.2	43.8	30.3
Professional service	4.7	1.8	2.5	1.1
Public and relief	6.3	23.6	16.1	21.4

SOURCE: California State Department of Employment, Division of Research and Statistics, *Analysis of Placements by Occupation and Industry.*

* Less than 0.05.

much larger proportions of placements. In 1936 and 1937 a smaller proportion of placements than of registrants were in industries classified as distribution and manufacturing. In 1938 the proportion of registrants from manufacturing industries increased greatly, but there was no parallel increase in placements in manufacturing.

Placements classified by industry and by occupation are available by county for 1938 only. The statistics of placements made by the county offices included in this study show that, as was true for the C.S.E.S. offices throughout the state, the largest number of placements were in the classification of domestic employments, the proportion varying from 30 to nearly 45 per cent. The order of importance of placements in other industries varied considerably among the counties studied. A relatively large proportion of total placements in San Francisco and Los Angeles counties were in the manufacturing industries, and these industries were represented by insignificant proportions in the other counties. In San Francisco nearly 30 per cent of the placements were in commerce and business,[50] in contrast with not more than 15 per cent in the other counties. Placements in public employment[51] made up nearly a fourth of total placements in Los Angeles, slightly less in Sacramento and Kern counties, and only 6 per cent in San Francisco. Agricultural placements were of importance only in Sacramento and Kern counties where their proportion to total placements was 17 and 29 per cent, respectively. Although Los Angeles County has a large agricultural population, less than 3 per cent of the placements by the offices in this county were in agriculture.

It is also of interest to compare the industries represented in the placements during the year 1938 in the counties included in this study with the industries represented in the active files of these offices in April 1938. As was true for the state as a whole, domestic service was represented by much larger proportions in placement than in the active file. The manufacturing industries, on the other hand, were much more heavily represented in the active file, and this difference was of particular significance in Sacramento County where about a third of the active file and only 4 per cent of the placements were in manu-

[50] Included in this category are wholesale and retail distribution, commercial and mechanical service, and finance.

[51] Included in this category are public construction, governmental service, and relief work projects. Although the county figures are not broken down by these categories, it is evident from the state figures that most of the public placements were in public construction.

facturing. In Sacramento and Kern counties, but particularly in Kern, agriculture was more heavily represented in the active files than in placements. In Kern County over 50 per cent of the active file and less than 30 per cent of the placements were in agriculture.

TABLE 20

OCCUPATIONAL GROUPING OF PLACEMENTS BY THE CALIFORNIA STATE EMPLOYMENT SERVICE AND THE NATIONAL REËMPLOYMENT SERVICE IN CALIFORNIA, 1936–1938

Occupation	1936		1937		1938	
	Number	Per cent	Number	Per cent	Number	Per cent
Total	442,520		275,434		223,297	
Total unclassified	443		336		39	
Total classified	442,077	100.0	275,098	100.0	223,258	100.0
White-collar workers	39,109	8.8	27,297	9.9	33,050	14.8
Domestic and service workers	69,107	15.6	67,807	24.7	60,680	27.2
Manual workers	333,861	75.6	179,994	65.4	129,528	58.0

SOURCE: Unpublished data from the California State Department of Employment, Division of Research and Statistics.

Placements by occupation.—It is to be expected that placements would represent a wide variety of occupations as well as industries. The tabulations prepared by the State Department of Employment show that placements were made in occupational groups ranging all the way from unskilled labor to professional pursuits.[52] There was, however, a large concentration in certain groups. Manual workers, including skilled, semiskilled, and unskilled workers were always the largest group. It is significant, however, to note that from 1936 to 1938 the

[52] Workers placed on relief works projects were given an occupational but not an industrial classification. This group was therefore included in placements classified by occupation, whereas it was excluded from placements classified by industry.

number of placements in manual occupations declined from over 300,000 to not quite 130,000, and that their proportion to total placements declined from 75 to not quite 60 per cent. This decline was undoubtedly due to a large extent to the fact

TABLE 20A

CLASSIFICATION OF PLACEMENTS WITHIN OCCUPATIONAL GROUPS BY THE CALIFORNIA STATE EMPLOYMENT SERVICE AND THE NATIONAL REËMPLOYMENT SERVICE IN CALIFORNIA, 1936–1938

Occupation	1936		1937		1938	
	Number	Per cent	Number	Per cent	Number	Per cent
White-collar workers	39,109	100.0	27,297	100.0	33,050	100.0
Professional	6,203	15.9	586	2.1	476	1.4
Semiprofessional*	11,494	29.4	7,968	29.2	10,358	31.4
Sales	6,177	15.8	8,182	30.0	11,147	33.7
Clerical	15,235	38.9	10,561	38.7	11,069	33.5
Domestic and service workers	69,107	100.0	67,807	100.0	60,680	100.0
Domestic	29,662	42.9	38,179	56.3	38,916	64.1
Other	39,445	57.1	29,628	43.7	21,764	35.9
Manual workers	333,861	100.0	179,994	100.0	129,528	100.0
Skilled	56,434	16.9	25,529	14.2	18,765	14.5
Semiskilled	67,833	20.3	38,127	21.2	30,860	23.8
Unskilled	209,594	62.8	116,338	64.6	79,903	61.7

SOURCE: Unpublished data from the California State Department of Employment, Division of Research and Statistics.

* Includes technicians and administrative and supervisory workers.

that in 1936 large numbers of manual workers had been placed on relief work projects, whereas in 1938 the responsibility for such placements had been removed from the C.S.E.S. The distribution of placements among skilled, semiskilled, and unskilled occupations did not change much in the period under discussion. About 15 per cent were skilled, 20 per cent semiskilled, and over 60 per cent unskilled. Service workers were the group next largest in size. In each of the years under discussion more than 60,000 placements were made in this occupational group—in the main, as domestics in households or in institutions. From nearly 30,000 to about 40,000 placements were made each year in white-collar occupations. Except in 1936, about 98 per cent of these placements were in clerical, sales, or semiprofessional pursuits. It is interesting to note that in 1936 over 6,000 professional workers were placed (about 16 per cent of the total placements in white-collar occupations), whereas in 1937 and 1938 less than 600 placements were made in these occupations. Although total placements in 1938 had declined to about half of 1936, the decline in professional placements was very much greater. This may have been to a large extent due to the fact that in 1936 large numbers of persons classified as professional workers were placed on relief works projects, whereas in 1938 the responsibility for relief works placements had been removed from the C.S.E.S. The decline may also be related to differences in classification[53] and possibly to some extent to the fact that fewer jobs in the professional category were listed with the C.S.E.S.

A comparison of the occupations represented in placements and by registrants in the active file for the state as a whole shows that the majority in each group was always in the category of manual workers. There was, however, a greater concentration of placements than of registrants in these occupations in 1936 and in 1937, whereas in 1938 about two-thirds of the active file and slightly less than 60 per cent of the placements were in manual occupations. There were considerable differences between the active file and placements within the group of manual workers. Over 60 per cent of the placements of manual workers were in unskilled occupations, whereas only

[53] In the industrial classification of placements the professional category always included between about 3,500 and 4,500. Since professional people attached to a particular industry are, in the industrial classification, included in the figures for that industry, it would be expected that the professional group in the industrial tabulation would always be smaller than in the occupational classification. This was true in 1936, but in 1937 and in 1938 more than five times as many were classified as professional in the industrial as in the occupational breakdown.

about a third of the registrants were in this group, and much larger proportions of the active file were semiskilled or skilled workers. The second largest group of placements were service workers, whereas in the active file white-collar workers were second in importance. There were also considerable differences of representation of the various categories within these two groups. Within the service group domestic service was represented by a larger proportion among placements, and other types of service employments were represented by larger numbers in the active file. There was a large difference between the representation of white-collar workers in the active file and in placements. From about 20 to 25 per cent of the active file at each of the inventories were white-collar workers, whereas placements of white-collar workers were always a smaller proportion of the total and only reached a figure as high as 15 per cent in 1938. Within the white-collar group there were also certain important differences. Professional workers made up from about 15 to 20 per cent of the white-collar workers in the active file. In 1936 about 15 per cent of the placements were professional persons, whereas in 1937 and 1938 only 1 or 2 per cent were in this category.

In general, the largest number of placements in the counties visited were in manual occupations. There were, however, wide divergences in the importance of this group. The proportion which this occupation made up of the total varied from a little over a third in San Francisco to nearly two-thirds in Kern County. Within this group the largest numbers were always placed in unskilled occupations, but there were considerable differences between the counties. For instance, about two-thirds of the manual workers were placed in unskilled occupations in Sacramento and Kern counties, in contrast with 40 to 50 per cent in San Francisco and Los Angeles counties, and in these two latter counties much larger proportions of skilled workers were placed. The greatest difference was in the white-collar

TABLE 21

OCCUPATIONAL GROUPING OF PLACEMENTS BY THE SAN FRANCISCO, LOS ANGELES, SACRAMENTO, AND KERN COUNTY OFFICES OF THE CALIFORNIA STATE EMPLOYMENT SERVICE, 1938

Occupation	San Francisco	Los Angeles	Sacramento	Kern
NUMBER				
Total	16,085	71,621	7,941	7,958
White-collar workers	4,663	19,549	1,661	398
Professional	226	9,496	114	24
Sales	1,755	5,686	410	144
Clerical	2,682	4,367	1,137	230
Domestic and service workers	5,614	21,157	3,222	2,317
Manual workers	5,808	30,915	3,058	5,243
Skilled	1,636	6,524	361	682
Semiskilled	1,936	8,457	664	1,031
Unskilled	2,236	15,934	2,033	3,530
PER CENT				
Total	100.0	100.0	100.0	100.0
White-collar workers	29.0	27.3	20.9	5.0
Professional	1.4	13.3	1.4	0.3
Sales	10.9	7.9	5.2	1.8
Clerical	16.7	6.1	14.3	2.9
Domestic and service workers	34.9	29.5	40.6	29.1
Manual workers	36.1	43.2	38.5	65.9
Skilled	10.2	9.1	4.5	8.6
Semiskilled	12.0	11.8	8.4	12.9
Unskilled	13.9	22.3	25.6	44.4

SOURCE: California State Department of Employment, Division of Research and Statistics, *Analysis of Placements by Occupation and Industry.*

occupations. This group included over 20 per cent of the total in all of the counties except Kern where only 5 per cent of the placements were in these occupations. Except in Los Angeles, about 95 per cent of the placements in the white-collar group were in sales and clerical work. In Los Angeles only slightly over half were in these occupations and nearly half in professional occupations, in contrast with only 5 or 6 per cent in the other areas.

A comparison of the occupations in which workers were placed with those represented by the registrants in the offices in

TABLE 22

AGE GROUPS OF PERSONS PLACED BY THE CALIFORNIA STATE EMPLOYMENT SERVICE AND THE NATIONAL REËMPLOYMENT SERVICE IN CALIFORNIA, 1936–1938

Age	1936		1937		1938	
	Number	Per cent	Number	Per cent	Number	Per cent
Total	442,520	100.0	275,434	100.0	223,297	100.0
19 years and under	17,145	3.9	15.128	5.5	12,203	5.5
20 to 24 years	63,612	14.4	48,141	17.5	41,288	18.5
25 to 34 years	120,902	27.3	79,167	28.8	67,123	30.0
35 to 44 years	114,576	25.9	68,652	24.9	51,574	23.1
45 to 54 years	82,326	18.6	44,659	16.2	35,725	16.0
55 to 64 years	36,589	8.2	17,372	6.3	13,707	6.1
65 years and over	7,370	1.7	2,315	0.8	1,677	0.8

SOURCE: Unpublished data from the California State Department of Employment, Division of Research and Statistics.

San Francisco, Los Angeles, Sacramento, and Kern counties in 1938 shows that with the exception of Sacramento placements, where domestic and service workers were the largest group, manual employments were represented by the largest numbers among both placements and registrants. Manual workers were, however, represented by a larger proportion of total registrants than of placements. The next largest group of workers placed (except in Sacramento) were those in domestic and service work, whereas among the registrants the white-collar occupations were second in order of size, except in Kern County, where domestic and service workers took second place. The general picture was that registrations were somewhat more heavily weighted with manual employments than were placements, that domestic workers made up a larger proportion of placements, and that except for Sacramento the proportion of white-collar workers among those placed and among registrants was quite similar.

Age of persons placed.—Since age is an important factor in securing employment, it is of interest to examine the age distribution of those placed by the C.S.E.S. There was considerable uniformity in the ages of persons placed in 1936, 1937, and 1938. From a little less than a fifth to nearly a quarter were under 25, a little more than half were between 25 and 44, from a little more than a fifth to about a quarter were between 45 and 64, and about 1 per cent were 65 and over. If the ages of those placed in 1937 are compared with the ages of the unemployed as found in the Unemployment Census, it is evident that the younger age groups were more heavily represented in placements. More than three-quarters of those placed, in contrast with a little more than 60 per cent of the unemployed, were under 45 years of age. Similarly, for the years 1936-38 the group placed were younger than the registrants. From about 70 to 75 per cent of those placed, in contrast with from about 60 to 65 per cent of the active file, were under 45 years of age.

Temporary vs. permanent placements.—No statistical information was available, at the time this study was made, as to the permanence of the jobs in which the placements described above were made. Total placements include many—no one knows how many—who were placed on jobs lasting only one or a few days, and it is probable that the proportion of jobs which were permanent varied greatly from year to year. In the offices of the C.S.E.S. which were visited, an attempt was made to determine in a general way the importance of permanent and temporary placements. The estimated proportion of placements in these two categories varied greatly in different departments. In the departments which placed industrial and agricultural workers the estimates of the proportion of temporary placements varied from "over 50 per cent" to "over 90 per cent," and in some instances those in charge of this type of placement said, "Nearly all of this year's placements have been temporary." The commercial department estimated that a larger proportion of the placements were permanent. These estimates were from "75 to 80 per cent" to "over 50 per cent." The comment was, however, frequently made that these figures did not apply to retail sales, where most of the jobs are temporary. The women's domestic departments reported that a majority of the orders were presumably for permanent employees, but that further investigation might show that a large proportion were actually temporary. It should be emphasized that estimates based on impressions rather than on statistical tabulations, such as those given above, are subject to a wide margin of error, and it is important that in the future more accurate information should be available. It has been suggested[54] that placements should be broken down into the following categories: regular, more than 1 month; temporary, more than 1 week to 1 month; and casual, 1 week or less. This would make it possible to determine whether the Employment Service has been able to break its way into the field of placements which are presumably permanent or whether it is chiefly called upon to supply an occasional temporary worker. Since the function of an employment agency is not merely to make placements but to fit the worker to the job, it is also important in some way to measure the extent to which workers keep the jobs in which they are placed or are fired because they lack the necessary qualifications. It would be difficult and unnecessarily expensive to collect this information on a wholesale basis; therefore it is suggested that sample studies should be made from time to time. Such studies would indicate the lines of activity in which new placement procedures should be adopted.

[54] Atkinson, Odencrantz, and Deming, *Public Employment Service in the United States*, p. 231.

Padding of placement statistics.—Coöperative arrangements between the C.S.E.S. and other community agencies are intended to supplement the files of the C.S.E.S. if orders are listed for which qualified applicants are not available. A somewhat different type of so-called "coöperative" arrangement, however, was sometimes reported. The purpose of these arrangements was to increase the reported number of placements, and they were in no way related to an attempt to find a person qualified for a particular job. A branch manager of an office of the C.S.E.S. in an agricultural area reported, "I know all of the labor contractors who operate in this area. They all coöperate with me by registering their workers, and when they go to work, the Employment Service takes credit for the placement." A manager of an employment department of an employers' association said, "The C.S.E.S. takes credit for all placements made by this association. A man from the C.S.E.S. comes to the office every week and gets our list of placements." When the manager was asked why he permitted this, his answer was: "Occasionally I need a man quickly who has no telephone; I telephone the C.S.E.S. and they send someone to notify him. Why should I care? They help me, and naturally I am willing to do them a favor in return."

Another type of "coöperative" arrangement, different from those described above but with the same purpose, was reported by a member of the staff of the C.S.E.S.:

> In the spring of 1938 a business prepared to open its season. There were some 24 or 30 openings, which were filled from applications directly to the office of the company. After these jobs were filled and the staff complete, a member of the staff of the C.S.E.S. registered the entire group and reported them as jobs filled by the service. This practice is so common as to have a name. It is called auditing the payroll.
>
> The claimants for unemployment insurance for benefits for partial unemployment are added to the list of placements of the C.S.E.S., although the claimant found the part-time job himself or was merely working part time for his regular employer.

According to these reports, there is no great secret about this practice, but, so far as is known, no disciplinary measures have been taken by officials of the department. A staff member in another office said there is considerable evidence that placement statistics are padded. "A few workers were placed in the X establishment; then a C.S.E.S. placement officer got a list of all employees of the X company and counted them as placements." This statement was made in relation to several companies, whose names were given, and the informant said, "I know this to be true."

In Los Angeles County there was a second public employment office—the Labor Coördinating Bureau, which limited its service to registered voters.[55] Within the city of Los Angeles these two employment agencies worked independently. In the outlying districts the offices of the C.S.E.S. were frequently the local representatives of the Labor Coördinating Bureau; thus orders for workers were filled from the files of the C.S.E.S., and apparently these placements were counted both by the Labor Coördinating Bureau, which makes an annual report to the Board of supervisors of Los Angeles County, and by the C.S.E.S. There were also in Los Angeles two educational institutions, the Los Angeles Junior College and the Frank Wiggins trade school,[56] which, while "affiliated" with the Central Employment Service, maintained independent employment departments. The only coöperative arrangements were that the C.S.E.S. forms were used, the franking privilege was granted, and their placements were counted as C.S.E.S. placements.

It was not possible in all cases to verify the existence of the so-called coöperative arrangements described above, but there was a rather widespread impression among the persons interviewed that there was a good deal of padding of placement

[55] For a description of the work of this organization see pages 169–172.

[56] For a description of the work of the Los Angeles Junior College and the Frank Wiggins trade school, see pages 188–191.

statistics. Clearly only an official of the C.S.E.S. with the power to inspect can determine whether such practices exist and to what extent. Since inaccurate statistics are worse than useless, and since the desire to make a good impression is an incentive to padding statistics, it is of great importance that the validity of placement statistics should be checked at frequent intervals by responsible persons and that administrative supervisors should not regard the number of placements as almost the sole measure of efficiency.

EMPLOYERS' AND COMMUNITY RELATIONS WITH THE C.S.E.S.

Employers' Use of the Service.—Employers' orders are as essential to an employment service as are two blades to a pair of scissors; and, since so little data were available on this subject from the offices of the Employment Service, an attempt was made to secure information as to the use of the C.S.E.S. from more than 350 employers who were visited in the course of this study. An examination of this material will provide some evidence as to the degree to which employers in certain areas of California were using the Employment Service in 1938, and, furthermore, comments of employers about the C.S.E.S will give some indication of their attitudes and whether it is likely to be easy or difficult to develop a strong employment service in the future.

Of the entire group of employers visited, only a little more than a fourth had used the Employment Service within a period of approximately two years preceding the study,[57] and, of this small group, only a few—slightly more than 10 per cent—claimed to have placed orders for any considerable number of

[57] It should be pointed out that this study was made in 1938, a time when labor surpluses were common in most fields of activity. A similar study made in a period when there was a labor shortage would undoubtedly show a larger proportion using the Service and, also, probably a change in employers' attitudes toward the Service.

workers. The situation was somewhat different among employers in industry and in agriculture. About a third of the industrial employers, in contrast with only a little more than 15 per cent of the agricultural employers, had made use of the Employment Service. Extensive use of the service was somewhat more frequent among employers in industry, but in both instances the vast majority reported only an ocasional order. These orders were almost entirely limited to situations in which there appeared to be a temporary shortage of workers and when other resources had failed. With one or two minor exceptions, the employers interviewed had no conception of the advantages of a state-wide system of state employment offices which would organize the labor market in times of surplus as well as of shortage, and, like a commodity exchange, would give the buyer and the seller the maximum opportunity of meeting.[58]

There were approximately 70 industrial employers who reported that they had employed workers through the Employment Service. About half of this group were satisfied with the Service, and the remaining 50 per cent expressed various types and degrees of dissatisfaction. The following quotations from interviews with these employers will serve as an indication of the various ways in which approval was expressed:

> Most of our employees apply at the gate; occasionally we have used the C.S.E.S. They have given us excellent service and coöperation.
>
> The Employment Service has given us good service for extra help.
>
> We don't have occasion to call the C.S.E.S very frequently, but we have called them four or five times and have had good service. If we call for an Elliott Fisher operator, we get just that.
>
> We use the C.S.E.S. whenever we have difficulty in getting engineers or other skilled men. The State Employment Service was recently most helpful in securing for us a national list of engineers with particular qualifications.
>
> Some of the companies in this business are trying to work out a coöperative arrangement with the C.S.E.S. The C.S.E.S. is now our chief

[58] For an interesting discussion on this subject see Don D. Lescohier, "A Clearing-House for Labor," *The Atlantic Monthly*, CXXI (June 1918), pp. 773–783.

source of workers, and when men are laid off we send information about them to the State Employment Service. We approve of this arrangement because the State Employment Service is in a position to keep a complete file of information as to the work history of applicants, and because it will make it possible to transfer workers from one company to another and thus avoid unemployment insurance payments.

During last winter we had a standing order with the C.S.E.S. for mechanics. All of the mechanics referred were employed and proved satisfactory.

The dissatisfied employers expressed a variety of opinions, of which the following are typical:

The men they sent out were never any good; they were inferior workers and knew little about the work required.

They are "reliefers," incompetents, and down-and-outers.

We tried the C.S.E.S. and had satisfactory results for a time, but we are now no longer getting competent service. Everyone we used to deal with has been transferred or ousted for political reasons, and we are frankly indifferent and will continue to be so until we are again convinced that it is a competent agency.

The main fault with the C.S.E.S. is lack of organization and too many shifts in personnel. At least half a dozen different employees of the C.S.E.S. have been here to try to sell us the service.

The C.S.E.S. is too slow in filling jobs. They send too many referrals, and those they send are incompetents.

The C.S.E.S. hasn't the first conception of interviewing. They don't check references to determine the person's work experience or the stability of the employee.

C.S.E.S employees don't understand the requirements of industry.

In general, the employers in industry who had called upon the C.S.E.S. for workers limited their calls to times when it was necessary to add to their staffs during a rush order or sale or to occasions when it was important to find a worker with a special skill. Only a very small group considered the Employment Service a really important source of labor. Whether or not the employer was "sold" on the Employment Service even in the circumstances mentioned above depended to a considerable degree on the skill with which the applicant was chosen, and apparently at times people were referred who were completely lacking in the necessary qualifications. It should be pointed out that no one, not even the employer himself, can be sure who is the right person for the job. But the fact remains that, if the man or woman sent by the Employment Service turned out to be the right person, the employer would call again; if not, the entire organization was subject to criticism. In addition, certain factors other than the qualifications of the worker were of importance. If an employer found that an applicant had been on relief, all the C.S.E.S. registrants were classed as "reliefers." If the order taker with whom the employer was accustomed to dealing was no longer at the office, as was frequently the case, the employer was annoyed and would not call again; and, if a member of the Employment Service staff did not understand in a particular instance the problems of the industry, this agency became worthless in the eyes of the employer.

The employers who had never called the Employment Service were questioned as to their reasons for not making use of this agency. The most frequent answers to this question were in such terms as:

No agency is necessary—we are swamped with workers who apply directly.

Our labor turnover is very small, and we always have a waiting list of experienced help.

Fee agencies have given us satisfactory help, and we have just never changed the habit.

A large proportion of our employees are hired through the union hiring hall, and we have no occasion to use the Employment Service.

A few stated that, although they had never called upon the C.S.E.S., they might do so if the need arose. This attitude is represented in the following quotation:

I favor a free agency. The local manager is a fine man, and I will use the C.S.E.S. if there is ever a shortage of skilled workers.

More frequently, however, this group expressed themselves in terms which did not indicate that they had confidence in the C.S.E.S.:

> I am not convinced that the Employment Service or any agency can separate the wheat from the chaff.
>
> The Employment Service has a poor type of applicant; a good applicant finds his own job.
>
> We sell style. The women we want do not need to apply to any employment agency; they can always sell their own services.
>
> Four or five field visitors called on us in one week, indicating bad organization. Two of them were badly dressed. If these persons are representative of the Employment Service, I would be afraid of the type of worker they would send for a job.
>
> They are not careful enough in their selection of referrals; politics enters in; they don't investigate labor agitators.
>
> The C.S.E.S. is no good; it is concerned with relief.
>
> If there is a shortage of good men, I send to a fee agency; the good men apply there. I would be afraid of taking a chance on men from the C.S.E.S.

It is apparent that the employers in industry who were interviewed in 1938 had not become convinced that the C.S.E.S. might become an agency of real value to them even at a time when employment opportunities were increasing. A few had used the Employment Service as a last resort when all other methods had failed; but many could not see that it would ever be needed, since existing methods of securing workers appeared to them to be satisfactory. A large number of employers were definitely critical of the C.S.E.S. Some of these criticisms were based on experience, and others were merely opinions; but in either case they indicate that there are barriers to the full development of a public employment service.

Of the 162 agricultural employers who were interviewed, only 27 (a little over 15 per cent) had ever used the C.S.E.S. as a source of labor, and only 2 had made any extensive use of this service. Slightly less than half of this group were content with the service they had received. Their attitude was frequently expressed in statements such as:

Occasionally, I have called the C.S.E.S. for men, and those they sent were satisfactory.

Others were more specific in their commendation:

My picking boss is on excellent terms with a Mexican in the nearby office of the C.S.E.S. He gave my boss a list of families on relief who could do the work. Some of these people did not want to work, but the C.S.E.S. office applied pressure; they came to work and were satisfactory.

Before harvest time arrangements were made with the manager of the local office of the C.S.E.S. whereby agricultural workers were classified according to the exact type of work they could do. The manager worked day and night and did a heck of a good job. The arrangement clicked.

The attitudes of those who had used the Service and were dissatisfied are illustrated by the following quotations:

The people they sent were no good. They send low white trash. Men who are any good won't register at the C.S.E.S.

They don't seem to be able to send men who can pick cotton.

The fee agency is easier to get at. They send out two advertising blotters every two weeks on which is printed their address and telephone number. I have to look up the number of the C.S.E.S., and I can never remember under what title it can be found. Furthermore, the fee agency accepts toll calls collect.

The better workers prefer the fee agencies. They think that they have better jobs, and that most of those who register at the C.S.E.S. are on relief.

Last year the C.S.E.S. called on a hop grower with glowing promises. They said that they had sent 800 men to pick hops. Only two showed up.

We can't get good workers from the C.S.E.S., and they won't stay on the job anyway; they work a few hours and quit.

I took one man from the C.S.E.S. At 10 minutes of 7 I told him that I was ready to show him about the work. He said, "I don't work until 7 o'clock." I left the man and went into the field to work. At 10 minutes after 7 the man picked up his blanket roll and left, with two meals under his belt and no work done.

Nearly 85 per cent of the agricultural employers had made no use of the Employment Service in the two years preceding this study. The vast majority of this group could see no need for such an agency. Their attitude was expressed in various ways but can be summarized in the following quotations:

Labor of all kinds comes in droves.

My foreman has a thousand friends.

If we just mention the date when we will need help, 300 are there in the morning.

They just flock in.

There is always a supply of labor. This company is well known, and the workers like to work for us.

Most of this group of agricultural employers simply could not see any place for an employment service, in view of the fact that there were always two men clamoring for every job. A few, however, were aware of the fact that such an agency might perform an important function if there were a shortage of labor. Occasional statements such as the following are illustrative of this attitude:

The C.S.E.S. is a good thing and deserves coöperation. We would use it if there were a shortage of labor.

Some who had never used the service expressed opinions which indicated a critical attitude, and in some instances actual opposition to the development of a state employment service. The following statements indicate the opinions of this group:

I won't have anything to do with a government agency. Unless a man pays for his job he won't stay. The free services are no good—the state is doing it for them and they expect a handout.

The cotton growers don't use the C.S.E.S. When there is a plentiful supply of labor, we don't need it; and, when there isn't, we won't, because we don't believe that we can get qualified workers.

The C.S.E.S. is not used at all as a source of farm labor; no one ever hears of it. Apparently the office which is supposed to serve this community has a very ineffective organization. It has done nothing to establish contacts with farmers.

The C.S.E.S. is not used to supply agricultural employers in this area. It has little to do with foreign groups. We employ Filipinos and have a practically foolproof system of labor contractors.

The C.S.E.S. has only Oklahomans, and they are completely and utterly no good.

If we used the C.S.E.S. we would have to send trucks for the men; the private agencies furnish transportation.

It is too expensive to use the C.S.E.S. It is necessary to spend money for gasoline and for toll calls. We find it cheaper and better to go to the corner near the post office where the men hang round.

Workers' Use of the Service.—The scope of this study did not include interviews with wage earners to discover what facilities they used for finding jobs. The only information concerning their use of the C.S.E.S. is from statements made by persons in close contact with job seekers.

Employees of the C.S.E.S. itself made the statement that up to 1938, when applicants for unemployment compensation benefits were required to register, the better type of worker would not register with the Employment Service because of the belief that it had only cheap jobs. This was apparently true for many occupational groups, but it particularly affected registration in professional, technical, and commercial occupations and in the skilled crafts. The Employment Service personnel, however, expected unemployment compensation to result in registration of qualified persons in all occupations in which there was a surplus of labor or a high labor turnover.

Inevitably, all unemployed workers covered by unemployment compensation will have to place their names on the active file of the Employment Service. There is still, however, the question as to whether the better workers in such noncovered occupations as domestic service will register, and whether those in the skilled crafts will register for the purpose of securing employment or merely in order to qualify for unemployment compensation. The attitude of some of the personnel of the C.S.E.S. is illustrated by a comment of a member of the staff of a men's industrial department who said, "Men who really want work won't register here."

Various other organizations in the communities visited were questioned as to their opinion of the quality of Employment Service registrants. In a good many instances the officials of these organizations had nothing to say on this subject, either because they had had no dealings with the C.S.E.S. or because they were, in general, sympathetic to its purpose but had no knowledge of the quality of those who registered. When an opinion was expressed on the quality of this group of the unemployed, it was usually in such terms as "good workers won't register at the Employment Service."

In San Francisco the private fee-charging employment agencies very frequently expressed their attitude in such phrases as: "Trained workers prefer to pay for jobs," or "Our workers are too proud to stand in line." In Los Angeles agencies of this sort made similar statements, such as: "The Employment Service has a poor type of client," and, "It is a good place for those who cannot pay for a job or for the unskilled."

The social service agencies in Los Angeles appeared to be particularly concerned with this problem, but in a way which was not very fortunate for the Employment Service.[59] It was characteristic of these agencies to refer their substandard clients to the C.S.E.S. on the theory that this agency was primarily concerned with people only capable of earning low wages. Two occupational associations in Los Angeles also concurred in this opinion. One said, "It may be all right for the unskilled and low class," and another, "We look on it as a place to dump our substandard members." In the Sacramento, Bakersfield, and Fresno areas few of the organizations had anything to say concerning the quality of Employment Service registrants, but occasionally, as in the case of a fruit growers' organization, the

[59] A much larger proportion of the social service agencies in Los Angeles than in the other areas visited had organized placement services. This probably made them more aware of the C.S.E.S. than those in the other communities.

statement was made that "Employment Service registrants are not reliable." An official of an industrial employers' association said, "Good men don't register with the Employment Service—they only have the broken-down man who is untrained or has lost his skill," and a man thoroughly familiar with the problems of agricultural labor said, "The Employment Service picks men up out of the gutter."

It must be remembered that the attitudes expressed above are frequently the opinions of agencies with a vested interest in the placement field, and therefore they must not be taken too seriously. Since, however, in many instances they probably represent the attitude of groups of unemployed workers and of others in the community, they must be considered as opinions which will have to be overcome if the Employment Service is to attract qualified workers in all fields.

Agriculture—A Special Problem and Two Suggestions for Its Solution.—Throughout this discussion of the work of the C.S.E.S., there has been recurrent mention of the special problems of agricultural placement—the migratory laborer with no permanent address, the uncoöperative farmer, the attempts of Farm Placement officers to direct the flow of labor. Obviously, in California one of the aims of the State Employment Service should be to introduce some degree of organization into this most disorganized portion of the general labor market.

The average industrial employer may hire and fire a good many workers in a year; but, except for such industries as canning, lumber, and textiles, he does not, in a period such as 1938, hire large groups of laborers for a few weeks and then lay them off. California's agriculture, on the other hand, is characterized not by the type of farming which depends on the year-round farm hand (who may have to be replaced occasionally but who, on the whole, stays with the same employer year after year), but by crops which during a few weeks require hundreds of laborers, followed by a period in which few or no workers are needed. Clearly, in good and bad years alike, the employer in agriculture hires many workers each year, whereas in a depression the industrial employer may hire few, if any. Although the C.S.E.S. has reported each year a considerable number of placements in agriculture, the fact that these placements are an insignificant part of the total workers employed by farmers is indicated by comparing the C.S.E.S. agricultural placements with an estimate of the number of agricultural jobs which must be filled each year in California. Professor R. L. Adams of the Giannini Foundation of the University of California has made a rough estimate[60] that three-quarters of a million jobs must be filled in California agriculture each year. Clearly the C.S.E.S. agricultural placements, which in the years 1936 to 1938 varied between about 35,000 and 65,000, were unimportant in relation to the needs of this industry.

California's agricultural employers are accustomed, in the main, to hit-and-miss hiring from large groups who just turn off the highway when a "help wanted" sign is put up, and in many instances not even this is necessary. Many farmers said, "We don't need the Employment Service," or, "The Employment Service has no place in our situation." But it must not be concluded that the present system of rumors, causing workers to move in droves up and down the highways of California (frequently only to find that the crop yield has been overestimated or that the labor market is already glutted), is not to the disadvantage of the worker, who must often begin his travels again without earning a cent, and also to the employer, who must choose in a largely hit-and-miss fashion from among hundreds of workers clamoring for jobs. The fact is, rather, that California farmers have not yet been convinced that the

[60] This estimate was based on the number and size of farm units, the number of man-days required per acre, and the number of days during which each operation lasts in California's chief crops, which require widely varying seasonal labor supplies.

C.S.E.S., as now organized, can fulfill the function of bringing together unemployed workers and farmers in need of labor. The task of changing attitudes which are based on habits of long standing is always difficult; and, when in some instances there must be added previous experiences with a none too efficient employment service, the problem becomes even more difficult.

The experience of the Texas State Employment Service is, however, an illustration of the fact that farmers can be convinced that a state-wide employment service can be of assistance in preventing much useless wandering and loss of time and money to both workers and employers.[61]

The Employment Service of Texas reports that during 1936 the first real attempt to handle migratory labor was made through a systematized, centralized method of control. The following measures were taken to facilitate the work:

> An assistant director of the Employment Service was placed in charge of all farm placement activities, and the Federal Farm Placement Supervisors worked under his direction, although they remained directly accountable to Washington.
>
> Seasonal calendars were worked out for each district to show planting, cultivating, and harvesting periods for each crop. This brought out the weak points in office locations.
>
> Steps were taken to move offices to the most strategic points, and itinerant services were provided in counties where no offices were located and where there were short periods of heavy labor turnover.
>
> A program was inaugurated to educate growers, shippers, contractors, and laborers as to the advantages to be gained from more orderly movements of labor through a centralized agency.

In a report covering the year 1936 the following statement is made:

> In spite of the fact that control was not absolute or without missteps or weaknesses in points, . . . it had proved that, in spite of the enormity of the task, it could be done.

[61] Texas State Employment Service, *Survey of Farm Placement in Texas, 1936 and 1937*, prepared by the Farm Placement Service (Austin: 1938).

In 1937 there was a further development of the methods which had been inaugurated in 1936:

> To handle more effectively the spinach harvest in Zavala County, men especially experienced in the handling of Mexican labor were transferred in.
>
> When word was received that migratory labor was moving, preparations were made to intercept the transients at strategic points and to reroute them to points where the demand was greatest.
>
> A "farm crew" of 18 interviewers was appointed, who were stationed in the various crop areas during peak seasons. These men moved from one station to another as their services were made necessary by harvesting. It is their work to contact both growers and workers to adjust the supply and demand for workers.
>
> A policy was established whereby no labor is directed from one district to another until the administrative office has been advised that all local labor has been placed and a shortage actually exists. This must be substantiated by specific orders from employers.

Frequent statements as to the success of the above program are found in the Texas report. Although these statements may be somewhat over-optimistic, statistics bear out the conclusion that the Texas State Employment Service has become a significant factor in the placement of agricultural labor. In 1936, the year that this plan was put into operation, approximately 70,000 agricultural placements were made by the Texas State Employment Service, and in 1937 the number increased to nearly 160,000. That the C.S.E.S. has accomplished little in the field of agricultural placements is evident from the fact that in 1936 this agency made about 58,000 farm placements; in 1937, 65,000; and in 1938, 32,000.

Although the problems of orderly movement of agricultural labor in California are in some respects different from those of Texas, and therefore the Texas system could not be adopted without modification, the objective as stated in the concluding paragraph of the Texas report might well be given serious consideration by the C.S.E.S.:

> With all the facts at hand, there is but one possible objective—to organize the greatest possible number of migrants in an orderly army

of productive workers, moving steadily from one scene of operations to another without confusion and with the minimum amount of lost motion, and gradually to provide year-round employment for as many as possible, with subsequent higher incomes and higher standards of living. It is an end which merits any amount of time and effort which may be required for accomplishment.

An interesting plan to control the movement of migratory labor in California was suggested to the Secretary of Labor in 1934 by a member of a committee appointed to investigate a strike in the Imperial Valley.[62] In brief, this proposal involved agreements with employers in agriculture to employ all workers through the C.S.E.S. if this agency was able to furnish the labor.

The steps outlined as necessary to carry out such an experiment were: first, employers must furnish an estimate of the number of workers required a month in advance of the harvest season; second, the Employment Service must agree to register in advance former employees and resident qualified workers and to give these people work authorization cards for the harvest season; third, the C.S.E.S. must make an estimate of the labor shortage or surplus and make arrangements for the necessary movement of labor. These movements must be controlled through the use of work authorization cards and not by posting notices that workers are needed in beets, cotton, or hops. It was further suggested that transportation loans should be made on agreement on the part of the worker to repay the sum from the proceeds of his labor. This report stated that the success of this experiment would depend largely upon the proportion of growers and shippers who could be induced to become parties to the agreement and on the ability of the Employment Service to furnish satisfactory workers. In order that the above plan should not be viewed with too much optimism, the author stated, in conclusion, that it could not be expected that such a system of labor control and registration would at once result in stabiliza-

[62] Pelham D. Glassford, *Control of Migratory Labor in Imperial Valley*, Report to the Secretary of Labor (June 23, 1934). Mimeographed.

tion of migratory labor. Workers would drift to the Imperial Valley and elsewhere without knowing of the registration and transfer requirements. However, he suggested that, before long, familiarity with the system would become widespread, and the uncontrolled movements of labor would be materially reduced.

It is important to recognize that the plan described above, or any other plan designed to regulate movements of labor through the use of work authorization cards, might be subject to abuse. If it came to a point where workers would not be employed if they did not have work authorization cards, and if there were any tendency to refuse such cards because of trade union or political affiliations, a system of blacklisting might develop. It would appear, however, that some system along these lines, honestly and fairly administered, is essential to the orderly transference of agricultural labor at the time and to the places where it is needed.

The writer has been informed that since the spring of 1941 a number of important steps have been taken to improve the efficiency of the agricultural placement service in California. Agricultural labor reports are issued to the field offices within seven days after the estimates of labor needs are received. Highway signs have been placed at the entrance to about 60 cities and towns. These signs inform both the worker and the farmer that farm labor information is available at the nearest office of the C.S.E.S. Cards have been posted in gasoline stations and country stores indicating the type of workers wanted and the place and probable duration of the work. A careful check is kept and the cards removed as soon as the labor need has been met. Temporary offices have been set up at strategic points throughout the state, and full coöperation has been established with the F.S.A. camps and also with the F.S.A. grant offices. A special identification and work history card has been prepared for the use of migratory laborers for whom it is useless to keep a card on file in a particular office. This card, which remains in the possession of the worker, contains information secured at an original interview as to his agricultural and other experience. It serves as an introduction to all offices of the C.S.E.S., makes reinterviews unnecessary, keeps the files clear of large numbers of cards of workers who within a few weeks have moved out of the locality, and furthermore it helps to educate the worker in the use of the Employment Service.

Place of the C.S.E.S. in the Community.—The purpose of a system of public employment exchanges is to bring some order into the chaotic conditions which exist in the marketing of labor. It can never be expected that a public employment service will be able to bring about a complete organization of the labor market, nor can it be expected to increase the number of available jobs; but, if its field of operation is sufficiently broad, and if it is efficient, it can reduce the frictions in the labor market by quickly placing qualified persons in whatever jobs are available.

Although statistics are not available as to the proportion of total jobs which are filled by the C.S.E.S.,[63] interviews with employers in the course of this investigation indicated that this agency acted as an intermediary in only a small proportion of the total job openings in private industry[64] and in agriculture. There were a number of reasons for the failure of employers to list such job openings as they had with the Employment Service. The Employment Service, a young and rapidly expanding or-

[63] For a discussion of the proportion of placements made by the public labor exchanges in Great Britain see T. S. Chegwidden and G. Myrddin-Evans, *The Employment Exchange Service of Great Britain* (New York: Industrial Relations Counselors, 1934), p. 176; Walter Matscheck, *Administration of Unemployment Insurance and the Public Employment Service in Great Britain*, report of the Committee on Public Administration of the Social Science Research Council to the Social Security Board, p. 77. Multilithed.

[64] Although this study was made at a time when there were large pools of unemployed labor in relation to the number of jobs, it must be recognized that, even in a time of depression, some industries are taking on workers while others are laying off, and that some industries require workers at one season and others at another; consequently there are always movements from job to job.

ganization, was in many respects inefficient. It had to function with untrained administrators, interviewers, and placement officers who knew little or nothing of the special techniques of their jobs, of their communities, or of the needs of industry. Furthermore, the pressure of registering large numbers of applicants for relief and for unemployment compensation by personnel who were overworked and who frequently had no understanding of the great importance of integrating the entire program of work of the Employment Service often resulted in almost hopeless confusion.

Another barrier to an increase in the job openings listed with the C.S.E.S. was the fact that organization of the labor market was foreign to most employers. A new idea is always faced with the necessity of overcoming established habits and prejudices; and, when the new idea is a government agency offering a service hitherto left to chance or to private individuals, it is confronted with the whole gamut of prejudices against anything in which the government has a hand. It must be recognized that these prejudices were certainly not lessened by experiences which resulted in a common feeling that "politics" and dissension were rife within the organization.

A final difficulty can best be expressed in the words of employers who said, "There are always plenty of workers at the gate—there is no need for an intermediate agency." At the time this study was made, there were more unemployed workers than job openings, but isn't it probable that a central employment agency, if efficient, could more quickly bring about the connection between job and worker even when jobs were few and workers plentiful? The employer would benefit by more careful selection of workers and the worker by shorter periods of unemployment and by an elimination of the costs of door-to-door job hunting.

If the C.S.E.S. is to become a real factor in the organization of the labor market, it must "put its house in order" and prove that it can do its job efficiently. In spite of all possible success in overcoming inefficiencies, however, the development of a strong employment service will be slow, since long-established habits must be overcome. Nothing, however, will be as effective in creating a demand for the Employment Service as a job well done.

V. Governmental Agencies Other Than the California State Employment Service

ALTHOUGH THE California State Employment Service was the only governmental agency organized solely as a placement service on a state-wide basis at the time this study was made, there were a number of other governmental agencies which had concerned themselves with the problem of finding jobs for the unemployed. With one exception these bureaus were not independent organizations with placement work as their sole function; rather, they were subsidiary to a department of the government set up for some other purpose, frequently education or relief.

THE LABOR COÖRDINATING BUREAU

The Labor Coördinating Bureau of Los Angeles County was the only governmental agency, other than the State Employment Service, whose work was confined entirely to registering jobs and workers and making placements. In 1931 the Board of Supervisors of Los Angeles County set up the Employment Stabilization Bureau to find jobs for residents. This bureau was organized in an attempt to reduce the heavy burden of unemployment relief on the taxpayer. In the following years its activities were expanded to include the placement of workers on the C.W.A., and it exercised some of the functions subsequently taken over by the S.R.A. By December 1933, however, relief work placements had been taken over by the S.R.A., and the employment bureau set up by the Los Angeles Board of Supervisors was reorganized with a smaller personnel and renamed the Labor Coördinating Bureau. The services of this bureau were limited to registered voters of the county, in proof of which a voters' registration certificate was required. The only exception to this rule was in the case of Mexicans, usually aliens, who were placed in agricultural work. This exception was made because large numbers of Mexicans were on the relief rolls.

In 1938 the Labor Coördinating Bureau had a staff of 16 in a central downtown office. In addition, there were between 50 and 60 unpaid "registrars" in the small towns surrounding Los Angeles. Their responsibility was limited to registering workers and filling such orders as were transmitted to them from the central office. The staff members interviewed reported that these "registrars" were city officials (such as the city engineer or fire chief) or secretaries of the local Chambers of Commerce, and that occasionally a branch office of the California State Employment Service had accepted this responsibility. It is probable that these offices were "registrars" more frequently than the above statement indicates, since five out of six offices of the California State Employment Service visited in these communities were the local representatives of the Labor Coördinating Bureau.

The Labor Coördinating Bureau reported that 14,000 persons had been registered during 1937; and from January 1934 to March 1938, 52,000. These figures did not include agricultural workers, who, in the main, were not voters and were therefore not registered. There was no publicity to encourage registration—"they just come in." In the main, those who registered were men (white and Negro), although about a fourth were women. It was reported that no orientals registered, although those born in this country would not have been refused registration.

Approximately 12,000 placements, exclusive of those in agriculture, were made in 1937, and in the three years prior to this the number of placements had varied from about 7,000 to 10,000.[1] Annual placement figures for agricultural placements were not available, but it was reported that from July 1935 through March 1938, 4,200 workers had been placed in agriculture.

Apparently an overwhelming proportion of the placements made by the Labor Coördinating Bureau were on county work. It was reported that all county construction contracts specified that workers must be secured through this bureau. In addition, this agency filled all county non-civil-service jobs, as well as those for which the civil-service lists had been exhausted—for example, emergency typists and nurses at the county hospital. Several field visitors attempted to secure orders from private business, but no data could be obtained as to the number of such orders. The agricultural placements were in charge of a Mexican who visited growers and labor contractors and secured information as to their future labor needs. He visited camps, found families who were out of work or finishing another job, and sent them where they were needed. In the main, he placed Mexicans in the citrus and walnut area east of Los Angeles.

The technique of placement appeared to be quite informal, and, at least in the central office, the man on the spot probably most frequently got the job. A list of the day's vacancies was kept on the information and placement desks, and applicants might come in at will, examine the list, and ask to be referred to the job of their choice. Job orders in outlying communities were sent to the local registrars, since it was the policy to attempt to fill orders from the community where the job was located. Since these offices, with the exception of those which

[1] It was impossible to determine what proportion of the registrations and placements were the entire responsibility of the Labor Coördinating Bureau and what proportion were registered and placed by the offices of the California State Employment Service. In the latter case they were included in the statistics of both organizations.

were also offices of the California State Employment Service, were in charge of personnel whose primary job was something other than placement work, it is doubtful whether placements were made on a highly selective basis. In the one local office visited it was obvious that, although an attempt was made to fill orders sent by the central office, there was little effort to select men particularly fitted for the job.

It did not appear that the Labor Coördinating Bureau was used to any considerable extent by other agencies or by employers in private industry. Some of the philanthropic agencies and business colleges which had placement offices reported that they referred calls which they could not fill to this bureau. None of the employers interviewed would admit ever having called on this bureau for assistance in getting workers.

In general, this bureau was disliked by other organizations in the community. The most common allegation was that it was a political racket for the benefit of the county supervisors and their constituents. A representative of an important employers' group alleged that it was a political racket to get jobs for people in a supervisor's district in order to get votes. Certainly the restriction of its services to registered voters lent some color to this accusation.

The Labor Coördinating Bureau of Los Angeles County was obviously an employment agency operating within a very limited field. The fact that its primary function was to place registered voters was of particular significance at a time when large numbers of people in California were recent residents who had not yet established the right to the ballot. Furthermore, it should be pointed out that being unemployed and being a registered voter are likely to be quite unrelated facts. The welfare of the community, as well as of a particular individual, demands an employment bureau which concerns itself with placing the unemployed without regard to such an extraneous fact as the possession of a voter's certificate.

GOVERNMENTAL RELIEF ORGANIZATIONS

Although the State Employment Service was presumably the only state agency engaged in placement work at the time this study was made, it soon came to light that at least in one instance, and possibly in others, a government relief agency had assumed some of the functions of an employment agency. For this reason it was essential to visit the offices of the various relief agencies in order to determine whether or not they considered job finding as one of their functions. The State Relief Administration was visited in all of the areas included in this study. Other government relief departments visited in some but not in all areas included the W.P.A., N.Y.A., State camps for single men, and an office of the Farm Security Administration grant program.

S.R.A.—The S.R.A. was responsible for certifying applicants for W.P.A. and for C.C.C. and for furnishing temporary relief to employable persons who were waiting for assignments to work projects. All clients of the S.R.A. were required to register at the California State Employment Service in order that they might be given an occupational classification and be available for placement. As has already been pointed out in chapter IV, the California State Employment Service had assumed in 1938 the responsibility for registering applicants for unemployment insurance, as well as for the large group of those certified for relief. These offices were not equipped to interview carefully and classify the large numbers for whose registration they were responsible. The registration of applicants for unemployment insurance was an immediate and pressing problem, which not unnaturally took precedence over all others, particularly over any efforts to secure job orders.

The S.R.A. became convinced that the California State Employment Service was not doing an adequate job in placing relief clients, particularly in the larger counties. Prior to 1938 some of the S.R.A. county offices placed personnel in the offices of the California State Employment Service in order that special consideration might be given to those who were certified for relief. This was, however, an unsatisfactory administrative set up, and in 1938 the S.R.A. inaugurated a plan whereby the offices might organize their own reëmployment services. The purpose and plan of organization of these services was described in a field letter issued in May of 1938 in the following words:

> It is our plan to supplement and assist the California State Employment Service . . . to the degree that such activity is necessary, county by county, in order to secure placement of S.R.A. clients in private employment. According to local needs counties are authorized to establish simple placement files and employ where necessary a staff with which to operate these files and assist in the assignment of clients to job openings.[2]

Although the reëmployment service of the S.R.A. was described as a plan to "supplement and assist" the California State Employment Service, the more detailed description of the activities to be undertaken indicated the possibility of a considerable degree of overlapping of functions between the two organizations. Although the rule that all clients of the S.R.A. were required to register at the California State Employment Service was not rescinded,[3] the S.R.A. offices were instructed to establish placement files, which were to be coded by occupations and in accordance with employability. The personnel of the S.R.A. reëmployment service were also charged with the responsibility of soliciting jobs from employers. That there was to be some attempt at "coöperation" with the California State Employment Service in respect to these activities is

[2] State Relief Administration of California, *Field Letter No. 142* (May 6, 1938). Mimeographed.

[3] Letter from Martin Ruderman, Director, Division of County Administration, State Relief Administration of California (Dec. 20, 1938).

indicated by the following section of the field letter of May 1938:

. . . if the Employment Service has a field representative contacting employers in a certain locality and requisitions persons from relief rolls to fill such jobs, the S.R.A. Placement Interviewer would not knowingly attempt to contact such employers. It is known, however, that in certain communities the community is not being serviced as far as solicitation of employment is concerned, or if serviced, only in a superficial manner. Therefore, we should have no hesitancy in making such contacts in these communities for the benefit of our relief clients.[4]

The S.R.A. offices were instructed to make placements from two sources of job orders: The California State Employment Service, with which daily contacts were recommended, and direct orders from employers who listed their labor needs with the S.R.A. In the latter case workers were to be referred directly, although it was suggested that "it might be desirable and serve to verify conditions of employment to telephone the C.S.E.S. first for information regarding the employer."[5] It was also suggested that the S.R.A. placement office should interview available workers in anticipation of a seasonal demand in certain industries and that "in so far as possible, there should be a follow up on assignments with the employer or C.S.E.S."[6] The instructions also contained a clause to the effect that aid should be discontinued if the client, for no valid reason, refused to accept a job.

It is obvious from the above that if the plan as described were set up, there would be two state agencies engaged in registering and classifying workers who were available for employment, in securing job orders, and in making placements.

The county offices of the S.R.A. visited in the course of this study exhibited wide gradations of placement activity. Only in Los Angeles was there found a separate placement bureau with a large staff actively engaged in the work of an em-

[4] State Relief Administration of California, *op. cit.*
[5] *Ibid.* [6] *Ibid.*

ployment bureau. In San Francisco there had been spasmodic attempts to place relief clients in private industry by the S.R.A., but the chief reliance was upon the State Employment Service. In Sacramento and in Bakersfield, with the exception of special efforts on behalf of Negroes in the latter city, the placement of relief clients remained the responsibility of the State Employment Service.

The Los Angeles S.R.A. had assumed the functions of an employment agency since 1935, and at the time this office was visited (June 1938) the reëmployment division was staffed by a personnel of 27. Headquarters were in downtown Los Angeles, but interviewers were sent out daily to 11 of the 14 district offices.

The reëmployment division registered all who were certified for relief by the S.R.A. and who "looked employable" and all employable persons in these families. It was reported that when assignments were made to the W.P.A. the names were removed from the file of the S.R.A., and no further efforts were made to place this group of people. During the year 1937–38 approximately 115,000 "employable" persons were registered by this office.[7] It was reported that 6,915 placements[8] were made in this year and that nearly 10,000 jobs were offered and refused. No occupational or industrial classification of placements was available, but the statement was made that this office had been fairly successful in placing workers in a variety of occupations—domestic, commercial, and industrial—as well as in agriculture. The official interviewed, however, laid particular stress on his success in selling S.R.A. clients to farmers. Apparently special efforts were being made to force Mexicans into agriculture, as against industrial work, on the ground that their past experience in most instances had been in farm work.

[7] There were 125,200 persons referred for registration, but 10,306 of this group were subsequently judged to be unemployable.

[8] This figure is the number of jobs filled, not the number of different people placed.

In order to encourage farmers to accept workers from this source, arrangements had been made to transport workers to the job and to furnish blankets, if necessary. That transportation is an important factor in agricultural placements is apparent from statements from a number of farmers that they would not use the California State Employment Service because it could not furnish transportation from the office to the job.

Officials of the S.R.A. Reëmployment Division reported that every effort was being made to pick the best man for the job rather than to send the man who happened to be in the office or to give preference in terms of need or length of time on relief. Apparently, however, interviewers frequently filled jobs from among those who turned up in the office rather than making use of any selective procedures. After a placement was made, it was verified by either a personal or telephone call to the employer, and the results of this check-up were reported to the social service department, which had discretion in closing cases.

The interviewers on the staff of this reëmployment service spent half of each day visiting employers to secure orders and to convince employers that it was to their advantage to call this office. "We do your preliminary interviewing for you," they said, "and it will save you money to hire relief clients, because otherwise you pay taxes to support them." There appeared to be no fixed standards as to wages or working conditions for jobs which this office would register except in the field of domestic employment, for which a minimum of $25 a month and room and board had been adopted. The official interviewed said, "We don't fool with any job offer that is too low." But "too low" was not defined, and it was impossible to determine which jobs relief clients would be forced to accept or be dropped from the relief rolls. It was reported that, before making referrals to jobs in agriculture, this office investigated the available housing arrangements, and that attempts had been made to urge beet growers in one district to provide living quarters.

It appeared that the reëmployment service of the Los Angeles office of the S.R.A. had in a number of respects adopted good employment-office procedures for an office doing a considerable volume of business. From the available statistics, however, it was impossible to determine either the number of relief clients who were placed or the number for whom more or less permanent jobs were found. It is perhaps significant that of all the employers interviewed in the Los Angeles area, not one would admit ever having used the S.R.A. Reëmployment Service as a source of labor. While it must be remembered that the employers visited represented only an infinitely small sample of all those in the area, among those visited there were included two firms which the S.R.A. claimed specifically as customers, and farmers in an agricultural district where the S.R.A. reported many placements.

In San Francisco the S.R.A. reported that it depended upon the State Employment Service to place clients, and that it was fairly well satisfied with this procedure, although few relief clients had been placed. One of the officials expressed the opinion that few S.R.A. clients were placed because they were, in the main, the hard-to-place. This office of the S.R.A. had one person in charge of placement work. Although he occasionally made a placement in a job which he happened to hear about, his activities were almost entirely limited to placements on work relief projects, to vocational guidance and counseling, and to coöperation with the State Employment Service in connection with its responsibility for the clients of the S.R.A. The S.R.A. had for months made no use of the list of unfilled openings received daily from the California State Employment Service. The consensus in San Francisco was that a placement office in the S.R.A. like the one in Los Angeles would be undesirable, since it would simply duplicate the work of the C.S.E.S.

The Sacramento office of the S.R.A. expressed considerable dissatisfaction with the opportunities offered to relief clients through the State Employment Service. Officials expressed the opinion that, on humanitarian grounds and in order to reduce the tax burden, a qualified relief client should be given preference in placements over one not on relief. The California State Employment Service, however, refused such discrimination, and even such job orders as might come directly to the S.R.A. were referred to the California State Employment Service, whose offices were in the same building.

The Kern County central office of the S.R.A. had no placement department, and the administrators were well satisfied with the work being done by the California State Employment Service. However, the case worker in the Negro department in Bakersfield was making an informal attempt to place S.R.A. Negro clients on the grounds that persons in this racial group seldom found jobs through the California State Employment Service. She had interviewed farmers for the purpose of finding job openings and had received frequent calls for domestics but reported no great success in making placements. She accounted for this in terms of the racial situation in the area. In the district office of the S.R.A. visited no placement work was being done, although there was no branch of the California State Employment Service or other placement agency within convenient reach.

State Camps for Single Men.—The prevailing policy in California, at the time this study was made, was to assign employable single men who applied for relief to base camps from which they were distributed to work camps and to W.P.A. work projects. Since these camps were potential labor pools, it was considered important to determine whether any program had been set up whereby these men might secure information as to job openings. Two base camps were visited: one in Pacoima, which served Los Angeles County, and one in Waybur outside Sacramento, to which the men from all of the northern counties except those on the coast were assigned.

In neither of the camps visited had any plan been set up which would keep the residents in touch with job opportunities, and the fact that many were far from their homes and thus could not take advantage of informal contacts with prospective employers lessened still further their chances of securing employment.

The Pacoima camp was quite readily accessible to Los Angeles, but those registered at this camp were not required to register either at the California State Employment Service or at the S.R.A. Reëmployment Service in Los Angeles. Occasionally orders for workers came from these sources; but, since the residents of the camp were not registered with the employment services, the orders could not be based on their qualifications. It was reported that occasionally a farmer came to this camp looking for harvest hands, but no special efforts were made to secure jobs from this group of employers, and only a small number of those in the camp were employed on neighboring farms.

The camp at Waybur, 30 miles from Sacramento, was almost completely isolated from placement resources. The nearest active office of the State Employment Service was in Sacramento,[9] and the only camp residents who were registered there were those who had been sent from Sacramento. It was reported that in theory the Sacramento office of the California State Employment Service might send a blanket order for a group of men. Apparently this seldom if ever occurred, since the camp officials stated that they had not been in touch with the State Employment Service for many months. In only half a dozen instances had a neighboring farmer come to the camp looking for workers, and obviously no special efforts were being made to get farm jobs for the residents of the camp, although it was reported that a large proportion were experienced agricultural workers.

[9] There was an office of the California State Employment Service in Woodland, which was closer to Waybur, but this office was practically inoperative.

It must not be forgotten that, at the time this study was made, the job market was overcrowded, and efforts to secure employment for the men assigned to the camps would probably have been largely unsuccessful. Nevertheless, it was significant that the men in the state camps were isolated from whatever jobs might be available, and apparently no real efforts were being made or even contemplated whereby this isolation might be broken down. One official stated that the only way these men ever returned to private employment was to make a stake on a W.P.A. project and then set out to hunt their own jobs.

C.C.C.—None of the camps of the C.C.C. was visited on the grounds that they were probably too isolated to be an effective factor in the labor market, and because the exigencies of time and money available made it necessary to omit from this study certain of the outlying agencies. However, a letter was sent to the regional office asking whether any steps had been taken to find jobs for those enrolled in the C.C.C. camps. The following is the official statement from the director's office from a letter dated April 5, 1939:

> In its placement activities the Civilian Conservation Corps coöperates with the established and recognized agencies such as the State-Federal Employment Service Offices in California. In addition to this work practically every camp is active in establishing its own contacts with firms and individuals who may afford employment opportunities to enrollees within specific camps. These contacts are made in person by camp officials and enrollees interviewing prospective employers during free time, by letters, and by inviting prospective employers to the camps to see for themselves the types of work being done by enrollees and to judge individual fitness and desirability of enrollees, insofar as specific employment is concerned. In a great many camps, a formalized course in "job getting technique" is given to enrollees, in order to enable them to know how to apply for a job, how to meet and interview prospective employers, write effective letters, use the telephone effectively for making appointments, and other allied skills.

No attempt can be made to judge the effectiveness of the program described above, as the C.C.C. camps were not visited.

W.P.A.—In the two areas in which W.P.A. offices were visited—San Francisco and Bakersfield—the W.P.A. had set up no independent organization to place workers from their projects in private industry. Responsibility for securing employment rested on the individual or on the State Employment Service, at which agency all were registered. In San Francisco there was a W.P.A. labor coördinator making efforts to speed up the placement of W.P.A. workers by selecting from W.P.A. rolls workers who might be suitable for available openings in the California State Employment Service office and calling them in for reinterview by the Employment Service. It was, however, entirely within the discretion of the Employment Service as to whether or not they were referred to jobs. No calls for workers which might come directly to the W.P.A., such as those for domestic workers trained by the W.P.A. for household service, were filled by the W.P.A.; all employers were referred to the California State Employment Service. In Bakersfield it was frequently stated that the W.P.A. had dispatched agricultural workers. This was, however, emphatically denied by the W.P.A. official interviewed.

N.Y.A.—In San Francisco the responsibility for securing employment for the young people on N.Y.A. was again placed on the youngster himself or on the Junior Department of the California State Employment Service. The N.Y.A. had set up a division of guidance and placement in the office of the California State Employment Service, but the work of this department was limited to vocational counseling and testing. At the time this study was made, the California State Employment Service reported little success in placing juniors; not a single placement had been made in the last six months and less than 10 a month in the preceding months. Occasionally a project supervisor knew of an opening to which he could refer an N.Y.A. worker directly, but, on the whole, the only way a young person from the N.Y.A. found a job was to hunt it for himself.

In Bakersfield, the other area where the N.Y.A. was visited, a division of guidance and placement was about to be set up by the N.Y.A. The plan included contacts with employers to solicit jobs for N.Y.A. workers; but the only agency currently available to place youth from N.Y.A. was the California State Employment Service, which had no separate junior department, and which did not encourage the registration of young people just out of school.

F.S.A.–Grant Program.—The F.S.A., which operated camps for migratory agricultural laborers (see pp. 202–206), also gave relief in cash and kind to nonresident farm families who were not eligible for relief from S.R.A. Bakersfield was the only office of this program visited. Because the laborers must collect their grants at the office, it was a potential source of agricultural labor, but the staff did no placement work other than the dissemination of information as to where work was available. Since the F.S.A. is a federal body with offices throughout the country which constantly exchange information on work opportunities, it was possible through this medium to encourage the shift of agricultural labor between states to meet crop requirements. For example, at the time of the visit in Bakersfield, cotton pickers were being encouraged to go to Arizona and given money for transportation there. The local representative did not recommend to his relief clients that they register at the State Employment Service, on the grounds that it was useless, but told them instead to solicit their own jobs directly from the farmers.

EDUCATIONAL INSTITUTIONS

California law requires that children shall remain in full-time school until they are 16, with the exception that work permits may be given to children of 14 and 15 if their families are in great need. It is further required that unless a child has finished high school he must attend part-time continuation school until he is 18.[10] Thus most young people are not faced with the necessity of finding a full-time job until they are 17 or 18 years of age; and, for those who continue their education, job hunting may not begin until 21 or 22, or even later.

The last school day, whatever may be the level of education attained, is most frequently followed immediately by excursions into the job market. It might be expected therefore that educational institutions would have developed methods of assisting in the transition from school to job.

Since the vast majority of young people in California secure their education in our public institutions, it is important to devote considerable attention to the efforts of our public-school system to assist in the job-finding process.[11] The types of public schools which might be expected to be of importance in the placement field are high schools, continuation high schools, trade schools, junior colleges, and universities. The placement activities of the school systems were investigated in three of the four areas visited—San Francisco, Los Angeles, and Bakersfield. In each of these districts the schools had established placement facilities for their graduates. Their organization and effectiveness, however, varied considerably, and nowhere was the school placement system sufficiently developed to take over all or even a dominant part of the task of placing graduates in jobs. The majority of the young people in all these communities had to rely on their own efforts or on other agencies.

High Schools, Trade Schools, and Junior Colleges

San Francisco.—In San Francisco the only part of the school system which had set up an employment office as a separate department with full-time personnel was the Continuation School. The services of this office were available to students of the high schools of the city, as well as to those enrolled in the

[10] *School Code of the State of California* (1935), Div. 1, Pt. II, chaps. i and ii.

[11] The placement department of one privately supported university was visited and is included in the group of institutions discussed in this chapter.

Continuation School. At the time this study was made, it was administered by two full-time workers. In addition, five teachers from the Continuation School gave a half day a week to visiting employers. The statement was made that the children in the school system were informed that there was a placement office where they were free to register. Apparently, however, there was no very careful check as to whether or not this information was actually given to the children. A person thoroughly familiar with this organization said, "Some of the students at the Continuation School don't even know that a placement service exists. . . . Some of the other schools are not interested in placement and do not coöperate to any extent."

The Continuation School placement office registered young people up to the age of 25, but the most usual type of applicant was a boy or girl under 21. Young people of all races could register, but it was reported that those who took advantage of this opportunity were, in the main, of the white race. This bureau aimed to serve high-school graduates as well as others, but only a relatively small proportion of their registrants were from schools other than the Continuation School.

The Continuation School reported to the Community Chest that it made placements in occupations described as commercial, salesmanship, stock-room work, wrapping and packing, domestic, journalism, advertising, carpentry, cabinet making, millinery, dressmaking, and show-card writing. The person interviewed in the course of this study stated that most of the 1,260[12] placements made during 1937 were in jobs requiring little skill or training. Although this as well as other schools laid considerable emphasis on vocational guidance,[13] it ap-

[12] It was impossible from the available data to determine the number of young people who were eligible for placement through this office, that is, high-school graduates, those leaving school to work, students in Continuation School, and deductions for those going on to college.

[13] Every educational institution visited laid stress on vocational guidance; but these programs, although of importance in adjusting the flow of new labor into the market, were not included within the limits of this study.

peared that vocational interest or aptitude had little relation to placement. It was pointed out that this office must meet the competition of other agencies to whom the employer has applied; therefore its basic policy was "the most important thing in filling a job is to fill it quickly." Most of the openings were filled by "spot placements" from the applicants nearest to hand. First choice was usually given to those who filled out daily registration slips or who were "hanging around" the office. If no one was available from these sources, an attempt was made to fill the job from students in the classrooms at the Continuation School. The next source was the current file of applications. Finally, if the job remained unfilled, the teacher in charge of placements in certain high schools was asked to refer someone. Where qualifications and availability were equal, preference was given to those most in need.

Although the placement office conducted by the Continuation School was available to high-school students, there were, in addition, special teachers in many of the high schools who assumed some responsibility for securing jobs for their pupils or graduates. These teachers were not visited, but their work was described by persons familiar with this activity of the school system as primarily that of finding part-time employment for students in school. It is probable that they placed few graduates in full-time employment.

At the time this study was made, no placement bureau had been established in the Samuel Gompers Trade School. This school had been open only a short time, and the hope was expressed that in the future employers and unions would come to the school for workers so that the boys need not tramp the streets or beg friends or relations for jobs.

Although 76 San Francisco employers interviewed in the course of this study were questioned as to their use of the placement offices in the school department as a source of labor, only seven reported that they had obtained workers from this source.

Several of these were retail stores which secured sales personnel, and the others were, in the main, hiring for office and clerical work. Insofar as evidence was available, it did not appear that San Francisco employers considered the placement facilities of the school department to be an important source of labor.

The San Francisco Junior College made no organized or coordinated efforts to obtain jobs for its graduates, with the exception of the department in charge of the hotel-management course. The assistant dean of men and the girls' counselor did a little placement work, and the commercial teacher spent two hours a day in the field "trying to work up business for her students." The man in charge of the hotel-management course said that he assumed full responsibility for the placement of students in this course.[14]

Most of the placements made by the San Francisco Junior College were in part-time work for students who were enrolled in the college. It was reported that 15 or 20 "outside jobs" (that is, exclusive of N.Y.A.) were obtained for students from August to December 1937. At this time there was an enrollment of 1,750. With the exceptions mentioned above, the Junior College had no planned program to secure job openings, and little attempt was made to urge students to register at an alternative placement agency, such as the State Employment Service or the Continuation School. The following statement made by a member of the staff of the Junior College undoubtedly accounted, at least in part, for this policy: "A capable student should be able to get his own job. I am bothered by the tendency of students to expect someone else to take care of them. I fear it means loss of initiative."

Although it is probable that a considerable proportion of the junior-college students transfer to a university, some terminate

[14] Although the first class in this course had not graduated, most of the students had already been placed, since the last semester included part-time work in a hotel which agreed to hire the student on graduation.

their education at the junior college level; and it was obvious, at the time this study was made, that little had been done to assist this group in the job-finding process.

Los Angeles.—In Los Angeles the central placement bureau for the city high schools was affiliated with the State Employment Service. It was, in fact, the Junior Department of the State Employment Service and has been described in chapter IV. This was in contrast to the situation in San Francisco, where the placement work of the school department was entirely independent of the State Employment Service, and there was very little coöperation between the two.

In Los Angeles there was a large and well-organized trade school (the Frank Wiggins Trade School) which gave trade preparatory courses in aircraft, art, automotive and metal, building, building operation, clothing, drafting, electrical and communication, food, printing, and office trades.[15] Both boys and girls were enrolled. In 1936–37 the number of boys was slightly larger than the number of girls. The minimum age at which students were accepted was 16. In 1936–37 the median age of these young people was 23. Enrollment was limited to those who could meet the occupational specifications set up by industry as to physical fitness and intelligence. Available facilities and the probability of job openings were further limitations on the numbers accepted. The school was closely geared to the industrial life of the community through trade advisory committees and constant field visits by the teachers to keep abreast of trade developments and opportunities.

The Frank Wiggins School considered the placement of those whom it had trained as one of its major responsibilities, although, of course, it could not guarantee jobs. This work was the responsibility of an employment office with a personnel of three full-time employees, and, in addition, teachers were

[15] There were also trade extension and apprentice courses, but, since these were for persons already employed, there was no placement problem involved.

charged with the responsibility of placement.[16] As was mentioned above, the teachers were in constant contact with employers, and in the course of these visits they sought job openings to be listed with the employment office.

During the year ending June 1937 the Frank Wiggins Trade School made 3,450 placements, about two-thirds of which were classified as permanent, since they lasted more than 30 days. Approximately 2,000 were placed in the calendar year of 1937; and in April 1938, 200 jobs were filled. All placements were followed up carefully because diplomas were issued only after six months' successful trade experience. It was reported that about 75 per cent of the students in most of the courses were placed by the school. The fact that the school met with greater success in placements in some fields than in others was illustrated by the statement that in aircraft and in hair-dressing and cosmetology all students were placed, whereas jobs were found for only about 30 per cent of those trained to operate elevators.

The most striking feature of the Frank Wiggins School and its program was the general esteem in which it was held by employers and agencies of all types in the community. It was not always possible to determine whether employers obtained workers directly from the Frank Wiggins School or from the Central Employment Service. Of 74 industrial employers visited, 15 said that they employed Frank Wiggins graduates, and 6 others said the schools were one of their sources of labor supply but did not specify which school. Trade associations and charitable organizations praised the training courses, and one trade association which conducted an employment bureau coöperated with Frank Wiggins in the placement of juniors. The general approval of employers was exemplified by those

[16] The Frank Wiggins Trade School was affiliated with the Central Employment Service of the Los Angeles public schools. California State Employment Service forms were used, and placements were reported to the Central Employment Service. In other respects this school operated an independent employment bureau.

who said, "Frank Wiggins sends the boy that fits, not the one who needs the job as the rest of them do," and "Frank Wiggins is familiar with our work and knows whether the applicants they send can fill the job." To a less frequent degree the same approbation was expressed for the Central Employment Service.

The Los Angeles Junior College also had its own placement office, which was very active and which reported considerable success in placing its graduates. The importance of the placement bureau of this junior college was indicated by the fact that about 75 per cent of the students were enrolled in semiprofessional vocational training courses in a wide variety of fields and did not go on to universities.

The staff of this placement office consisted of a full-time director and a secretary.[17] Its services were available to all graduates of the junior college. Among the schools visited, this one was unique in its efforts to keep in touch with former graduates and to give them assistance in finding new and better jobs. Periodic follow-up letters were sent to alumni to secure information as to their work experience and to ask them to notify this bureau as to the notices of civil-service examinations in which they were interested. The work of finding part-time jobs for those who were enrolled as students, which swamps so many school placement bureaus, was not the responsibility of this office.

The director of this bureau placed great emphasis on the necessity of selling the placement service to employers, and for this reason she spent a considerable portion of her time in visiting employers. The purpose of these visits was not only to secure job orders but also to determine the type of training which was necessary for various jobs and where there were likely to be openings in the future. Other publicity methods

[17] Vocational guidance was given by a vocational counselor with a separate office and staff.

included employers' luncheons on the junior-college campus, radio talks, and a folder listing the types of graduates, which was sent to the Chamber of Commerce mailing list.

During the school year 1937–38 this office made 1,111 placements.[18] The director estimated roughly that 70 per cent of the graduates of the semi-professional training courses were placed through this office. The greatest success in placements had been attained among those who graduated in the courses for accountants and bookkeepers, bank clerks, dentists' assistants, engineers—mechanical, civil, and aviation—library clerical aids, playground directing, and peace officers. Although this office would register any graduate of the junior college, it was pointed out that racial prejudice in Los Angeles makes it difficult to place Jewish graduates, and that it is almost impossible to place orientals.

Bakersfield and Taft.—In Bakersfield and in Taft the local high schools and junior colleges had joint placement offices. Apparently neither of them played a dominant role in placing high-school or junior-college graduates in industry. In both cases the primary purpose was to find part-time jobs for school children. The Bakersfield office was in charge of a part-time secretary who reported that during the last year only 300 students registered for placement, although the graduating classes alone amounted to 700. Statistics of placements were not available, but it was reported that 15 to 20 job orders were received a month, not all of which were filled. No attempts were made to secure job orders by visits to employers or other methods. The school placement bureau in Taft, which had a full-time director, had been established by a community welfare organization only three days before the investigator's visit, although there had been experimental work the year before. This bureau was intended to serve students in both the high school and the junior

[18] The total enrollment at the time of the visit to the Los Angeles Junior College was 5,030.

college. Its primary purpose was to get part-time jobs for students in school so that they could continue their education. It was obviously too early to appraise the work of this bureau, but the manager was of the opinion that the greatest difficulty would be found in placing high-school graduates. Assistance in finding jobs was given to junior-college graduates by teachers in the trade preparatory courses. One of the men interviewed reported that it was relatively easy to place graduates of these courses, but another said only 6 out of 20 boys graduating from junior college and not continuing in universities were placed in the trades which they had studied. Obviously, at the time this study was made, the school placement bureaus in Bakersfield and in Taft had not done much to assist their graduates to make the transition from school to job. Only 5 of the 37 nonagricultural employers interviewed in the Bakersfield area reported that they employed workers through the school placement office. Five or six of the oil companies, however, said that they had employed junior-college graduates who had applied directly.

The schools and placements in agriculture.—The proportion of industrial employers who used school placement offices as a source of new workers was not large, but it is a striking fact that not a single agricultural employer in the areas visited got any of his workers through the schools. It was not part of this study to investigate the extent of child labor in California agriculture, but it was clear that any children who worked in the crops in the areas visited got their jobs through direct application or through a contractor who employed whole families. The schools were definitely attempting to act as a deterrent to the employment of children under working age and had no coordinated plan, if such were possible, for training students for agricultural work after graduation or placing untrained graduates in such work. The Kern County school system had for several years conducted a campaign to eliminate the illegal employment in agriculture during school hours of children subject to the compulsory school law and to limit the issuance of work permits. Imposition of fines on a few employers hiring children had produced widespread coöperation from employers, according to both the school authorities and to the growers who were interviewed. In Yolo County, near Sacramento, the school authorities reported that it was impossible to enforce the child labor laws, but here again the attitude of the schools was that it was their function to curb child labor rather than to aid in legal distribution of child workers to agricultural jobs.

The schools and the California State Employment Service.—Close coöperation might have been expected between the schools of California, from whose doors each year comes an army of young people in search of employment, and the State Employment Service, also an agency of the government, whose function is to place persons of all ages. There was, however, except in the case of the Central Employment Service in Los Angeles, little evidence of such coöperation.

In San Francisco there was little indication of any coöperation, although a member of the staff of the Continuation School said that if an employer's order could not be filled it would be referred to the State Employment Service. Apparently the San Francisco Junior College, which does little placement work, did not refer its graduates to the C.S.E.S.

Officials of the school department in San Francisco were definitely of the opinion that the schools should maintain placement bureaus distinct from the Junior Department of the State Employment Service. Although the school department expressed a willingness to "coöperate," the officials felt that the schools could do a better job. "We know our students, have time to study their individual needs, and have made wide contacts with employers." In addition, they were convinced that the files of the State Employment Service were so large that the juniors were lost in them and that the technique of interviewing left something to be desired. At the time this study was made, it did not appear, however, that the placement work of the San Francisco School Department was organized in accordance with the principles stated above. Most of the placements made by the Continuation School were "spot placements" with little attempt to fit the person to the job, and little attention had been given to the development of a placement service for high-school graduates. The Junior Department of the State Employment Service, on the other hand, was suffering from the difficulties of a new and rapidly growing organization and had certainly not developed an efficient organization to serve the young people. The State Employment Service in San Francisco recognized that no agency was offering a proper service to juniors. They deplored the lack of close connection between their Junior Department and the schools and confirmed the lack of coöperation between high-school principals and the Continuation School service.

As has already been pointed out, in Los Angeles the placement bureau for the city high schools was the Junior Department of the State Employment Service. All of the placement work for young people leaving school, however, was not coördinated in one department. There were independent placement offices in the Frank Wiggins School and in the Los Angeles Junior College, and some placement work was done by teachers in the various high schools. There was, in one sense, "Coöperation" between the Frank Wiggins and the Los Angeles Junior College bureaus and the State Employment Service. Both of these were affiliated with the State Service; but, as far as could be determined, the only meaning of this was that their placements were reported to the Central Employment Service and thus to the California State Employment Service, and the junior college bureau received franking privileges and State Employment Service forms. There was apparently no real coöperation in regard to referral of applicants[19] or of employers' orders

[19] Withdrawals from the Los Angeles Junior College were referred to the State Employment Service because the placement office handled only graduates.

between these agencies. Each tried to place its own students and did its own field work to find job openings.

In Bakersfield the State Employment Service had no junior department and expressed the opinion that it did not want school graduates to register, since they would swamp the office. The state office occasionally called the school placement bureau for applicants for a job which could not be filled, but it was reported that the school placement bureau did not reciprocate. In Taft there was only an itinerant office of the State Service which did little placement, and thus the juniors were left wholly to the schools.

Universities.—The two universities visited, one in the northern and the other in the southern part of the state, had organized separate placement offices for teachers and for all other types of work. The only teachers placement bureau visited was at the University of California in Berkeley. It was staffed by six full-time persons. Registration with this bureau was limited to those who had taken work at either the northern or the southern branch of the university. Each person who registered was required to pay a fee of $5 to cover the cost of clerical service and of writing letters, and an additional sum was charged when the original fee was exhausted. A university regulation that all who expected to enter the teaching profession must register had apparently been successful, since it was reported that only 1 or 2 per cent of this group fail to register. Although graduates of the university with Ph.D. degrees in search of teaching positions were required to register,[20] the work of this bureau was, in the main, confined to placements in secondary schools, which was the teacher-training field in which this branch of the university specialized. In 1937–38 this office placed 403 teachers and furnished credentials for

[20] The primary purpose of this registration was to centralize the handling of credentials, since most of this group were placed through the professors in the various departments. Librarians and public health nurses were also required to register for the same reason; but, again, most of the jobs in these fields were found through other sources. Less than 5 per cent of the placements of this office were in these fields.

256 teachers who had come to the attention of prospective employers through some other source. Of the 659 teachers who were assisted in securing employment, about two-thirds were experienced and about one-third inexperienced. It is interesting to note that, of the 383 who were granted secondary credentials in 1937–38, over 200 (about 60 per cent) were assisted in securing employment by the university bureau. In addition, this office made some placements in public schools other than at the secondary level, in junior colleges, in private schools, colleges, and universities, and in librarianship and public health nursing.

Although the teachers placement bureau of the University of California placed nearly 400 teachers in schools each year and provided credentials for about another 200, there was evidence that a considerable number of openings in the secondary schools in California were filled from some other source. In 1937–38 the University of California placement bureau received 1,408 requests from schools for teachers to fill vacancies. In this same period only about 400 teachers were placed, less than 30 per cent of the total openings offered. It is probable that principals in search of new teachers registered the openings with the California Teachers Association[21] and possibly with other organizations, as well as with the University of California.

Two university placement bureaus for occupations other than teachers were visited. Each of these offices had a staff of three full-time persons. They registered graduates and former students of the university, certain other "superior" persons, and students enrolled in the university who were seeking part-time employment. This latter group—students in immediate need of part-time employment if they were to remain in college—represented a heavy load of work, and there was little doubt that this function absorbed most of the time of the staff.[22]

---

[21] See pages 241 ff. for a discussion of the California Teachers Association.

[22] No investigation of part-time work for students was made because it did not fall within the scope of this study. It may be noted, however, that the bureau which

There were no requirements that the members of the graduating class should register with these bureaus, and the manager of one said that the best students were placed directly by their professors. Thus those who registered with the bureau were, at least to some extent, not the most promising group. In one instance the service of the employment office was free; in the other, graduates of the university were charged a fee of $1 and other persons paid $5.

Both of these offices reported that they placed only a small proportion of the graduating class. One refused to give statistics of placements; the other reported 900 placements in full-time jobs in the year 1936–37. Since few statistical reports were kept by these bureaus, it was difficult to secure much information as to the types of occupations in which placements were made. One manager refused to give any information on this subject, whereas the other merely made the general statement that the largest groups placed were engineers and stenographers, but that considerable numbers were also placed as "trainees" for large companies and in merchandising. It was obvious that neither of these offices was a clearing house for all persons placed from the campus. One manager said, "All departments place a considerable number of their own people, and the departments which are vocational in nature, such as law, medicine, social service, and librarianship, place almost all of their own students."

Each of these offices recognized the importance of maintaining contacts with local employers through a field-visiting program and vocational conferences on the college campus to which employers were invited. One advertised its services to employers in trade journals and other media, and the other sent 5,000 letters a year to a mailing list of firms throughout the country. Another method of keeping the bureau in the minds of employ-

reported statistics of placements secured over 8,000 part-time jobs for students enrolled in the university, and in the same year (1936–37) 900 jobs were found for former students or graduates.

ers was to give promising applicants cards of introduction and send them out to "free lance" for jobs with employers who might have an unreported opening.

Only a handful of industrial employers in San Francisco and in Los Angeles reported that they used the university placement bureau as a source of new workers. In Bakersfield, on the other hand, practically all of the oil companies got at least their technical force from the universities, in most instances through the placement office. The fact that all of the employers interviewed expressed friendly sentiments toward university placement offices indicated perhaps that, if these offices were not so overburdened with part-time student placements, it might be possible to convince a larger group of employers of the advantages of a specialized agency which had many trained applicants available from whom to choose. One employers' association in Los Angeles, where there are a number of colleges and junior colleges, pointed out that there were too many college employment offices, a situation uneconomical both for the colleges and for the employer, who must call many different places. The suggestion had been made that a central clearing house be set up, but the colleges refused to coöperate.

At the time this study was made, there was apparently no coöperation between the college employment bureaus and the State Employment Service. One manager said, "Quite frequently the California State Employment Service calls this bureau for our entire list of persons in a given occupation. These are not bona fide jobs, and there is no use to spend the time going through our files. I do nothing about it." The other manager expressed the opinion that the California State Employment Service was so badly run that employers would not patronize it. Furthermore, he emphasized the importance of a thorough knowledge of applicants and of the "personal touch," which he believed was not posible in a state service. It was obvious that the State Service was in no position to perform the specialized service given by university employment offices. It was impossible to determine whether certain of the specific criticisms of the managers of the college bureaus were based on experience or on prejudice, but it will be regrettable if in the future all bureaus whose purpose is to lessen the frictions in the labor market cannot coöperate when jobs are available in one place and workers in another. It is certain, however, that this will not be possible until the State Service has improved its interviewing and placement procedures and until it proves that in asking another agency to refer workers it has bona fide jobs and is not merely "making activity" for itself.

MISCELLANEOUS GOVERNMENTAL AGENCIES

In addition to the governmental agencies discussed above, three other agencies of the government which did some placement work were visited—the Bureau of Vocational Rehabilitation, the Indian Bureau, and the F.S.A. camps. It is quite possible that among the multiple ramifications of federal, state, and local government, there were other offices that did some limited placement work for a small group in conjunction with their regular duties, but it is doubtful that any operating on a large scale in the localities visited were missed.

Bureau of Vocational Rehabilitation.—The Bureau of Vocational Rehabilitation, a division of the State Department of Education, arranged for vocational training and gave financial assistance during the period of such training to handicapped persons whom it believed could be made self-supporting. At the time this study was made, between 2,700 and 2,800 persons were being aided throughout the state. Most of the referrals were from the California Industrial Accident Commission.

The San Francisco office of this bureau was the only one visited. This office maintained a placement service for its clients. Field workers were employed, whose responsibility it was to find openings and to escort handicapped applicants to prospective employers to assist them in selling themselves. It was reported that this office had had considerable success in making placements, and that most of the retrained applicants had become self-supporting.

The Wagner-Peyser Act contemplated coöperation between state employment services and state bureaus of vocational rehabilitation[28] in the placement of handicapped persons. It was, however, reported that in San Francisco the State Employment Service did not coöperate with the Bureau of Vocational Rehabilitation. The State Employment Service was supposed to refer all handicapped persons to the Bureau. This was done occasionally, but the number of referrals was disproportionately small. It must be remembered that the Bureau of Vocational Rehabilitation was in a position to do intensive case work for handicapped persons, whereas the State Employment Service was attempting to do a placement job on a large scale and was in no position to discriminate in favor of handicapped persons. Officials of the State Service apparently felt that employers would object to any suggestion or request that they employ handicapped persons and that any attempts in this direction would result in a loss of patronage. It was, however, alleged that the State Service refused to notify the Bureau of Vocational Rehabilitation of job openings in which handicapped persons might be placed, although the Bureau would take the entire responsibility for such placements.

Although it is quite understandable that the State Employment Service should concern itself primarily with the person without a handicap, there appeared to be no good reason why these two governmental agencies should not coöperate to the extent of the State Service's referring all handicapped workers and any jobs into which such persons might fit to the Bureau of Vocational Rehabilitation.

[28] 48 U. S. Stat. at L. 113. Sec. 8.

Indian Bureau Placement Office.—Placement work was an important part of the activities of the Los Angeles office of the United States Bureau of Indian Affairs.[24] A staff of two spent about half their time on placement work and the remainder on miscellaneous types of social work for persons of Indian blood resident in or passing through this community.

The direct placement work of this office was limited almost entirely to finding housework jobs for women and girls over 18 years of age. Occasionally men were placed in temporary cleaning jobs, but the policy was to refer men and boys to the State Employment Service, to an Indian irrigation project, or to large companies that were likely to have job openings. This office also acted as a clearance agent for Indians applying for jobs in the Indian Bureau.

Most of the applicants to this agency had been referred by one or another of the Indian agencies, or they had heard of it through friends. Job openings were secured through those who had used this office, had been satisfied, and had referred their friends. New employers, also, frequently called this office because of the generally good reputation of the Sherman Institute, where most of the Indian girls have received training in home economics. There were always more vacancies for domestics than this office could fill. Every job was carefully investigated, and girls were not referred unless the conditions of work met accepted standards, and apparently referrals were seldom made at a wage less than $30 a month and room and board. During the year 1936–37 this office filled 383 jobs, of which about three-quarters were full-time jobs.

This government bureau worked in close coöperation with the State Employment Service. All of the men, boys, and adult women were instructed to register at the State Service. The latter agency was supposed to refer all Indian applicants to this

[24] This was the only placement office organized by the Indian Bureau in California. However, some placement work was done by the Indian schools and agencies incidental to their other work.

bureau. It was reported, however, that the State Employment Service did not refer all Indians to the office of the Indian Bureau, and that an investigation indicated that Indians have "practically never" been placed by the State Service. In spite of the above-mentioned facts, the attitude of this bureau toward the State Employment Service was unusually cordial.

Since the placement of Indians might present difficulties for the State Employment Service, and since a government bureau had set up an employment bureau for the women of this racial group, there was again, as in the case of the handicapped, no reason why the State Service should not make every possible use of this agency.

F.S.A. Camps.—The F.S.A. of the United States Department of Agriculture has during the past few years opened a series of camps for migratory farm workers in California and in other states. These camps are located in areas in which customarily there is a large influx of agricultural labor for seasonal work. They are designed to provide decent camping facilities and to remove the menace to community health of promiscuous ditch-bank camping. Eight camps had been opened in California at the time of this investigation, three of which were in the areas visited—Winters near Sacramento, and Arvin and Shafter near Bakersfield. These camps accommodated from 100 to 240 families each. Admission was restricted to families in which one or more members were "genuine agricultural workers." Single men were not admitted. Although there were no racial restrictions, very few Mexican or Negro families had applied for admission. The absence of single men and of nonwhite races meant that a very large proportion of California's migrant agricultural labor was not represented. The largest group of residents in these camps were recent arrivals from the Southwest. Camp managers estimated that a large proportion were from Oklahoma. In one camp where the records were checked, two-thirds of the families in camp at that time came from Oklahoma and 30 per cent more from Texas, Arkansas, and Missouri; 82 per cent of all families ever admitted to this camp were from these four states.

Obviously these camps were focal points for the flood of homeless labor trying to gain a foothold in California agriculture that represents one of the chief problems in the organization of the labor market in this state. The following statement indicated that job finding was not considered to be a function of these camps: "In operating the camps the Farm Security Administration does not undertake functions, such as . . . employment service, now performed by established Government agencies. The province of the camp administration shall be, rather, to assemble and impart information which will facilitate the work of such agencies and to enlist the coöperation of . . . employment offices when the need becomes apparent. It is to be expected that employers will in many cases come directly to the camps to hire their help. The camp manager shall, in such instances, arrange for contact between employer and workers or representatives of the workers, who shall deal directly and reach their own agreements regarding terms of employment."[25] Camp managers had originally been instructed to urge all migrants to register at the State Employment Service. Unfortunately few of the camps—none of those visited—were within practicable distance of the Employment Service offices. Round trips to the nearest Employment Service office for registration and for subsequent visits would amount to about 50 miles for residents of any of the camps visited. As a consequence few registered, and the camp managers were agreed that the Employment Service seldom or never found jobs for camp residents even when they were registered. Although it must be recognized that the Employment Service was unable because of a shortage

[25] U. S. Department of Agriculture, Farm Security Administration, *Administration Letter 161* (Washington: Apr. 18, 1938).

of funds to do effective work in rural territory, it appeared significant that these two governmental agencies had made no attempt to work out a coöperative arrangement to assist camp residents to secure employment.

Although the camp managers did no placement work, they had assumed certain functions which contributed to a smoother flow of labor. They disseminated information about work or the lack of it in other communities and tried to encourage local farmers to use the camps as a source of labor supply. Information as to work available in other communities was posted on a bulletin board, published in the camp's weekly newspaper, or spread by word of mouth. In September 1938 a notice from the Farm Placement Service that 2,000 cotton pickers were needed in Arizona was posted in the camps near Bakersfield. The camp managers recognized that an important part of the task of spreading information about work opportunities was to counteract the rumors of jobs in localities that were already overstocked with labor and to attempt to check the disastrous surges of labor into communities that could not offer adequate employment. It is, however, hard to visualize how thousands can be prevented from going where only hundreds are needed if a sign is posted that 2,000 are needed, and no mechanism is set up to refer a reasonable number to the jobs.

The camp managers had not been very successful in getting farmers to come to the camp to secure workers, although those who lived in the camps worked on farms in the neighborhood along with those who had other types of living arrangements. A considerable group of farmers expressed the opinion that they preferred not to hire residents of the F.S.A. camps. The most common complaint was that the camps were "headquarters for radicals and trouble makers" and administered by "reds."[26] These objections were undoubtedly related to the fact

[26] This point of view is also found in a statement to the Tolan Committee by the Associated Farmers in 1940: "We find that . . . they are in many instances a rallying point for radical and subversive elements, housing saboteurs who work from

that the agricultural districts were strongly antiunion. Camp residents were not evicted from the F.S.A. camps for union activities as was customary in privately owned local camps. Although the opposition was specifically against the federal camps, there was a widespread conviction that all large congregations of agricultural workers were dangerous as possible headquarters for "radicals," and that growers' camps on individual ranches were far more desirable. This was an important point of view because it militated against the establishment under any auspices of centers from which farm labor might be dispatched on demand or to which farmers might go to obtain workers and thus tended to perpetuate the wasteful system of door-to-door solicitation of work.[27]

Other complaints about the F.S.A. camps were that they were too far away from many of the ranches, that too much money had been spent on them, that they did not take in single men or Mexicans (in the Sacramento area, where these were important elements in the labor supply), and that workers from the camps were lazy or unskilled.

Although not all of the growers interviewed objected to the F.S.A. camps, and a few went to the camps in search of labor, more commonly they chose their workers from those who ap-

---

them because inside the camp they cannot be touched by local, county, or State law-enforcement agencies." *Hearings before the Select Committee to Investigate the Interstate Migration of Destitute Citizens, House of Representatives,* 76th Cong., 3d sess., Part 6, San Francisco Hearings, p. 2752.

[27] It should be noted that these opinions were expressed at a time when there was an oversupply of farm labor, and most growers could obtain all they needed by sitting and waiting for it to apply at their gates. There might be less reluctance to establish distribution centers at a time when farmers were having difficulty finding enough workers. It is interesting to note that in 1940 the California State Chamber of Commerce recommended a modified extension of the F.S.A. migratory labor camps. "These camps have served a useful purpose as demonstrational projects in providing healthful temporary semipermanent types of housing to a limited number of migratory families in need of housing. The nature of the housing problem . . . makes it necessary to continue various types of experimental or demonstrational efforts in the housing field. . . . While many persons . . . were of the opinion that the Farm Security Administration program should be discouraged, the committee takes the position that the provision of housing is so vital that all intelligent approaches should receive encouragement." *Ibid.,* p. 2775.

plied at the gate—residents of the camps along with others. In two instances producers' associations in areas where there were no F.S.A. camps expressed their approval of this type of camp. It is perhaps significant that one of these was an association of hop growers. Hop growers employ large quantities of unskilled family labor and were almost the only farming group that reported any difficulties in finding an adequate labor supply.

Although it was impossible to interview an adequate sample of camp residents, about a half dozen from a camp near Bakersfield confirmed the general story of having to rustle their own jobs. In summary each of them said, "We have registered at the State Employment Service, but it is never any use. The only way we get jobs is to go from grower to grower. After you have been here a little while you get to know who the growers are and where labor is needed, and you just turn up and ask for work."

SUMMARY

At the time this study was made, the worker in search of employment in California might use placement bureaus which had been organized by a number of government agencies, in addition to the State Employment Service. These bureaus differed from the California State Employment Service in that they were designed to serve special groups—relief clients, registered voters, the handicapped, Indians, or graduates of schools and colleges. The services of the California State Employment Service were—in theory, at least—available to all of the above groups, and relief clients were a specific responsibility of this agency. The heavy relief load, however, made for pressure for special consideration to relief clients, and thus the S.R.A. in Los Angeles had set up an independent employment bureau which necessarily overlapped with the California State Employment Service. Clearly the Los Angeles Labor Coördinating Bureau appeared to be a duplicating service. The special services for the handicapped and for Indians were perhaps in a somewhat different category, since they concerned themselves with groups which presented special difficulties in placement. Ultimately these groups may be taken over by the California State Employment Service. Attempts in this direction, however, should not be undertaken until the State Service is equipped to handle the special problems involved, but in the meantime there should be more coöperation between the California State Employment Service and the agencies serving special groups.

In a number of cities, school departments had organized placement services for their graduates. The offices of the California State Employment Service were supposed to have a special department to serve young people just entering the labor market. Where such departments had been set up there was, except in Los Angeles, an overlap in the functions of the two government agencies. In Los Angeles the placement bureau of the city high schools was the Junior Department of the State Employment Service, and thus there was no duplication. There were several reasons why coöperative arrangements had not been worked out between the California State Employment Service and the school departments. In some instances the California State Employment Service was quite openly opposed to taking any responsibility for this group of job seekers, and in others the Junior Department of the California State Employment Service had not as yet developed its work to the point where it could give efficient service. There was also a strong conviction in some areas that the schools could do a better job—thus, an unwillingness to work with or through the California State Employment Service. It seems obvious that it is wasteful for two governmental agencies to set up departments to do the same job, and that good organization points in the direction of one coöperative agency.

The employment bureaus set up by universities, in the main, served a special group seeking jobs which in most instances were not listed with the California State Employment Service.

It may be that in the future the California State Employment Service will develop a service for those at the college level, but it is doubtful that the State Service, because of the large volume of work it must handle, will ever be able to do on a large scale the careful and probably somewhat expensive job of placing college graduates. It is important, however, to recognize that because of unemployment insurance, if for no other reason, college graduates will register at the California State Employment Service, and for the same reason employers will probably in some instances list their job orders for persons in this group with the State Service. It is therefore essential that efforts be made to overcome the present antagonism on the part of some college placement bureaus, and that there should be at least some sort of informal coöperation between these two types of agencies in order that jobs and applicants can be brought together as speedily as possible.

VI. Nongovernmental Free Agencies

In addition to the somewhat varied group of governmental agencies in which placement work was a subsidiary[1] to other functions, there were a number of different types of private organizations which, though almost always in business for another purpose, offered some sort of a free placement service to workers seeking employment and to employers who needed labor. This group of organizations included social service agencies, private trade schools, businesses which had developed an employment service for the benefit of their customers, occupational, fraternal, and veterans associations, and a small miscellaneous category. It is obvious, of course, that the organizations listed above were each in business for a quite different purpose. The only characteristic which they possessed in common was that they had all included placement work within the scope of their activities.[2] In some instances they had set up highly organized employment bureaus, whereas in others their methods of distributing job information were of the most informal sort.

SOCIAL SERVICE AGENCIES

Many welfare agencies in the larger cities functioned to some extent as employment bureaus, frequently in an informal fashion. In the smaller towns visited these agencies did little or no placement work; in Los Angeles this function was much further

[1] The Los Angeles Labor Coördinating Bureau was the one governmental agency other than the California State Employment Service which was set up for the sole purpose of placement work. See chap. v.

[2] An attempt was made to visit examples of all types of free nongovernmental placement services which could be discovered. It should, however, be pointed out that other agencies of this sort probably existed, but it is unlikely that they were operating on any considerable scale. In one or two instances, such as the associations of foreign-born groups, it was found that little if any placement work was done. Since, however, it appeared likely that these organizations might concern themselves with this problem, a brief comment as to their activities has been included in this chapter.

developed than in San Francisco. Placement work was usually incidental to the agency's other activities; there were only a few instances of private philanthropic agencies set up exclusively for placement work and vocational guidance. The employment facilities were usually available to anyone, with certain racial restrictions, rather than limited to the agency's own cases. Typically, the placement work was designed to aid a special underprivileged group—particular races or nationalities, the middle-aged, or the maladjusted. The great majority of openings which these agencies filled were for domestic servants or odd jobs in private homes, and these were not usually the most skilled or best paid. Very few social service agencies filled any jobs with business houses in the commercial or industrial fields. A corollary of this was that there was very little solicitation of orders from employers. Most of the agencies depended on orders telephoned in by employers who had used the agency before or knew it by reputation. The number of placements indicated how small was the scale of operations; four-fifths of the social service agencies visited in Los Angeles and San Francisco made less than two placements per working day, and in most agencies a considerable proportion of the placements were in temporary jobs. Most of the welfare agencies advised their applicants for employment to register with the State Employment Service, and many agencies told applicants about the other free placement resources in the city or recommended "reputable" fee-charging agencies. But, in spite of the fact that the welfare agencies (in Los Angeles, at least) failed to fill a considerable proportion of the employers' orders which they received, there was very little clearance of such orders between the different agencies. The general picture was one of quite uncoördinated efforts, on a small scale and in a somewhat haphazard fashion.

Number and Type of Agencies That Did Placement Work.— As has been mentioned in an earlier chapter, it was impossible to determine just how many philanthropic agencies in each community conducted an employment service, and time and funds did not permit visiting a random sample of such agencies. The agencies visited were selected from those which the local Community Chest or its equivalent indicated as doing placement work, together with a few others suggested by other sources. Fourteen agencies which did placement work were visited in San Francisco, 18 in Los Angeles, and 1 each in Bakersfield and Sacramento. Those visited in San Francisco were primarily family welfare agencies and character-building agencies, such as the Y.W.C.A. and the Y.M.C.A., including agencies representing the chief foreign groups of the city. In Los Angeles, in addition to these two types, the sample included church organizations and several community centers for Negroes and Mexicans. It is possible that churches, community centers, boys' clubs, agencies interested in health rehabilitation and housing, and agencies outside the Community Chest were doing some placement work in both cities, but it is improbable that their methods or the extent of their work differed radically from the sample visited.

The Sacramento Community Chest reported by letter that it maintained an employment agency prior to 1936 which "did not function satisfactorily and its usefulness at that time was questionable. . . . There are no Community Chest agencies in Sacramento which have placement departments or perform a placement service for any considerable number of clients. . . . Naturally, certain of the agencies occasionally find a position for a client in whom they are especially interested, but such placements are very infrequent." One of these agencies, dealing primarily with Mexicans, was visited. In Bakersfield the Community Chest indicated that only one agency did any placement work, and that of the same informal type as in Sacramento.

Philanthropic agencies organized exclusively for placement work and vocational guidance were rare even in the large cities.

One was found in San Francisco and one in Los Angeles, both of them for the benefit of women. In the other agencies finding jobs had developed as a corollary of the agency's primary functions.

The central organization of philanthropic agencies in the large cities disapproved of the multiplication of placement bureaus among their members. The Community Chest of San Francisco in April 1935 formulated the general principle that "the provision of employment service in relief agencies is unsound" and recommended its discontinuance. Three years later, however, the same agencies were continuing placement work. The Los Angeles Community Welfare Federation made a study of employment services of member agencies in the same year[3] and recommended that the 15 agencies studied consolidate their employment services into one agency by November 1936, but it was not done.

Administration.—In San Francisco the social service agencies, with two exceptions, did not have a full-time person in charge of placement work. In Los Angeles, on the other hand, about half of the agencies which considered placement as one of their functions employed one or more full-time persons whose duties were restricted to the placement field.[4] When there was no full-time employment secretary, the work was done by a staff member, either interspersed with regular duties or for stated hours each day. In a few instances these offices were staffed by skilled personnel, but the following statement from the Los Angeles Community Welfare Federation study in 1935 can probably be considered descriptive of the situation in 1938 in both San Francisco and Los Angeles: "The employees in

[3] Los Angeles Community Welfare Federation, *Employment and Counseling Service in Agencies in Membership in the Los Angeles Community Welfare Federation* (Oct. 21, 1935). Mimeographed.

[4] It should be noted that a number of the agencies visited had full-time employment bureaus prior to the depression which were abandoned for lack of funds and difficulty in finding jobs.

these agencies are in the majority of cases not technically trained for employment work, and have had no experience in this type of work previous to their employment in their present positions."[5]

Type of Applicants.—Although, in the main, the social service agencies did not limit registration to their own clients or members, their services were to a large extent limited to a particular group which was felt to be at a disadvantage in seeking employment in the open market. Examples were age and racial groups which presented special placement problems.

In San Francisco a guidance and placement bureau was organized by a group of business and professional women's clubs in 1936. The purpose of this organization was to "counsel and befriend," to give vocational information, and to find suitable positions for the unemployed working woman over 40. This organization was particularly interested in women in the business field, although it was recognized that probably a number would have to be shifted to other fields, particularly to domestic service.[6] In Los Angeles a church organization had set up an employment service which, in the main, placed middle-aged and older women. Unlike the San Francisco office serving a similar group, this Los Angeles agency only made placements in domestic service.

There were also agencies in both San Francisco and Los Angeles which specialized in service to a younger group of women. In San Francisco the Y.W.C.A. had a special vocational counselor who, in the main, gave advice and assistance to women under 35. This organization made some placements, usually in commercial and industrial occupations, but this work was incidental to that of giving vocational advice. The Bureau of

[5] Los Angeles Community Welfare Federation, *op. cit.*, pp. 4–5.

[6] In October 1940 this bureau was taken over by the California State Employment Service. The staff of the bureau was transferred to the State Employment Service and the sponsorship of the Council of Club Presidents continued. *San Francisco Chronicle* (California), Oct. 18, 1940.

Vocational Service in Los Angeles was organized with a twofold purpose: to secure jobs and to give vocational information and advice to women in professional and commercial occupations. Most of the women registered with this bureau were between 25 and 35 years of age. This organization was formerly supported entirely by the Community Chest, but in 1938 an agreement was made with the California State Employment Service whereby the salary of one interviewer was paid by the State Employment Service.

Social service agencies had not set up organized placement services for the young person just entering the job market, although in San Francisco the private welfare agencies that handled cases of state aid to children attempted in an informal way to find jobs for young people no longer eligible to receive state aid.

Several agencies were attempting to give special assistance to certain racial groups. In San Francisco the Jewish charities had no organized employment department, although they accepted orders for domestics and made some placements. In Los Angeles, on the other hand, the Jewish Social Service Bureau had organized an employment bureau which was maintained as a distinct and quite independent branch of its parent organization. This office, one of the best equipped in the city, had been set up because racial prejudice in Los Angeles made special efforts on behalf of this group necessary. Persons in all occupations except domestic service were registered, and, since this organization was intended to serve the Jewish community in general, most of the registrants were not relief clients.

In San Francisco the Chinese and Japanese branches of the Y.M.C.A. and in Los Angeles the Japanese branch of this organization did a little placement work for young people of these races. In Los Angeles four agencies had organized placement work for Negroes and one for Mexicans. These organizations were usually under religious auspices.

Less than a third of these agencies restricted their registrations to women, but at least half reported that few or no men registered because most of the jobs they had to offer were domestic. Only the Y.M.C.A.'s registered men exclusively.

None of the social service agencies was anxious to get job applicants, and many said that certain applicants were discouraged because funds and personnel were inadequate. There was no soliciting of workers by advertisement or any type of publicity. Applicants were attracted to the organization through its word-of-mouth reputation, were referred to it by other agencies or churches, or were relief clients.

Placements.—The job openings which social service agencies had to offer were to a large extent limited to domestic service and odd jobs in private families. Two-thirds of those visited reported that they seldom or never had calls for any other type of work, and in most of the other agencies the proportion of domestic openings bulked large. Only 3 of the 34 social service placement departments visited reported that all or the majority of their placements were in other fields; 2 of these specialized in vocational guidance for young women, and 1 was the Jewish agency in Los Angeles.

It is always difficult to determine cause and effect in such a situation. The great proportion of applicants at most of these agencies were untrained women who could not be placed outside the domestic field, but it may be that only this type registered because the agency could offer nothing else. Similarly, openings in industry could not be obtained without a publicity campaign and soliciting among employers, such as few of these agencies had ever attempted. The absence of publicity and solicitation of employers may be attributed either to lack of funds or to a definite policy on the agency's part. The Los Angeles Community Welfare Federation study decided that specialization in domestic placement "is not due to any desire on the part of the agencies, but is largely a result of present conditions and the connotation placed upon the agencies by the employers of this area."[7]

It is impossible to be precise, but the general impression of interviewers was that the domestic service jobs offered to these agencies were usually general housework and by no means the best paid or most highly skilled. The Los Angeles study confirmed this opinion: "In general the domestic agencies are receiving a number of orders in the lower wage groups."[8] Jobs for men were apt to be housecleaning or such odd jobs as repair work in private houses, rough gardening, distributing handbills, or carrying salesmen's sample cases. They were usually temporary, rarely with an industrial firm, and often described as "substandard" by the placement officer.

The few agencies which made placements outside the domestic and odd-jobs fields were generally operating in commercial and professional lines. There was very little placement by philanthropic agencies in industry. One Los Angeles agency which used to do field work among employers reported some placements in factory needle trades. One of the Negro organizations in Los Angeles made a point of persuading firms that sought Negro trade to employ Negro help; grocery stores were cited as an example. Other racial or religious group agencies found openings in firms run by their own people. One or two women's agencies made placements in such professions as social worker and dietitian. On the whole, the nondomestic placements were clerical occupations.

Another characteristic of jobs furnished by philanthropic agencies was the high proportion which were only temporary. In more than 40 per cent of the agencies visited in Los Angeles and San Francisco which reported on this topic the majority of jobs furnished were temporary.

[7] Los Angeles Community Welfare Federation, *op. cit.*, p. 27.

[8] *Ibid.*, p. 29.

Not only the scope but the extent of placements by philanthropic agencies was very limited. In San Francisco the 14 agencies visited placed around 200 people a month;[9] in Los Angeles 18 agencies placed 1,200 a month. Obviously this was an insignificant fraction of the total labor turnover in these cities, even in a depression year. In each city two-thirds or more of these placements were made by only three or four agencies. In San Francisco there was not a single agency that made more than 50 placements a month; in Los Angeles the average was larger, but only two agencies made more than 100 placements a month. For the two cities combined, half the agencies made less than 25 placements a month, or 1 per working day, and four-fifths made less than 50 a month. Of the agencies with full-time staff members for employment work, more than half made less than 50 placements a month. The wastefulness of operation on such a scale is obvious and explains the attempts of coördinating bodies to abolish employment services in private charitable agencies.

A criticism of procedure brought out in the Los Angeles Community Welfare Federation study in 1935 was that placement officers in these agencies depended on their personal knowledge of applicants to select them for referral to a job or upon those who happened to call into the office at the time a job was open rather than on a thorough analysis of applications on file to select the one best fitted for the job. A number of factors explained this: the case-work attitude of finding work for a given client, the inadequacy of information in application files, and the difficulty and expense of reaching applicants (who frequently had no telephone) in time to refer them to the job before

[9] It was impossible to obtain adequate statistics from most of these agencies. Frequently they had no recent reports on work done, or the figures given were vague and ambiguous. Resources were not available to compile data from agency files, even when the files were complete. One of the worst features of their statistics was the lack of uniform definitions; it was impossible always to determine precisely even what constituted a placement. Figures available were usually estimates and for varying dates, but they are cited as indicative of the volume of work done. The latest date available has always been used.

it was filled from another agency. But the obvious result was that the employer got the worker who was most readily available rather than the one best suited to his requirements. Although complete information on this subject was not obtained in the present study, the interviews indicated that the same criticism was still widely applicable in both Los Angeles and San Francisco. In both years, however, there were a few agencies with trained staff members who made a point of fitting the applicant to the job. These were usually in the commercial rather than the domestic field.

One of the chief criticisms of current practice made by the Los Angeles Community Welfare Federation was that many of the agencies, particularly those placing domestics, failed to follow up promptly after they had referred an applicant to an opening. Since they seldom referred more than one applicant to an opening, this meant that if the employer was not suited the agency usually did not learn of it in time to send another applicant and thus lost not only an existing opening but perhaps the employer's future patronage.[10] The answers given to interviewers on follow-up procedure were very vague; usually the agency said that they telephoned if the applicant failed to notify them. Probably the 1935 criticism was still valid. Certainly the habit of sending only one applicant to a job still persisted in the majority of agencies.

It was impossible to obtain usable estimates of the number of openings and the proportion filled from any appreciable number of agencies. In 1935 special records were kept for the Federation study, which found that placements were 69 per cent of openings for all agencies studied in Los Angeles and only 56 per cent for placement bureaus specializing in domestic service.[11] Quite a number of the agencies visited in 1938 reported that they always had more domestic service jobs than they could fill, either because wages or working conditions were

[10] *Ibid.*, p. 13. [11] *Ibid.*, p. 23.

substandard or because of the difficulty of finding competent people willing to do housework.

Employers' Orders.—The majority of agencies visited made no effort to solicit patronage for their employment services but depended on their previously established reputation with employers whom they had served. The activities of the agencies who solicited business in any fashion varied from an advertisement in the classified section of the telephone book or in the agency's own periodical to a regular program of field visits to employers. Even this group of agencies got the majority of their orders from word-of-mouth reputation. Obviously domestic service agencies found it harder to reach their potential employers—housewives—than did those attempting to find openings in business firms. However, one or two of the former reported speeches to women's groups and circulars to churches as a method of publicity for their service. Six of the 32 agencies visited in Los Angeles and San Francisco had a program of field visits to business firms. A few others had recently abandoned such a program for reasons of economy.

A common complaint was that the employers who called a charitable agency expected to get a worker at substandard wages. A majority of the agencies indicated that they would not accept orders or would "try not to send a worker out" to jobs paying below a certain minimum, particularly for domestic work. However, the Los Angeles study in 1935 indicated that "the majority of them do not always adhere to the standards and restrictions indicated in their policies."[12] There was no reason to believe that the situation had altered since that time.

Relationships with Other Agencies.—The picture of placement work among social service agencies was one of a large number of organizations operating on a small scale in much the same field. In the interests of economy, close coöperation

[12] *Ibid.*, p. 4.

with each other, with the State Employment Service, and with other free agencies in the community would be highly desirable. Unfortunately there was little indication of this. Apparently the majority of such agencies handled the applicants and the employers' orders that came to them and, if the applicants could not find jobs or if the employers' orders could not be filled, did not suggest other philanthropic agencies that might be of use. Obviously there were exceptions. Agencies that specialized in guidance referred their applicants to other free placement resources, and some of the other agencies reported an informal exchange of applicants and openings. The Los Angeles Community Welfare Federation study in 1935 found that "there is not much coöperation among the domestic agencies. There is no definite plan of referring orders which cannot be filled to other agencies. Some agencies refer a few orders and coöperate with two or three other agencies, but there is a need for more complete coöperation among all agencies. Until there is such coöperation, a large number of orders will remain unfilled because no applicant is referred to them." Probably this situation explained another of their findings—that there was greater duplication between agencies in employers' orders than in applicants' registrations.[18] The Federation recommended a central clearing agency for employers' orders, but three years later there was little indication that the situation had improved.

The question might perhaps be raised of the desirability of employment services in philanthropic agencies competing with a free state employment service. The justification by the agencies was either that the Employment Service was not actually finding jobs for their clients or that they served a special group who needed particular efforts to combat prejudice against them. Usually they were sympathetic toward the idea of a state employment service but felt it could not take over their work. A typical statement from the placement officer of a San Francisco

[18] *Ibid.*, p. 27.

agency, thoroughly in sympathy with the Employment Service's aims, was that people referred by the agency were lost in the crowd, waited all day for interviews, never heard from their applications, and got results only when sent with a personal note to one of the Employment Service interviewers. An example of the special group was the Negroes in Los Angeles. Their agencies declared either that the State Employment Service had no interest in Negroes or that special field work was needed to open new types of jobs to Negroes. Another type of special work was vocational guidance for women and the commercial and professional placement connected with it. The Los Angeles agency doing this work was partly subsidized by the Employment Service on the theory, apparently, that the latter was not equipped in time or personnel to do the careful interviewing and selection for this specialized placement job but would eventually take it over. The Los Angeles Community Welfare Federation study stated: "The State Employment Service is not as yet ready to assume the entire burden of employment service. Until this public agency has had an opportunity to develop, some private free employment service has a definite place in Los Angeles."

The social service agencies appeared to be coöperating more closely with the State Employment Service than with each other. Half of the agencies visited in Los Angeles and San Francisco recommended to some or all of their own applicants that they also register with the State Employment Service; and half of them, much more commonly in Los Angeles than in San Francisco, referred to the Employment Service applicants and jobs of a type they did not handle. The State Employment Service for its part referred applicants to social agencies giving special service, such as religious or racial groups or vocational guidance agencies, and occasionally called one of the charitable agencies for an applicant to fill a job. Only four agencies in the two cities reported no dealings with the State Employment Service. However, this appearance of coöperation may have been greater than the reality. It is at least open to question whether duplicate registration at many different agencies is desirable as a permanent feature of the labor market. The agency reports on referring applicants and jobs of a type never handled to the State Employment Service indicated that in many cases these were unplaceable applicants and substandard jobs, which injured the community reputation of the Employment Service and loaded its files with workers and job openings that could never be disposed of. The State Employment Service in Los Angeles, where this was most common, said that all free domestic service agencies had agreed not to dump on each other, but in practice apparently many of them did.

In Sacramento the State Employment Service had very largely taken over the placement functions of social service agencies, with the exception of the informal activities already cited. The Community Chest wrote, "All local agencies refer applicants for positions and prospective employers to the local office of the California State Employment Service." In Bakersfield interviewers found no indication that philanthropic agencies had ever done much placement work.

Although none of the charitable agencies condoned the worst practices of fee-charging agencies, nearly half of them referred certain of their clients—the more skilled or those with money to pay fees—to the "reputable" licensed agencies on the grounds that their chances of a good job were better there than at the free agencies. In San Francisco some of the philanthropic agencies would either pay or guarantee the fee for their clients under certain circumstances.

PRIVATE TRADE SCHOOLS

It is a well-known fact that private trade schools concern themselves with the placement of those to whom they offer training. Students enroll in schools of this sort for the purpose of securing training for a specific occupation, and thus it is not unnatural that they should expect more assistance in finding a job than in the case of students in the academic institutions. Furthermore, the fact that, with one or two exceptions, the student in these schools must pay a fee for his training perhaps leads him to expect a job when the course is completed. Competition among trade schools for students, on which the profits of the business depend, also stimulates their interest in placing their graduates. These schools recognized the fact that the likelihood of getting a job was the most cogent reason for choosing a particular school.

An examination of the classified telephone books in San Francisco and Los Angeles showed over 250 trade schools in these two cities. The largest single group was the business and secretarial schools; the others covered a tremendous variety of occupations, from modeling to sheet metal working. It was impossible to visit any adequate sample from which the importance of schools of each type in the total sum of placements for the community could be calculated; instead, a few examples were investigated.

The wide variety of training made it impossible to generalize closely about the activities of the schools as a group. In certain respects the reports received from them were similar. They all purported to find the first jobs for a great majority of their graduating classes. Most of them officially offered placement facilities to former graduates, but apparently few former students returned to have jobs found for them in later years. Consequently the schools furnished only the inexperienced element among job seekers. Very few did employment work for nongraduates. Usually there was no employment secretary in the school, but the placement work was done by one of the school officials. For openings the schools depended chiefly upon a clientele of regular patrons, the reputation built up by advertising the school to get students, and the contacts of school officials with business firms in connection with the work of the school, rather than upon field visits for placement work alone. A few schools had clearance arrangements with the State Employment Service or fee-charging agencies, but, on the whole, they placed students without reference to other placement agencies. With very few exceptions they were not on good terms with the unions, and there were no arrangements to admit their graduates as apprentices. The employers visited in the course of the study reported a wide use of the secretarial schools, and the firms manufacturing airplanes obtained many of the beginners from trade schools training for this industry. Otherwise there was little mention of private trade schools as a source of employees, although the public trade school in Los Angeles was frequently cited.

Business and Secretarial Schools.—There were approximately 75 privately owned schools in the two cities of Los Angeles and San Francisco which offered training in some aspect of the general field of business. Five schools of this type were visited—three large and long-established business colleges offering a variety of courses from the simple secretarial to three-year courses in "business administration," one small specialized school for high-class private secretaries, and a large night school. Small as was the sample, it was probably an adequate indication of how the reputable schools operated.

Night schools may apparently be ruled out as an important factor in the community system of placement facilities. Most, if not all, of their pupils were already employed, and the schools did very little to help them find new jobs when training was completed. The example visited had 800 pupils during the school year and made only 14 placements. These were cases in which the school received an unsolicited order or in which one of the instructors happened to know of an opening. Similarly, one of the business colleges reported that students in the night classes rarely registered with the placement office, although its services were open to them.

The large business colleges placed only their own pupils, sometimes only their graduates; but, since each of them trained several hundred young people a year, and since their existence depended on the ease with which their graduates found jobs, they were obviously an important source of placements. To judge from those studied, however, their placement activities in practice were usually limited to the beginner's first job and were not a factor in finding new employment for experienced workers. All schools offered "life-time service" to their graduates, but the placement officers interviewed gave little indication that many returned for new or better jobs. No reputable school guaranteed placement to its graduates; inducements to prospective pupils were along the line of "Blank School has successfully placed its graduates in good positions throughout the depression." Of the three business colleges visited, one said that, with the exception of a few students who found their own jobs, every graduate was placed; the employment manager found him job after job until one proved permanent. Another said that a sample over the last 10 years showed that 95 per cent of the graduates were placed by the school. The third said that it could place all graduates who wanted placement but that this was only 50 per cent last year. The number of placements reported varied from 200 a year to 2,000; it was impossible to estimate the total volume of placements from all business colleges in either city, although it was obviously very large. Confirmation of the importance of placements from this source was the fact that one-fifth of the industrial employers interviewed in San Francisco and Los Angeles reported that they called upon secretarial schools to fill at least some of their office jobs.

The mechanics of placing students differed in different schools. There might be a full-time employment secretary, or one of the school officials might handle placement work. The most profitable sources of openings were a clientele of long-established patrons and the school's reputation in the community. One school spoke of an "aggressive" program of field visits to employers; another did field work only when the supply of graduates began to exceed openings; the third had no organized field visiting program.

Relations with other placement agencies apparently were not close. It was reported that the State Employment Service or the fee-charging agencies occasionally called the schools for an applicant to fill a job. Orders that the school could not fill were sometimes passed on to other free agencies or to the universities. One school sent to fee-charging agencies those graduates who were difficult to place and frequently paid the fee.

The small secretarial school visited did not differ markedly in its placement policies from the larger schools. Ninety-eight per cent of the graduates were placed, usually "for life." Openings came primarily from an established clientele and the school's reputation. This school did no advertising. When openings became scarce, the head of the school "put on her hat and went out to find jobs for her girls." Because of the high type of student, only "select positions" in the better commercial houses were accepted. The school placed 35 girls in 1937. It had no dealings with the State Employment Service, but there was a coöperative arrangement with one of the best of the fee-charging agencies to clear openings which they could not fill.

All placements through schools of the type described were, of course, free. In addition, a limited number of fee-charging agencies also operated business schools. Two of these were visited in San Francisco, of which one (a business machine agency) gave school graduates free placement, and the other placed them through the usual routine and charged the usual fees. Other business machine companies with free placement bureaus also operated schools; these are discussed in a later section.

Trade Schools of Other Types.—There were more than 175 private trade schools in San Francisco and Los Angeles in addition to the business and secretarial schools.

The aircraft schools were the only trade schools other than secretarial and business colleges which employers gave any indication of patronizing extensively.[14] All three airplane manufacturing companies which were visited indicated that most, if not all, of their beginning mechanics came from these schools, which were highly praised for keeping in close touch with the industry and adapting their courses to its needs. The union situation in the industry may also have been a factor; in at least one plant the union was violently opposed to "company controlled" schools, and the schools "steered clear" of unions. But, from whatever cause, the private aircraft schools were a direct road to a job. Three of about a dozen such schools were visited in Los Angeles. Two schools reported 90 to 95 per cent of their graduates placed by them; the third, with many students from foreign countries and other states who went home to get jobs, stated that "there is no recommended graduate of this Institute out of employment," and that many students not yet graduated had jobs waiting for them. It is difficult to estimate the total volume of students coming from these schools on the basis of the sample visited; one school had graduated 150 in 10 months of operation; another, 1,403 in 19 months; another, around 400 a year. None of the schools guaranteed placement, but one offered to refund tuition if the student was not placed. Apparently it was customary for the school to place the student in his first job only, since it was reported that students did not return for later placements. The schools' explanation was that their graduates remained in their first job. All of the schools did a great deal of soliciting for students, such as national advertis-

[14] This applies only to privately operated schools. The public trade school in Los Angeles was widely used (see pp. 188–190). In addition, the schools may have been effective in placing their graduates in trades, such as beauty parlor operation, which were not included in our sample of employers.

ing, pamphlets, and salesmen posted at the hiring gate of airplane plants, and one belonged to a sales organization that pushed a group of trade schools. The publicity included much stress on the openings in the industry and the ease with which students were placed. Jobs were apparently found largely through the schools' current contacts with the relatively few plants in the locality and direct calls to them for workers rather than through any organized program to hunt openings, although one school reported an employment director. There were no contacts between the schools and the State Employment Service, fee-charging agencies, or any other type of placement service.

Of the miscellaneous types of trade schools visited, two were schools of beauty culture in San Francisco—one large and one small. Both reported placing practically all their graduates. The smaller advertised that positions were guaranteed; the larger said that all students who did not secure their own jobs were placed by the school, that all were placed within three weeks after graduation, and that it often had more openings than students to fill them. This amounted to about 300 placements in 1937 for the large school and 36 for the small. Employers were said to call the schools when they wanted an operator[15] or to call the wholesale supply houses (see p. 236), which in turn called the schools, and one of the schools circularized a mailing list of employers and did some field visiting to be sure of placing its graduates. Neither school had a separate placement officer. Both schools gave placement service to former graduates who asked for it; but in one, at least, the proportion was small. The larger school exchanged applicants and openings with the State Employment Service, which usually had more experienced operators registered than had the schools; the smaller school did not. Fee-charging agencies did not operate in this field. The placement agency with which the schools were in direct competition was the union, which was attempting

[15] No beauty parlors were included in the sample of employers to check this statement.

to set up a placement office through which all beauty operators would be hired. The union regarded the schools as its "keenest competitors," was pushing legislation to restrict their activities and to increase the stringency of state licensing examinations so that the supply of operators would be reduced, and was making it extremely difficult for recent graduates to obtain membership in the union. The small school said that in spite of these activities it expected to continue to be able to find openings for its limited graduating class. The larger school was extremely doubtful of its ability to place all graduates in the future, although it was on relatively good terms with the union because it often advised girls to register with the union and refused to send out strikebreakers. The union, however, had as yet obtained little control over the field, having made only three placements in the month preceding the interview.

One hotel training school was visited in San Francisco, which offered courses in dining-room training, bartending, "executive housekeeping," etc. Its advertisements stressed the supervisory and administrative positions. The school authorities said that 95 per cent of their graduates were placed, "a hundred or so a year." Placements were all in hotels, restaurants, apartment houses, and cocktail bars, not in private homes. Openings were obtained primarily from a steady clientele; some were referred by business associations, such as the Chamber of Commerce; others were obtained by field visits to employers. The school had no coöperative arrangements with the State Employment Service because it "didn't like their policy" but cleared unfilled openings with certain fee-charging agencies that did the school favors in turn. It reported that it made "no attempt to buck union rules," but when the union obtained control of a trade and made entrance into the union difficult, the school closed out its course in that trade or sharply limited enrollment. The unions in this industry made no comment on trade schools.

The mechanical and engineering trade schools, other than

aircraft manufacture, were represented in this sample by three San Francisco schools: a free endowed vocational school offering courses in drafting, machine shop practice, radio, etc.; a well-known private "engineering college" which offered similar but much shorter "practical" courses and a two-year engineering course of "college grade"; and a school with short courses in Diesel operating, air conditioning and refrigeration, and aircraft manufacture. The two latter charged tuition, whereas fees were not required in the endowed school. Curricula and standards varied so greatly between schools in this category that the three visited cannot be considered other than isolated examples not necessarily representative of all or of a majority of this type of school.

The endowed trade school limited its enrollment to 250 boys who were graduates of junior or of senior high schools. The training offered was primarily in mechanical and industrial "arts," although preparation for university entrance was also offered. This school had not set up a placement department, but the dean considered placement work to be one of his responsibilities and reported that boys were referred to employers who call the school for assistance in filling jobs. Because of the wide reputation of the school, a majority of the students found their own jobs, and thus it had not appeared necessary for the school to assume much responsibility for placing its graduates. Students were not referred to the State Employment Service, probably not because of any antagonism to this agency, but rather because it had not been necessary to use this resource.

Neither of the two engineering schools which charged tuition had organized placement departments. In both, however, someone on the staff considered placement work as one of his responsibilities. Not unnaturally, these schools were unwilling to give definite information as to the number of placements made by the school. One said, "We can place all who want to be placed"; the other, "Seventy-five per cent of our graduates are placed either through their own efforts or through this office." Statements of this sort must, of course, be interpreted with caution, since attendance at these schools was probably dependent to a considerable extent on the impression created as to the likelihood of employment after a course was completed. It was impossible to estimate the importance in the larbor market of schools of this character, but it may be significant that practically none of the employers visited cited them as a source of labor supply.

In San Francisco an endowed vocational school for girls and a private school for models were visited. The endowed school gave courses for medical and dental assistants, saleswomen, dressmakers and milliners, courses preparing for food industries and for the decorative arts, and a prenursing course. As was the case of the endowed vocational school for boys, the enrollment was limited to 250 graduates of junior and senior high schools. This school had no placement department. The dean and teachers kept their eyes open for available jobs, but it was reported that the girls were likely to find openings through the field work done before graduation. There was apparently not much of a placement problem, which perhaps accounted for the fact that there were no contacts with the State Employment Service.

The school for models was a profit-making venture which, for a fee, gave courses in modeling and "personality development." This was a small organization run by an owner-manager who had no record of placements. It was reported that placement was considered one of the functions of the organization and that "graduates" were placed in wholesale and retail trade, in fashion films, and with photographers. It appeared probable that finding jobs for students was of importance primarily as an advertisement for pupils.

Summary.—It was difficult to estimate the value of private trade schools in the placement field. It appeared, however, that the business and secretarial schools had, in general, earned a good reputation as a resource for labor, and that the endowed free vocational schools for boys and girls, although doing little organized placement work, actually provided a fairly easy step into the labor market. The situation in regard to the private trade schools in other fields which operated on a fee basis was somewhat more doubtful. While it was not possible in the course of this study to secure evidence as to the validity of a quite general opinion that many of these schools taught little or nothing in exchange for tuition paid and gave little security of employment upon graduation, it appeared likely that some of the schools visited operated on this basis, and it is probable that there were many more of this sort. Just as there is danger that a fee-charging employment agency will be more concerned with collecting a fee for a job than with placing the right person in a job, unless a private trade school is run by personnel with the highest standards, admission may be granted to all who can pay the fee, qualifications for the training and for subsequent placement being of secondary importance. Furthermore, such placements as are made will not be in accordance with good placement practice—the right man for the job—but rather an attempt will be made to make placements in any jobs which turn up.

BUSINESSES GIVING SERVICE TO CUSTOMERS

Another type of free placement service was that which commercial organizations, usually wholesale or retail houses, had instituted to supply workers to their customers or, when the workers themselves are the customers, to find them jobs. The motives inspiring such undertakings were to keep the good will of the employer by finding workers for him, to push the sale of products by placing workers who were either accustomed to using them or felt a debt of gratitude to the company, to guarantee the workers' patronage of a store by making placement contingent upon it, and to guarantee workers' bills by assignment of wages or less formal arrangements. The investigators obtained no evidence of illegal fee charging or rake-offs, if any existed.

The most common type of business which had organized a service as described above was the business machine and typewriter company, which supplied operators for their own machines, stenographers, and other types of office help. Similarly, establishments selling wholesale drugs and beauty parlor supplies dispatched pharmacists and beauty parlor operators. An ambulance service supplied nurses to patients in their own homes. Japanese boarding houses were the clearing agency between Japanese farmers and agricultural laborers of their own race. A landholding company occasionally hunted up a skilled farm worker for its lessees. Grocers in rural towns found agricultural work for Filipinos in exchange for their trade and, according to one authority, for a "cash bond." Two chains of retail stores, patronized by Mexicans who worked on the railroads, had close to a monopoly in selecting Mexicans for the "extra gangs," and, in exchange, at least one of them took an assignment of wages for debts incurred at the store. Some of the packing and shipping sheds for agricultural products reported that during the season a stream of migratory labor asked for directions to ranches that needed harvest hands. Since these sheds frequently belonged to the farmer or were coöperatives, they are discussed in a later section.[16] Some, at least, of the sugar refineries had long made a business of providing labor contractors[17] to the growers when they were needed. One of the jobs of their field man was to keep on hand a list of available contractors and to make sure that every farmer who sold his sugar beets to the refinery had made adequate arrangements for

[16] See pages 400–401. Cotton gins are included there, although their relation to the farmer was more like that of the refineries.

[17] For the role which labor contractors play in the cultivation of sugar beets see pages 315–317.

harvest hands. Undoubtedly there were many other types of businesses which did a little placement work as a side line.[18] Those included in this study are examples of the way the system operated rather than any attempt at an adequate sample.

Most of the business houses visited made very few placements. One business machine company, however, was probably the most important source for operators of its widely used machine. So was the anonymous company. The ambulance service reported a volume of placements comparable to that of a small commercial agency. The rural groceries reported a number of placements, but their volume would be small compared with the total number of harvest hands in the area. The two chains of stores for Mexican railroad workers had close to a monopoly in this field. The importance of field labor placements via contractors provided to growers through the efforts of sugar refineries was undoubtedly large but impossible to estimate. The contractors themselves were only an intermediate step in procuring the actual workers, and many of the growers had contractors of long years' standing and so did not need the refineries' services. To judge from our sample, the free services offered as a side line by commercial companies were an important factor in only a few instances or a few specific types of occupation and industry.

Business Machine and Typewriter Companies.—It has become established practice that most typewriter and business machine companies shall run an informal placement service to supply their customers with operators for the machines they sell and frequently with stenographers and other classes of office workers. Of 14 different companies investigated in San Francisco and Los Angeles,[19] only 2 had no employment service.

[18] In addition, a very large corporation was visited which did quite an appreciable amount of placement for its customers, but which was insistent on the preservation of its anonymity.

[19] This probably covers all the larger companies of this type. Most of the information was gathered by telephone and consequently is limited in scope.

Two in each city operated fee-charging, licensed employment agencies; another in each city employed a full-time placement secretary. The majority of companies, however, simply kept a list of applicants, sometimes tested for competence in machine work, from which they made referrals when employers called for a worker. Placement service was free except in the licensed agencies. The placement facilities were maintained "as a service to the customer," and consequently there was practically no soliciting of business aside from information given to new customers by the companies' salesmen. The number of placements through these agencies was usually low; excluding the licensed companies and one other, the average was less than a dozen placements a month for companies reporting, and the majority of these placements were usually temporary jobs. The exception was a large company selling a widely used machine for which a course of special training is necessary. Their offices reported 100 to 150 placements a month in each city. In spite of the small number of placements, a large number of employers reported that they used the placement services offered by these companies. These calls were probably infrequent, however, because such employees were a small proportion of the total labor force and usually stable. Nearly a third of the employers interviewed in the two cities[20] reported calling such companies for office workers of various types, usually after files of direct applications had been exhausted.

About one-third of the companies operated schools or classes to instruct workers in the use of the company's machines, usually for a fee, and then sent these operators to their customers through the placement bureau. One of the larger ones was visited. The course required three or four months, cost $50, and furnished a certificate of competency on the passing of a rigor-

[20] The proportions were 43 per cent in San Francisco and 18 per cent in Los Angeles, but this difference may be partly or wholly attributable to the use in San Francisco of an experimental schedule on which business machine companies were specified as a possible source of workers. In Los Angeles the interviewers did not prompt employers by suggesting possible sources.

ous test. It was concerned solely with the operation of the company's machine. Both school graduates and others who could pass the test were placed through the employment bureau run in connection with the school, which got its orders through salesmen of the company's machines, regular patrons, and some soliciting. This was one of the companies most frequently called by employers for operators.

Other Types of Businesses.—Wholesale supply houses for drugs and for beauty parlor supplies, to judge from the two visited in San Francisco, operated in much the same manner as business machine companies in keeping a list of applicants on whom their customers might call. Those visited placed pharmacists and beauty parlor operators, respectively. Neither had a regular employment secretary; neither solicited openings but depended on calls from customers or information spread by its salesmen. The schools of beauty culture recommended to their graduates that they register there; otherwise applicants just came. It was impossible to determine the number of pharmacists placed through this supply house, but it was obviously not large. The beauty parlor supply house made only one permanent placement a month; most of its calls were for extra help in the rush seasons, and no estimate of the volume of this business was available. It might be noted that this latter company expressed open hostility to the union which was attempting to control placements in the field and was willing to furnish strikebreakers if asked to do so. Neither of the companies cleared with any other placement source.

Another large company in San Francisco maintained a placement bureau to furnish operators of a mechanical device[21] to its customers. Applicants were tested not only for their ability with this device but also for typing and stenography, since employers frequently called for a combination of abilities. Openings came

[21] In order to avoid identification, at the company's specific request, no more details are given.

only from direct, unsolicited requests. Several hundred openings were filled in 1937, of which about one-third were "intended to be permanent." The person interviewed made the point that temporary jobs often became permanent because the girl stayed on or was called back directly when there was an opening without going through the original placement office. Unlike other companies with this type of placement bureau, this company coöperated with other employment agencies, both free and fee-charging, calling them for a special type of applicant or referring someone from their list on request.

An ambulance service, which maintained a free employment service for trained and practical nurses, differed from the companies previously described in that its customers were private individuals, not business or industrial enterprises. Nurses registered with it because it was a long-established institution, and doctors recommended it to patients who needed a nurse at home. All placements were transacted by telephone and amounted to between 75 and 100 calls a month.

Still another type of business which occasionally supplied workers was a large landholding company whose local office near Bakersfield was sometimes asked to find a special type of agricultural worker, such as a tractor driver, for its lessees. The usual method apparently was to get in touch with an employment agency rather than to keep a file of applicants.

Some businesses found jobs for workers as a side line because the workers, not the employers, were their customers. In Los Angeles and probably elsewhere in the state there were boarding houses run by and for Japanese, usually from a single district of Japan. A Japanese farmer in search of agricultural labor got in touch with these boarding houses, preferably one operated by people from his own province, and asked that a certain number of workers be sent him. There were no fees to worker or employer for this placement service. Two such boarding houses were visited in Los Angeles. The interviewer spoke of the atmosphere as one of a social club rather than a purely commercial enterprise. Members of the Japanese community in San Francisco, interviewed in regard to the placement facilities open to their nationals, spoke of these boarding houses as a common institution through rural districts where Japanese agricultural labor was employed. They also assumed that there would be no charge for placement. A Japanese lawyer in San Francisco said that these boarding houses advertised for farm labor in the Japanese newspapers. Several fruit and asparagus growers and a contractor near Sacramento mentioned them as an agency through which they obtained oriental labor.

Another type of business where the worker was the customer was the store which sold him food and other supplies, and which frequently extended him credit during periods of unemployment. Two stores of this type, catering to Filipinos, were visited in a town of the Sacramento River Delta where Filipinos were the principal labor used on asparagus. These stores reported finding jobs for several hundred workers each season, both for workers directly and for labor contractors. The managers said they referred job seekers to growers who were likely to be hiring or, if necessary, went about the countryside inquiring for jobs. They said there was no charge for this placement service, but that the workers and contractors so placed would thereafter patronize the store. A prominent member of the Filipino community in Sacramento had a less favorable story to tell of this type of store, though he was not necessarily referring to the particular stores visited. His version was that the common practice of stores in the Delta was to require a cash bond from the men placed, as well as a promise to do all their trading at the store, whose prices were always exorbitant—sometimes 100 per cent above current prices. Men were "guaranteed" to the farmer by the grocer, and in return they were fired if they defaulted in payments to the store. There was no possibility of checking the accuracy of these claims within the scope of the present investigation. Some of the fruit and asparagus growers near Sacramento spoke of obtaining workers, usually Filipinos, through local stores, either directly or through contractors. Such storekeepers were usually Chinese or Japanese and they often gave credit to workers before the season opened.

The supply houses which did the greatest amount of placement were two with branches in a number of California cities and towns which supplied the two largest railroad systems of the state with a very high proportion of their Mexican maintenance-of-way workers—section hands, trackmen, and extra gangs. The local stores sold food, clothing, and all types of equipment to the Mexican workers and gave them credit between jobs. When the railroad officials needed a gang of men they called the store, and the manager collected a crew and told them to report to the railroad foreman, who did the actual hiring. According to company officials, the managers picked up men from the idlers who were always hanging around the offices and stores, and also sent the word out by "grapevine," which worked with unbelievable rapidity through the Mexican community and brought men flocking to the office. If necessary, one of the office staff was sent into the Mexican pool halls to round up men for the crew. There was never any need to apply to one of the regular employment agencies to find men. Instead, one of the offices of the State Employment Service reported calling on these stores for some Mexicans to fill agricultural jobs. It was impossible to obtain any estimates of the number of jobs filled through even one branch of these chains of stores. One manager estimated that his office supplied 50 per cent of the maintenance-of-way men used in his district by the railroad that patronized him. Apparently these companies were the greatest single factor in placing unskilled workers in railroad jobs in the state.

There was a widely disseminated story that one of these companies did "labor contracting" in the sense of exacting a fee for placing workers on a job. There was no evidence of this so far as the investigators could discover. All the company officials and store managers insisted that placements were absolutely free. Probably the explanation for the existence of this rumor lay in the clause at the foot of the itemized bill form used by one company: ". . . and this will authorize the Atchison, Topeka, and Santa Fe Railway to pay out of any wages due me the amount charged therefor." It was signed by laborer and foreman, and the foreman filled in the number of days worked.[22] The practical monopoly of placements guaranteed customers to the store, and the wage assignment guaranteed their bills. The opportunities for abuse in such a system are obvious, but the limits of the investigation made it impossible to say whether or not any were practiced. The investigator reported that the prices charged at one store were not excessive.

The sugar refining companies, at least in certain instances, exercised a very complete control over the operations of the growers who sold to them and who were financed by them. The field man of one company estimated the proportion of growers financed by the refinery as 90 per cent of all beet growers. To this large group checks were given for their wage bills. Part of this control consisted in making certain that each grower had an adequate labor supply for thinning and for harvesting. All beet labor was hired through contractors.[23] Representatives of the sugar company kept a list of contractors to be referred to any grower who had none of his own, a system described by one grower as a "clearing house" for labor. The company also kept a list of undesirable contractors and urged growers not to employ them. It was impossible to determine the proportion of growers who obtained their workers from this source, as a contractor obtained through the company one year might be hired directly in subsequent years. At the time of this investigation

[22] Assignments of wages before they are earned to be valid in California law must be for necessities of life only and must have the approval of the spouse attached.

[23] See pages 310, 315–317.

labor was easily obtained. In earlier years when there had been a shortage, officials of the sugar company recruited field labor for the growers by advertising, radio programs, and trips through the southern part of the state. Apparently only about one-half the beet growers signed a written contract with their labor contractors, but those who did so used a form furnished by the sugar company, which provided that the company was to be the judge of the work performed and was to arbitrate any disputes arising under the contract.

OCCUPATIONAL ASSOCIATIONS

People in those occupations, mainly professional and clerical, where trade unionism had made no headway frequently had organized themselves into local and even national associations, primarily for sociability or professional advancement. Sometimes such organizations operated a busy, expertly run placement bureau; more often they simply served as an informal clearing house where members, meeting for another purpose, exchanged information on openings they happened to know about. The scope of this study did not permit investigation of the latter type, whose importance in the labor market is very difficult to appraise. Nor did it permit an extensive sampling of organizations with placement bureaus. Merely as examples, two state-wide professional organizations which controlled a large share of the placements in their respective fields were visited in both Los Angeles and San Francisco, and two smaller local associations were visited in each of the two metropolitan areas.[34]

Teachers and Nurses

The parent organizations.—The California Teachers Association is a state-wide organization of both classroom teachers and

[34] In addition, a models club was visited in San Francisco, but it proved to depend for its placement work entirely on the activities of a small school with which it was closely connected.

school administrators, open to anyone connected with or interested in education, and claiming a membership in 1938 of 36,000—90 per cent of the teachers of the state. It was founded some 30 years ago for the usual meetings and exchange of information of a professional group and for legislative pressure in the interests of teachers. A placement service was organized by the association in 1920—the earliest experiment in this field by a state teachers association. The California State Nurses' Association is a similar state-wide, long-established organization of graduate nurses registered in California who are either citizens or have their first papers. Its administration is considerably more decentralized than is that of the Teachers Association. Placement work is a secondary development in this organization also, since 1905 in San Francisco and since 1922 in Los Angeles.

Organization of the placement bureaus.—Although finding jobs for members was not the primary purpose for which either of these associations was organized, it had become one of their most important functions. The Teachers Association had two placement offices for the state, one in Berkeley and one in Los Angeles, each staffed by several full-time workers. The placement service was limited to members. Any member of the Association might register for placement, but the officials discouraged registration of the middle-aged and of nonwhite persons because they were difficult to place. Dues for the Association were $3 a year, of which $1 was credited to the local placement bureau. Those who were placed through the office were charged a fee of 2½ per cent of the first year's salary.[25] "The modest fees charged for this service do not cover the actual costs of operating the placement offices, and are nominal as compared with the fees charged by commercial agencies. Commercial employment agencies charge 6 per cent or more for the same

[25] In cases where the teacher found the job and the Association merely furnished copies of her "papers"—the elaborate records of education, experience, and recommendations kept on file for each applicant—the charge was 1 per cent.

type of service. The difference thus saved the teachers of the State already has amounted to many thousands of dollars."[26] The northern office reported losing money for the past 10 years; the southern one operated at a loss only during 1932–35 and had made a profit of nearly $2,000 in 1936 and in 1937. A report of the Association quoted a 1925 study in California which estimated that the cost of placing a teacher through any agency in the state was $25 or more.[27] No figures were given for the average fee per placement at the time of this investigation, but it was almost certainly in excess of $25.

The Nurses' Association was divided into a number of largely autonomous districts, 13 of which had placement offices. Of these, the San Francisco and Los Angeles offices were visited. The placement office was not a department of the district office, as in the Teachers Association, but was a separate organization called the Registry or Nursing Bureau. Dues for district membership in the Association were $4 or $5 a year; for membership in the local registries, separate dues of $10 a year were charged. Ordinarily any Association member might also take out membership in the local registry, which was not open to nonmembers. Since the fall of 1937 the San Francisco Registry, however, "because of the recession" had refused all applicants except graduates of local hospitals. The Los Angeles Bureau reported that it refused Negroes and orientals because of placement difficulties. Because of the extra charge, only nurses wanting the type of jobs in which the registries specialized joined them, so that the membership was considerably smaller than that of the district association—40 per cent in Los Angeles, for example. At the time of the investigation the San Francisco Registry reported about 1,200 members; the Los Angeles Bureau, about 1,000. In Los Angeles officials reported that they could

[26] California Teachers Association, *Manual of Information, 1935–1936* (San Francisco), p. 21.

[27] California Teachers Association, Southern Section, *Committee Report [on the] Placement Bureau* (Los Angeles, 1938), p. 5. Mimeographed.

not disentangle the costs of District Office and of Nursing Bureau to determine whether the latter were self-supporting; the San Francisco office reported that the Registry "was supported by the Association."

Relation to the Employment Agency Act.—The placement work of both these associations was fundamentally on a nonprofit basis and was limited to members, exempting them from the licensing requirements of fee-charging agencies. But it is interesting to note, if only as a commentary on the enforcement of the Employment Agency Law, that both of these large and respected professional organizations were operating in violation of the clause of the law which requires an annual application for exemption. At the time of this investigation there had apparently never been such an application from either of them. The very small group of requests for exemption on file in the Labor Commissioner's office were from small local clubs. It might also be noted that these requests for exemption were seldom renewed annually. Consequently the Labor Commissioner's office had nothing approximating a record of the coöperative, nonprofit-making employment agencies of the state.

Placements.—The two associations differed considerably in the portion of their respective job fields that they covered and in the degree of control they exercised within those portions. Much of the difference was attributable to the temporary and therefore repetitious quality of nurses' jobs, contrasted with the permanence of a teacher's appointment. The Teachers Association was one of the several agencies to which superintendents of the state public schools applied when they wished to hire a teacher; it took its share of the general field of placements in the school system with apparently little specialization, competing with such other agencies as colleges, normal schools, and commercial fee agencies. The nurses' registries, on the other hand, were the only means through which private-duty jobs were filled in the coöperating hospitals; in San Francisco the

Registry also placed many nurses in private homes; in Los Angeles, where the competition of other agencies was keener, the placements in private homes were relatively few.

The number of members of the Teachers Association who were registered for placement was very large—over 2,000 each in the northern and southern offices in 1936–37—but from one-third to one-half of them were already employed and merely hoping for a better offer. For each of these applicants the office kept an elaborate confidential file of experience records, references, letters of recommendation, etc. When the office was notified of a job opening, it selected a very few candidates who appeared to meet specifications and arranged interviews with the school superintendent or other prospective employer. According to the placement officers, this ability to choose a small group of desirable applicants and thereby reduce the employer's interviewing task constituted the Association's most important advantage over their competitors in placement work and was due to their intimate knowledge of their membership, which included both the employing superintendents and principals and the job-seeking teachers, and of local school situations through contacts in the course of other Association business.

Approximately 1,000 placements were made in 1936–37 out of the two offices, principally in the elementary and high schools of the California public school system; few were made in junior colleges or universities or in private schools. Not more than 10 per cent of the placements were temporary, i.e., substitute teachers. Many of the openings were received through unsolicited telephone calls or correspondence. Others were obtained from a form mailed to district superintendents, principals, etc., asking them to list vacancies, from contacts at the annual Association convention, from field visits (both on placement bureau and on other Association business), and from the publicity about placement work sent to all Association members, whether prospective employers or prospective job seekers.

The nurses' Registries visited in San Francisco and Los Angeles operated in a quite different fashion—primarily as a clearing house for short-time private-duty calls from member hospitals. Most of the private hospitals in both cities coöperated with the Registry, and those which did so got all their private-duty nurses here. Each Registry had a 24-hour switchboard with several operators and a visible file system of the panels of preferred nurses for each hospital—in San Francisco primarily the hospital's own graduates. When the hospital wanted a nurse for a special case, for group nursing, or for staff relief, the superintendent of nurses or her deputy called the Registry and asked for a specific nurse. If she was not on call, or could not be reached in time, the switchboard operator called other nurses down the panel until one was secured. The process was completely mechanical, with no scope for discrimination on the part of the Registry. In San Francisco a large but unspecified number of calls were for cases in private homes. According to the informant, the doctor usually put in this type of call,[28] either directly or by asking someone in the hospital to call for him; in either case a particular nurse was specified, and the procedure was that already described. In Los Angeles, with greater competition from other placement agencies (see below), private duty in homes constituted only 5 per cent of all calls. Of these, about half came from the family, not the doctor, and were the only calls in which the Registry exercised any discretion in selecting a nurse to fill the job. Occasionally hospitals or such other institutions as airlines obtained a nurse from the Registry for a permanent staff position, but such placements were less than 1 per cent of all calls in both cities, and, moreover, these were not exclusive commissions; in Los Angeles less than half of such calls received during 1937–38 were filled by the Registry. The total volume of business handled was very large in both agencies visited. San Francisco had filled 2,400 calls

[28] Nurses were sent out by the Registries only to cases with a doctor in attendance.

in March 1938, "a typical month"; Los Angeles, 2,000 calls in May in spite of the recent defection of two hospitals that had set up their own placement service, which accounted for a considerable part of the reduction from 3,400 calls in May 1937. Neither Registry needed to do any soliciting of registrants because of the connection with the local Nurses' Association. The San Francisco office said that they made no attempt to solicit openings. In Los Angeles the Nursing Bureau was attempting to increase its share of the home nursing field, chiefly by mailing advertising leaflets and letters to local doctors.[29]

These two organizations were in a particularly advantageous position for placement work, because through their membership they had access to almost all the qualified job seekers in their respective fields and knew intimately not only the individual applicants but also the employers and the circumstances of each job. The Teachers Association enjoyed the additional advantage of including within their organization both employers and prospective employees. However, despite this potential control of the labor supply, neither organization made any effort at monopoly through such means as forbidding their members to seek jobs by direct application or to accept offers through other placement agencies; at least the interviews and published material supplied by the offices gave no hint of any such policy.[30] Nor did either agency attempt to influence employer choices so as to spread work evenly through the membership—a sharp contrast to common union policy. It was impossible to appraise precisely the proportion of the total placements in the state that were made through each of these associations, although it was certainly large. The two offices of the

[29] The Association's lawyer had assured them that public advertisements, other than a small box in the classified section of the telephone book, would render them liable to the licensing provisions of the Employment Agency Law.

[30] This does not apply to a campaign against the private fee-charging agencies supposedly conducted for the benefit of members rather than for the aggrandizement of the placement bureau. Teachers were urged through publicity to save themselves money by not registering with fee agencies but were never disciplined for so doing.

Teachers Association covered the entire state. Its chief competitors were the placement bureaus of the universities and state teachers colleges. Although a few fee-charging employment agencies for teachers persisted, the volume of business done by them was relatively very small. Some indication of the relative positions of the Association and the teacher training institutions may be indicated by the fact that the northern office of the Association filled about two-thirds as many jobs as did the University of California teacher placement office at Berkeley. Apparently superintendents in search of a teacher tended to shop around through the various placement bureaus; only 60 per cent of the vacancies reported to the southern office of the Association in 1937 were filled through that office.

The Nurses' Association, on the other hand, had a monopoly of placements in the coöperating hospitals of the two bureaus visited, but no estimates were obtained of the proportion this represented of all hospital jobs within the two cities. Moreover, the 13 autonomous Registries did not constitute complete coverage of the state. It was impossible to determine what proportion of the calls for nurses in private homes passed through the Registries in the two cities. In San Francisco it appeared to be high. According to the report from the Registry, only one of the fee-charging agencies handled nurses;[81] and miscellaneous placement resources, such as ambulance services,[82] tended to handle practical nurses, those who had failed to graduate, or graduate nurses not registered in California. In Los Angeles, on the contrary, the home-duty field was reported as largely in the hands of fee-charging agencies and of practical nurses. There were several agencies that placed only nurses, both for home duty and in hospitals not connected with the Registry, and others handled nurses along with other business. The attempts of the

[81] At the time of the investigation a new agency had just been licensed which expected to handle registered nurses, and another agency was organizing a department for nurses.

[82] See page 237.

Association to increase its placements in this field through advertisements to physicians have already been described.

The State Employment Service was not a serious competitor of the association placement services of either nurses or teachers, but it is worthy of note that these two nonprofit, professional organizations were either openly opposing the entry of the State Employment Service into their field or else were quietly sabotaging it. The attitude of the California Teachers Association is best shown by quotations from a 1938 report[88] apropos of a bill introduced into the 1937 legislature making it obligatory for the school authorities to notify the State Employment Service of vacancies. This was intended to remedy a situation in which the Employment Service could be of no use to unemployed teachers because it could not get the employers' coöperation; the bill did not pass, and the situation remains virtually unchanged. The report comments: "School trustees and administrators saw the many problems which would arise from being compelled to notify the State Employment Agencies of each vacancy on their staffs. Also, they objected to having teachers for those vacancies recommended by nonschool people." "If such a free State Employment Agency were to be set up, two things would probably happen: (1) The C.T.A. Placement Bureau would discontinue its *service at cost* to the teachers. The excellent staff of school people, the hundreds of complete records and the necessary office space to serve the schools and teachers would all be discontinued. It would be only a matter of time until the teachers and schools would want this same service again. The whole institution would have to be reëstablished. (2) The private agencies would reappear and do a fine business alongside the State Agencies. The teachers would find themselves very pleased to pay the private agency 5 per cent for a position and would wish for the C.T.A. rate of 2½ per

[88] California Teachers Association, *Committee Report* [*on the*] *Placement Bureau*, pp. 6 and 8.

cent." The California Teachers Association official interviewed clarified the opposition by saying that the State Employment Service would give publicity to confidential information about vacancies, that it would swamp the superintendents with applicants to interview, and that satisfactory teacher placements could only be made by people who knew both employer and applicant personally. It should be remembered in connection with this organized opposition that the great bulk of the membership of the Association was employed in the public schools, a branch of the state government of which the State Employment Service is also a branch, and that the employing superintendents, principals, and so forth, members of the Teachers Association who refuse to coöperate with a free State Employment Service, are themselves state employees.

The opposition of the California Teachers Association to relinquishing its placement service to the State Employment Service was, at least in part, founded upon important weaknesses in the State Service. It would undoubtedly have been unfortunate, to say the least, if the California State Employment Service had been given the responsibility for placing teachers at a time when the entire organization was in a state of considerable chaos. (See chapter iv.) It might be possible for a well-organized and properly staffed state service to set up a separate department to assume this responsibility. It is hardly fair to suggest that teachers would be "pleased to pay private agencies 5 per cent," and certainly a state service organized in accordance with good placement procedures would not "give publicity to confidential information about vacancies." Since, however, the placement of teachers presents special problems, it is more likely that the free employment services operated by educational institutions would do a better job.

The Nurses' Association showed no such outspoken antagonism, but there was no evidence of coöperation in the offices visited or of any future intention to share its placement functions with the State Service. Either there were no contacts or the Association referred to the Employment Service those women who were elderly or otherwise substandard and therefore unlikely to find work through the Registry.

It is not unfair, perhaps, to sum up the attitude of both agencies towards the State Employment Service as the view that it was a low-grade institution which might be good for unskilled, casual workers, but which must be prevented from intruding upon their vested interests in the professional field.

Smaller Local Groups

Women office workers.—As examples of local occupational associations—"clubs" might be a better description—which were primarily social and educational in character, but which also did some placement work for their members, this study included secretaries in law offices and in insurance work and a larger group of "business women," primarily, apparently, also in the clerical occupations. Dues ranged from $3 to $10 a year. The placement service was for members only. There were no fees, and the work was done entirely by volunteers, officers of the organization, on their own or their employers' time. The organizations had no offices or telephones of their own.[34]

The experience of these organizations suggests that effective placement work, even on a very small scale and in a limited and familiar field, was too time-consuming an undertaking for volunteers who were employed full time at another job. In one association there was no attempt to solicit openings; the employment service consisted only of keeping records of members who were seeking jobs, receiving employers' orders by phone, and matching the two. This work was supposed to rotate among officials of the organization who handled it in their employers' offices along with their other duties. The official in charge of placement work at the time of the investigation was dropping

[34] The largest group had a telephone listing under "Employment Agencies" which was the telephone of the business firm employing the association's secretary.

it the next month at her employer's request because it took more time than the office could afford. "Mr. Blank has been very generous, but the work takes several hours a day." She did not know who, if anyone, could take it over; it was obviously a job for a paid employee. A similar organization was attempting to solve the problem by minutely subdividing the placement work among a number of association officers, with, in the judgment of the investigator, a loss of efficiency and coördination. One girl solicited openings in the course of contacts made for her regular office work; another was in charge of memberships; another kept a file of unemployed members. The great advantage enjoyed by small specialized groups, of which the two secretarial groups are examples, was, of course, familiarity with the field. They knew intimately the abilities, personalities, and present employment status of their own membership and had a body of experienced workers available without solicitation. Similarly, they were familiar with the requirements of most, if not all, employers in their field. Most important of all, perhaps, they had the employers' confidence and could easily become the first agency that the employer called, with little need for solicitation of openings.

During 1937 each of these three organizations made between 60 and 100 placements. One of the secretarial groups placed five a month, said to be mostly permanent; the other made about six temporary placements a month and one or two that were permanent.[85] The general business women's organization could give no exact figures, but placements were less than 100 a year, and about one-fourth were domestics, girls who were "desperate" and willing to take any sort of job.

It is interesting to note the relationship of the two San Francisco associations with the State Employment Service in the face

[85] It might be noted that this was the organization that reported several hours a day spent on placement work as an indication of the cost in time of doing any employment work, even in a familiar field. The investigator was convinced that there was no time lost here through inefficiency.

of claims made by the latter agency. Both of them reported that the Employment Service had called once or twice for a girl to fill a job. One occasionally sent members to the Employment Service to register for work; the other referred only nonmembers whom they could not themselves register. The Employment Service had stated several months before that both of these associations had turned over all their placement work to the state office. In Los Angeles the organization studied and the State Employment Service sometimes referred applicants to each other for registration but never asked aid in filling jobs. This same group sometimes found "mother's helper" jobs for clients of some of the philanthropic agencies. In San Francisco the two organizations studied had no contact with any other agencies.

Skilled craftsmen.—Only one organization of skilled craftsmen (outside of trade unions) which did placement work was found in the course of this study. Others of a similar type undoubtedly existed, but, in the main, this type of organization had been superseded by union placement services.

The organization mentioned above was a social and mutual benefit association of chefs, which included placement as one of its functions. Originally this was an organization of head chefs—very exalted personages—in "well-known establishments," but during the depression junior membership was opened to other kitchen workers and associate membership to "any man interested in the hotel catering or allied industries." It was difficult to determine the relationship of this organization to the unions in the trade, but the official interviewed stated that many of the members belonged to unions and worked in closed shops. He said, "We have nothing against the unions."

The placement work, which was free to a membership of 600, was done by a full-time, salaried manager along with his other duties. There were no placement statistics, but the manager estimated that from 75 to 100 were placed each month. This large proportion of placements to membership was explained by the great mobility in the industry. Apparently placements were considered an important function, since the bylaws included a number of rules and regulations governing this work. One rule which simplified the work was to the effect that members should notify the employment department of the association of their intention of leaving a position. The manager reported that very little solicitation of orders was necessary. In the large kitchens, chefs who belonged to the association did the hiring, and in other cases members gave publicity to the employment department of the association. Although this association included in its membership some of the lower-skilled kitchen help, it is probable that most of its placements were in the higher-skilled brackets. The manager said that the fee-charging agencies filled many of the smaller jobs, and in some instances the State Employment Service and the Masonic employment office made placements in the lower-skilled restaurant jobs. These employment bureaus occasionally called the association of chefs if a job came in that they could not fill, but there were no formal arrangements for coöperation.

FRATERNAL ORDERS

Only one fraternal order operated full-fledged employment bureaus in both San Francisco and Los Angeles; a second was starting an employment office in the latter city. In most other fraternal organizations information on job openings was exchanged in an informal fashion at lodge meetings, or the secretary looked up an unemployed member when he heard of a job. Some orders did no placement work, not even of this informal type, and a few had experimented with employment services in earlier years and discontinued them.

In each of the major cities an attempt was made to reach, chiefly by telephone, all the fraternal organizations in which the membership was not limited to women or to specific national groups. This amounted to a total of 15 in San Francisco and 12 in Los Angeles, largely the same organizations in both cities. The Masons maintained a separate employment department with a full-time staff in both cities. Another fraternal order in Los Angeles, which in 1938 registered unemployed members and accepted but did not solicit orders, was inaugurating a regular employment service to include nonmembers as well. Five organizations in San Francisco and one in Los Angeles said that they did no employment work of any sort, not even the most informal passing about of information by the secretary or at lodge meetings. Three of these San Francisco organizations, another in that city, and four in Los Angeles reported employment services which had been abandoned in recent years, usually because they received many applications for jobs but very few openings. Most of the lodges, nine in each city, operated as a sort of labor pool, circulating information about jobs but rarely registering workers or openings.

Organizations which met regularly in small groups, and which had a secretary who might be reached by telephone and who was well acquainted with the personnel of the organization, offered opportunities as a clearing house for job information, and that appeared to be the function of most fraternal orders in relation to the labor market. In some, members were asked at each meeting if they knew of any jobs; or openings which had been reported were announced for the benefit of unemployed members. In others it was the secretary's duty to notify unemployed members of any jobs that came to his attention. In others, the only activity was word-of-mouth exchange of information among members at lodge meetings. It was impossible to get any figures on how many placements were made through these organizations, but the number was obviously very small. One or two suggested four or five placements a month.

The Masons were the only fraternal order with free employment offices with a full-time staff. There were six such offices in

California. Only those in San Francisco and Los Angeles were visited. Both of these offices had been operating for more than 25 years. They placed only Masons and members of their immediate families. The majority of placements in San Francisco were in domestic service for women and in office work for both men and women. In Los Angeles the types of jobs for men were more varied, including building trades and machinists, clerks in stores, and some professions. There were few placements in factories. Most orders were obtained by voluntary calls from employers, but this good will had been built up and maintained by publicity for the service in the form of post cards, periodic bulletins, and blotters to large mailing lists, telephone solicitation, speeches, and some field work. Both offices reported about 1,800 employers who were regular patrons; one said that the majority were Masons. Both offices did a considerable volume of business, although the Los Angeles office was much the larger. During 1937, 2,000 placements were made in San Francisco, or about 160 a month; in the early months of 1938 the volume decreased to about 100 a month. In Los Angeles in 1937 there were nearly 6,000 placements, about 475 a month, and by May 1938 the office was making between 500 and 600 placements monthly. Roughly equal numbers of men and of women were placed in both cities. The proportion of temporary jobs varied. Los Angeles reported about 40 per cent temporary; in San Francisco 60 per cent of the clerical jobs were temporary in 1937 and very few of the domestic, but in 1938 there were few temporary openings in any class. In San Francisco in 1937 two-thirds of the openings offered to the office were filled. In both cities the employment bureaus checked with certain other free agencies to find applicants to fill jobs after their own lists were exhausted. The interviewers received the impression that the Masonic employment bureaus were efficiently administered and doing a good job of placement for the group they were designed to serve.

VETERANS ASSOCIATIONS

Another special group whose associations were investigated were the war veterans. In San Francisco the American Legion reported that it did no placement work. In Bakersfield the American Legion "tried to help unemployed members find work" in a wholly informal fashion, saying that it could not run an employment bureau in competition with the State Employment Service on the next corner, which had been helpful in placing veterans. In Los Angeles 13 veterans organizations were combined into a single employment bureau, supported financially by the Community Welfare Federation, which was in direct competition with the State Employment Service.[36]

The Los Angeles Veterans Bureau maintained a staff of four full-time workers. It accepted applications from any veteran of the United States Army or of its World War allies and a few of their dependents, mainly boys. It made 8,600 placements in 1937. Most of the work supplied was common labor, and two-thirds of the jobs in 1937 were temporary. The most striking feature of the jobs filled by this office was that 70 per cent of them in 1937 were with public agencies, not private employers. The largest proportion of jobs were with the Metropolitan Water District and the Post Office, the latter for extra work in the holidays. Fifteen per cent of the openings filled in 1937 were listed as "Los Angeles County Labor Coördinating Bureau," the employment agency already described. Two of the staff regularly did field work; another, "political work and contacts." A door-to-door canvass of employers was made in 1925 when the bureau was opened; in 1938 it was reported that 3,000 employers were on file. Nevertheless, the 2,600 placements in commercial and industrial private employment represented only a fraction of the total placements of veterans. A type of private employ-

[36] For a description of the State Employment Service's function in placing war veterans see pages 124–125.

ment specifically cited was warehouse labor, and there were some placements in the mechanical trades. Characteristically, the jobs furnished were stopgaps filled by spot placements of men on hand in the office, a practice which reduced the skilled and unskilled to a common level. The bureau maintained "co-operative arrangements" with other free organizations in the city, calling them for applicants on the rare occasions when a job could not be filled from their own files. It is interesting to note in this connection that the 1937 report shows 99 per cent of orders filled—very high in comparison to most other placement offices.

ASSOCIATIONS OF FOREIGN-BORN AND NONWHITE GROUPS

In a state with as large a proportion of foreign-born and of non-white races as California it seemed probable that the numerous societies in which these groups were organized would do some placement work for their membership. This assumption proved false. A few of the associations acted as a completely informal clearing house for job information, but the majority denied exercising any employment function. In each area visited the procedure was to interview authorities for some of the principal foreign or racial groups in order to determine which, if any, of their societies did placement work.[87] These groups included British, German, Italian, Chinese, and Japanese in San Francisco; Filipinos, Japanese, Mexicans, and Negroes in Los Angeles;[88] Chinese, Filipinos, Italians, Japanese, and Mexicans in Sacramento; and Chinese, Mexicans, and Negroes in Bakers-

[87] It was not always possible to distinguish associations of the type discussed here from "social service agencies" or fraternal orders. For example, Negro organizations in Los Angeles, such as the Urban League, have already been discussed in the category of social service agencies; some of the fraternal orders in San Francisco had a large German membership; all Jewish activities in both San Francisco and Los Angeles were included in one or the other of these categories.

[88] In addition, the International Institute reported that none of the foreign groups in Los Angeles had any associations that did placement work.

field. In all this large field not a single association was found that ran a placement bureau for members of its national or racial group, with the exception of those already discussed under "social service agencies." The recurrent story was that their activities were benevolent and social but did not include any attempt to find jobs for their members or even to act as a clearing house for information on where jobs might be found. Three were visited in San Francisco which reported a little informal exchange of information between members or through the medium of the secretary. On the whole, members of foreign groups depended on finding jobs through the media open to all residents of the community rather than through any coöperative efforts of their own.

OTHER FREE, NONGOVERNMENTAL PLACEMENT AGENCIES

There were a variety of free nongovernmental placement resources other than those listed above or in the class of employers' and workers' associations, which will be discussed later. Probably none of these in the areas covered were of very great importance. Only a few were visited. Among these were two foreign-language newspapers in San Francisco which ran "position wanted" ads free. The staff of one would also make informal inquiries for an opening if one of their nationals came into the office and asked for help. The other one kept rough memoranda of calls for office workers and domestics, which were available to any job seeker who came into the office. Other foreign-language newspapers did none of this sort of work. Consular offices apparently did little or nothing beyond referring the applicant to free employment services elsewhere. A curious institution of Los Angeles was a certain street corner[89] near Beverly Hills, at a terminus of a street-car line, where un-

[89] The writer has been informed that similar centers of labor collection exist in Imperial Valley, and it is possible that they also exist in other parts of the state.

skilled labor for building and gardening work congregated early in the morning. Contractors and private employers came there in cars to pick up men for a few days' or hours' work. Apparently about 10 men a morning got jobs this way.

Such placement facilities are interesting curiosities but certainly do not bulk large as a factor in total community placements.

VII. Fee-charging Employment Agencies

FOR MANY decades the commercial fee-charging employment agency has been one of the methods of job seeking available to the unemployed worker. These agencies are private, profit-making organizations. They charge a fee for their services, and this fee in most instances is paid by the applicant for work, although occasionally it is paid by the employer.

LEGISLATIVE REGULATION[1]

There is considerable literature on the subject of private employment agencies and their abuses. Mention is often made of such practices as the collection of exorbitant fees; sending workers long distances from their homes to nonexistent jobs; collusion between employer and agency, whereby fees are split and the worker fired after a short period; and refusal to refund fees when the worker leaves because the job was misrepresented or because he has been placed in a job for which he obviously lacks the necessary skills. Because of these and other possible abuses, practically every state has legislation on its statute books regulating the activities of private employment agencies. Since 1903 California has regulated these agencies in some fashion, but only since 1913 have they been required to secure a license.[2] All agencies which are in the business of securing employment in return for a fee must annually secure a license from the Labor Commissioner. Nonprofit organizations performing a placement function are not required to secure a

[1] Cal. Stats. (1937), ch. 90, pt. 6.

[2] State of California, Department of Industrial Relations, *First Biennial Report, 1927–1930* (Sacramento: California State Printing Office, 1931), p. 98.

license if they meet certain requirements, the most important of which is that they charge no fee other than a membership fee. However, organizations which charge a membership fee are required each year to file a request for exemption.

In order to secure a license, an employment agency is required to pay a fee and to deposit a bond. Agencies in cities with a population in excess of 100,000 must pay a license fee of $100 and deposit a bond of $2,000; in cities with a population of 25,000 to 100,000, a $50 license fee and a bond of $1,000; and in cities with a population of less than 25,000, a license fee of $10 and a bond of $500.

The Employment Agency Law sets up certain conditions which must be fulfilled by licensed agencies. A number of these refer to records which must be filed with the Labor Commissioner or open to his inspection. The agency is required to file with the Labor Commissioner a schedule of fees, and this schedule must also be posted in a conspicuous place in the employment agency. A register must be kept of employers' orders, of applicants referred to employment, and of the amount of fees collected. Every person who is placed must be given a uniform contract or receipt on which is entered the amount of the fee and the place and conditions of employment, and a duplicate copy of this receipt must be retained by the agency.

Certain other provisions of the law are of importance in that they are, in the main, for the purpose of prohibiting certain practices which would be injurious to the workers. A copy of the Employment Agency Law must be posted in a conspicuous place in each room of the agency. Agencies are prohibited from charging registration fees, and if an applicant pays for a job which he does not get, the fee must be returned within 48 hours after the application for refund has been made. If the fee is not returned within this time, the agency is liable for double the fee. It is also provided that if an applicant is employed and if the employment lasts less than seven days by reason of his discharge, the employment agency must return the fee or such portion of it as the Labor Commissioner requires. Other prohibited practices include the following: false advertising, sending a woman or minor to a house of ill fame or to a gambling house, sending a minor under 18 years to any place where intoxicating liquors are sold to be consumed upon the premises, accepting any order which will violate the child labor law, sending an applicant to a place where a strike, lockout, or other labor dispute exists without notifying the applicant of the conditions and entering a statement of such facts upon a receipt given to the applicant, splitting fees with employer or employers' representatives, and operating agencies in connection with lodginghouses, restaurants, pool rooms, or saloons.

The Private Employment Agency Law is administered by the Labor Commissioner, and disputes arising under the act must be submitted to the Labor Commissioner for adjudication but may be appealed to the Superior Court.[3] The penalty for violation of the Employment Agency Law is a fine of not less than $25 nor more than $250 or imprisonment for a period of not more than 60 days, or both.

NUMBER AND TYPE

At the time this study was made (in the spring and summer of 1938), there were approximately 366 licensed employment agencies in San Francisco, Los Angeles, and Sacramento.[4]

[3] The law as amended in 1939 provides that controversies need not be referred to the Labor Commissioner if the contract between the agency and the person seeking employment provides for arbitration of controversies.

[4] This number included two agencies charging a fee to the employer and thus requiring a city but not a state license. An effort was made to secure a complete list of licensed agencies in the areas visited. It is, however, possible that a few more existed than the total shown in table 23. In a few instances the license may have been removed from the files at the time the search was made. At the time this study was made, information was not available as to the total number of licensed agencies in the state. Data for earlier years, however, indicate that the 366 agencies in the areas studied constituted a substantial proportion of the fee-charging agencies in the state. In 1931–32 and in 1935–36 approximately 60 per cent of the licensed fee-charging agencies were in San Francisco and in Los

Licenses were found in the Department of Industrial Relations for 54 agencies in San Francisco,[5] for 301 in Los Angeles, and for 9 in Sacramento. Although data as to the number of licensed agencies at earlier dates are available only for San Francisco and Los Angeles, it is significant that there were a larger number of licensed agencies in these two cities in 1938 than in the preceding years—355 licenses were issued in 1938 and from 150 to 240 in the four preceding years.[6]

In 1938 approximately 60 per cent of the agencies in San Francisco, Los Angeles, and Sacramento were operating in the theatrical field, and the remainder served a variety of other occupational groups. The following discussion will be divided into two parts; the first will deal with nontheatrical and the second with theatrical agencies. Theatrical agencies will be considered separately because they differed from the others in many respects, and because the report form used by these agencies was not the same as that used by the others, and thus different information was available regarding their activities.

NONTHEATRICAL AGENCIES

Of the 152 licensed nontheatrical agencies for which a record was found, 98 were in Los Angeles, 46 in San Francisco, and 8 in Sacramento. From the Department of Industrial Relations it was possible to secure information as to type of agency, number of jobs furnished, fees, refunds, and complaints for most

Angeles, and in 1933–34 over 50 per cent were in these two areas. Figures for 1931–32 from State of California, Department of Industrial Relations, *Second Biennial Report, 1930–1932* (Sacramento: California State Printing Office, 1932), p. 79; figures for 1933–34 and 1935–36 supplied by the Department of Industrial Relations from unpublished data.

[5] In addition, there were two agencies in San Francisco which had city but not state licenses.

[6] Figures for 1929–30 from California Department of Industrial Relations, *First Biennial Report, 1927–1930,* p. 101; figures for 1931–32 from California Department of Industrial Relations, *Second Biennial Report, 1930–1932,* p. 79; figures for 1933–34 and 1935–36 from unpublished data from the California Department of Industrial Relations.

TABLE 23

LICENSED FEE-CHARGING EMPLOYMENT AGENCIES IN SAN FRANCISCO, LOS ANGELES, AND SACRAMENTO, 1938*

City	Total	Total non-theatrical	Commercial	Domestic	Oriental	General	General-commercial	Nurses	Teachers	Miscellaneous	Total theatrical
Grand total	366	152	34	12	15	44	25	10	2	10	214
San Francisco†	56	46	15	5	8	10	6	—	—	2	10
Los Angeles	301	98	19	7	7	27	19	9	2	8	203
Sacramento	9	8	—	—	—	7	—	1	—	—	1
Sample	65	51	11	3	6	21	2	4	2	2	14
San Francisco	19	15	4	2	2	5	—	—	—	2	4
Los Angeles	40	30	7	1	4	10	2	4	2	—	10
Sacramento	6	6	—	—	—	6	—	—	—	—	—
Not visited	301	101	23	9	9	23	23	6	—	8	200
San Francisco	37	31	11	3	6	5	6	—	—	—	6
Los Angeles	261	68	12	6	3	17	17	5	—	8	193
Sacramento	3	2	—	—	—	1	—	1	—	—	1

* Count made from licenses in Department of Industrial Relations and from the Bureau of Licenses, Tax Collection Office of San Francisco.

† Includes two agencies licensed by the city and not by the state. These agencies charged a fee to the employer and therefore were not required to have a state license.

of the licensed agencies.[7] Additional information as to their activities was secured through visits to a sample of 65 of these agencies.[8]

Since fee-charging employment agencies operated in a wide variety of occupational fields, it appeared important to attempt to classify them in accordance with the occupational groups which they served. Although every employment agency must, in its application for a license, state the field in which it operates, certain difficulties arose in connection with the classification. A number of the agencies operated in more than one category of occupations, and, furthermore, the field investigation disclosed that in some instances agencies were not placing in certain occupations which were included in their license classification. Table 23 represents an attempt to classify these agencies in accordance with their major field of operations. Certain of the categories require special comment. Those classified as "General" placed workers in a wide variety of occupations. Their placements appeared, in the main, to be in unskilled or semiskilled occupations in industry and agriculture and in various types of hotel and restaurant employments. Some of these agencies placed domestics in private homes, but the agencies specializing in this type of placement have been classified as "Domestic." The agencies classified as "General-Commercial" apparently placed workers in the occupations mentioned above and also in office employments. It was impossible to determine the proportions in the various categories.

[7] In some instances the reports to the Department of Industrial Relations were lacking or incomplete, and thus it was necessary to base the analysis on those agencies for which information was available. After this study was completed, the California Department of Industrial Relations published a report on private employment agencies in California. According to this report, in 1939 there were 108 nontheatrical fee-charging agencies in Los Angeles and 46 in San Francisco; the number in Sacramento was not given. See California Department of Industrial Relations, Division of Labor Statistics and Law Enforcement, *Fees Charged by Private Employment Agencies in California* (San Francisco: Oct. 1940), p. 3. Mimeographed.

[8] For a discussion of the method of sampling see pages 32–35.

Almost all of the types of employment agencies were represented in San Francisco and in Los Angeles, whereas in Sacramento with the exception of one nurses agency all of the private fee-charging agencies were in the "General" category. Approximately 30 per cent of the agencies in the areas covered were operating as general agencies, slightly over 15 per cent were general-commercial agencies, and about 20 per cent specialized in commercial placements. Another considerable group, including those classified as "Domestic" and as "Oriental," operated primarily in the field of domestic employment in private homes. There were also a number of highly specialized agencies, such as those placing teachers and nurses and various sorts of physicians' assistants. Although each type of agency was not always represented in the sample in the same proportions as in the total group of agencies, table 23 shows that agencies of all types were visited, and it is believed that the sample gives a fairly complete picture of the activities of fee-charging employment agencies in nontheatrical fields.

Office Organization.—The licensed fee-charging agencies visited were not a fly-by-night group. Nearly 70 per cent of all the agencies visited had been in business over 10 years, and more than 40 per cent had been in business over 20 years. In general, these agencies were operated in one city only. Only 5 of the 51 agencies visited had branches in other cities. One general and one commercial agency had offices in San Francisco and in Los Angeles, and one commercial agency in San Francisco had a branch in Oakland. An engineering society which ran an employment bureau in San Francisco had offices in New York and Chicago, and one commercial agency, affiliated with a typewriter company, had branches in all sales offices of the typewriter company.

In the main, these agencies were operated with a small personnel. Over a quarter were one-man offices, and 60 per cent had between 2 and 5 employees, including the owner or manager. Only 2 reported over 10 employees—a commercial agency in San Francisco and a nurses agency in Los Angeles—each of which operated a school in connection with an employment agency.

They were usually located with reference to the type of applicants served and orders filled. The general agencies were in the poorer and older business districts; the domestic agencies, usually in the somewhat poor residential districts; commercial and teachers agencies in the shopping, financial, and main business districts; those which placed nurses, in the residential and downtown business districts; and the oriental, always in the part of the city where the particular race lived.

Nine of the agencies visited were conducted in connection with some other business. Two typewriter and business machine companies also operated an employment agency, and in one instance a business school and an employment agency were under the same management. Two nurses agencies were conducted in connection with another business—with a switchboard service for doctors, and with a school for practical nurses. Other combinations with employment agencies were a letter-writing and brokerage service, a wholesale grocery, and pool halls.[9]

The fact that in San Francisco, Los Angeles, and Sacramento there were a considerable number of fee-charging employment agencies operating in the same field indicated that this was a competitive business. It appeared possible, however, that, since some agencies specialized in placing one or another of the occupational groups, some coöperative arrangement might exist whereby referrals were made from one agency to another or even that competing agencies might have informal arrange-

[9] It will be shown later that one complaint was made against an agency for violation of that section of the Employment Agency Act which prohibits a licensed agency to be carried on in connection with a pool hall. No such complaint was made against the two agencies visited which were operated in connection with pool halls, although they were obviously operating in violation of the law.

ments whereby they called others in the same field if orders came in which they could not fill or if good applicants registered for whom the agency had no job opening. The licensed employment agencies visited reported no formal coöperative arrangements and almost none of even an informal sort. Occasionally an agency said, "We refer persons in occupations of the type we don't handle to other agencies," or, "Occasionally we telephone another agency if we have a position and no suitable applicant." On the whole, the theory seemed to be that both employers and workers registered at a number of agencies, and thus nothing was to be gained by calling another agency. Furthermore, an employment agency, like any profit-making business, is concerned with selling something—in this instance, the service of workers—and it can hardly be expected to take any considerable responsibility for placements from which it will not derive a profit. Why should an employment agency concern itself with the problem of the worker in occupations which it does not handle? And it is unlikely that an agency will give information as to who are its clients to another agency in the same field except in very special circumstances.

Restrictions on Registrations and on Job Orders.—The general classification of agencies discussed above indicates that there were certain restrictions as to workers registered by various agencies. For instance, a stenographer would not be registered by a general agency nor a farm laborer by a commercial agency, and those placing professional groups would presumably accept applications only from those with certain technical training. There were, however, certain types of restrictions which would not be apparent in the broad classification of agencies, and thus the agencies visited were questioned as to any restrictions which might have been adopted.

Only a few agencies—those limiting their placements to industrial and farm employments—restricted their placements to men. This group did not include all of the general agencies, since many of these placed both men and women, particularly in culinary employments. No agency had a formal rule restricting registration to women, but those operating in the commercial, nursing, teaching, and domestic fields obviously registered mainly women.

Except in the professional agencies a definite amount of education, training, or experience was seldom required for registration. In a few instances commercial agencies, specializing in placing highly-skilled workers, did not accept all applicants. One manager said, "Although there are no formal limitations, only about 10 per cent of the applicants are accepted for registration." The domestic agencies usually accepted only experienced workers. The managers of the general agencies said, "We will accept any qualified applicant for registration." Since these agencies placed in a wide variety of occupations, this probably meant that they would only refuse to register those who were obviously unfit for any employment.

Since the problem of placing the older worker and the junior entering industry for the first time has been a frequent subject of discussion in recent years, the agencies were asked a question as to their policy in regard to these groups. Only about 10 per cent of the agencies stated either that they refused to register older workers or that they preferred younger applicants, and only two specifically stated that they did not accept juniors, although others frequently stated that few juniors applied for registration. Since the managers of the agencies may have been unwilling to admit restrictions based on age, it is probable that the above statements are an underestimate of the extent of such restrictions.

A number of the agencies limited their registrants to certain racial groups. The oriental agencies frequently accepted applicants of one race—Japanese, Chinese, or Filipinos—although in some instances persons of all three of these races were accepted. A considerable group of the commercial agencies accepted only persons of the white race, and several stated that, although there was no such formal limitation, no Negroes and few orientals applied for registration. The general agencies in San Francisco in most cases would not accept orientals for registration. In Los Angeles and in Sacramento, on the other hand, agencies of this type almost without exception stated that they had no racial qualifications for registration. Of the three domestic agencies visited, only one accepted persons of any race. One refused to register Negroes; and one, orientals. Again, it was impossible to determine in how far there were actual, though not admitted, restrictions as to race; it is, however, probable that persons of the nonwhite races were not given much consideration except by those agencies set up to deal specifically with these groups.

A few restrictions on religious grounds were found in the Los Angeles agencies. Two general agencies would not permit Jewish people to register, and one teachers' agency would not register Catholics, Jews, or Seventh Day Adventists. Although the commercial agencies did not have any formal rules regarding religion, the investigator in Los Angeles reported a strong anti-Semitic feeling among the managers of the commercial agencies and stated that it was probable that most of these offices would not accept applications from Jewish people.

In the main, the formal restrictions as to applicants accepted for registration by the fee-charging employment agencies were along broad occupational lines. A few other types of limitations were admitted by some agencies, and it is possible that others actually refused applicants from certain age or racial groups or from those who lacked certain skills. It is probable, however, that these agencies will accept anyone who they think can be placed. They will concern themselves primarily, no doubt, with the experienced person in the prime of life of whatever racial or religious groups are preferred by employers. They will naturally be most interested in the group that can be placed most easily and in the higher wage brackets, since these applicants will yield the highest fees.

It was important not only to examine restrictions as to applicants registered but also any limitations which might exist as to job orders which would be accepted by these agencies. This was a subject upon which the agencies were loath to commit themselves, and thus the information was somewhat fragmentary. Only a very small number reported a policy of refusing to register jobs below a defined wage rate. A number, however, said that they would accept no jobs in which wages or hours were in violation of labor laws,[10] some refused to accept jobs on a straight commission basis, and others informed employers offering substandard wages that it would be impossible to fill the job.

At the time this study was made, the question as to whether these agencies would accept orders for strikebreakers appeared to be applicable only to the general agencies. Of the 20 general agencies from which answers to this question were obtained, 11 said that strike jobs would not be filled. Of the remaining nine agencies, three stated that they would send workers for strikebreaking only to old customers, and the rest would provide such workers to any employer who called. All claimed that the worker was informed that the job was a strike job. The manager of one of these agencies said, "I will break any strike I get a chance to," and he proudly asserted, "I take personal credit for breaking the Brown Derby strike last year." The manager of another said, "We seldom handle strike jobs," but immediately followed this with the statement: "During the waterfront strike in San Francisco in 1934 we sent 500 men and got $3 per man. It looked like good business and we took it." There thus appears to be evidence that a considerable pro-

[10] It is quite possible that in some instances the question was phrased by the investigator in such a way as to result in this answer, even though the agency had no such formal rule.

portion of the general agencies were a source of supply for workers when a strike was in progress. The proportion of agencies engaging in this type of work may have been greater than is indicated by this study, since it is possible that some of those which answered this question in the negative placed strikebreakers when it appeared to be good business.[11]

Although the employment agencies reported some restrictions as to jobs which they would register, it is probable that with a few exceptions they would register any job which they had reason to believe a worker would accept, if the fee which could be exacted made it worth their while to make a referral. Conditions of the labor market would to a considerable extent affect the policy as to refusal to accept certain job orders. In a time of depression the competition for jobs is severe, and it is probable that almost any kind of an order from an employer could be filled. Furthermore, agencies at such times are particularly anxious to collect even the smallest fee. If, on the other hand, there is a labor shortage, the employment agency will not wish to clutter up its files with orders at such low rates of pay that there will be difficulty in making referrals or to accept orders for strikebreakers, since jobs of this sort are likely to prejudice workers against the agency at a time when there is a shortage of applicants. At any time, fee-charging agencies will undoubtedly give preference to the higher-paying jobs, since it is for these jobs that the larger fees will be paid.

Methods of Securing Applicants and Job Orders.—If an employment agency is to function, it must have a supply of workers available for placement and orders for workers from employers. Statistics were not available as to the number of workers or job orders registered with the fee-charging agencies. Placements (which will be discussed later) provided some, although very incomplete, evidence on these subjects. It was,

[11] See chap. ix for a further discussion of this problem.

however, possible to obtain some information from the agencies visited as to the methods used in securing applicants and job orders.

Most of the agencies claimed that they obtained a large proportion of their applicants through word-of-mouth advertising—the recommendations of persons placed by them or of employers. Many said, "A satisfied worker or employer is an excellent source of future business." Very few, however, neglected other sources of advertising. With a few exceptions these agencies advertised in the classified section of the telephone directory; and with the exception of the oriental agencies a large proportion advertised in the newspapers—some daily and others only occasionally. A variety of other methods of bringing the agency to the attention of both workers and employers were also used. Commercial agencies called junior and business colleges; professional agencies advertised in trade journals; and the general agencies sent out handbills. Furthermore, the general agencies were usually located on the street floor in districts where workers tended to congregate, and they often had a blackboard either outside the building or just inside the door listing job openings.

All of the agencies claimed that the majority of employers' requests for workers were obtained through the reputation they had gained with their regular patrons to whom they had sent the right man for the job, and who thus not only continued to use the agency but recommended it to others. Most of the agencies, however, did not depend upon this alone. A large majority sent field agents to visit old patrons and new prospects and, in addition, maintained a mailing list to whom advertising material was sent. Sometimes this was in the form of circular letters or a blotter giving the name, address, and telephone number of the agency. Several commercial agencies and an agency specializing in the placement of engineers sent out elaborate bulletins giving in considerable detail the qualifications of persons available for employment. Only a small number used newspaper advertising as a method of informing employers as to available applicants. Occasionally an agency attempted to fill orders advertised by employers, but the consensus appeared to be that this was of little use. One agency said, "The jobs are never good ones."

There was no way to determine how much advertising was actually done or the relative importance of the various forms of advertising. At the time this study was made, there was a plentiful supply of most types of applicants, and probably little was being done to attract additional registrations. Employers' orders, on the other hand, were scarce, and it was evident that these agencies recognized the importance of keeping their names before prospective employers at all times and following up on their contacts at frequent intervals.

Placements.—Since employment agencies are in the business of bringing together jobs and workers, it is important to examine the available data as to the number of placements which they make. The State Labor Commissioner requires a monthly report of total placements from each agency. Since, however, these reports were frequently late in coming and in some instances reports for 1937 were not in the files at the time this study was made (in the spring and summer of 1938), it was not possible to compute total placements for a year. The only alternative appeared to be to compute the average number of placements per month for the period covered by those reports which were available for a considerable portion of the year.

There were wide variations in the number of placements per month not only for the group as a whole but also within each type of agency.[12] Several placed an average of only six or seven a month, and one general agency in Los Angeles reported over

[12] An analysis of the sample of agencies visited in the course of this study showed that, although the sample included both agencies making relatively small and large numbers of placements, there were included in the sample a somewhat larger proportion of agencies which made over 100 placements per month.

1,000 placements per month. More than 40 per cent of the agencies made less than 50 and two-thirds less than 100 placements a month. The largest number of placements were made by the general agencies. Over half of the agencies in this category placed more than 100 per month and over a third more than 200 a month, but only in a few instances were their placements as high as 500. Six of the eight nurses agencies for which these data were available made over 100 placements per month, the maximum being about 200. A majority of the other types of agencies made less than 50 placements per month, although in almost every category there were one or two which made 200 or even 300 placements a month.

Although the information as to placements was in a number of respects incomplete, it was obvious that in 1937 a large number of private employment agencies were competing with each other and that in many instances the number of placements was so small as hardly to make for a profitable business.[18]

[18] The total jobs furnished by nontheatrical agencies for the state as a whole as reported by the California Department of Industrial Relations for the period 1928 to 1939 are as follows:

1928	318,706	1934	119,909
1929	335,357	1935	146,603
1930	255,476	1936	207,636
1931	154,754	1937	202,864
1932	80,308	1938	150,507
1933	92,407	1939	174,637

Source: Figures for 1928–35 from California Department of Industrial Relations, *First Biennial Report, 1927–1930*, p. 103, *Second Biennial Report, 1930–1932*, p. 81, and unpublished data from this department; figures for 1936–39 from California Department of Industrial Relations, *Fees Charged by Private Employment Agencies in California*, p. 35.

Although the number of placements by these agencies declined in 1932 to less than a fourth of the 1929 figure, the fact that their placements increased considerably during the last two years indicates that at least until that time fee-charging agencies in California were not in the process of gradually passing out of existence. Further evidence of this fact is found in an estimate of total placements of 130 fee-charging agencies in San Francisco, Los Angeles, and Sacramento in 1937. These agencies made roughly 170,000 placements in 1937. It should, however, be pointed out that this is an understatement of placements by fee-charging agencies in these cities, since placement statistics were not available for 22 agencies. It is, however, significant that placements by the 130 agencies in these cities in 1937 were larger than the total placements for all fee-charging agencies in the state in 1935.

No information as to the types of jobs in which applicants were placed, except such as can be judged by the classification of the agency, was available from records in the office of the Labor Commissioner. Although an attempt was made to secure an answer to this question from the agencies visited, the information secured was very general in nature. Either the managers did not know or they were unwilling to reveal statistics as to the proportion of placements in various occupations. Considering the kind and quality of record keeping found in many of these offices, probably the former was more frequently the case than the latter.

The commercial agencies were of a variety of types. Some were chiefly concerned with the careful selection of skilled office workers, sometimes even specializing in a particular type of business, such as advertising. These were usually the smaller agencies, making not more than 50 placements a month, although one or two agencies of this type did a much larger volume of business. This group of agencies usually had a good reputation in the community and there were no complaints registered against them in the Labor Commissioner's office. At the other end of the scale was the large commercial agency, in certain respects competing with the type mentioned above but probably placing a larger proportion of less highly skilled office workers. In one or two instances these agencies appeared to be guilty of "sharp practices," such as persuading a worker to leave for a better job, which was not forthcoming, presumably with the hope that the agency would be called upon to fill the job again and thus could collect another fee.

Again, only a very general idea as to types of placements could be obtained from the general agencies. These agencies were of two types—those which specialized in placing in culinary employments, and those which placed all kinds of workers in industry and in agriculture. Discussion with the managers indicated that the former placed a majority of their applicants outside of the cities in which the offices were located—in resorts, construction, mining, and lumber camps—although one of the Los Angeles agencies claimed that a large proportion of their placements were in the better hotels, restaurants, and clubs, and they probably all placed some domestics in private homes. Although the other category of general agency claimed to place all kinds of workers in industry and agriculture, it appeared probable that most of their placements were outside the cities in which they were located. They frequently mentioned sending workers to construction projects and to mining and logging areas, and one of the managers said, "We supply all the workers for a chemical company on the Mojave Desert." Several said that they specialized in farm labor and sent workers not only to the farms of California but to surrounding states as well. Two managers said, "We are retained by sugar-beet companies in Washington, Idaho, Utah, and Wyoming to supply them with workers in the beet fields."

Some additional evidence as to the placements made by commercial and general agencies was obtained from the sample of employers visited. Of the nearly 200 employers in industry and commerce in San Francisco, Los Angeles, Sacramento, and Bakersfield, about 40 per cent said that they made some use of fee-charging employment agencies. It was, however, significant that nearly three-quarters of those who used this resource for workers called a fee-charging agency only for office help. Employers also said that the use of these agencies was, in the main, "a last resort" limited to an occasional call for extra help. This appears to verify the impression given by the agencies themselves that most of their industrial labor placements were outside the cities in which the agency was located. It should, however, be pointed out that the sample of employers visited were to a considerable extent the larger establishments, which may perhaps make less use of employment agencies than smaller establishments.

Although a number of the fee-charging agencies claimed that they placed large numbers of farm laborers, little verification of this was found in the interviews with more than 150 farmers. Again, however, it must be emphasized that the sample of farmers interviewed did not include all types of crops; in particular, field crops employing mainly permanent farm hands were excluded, and it is possible that the employment agencies may have made most of their placements in that type of work. Only one farmer in the Los Angeles district—a walnut grower—called upon fee-charging employment agencies for workers. About a half-dozen farmers in the Sacramento area used these agencies as a resource for workers. Two hop growers had a standing order with a fee-charging agency, although they reported that they had little luck in obtaining labor from this source. There was some difference of opinion as to the use of these agencies by the beet growers. One beet grower in Knights Landing said that fee agencies supplied from 25 to 30 per cent of the labor in the beet fields in this area, but others reported that this method of securing workers was seldom used. Only one employer in the fruit crops reported any but very occasional use of these agencies.

The fact that the commercial and general agencies were not extensively used at the time this study was made is probably related, at least in part, to the fact that there were labor surpluses in almost every field of employment, and it is possible that the situation might change if there were labor shortages. It is important, however, to recognize the fact that, in general, employers preferred other methods of securing workers and called upon an employment agency of any kind usually only when all other methods failed. In some instances employers expressed a preference for fee-charging agencies, in contrast to a free employment service, in such terms as: "They give better service; they transport men right to my door." "They are selling a service and take the trouble to find out just the kind of cook

I want." "The better workers prefer to pay for a job." Others, some of whom had used these agencies and some of whom had not, were critical of their service and practices. Several disapproved on principle of workers' having to pay for jobs; others said, "The fees are too high," or "They are rackets and supply incompetent help." One employer, who had himself sought employment through fee-charging agencies, said, "Employment agencies do nothing for their fees. They don't investigate either the job or the applicant, just send them out at random. . . . Any good man can do a better job for himself by going to the employer direct and asking for work. They ought to be abolished."

The domestic and oriental agencies, in the main, specialized in placing skilled cooks, waitresses, and other types of workers in private homes. The oriental agencies also reported some placement in hotels, and one such agency in Los Angeles reported that the major portion of its work was in clerical employments in Japanese firms. Although no evidence was available as to the proportion of placements in private homes which were made by fee-charging agencies, it is probable that it was considerable, since other methods were not as easily available to the housewife, and, furthermore, she was likely to consider—perhaps not always with justification—that the agency had knowledge at least of the honesty of the person referred. There were, of course, other agencies—the California State Employment Service and agencies conducted by various philanthropic organizations—which also placed domestics. It was impossible to determine in how far these agencies competed with the fee agencies; however, at the time this study was made, it appeared that the free agencies placed mainly the less skilled domestics and that the fee-charging agencies had considerable control over the market for the more highly skilled workers in this field.

The nurses agencies placed graduate, undergraduate, and practical nurses and some laboratory workers and assistants in doctors' offices. In the main, they placed nurses for short-time private duty in homes, although one specialized in hospital positions. It was impossible to determine the proportion of nurses placed by the fee-charging agencies specializing in this field. It was, however, quite clear that the bulk of the placements of nurses were handled by the California State Nurses' Association[14] rather than by the licensed fee-charging agencies. In San Francisco there were no fee-charging nurses' agencies licensed at the time this study was made,[15] and in this city, as in Los Angeles, the California State Nurses' Association undoubtedly handled a large proportion of the placement of nurses, although in both cities some nurses were placed through hospitals and private physicians.

A majority of the placements made by the fee-charging teachers agencies were probably certified teachers, although one of these said, "We place a few uncertified teachers and a few other workers in educational institutions." It became evident in the course of this study, however, that the fee-charging agencies were unimportant in the field of teacher placement. Throughout California the vast majority of teachers were placed by the California Teachers Association and by the various teacher-training institutions. According to a report of the California Teachers Association, the number of private fee-charging agencies in Los Angeles was reduced from seven to two or three. "Because of the C.T.A. Placement Bureau services and because of the improved appointment service of universities and colleges, the teacher placement agency field has ceased to be a lucrative one."[16]

Since an employment agency assumes responsibility for fitting together jobs and workers, it is of interest to examine the methods used to determine the qualifications of an applicant

[14] For a discussion of the work of this organization see pages 244–249.

[15] Two fee-charging nurses' agencies were licensed after the data for this study were gathered.

[16] California Teachers Association, Southern Section, *Committee Report* [*on the*] *Placement Bureau* (Los Angeles: 1938), p. 5. Mimeographed.

who is to be referred to an employer. It was evident from the sample of agencies visited that the care with which qualifications were examined varied greatly between different types of agencies. Only those agencies which placed in occupations requiring a definite educational background, such as teachers and nurses, checked school records. The commercial agencies in most instances gave tests for stenographers and typists. Some, although by no means all, of the agencies supplemented their information regarding applicants by checking with former employers. This was most common among the nurses, teachers, and commercial agencies. Some of these agencies always checked references; others did so only if specifically requested by the employer or if there was some special reason, such as the fact that the worker had been out of work for some time. A few of the agencies in the general and domestic categories checked references as a matter of routine but usually only if the employer specifically requested a reference, if the job to be filled demanded a special skill, or if the agency had some reason to be suspicious of the applicant. All of the agencies depended to a large extent on the skill of the interviewer in "sizing up" the applicant and on his knowledge of the requirements of the job.

These agencies stated almost universally that occupational qualification was the basis for referral of applicants. In a few instances order of registration or the relative need of applicants was taken into account if qualifications were equal. It appeared, however, that in the case of the general agencies, although theoretically a careful choice was made of the best man for the job, actually "the man on the spot" probably had the best chance of being referred. In these agencies, the jobs were posted on a blackboard, and it was likely that if a suitable applicant appeared at the desk he would be given the job, since this would save the time of waiting for a more qualified applicant who had registered earlier to come in again or the expense of a telephone call.

A majority of the fee-charging employment agencies referred one applicant to an employer, and, if he was not accepted, another was sent. Commercial agencies, however, frequently sent two or three applicants to be interviewed, probably because employers of this type of worker prefer a certain range of choice.

All employment agencies must concern themselves with placements actually made as an index of the success of their work. This is, however, of special importance to fee-charging agencies, since they are dependent on the fees from workers placed. The method of verifying placements by the fee-charging agencies depended to a large extent on the time at which the fee was collected. In general, those agencies which collected the fee before the applicant was placed assumed that the worker was employed unless he returned for a refund of his fee. Those which collected the fee after the worker was employed naturally expected him to report back; but, if he did not, the employer was called both as a means of checking on the worker and to maintain contact with the employer, who perhaps was not satisfied with the referrals.

Fees

Fees charged.—As a protection to the worker who goes to an employment agency to "buy a job," the Employment Agency Law requires that every licensed agency shall file a copy of its schedule of fees with the Commissioner of Labor. It was found that approximately 30 per cent of the nontheatrical agencies in the areas included in this study had not complied with this section of the law, since for these agencies there was no fee schedule on file. Apparently the law in this respect was most rigidly enforced in San Francisco, since fee schedules were lacking from only 16 per cent of the San Francisco agencies, in contrast with over a third in Los Angeles and a fourth in Sacramento.[17]

[17] Apparently this was no longer true in 1939. See California Department of Industrial Relations, *Fees Charged by Private Employment Agencies in California*, p. 3.

Several of the agencies visited were in the group which had not filed fee schedules with the Labor Commissioner. It is significant that these offices had been in business for periods of time ranging from 1 to 34 years; and thus it cannot be claimed that failure to file the schedule was because the office had been recently opened. It should also be mentioned that among the agencies visited there were 10 whose fee schedules were different from that on file with the Labor Commissioner.

The law also requires that a copy of the fee schedule shall be posted in a conspicuous place in each room of the employment agency frequented by applicants. Visits to employment agencies indicated that this provision of the law was not being enforced. In only 17 of the 65 offices visited were the schedules visible to the investigator, and, in addition, there were 5 offices in which the schedule was posted in the manager's office and not in the waiting rooms.[18]

Since in so many instances fee schedules were not available in the Labor Commissioner's office, and since some of those on file were not correct, the discussion of fees charged will be limited to the sample of agencies visited. There were wide variations in the fees charged.[19] Charges for permanent jobs ranged from 5 per cent of a month's salary, charged by an oriental agency placing domestics, to 50 or 60 per cent of a month's salary, required by some commercial agencies for placements in the higher brackets. One agency placing teachers charged an even higher amount—10 per cent of a year's salary.

The highest fees for permanent employment were charged by commercial agencies and by those serving professional groups—teachers, nurses, and engineers. Some commercial agencies charged a fixed rate on all salaries, usually from 20 to 30 per

[18] It is possible that in some of the oriental agencies the fees were posted in a foreign language and thus could not be read by the investigator. If, however, this were true of all oriental agencies, there would still be a large number in which the fee schedule was not visible.

[19] A detailed analysis of fees charged in 1939 was published after the completion of this manuscript. California Department of Industrial Relations, *op. cit.*, pp. 4 ff.

cent of a month's salary; others, most frequently the Los Angeles agencies, had adopted a sliding scale of fees. The agencies seldom charged less than 25 per cent of the first month's salary for those in the lower income brackets, and most frequently 50 per cent for those earning $150 or more a month. Fees paid in installments were frequently higher. There were only a small number of fee-charging teacher agencies, but those which operated in this field charged from 5 to 10 per cent of the first year's salary. The nurses agencies reported charges of from 20 to 50 per cent of the first month's salary for permanent jobs; and the engineering society, from about 18 to 25 per cent, the amount varying with the earnings.

The general and the domestic and oriental agencies for the most part charged 10 per cent of the first month's earnings, although a few had adopted fee schedules which varied with the amount of earnings and occasionally charged as much as 50 per cent of the first month's salary for those earning over $125 a month.

Most of the agencies reported that the charge for a temporary placement was 10 per cent of the amount earned, but there was usually a provision that the total sum paid should not be larger than for a permanent placement at the same salary. In some instances, however, the fee was charged on total earnings for a period up to 100 or 120 days, and some of the nurses agencies charged a fee for every placement with no provision as to a maximum. This was of considerable importance, since a large proportion of nursing jobs were temporary, and, if a nurse were required to pay 10 per cent for every job and were employed at 12 different jobs each of a month's duration, she would pay each year an amount greater than a month's earnings.[20] A few of the agencies set a minimum fee, such as a dollar, which, if

[20] It is interesting to note that an agency with this type of fee schedule also makes the following requirements: "Nurses affiliated with this Registry will not be permitted to register with any other registry and must agree to pay their commission for all cases however received."

the job was of short duration, might amount to much more than 10 per cent; and a few of the commercial agencies charged approximately 15 per cent for temporary placements.

It is not surprising to find that employment agencies charged fees which varied greatly from agency to agency, since there was no legal control of the sum which might be charged.[21] This study indicates that the person applying to a fee-charging agency for permanent employment in the commercial or professional fields will usually have to pay from 20 to 50 per cent of a month's salary, and one who applies for industrial, agricultural, or domestic employment, about 10 per cent. In almost every field there were, however, some agencies which charged fees considerably higher than those just mentioned.

There is no objective test as to what is a reasonable fee to be charged by an employment agency. Apparently competition between agencies and what the traffic will bear have been the controlling factors in determining the fee schedules. The available evidence appeared to point to the fact that in a good many instances the fees charged were a heavy burden on the worker. A 10 per cent fee, most frequently charged by agencies in the industrial, agricultural, and domestic fields, might perhaps be considered to be a reasonable fee, but it must be remembered that for the worker who is in and out of employment several times each year the cost is considerable. The fees charged by commercial and professional agencies often amounted to as

[21] The Supreme Court in 1928 handed down a decision under which a state is permitted to license and regulate employment agencies because "the general nature of the business is such that unless regulated many persons may be exposed to misfortunes against which the Legislature may properly protect them." The Legislature cannot prohibit the business entirely nor fix the fees collected by the agency. Ribnick v. McBride and Brazic v. Mich. See U. S. Bureau of Labor Statistics, *Laws Relating to Employment Agencies in the United States as of July 1, 1937*, Bulletin No. 630 (Washington: Government Printing Office, 1937), pp. 7–9.

On April 28, 1941, the Supreme Court overruled the 1928 decision and unanimously upheld a Nebraska law limiting the fees which may be charged by private employment agencies. Olsen v. State of Nebraska (61 Sup. Ct. 862). See *Monthly Labor Review*, 52 (June 1941), pp. 1451–1452. This decision will make it possible for other states to pass legislation regulating the fees charged by private employment agencies.

much as a half or a full month's salary. There appears to be little doubt that such sums are an undue hardship on the worker.

Students of this problem agree, in general, that the worker should not have to "buy a job." Such a payment, though in some instances small, is almost certain to be a real hardship, since it comes at a time when the man is out of work; and not only is there no weekly pay envelope, but weeks or even months of unemployment may have made it necessary for him to deplete whatever reserves he may have had. Furthermore, the mere fact that a fee is charged encourages fraudulent practices, which act as a hindrance to the worker in reëstablishing himself as quickly as possible in permanent employment. An employment agency may place a worker in a job for which he is obviously unfitted in the hope that he will return to get another job and thus pay another fee; or there may be collusion between an agency and an employer whereby workers are employed for a short time and then discharged and new workers employed, the fees being split between the agency and the employer.

Fees collected.—It is of interest to examine the economic position of the fee-charging agencies in terms of the sums which they collected from applicants for jobs. Although the Labor Commissioner requires a monthly report of total fees collected from each employment agency, it was found that—as was the case with the reports of placements—these reports in many instances were late in coming in and frequently were lacking for a number of months. Again, since in many cases information as to the total sum collected in 1937 was not available for the entire year, the average amount collected per month for those months for which reports were available was computed.[22]

[22] After this study was completed the following figures as to fees collected in 1939 by 204 of 216 fee-charging agencies in California were published:

San Francisco	$202,656
Los Angeles	431,606
Remainder of state	196,411
Total	$830,673

California Department of Industrial Relations, *op. cit.*, p. 33.

There were wide variations in the average monthly fees collected by the employment agencies included in this study, and this was true not only for the entire group of agencies but for each type of agency as well. About 15 per cent of the agencies collected less than $100 a month; over 40 per cent collected less than $200 a month; more than 60 per cent, less than $500 a month; and less than 5 per cent, as much as $2,000 a month.[23] Although some agencies in almost every category collected relatively low and others relatively high average monthly sums, it was found that commercial, general, and nurses agencies more frequently collected larger sums than did the other types of agencies. About half of the agencies in the categories mentioned above collected more than $400 a month. In contrast to this, about half of the domestic, oriental, and teachers agencies collected from $150 to $200 a month.

It was impossible to determine how large collections must be in order to place an employment agency on a profit-making basis. It would appear, however, that even a small agency, with possibly only one employee, could hardly even make ends meet unless at least $200 a month were collected in fees. Since this study has shown that over 40 per cent of the agencies collected less than $200 a month, it appears safe to hazard a guess that these agencies and probably others collecting somewhat larger amounts were, to say the least, in a precarious economic position, that their reports were incomplete, or that they had some unreported source of income.

Fees refunded.—As has already been pointed out, the law provides that the employment agency shall return the fee to the worker who fails to obtain employment or who is discharged in less than seven days. The Commissioner of Labor requires a monthly report of the number of applicants who received refunds and the amount and reasons for the refunds. The reports

[23] The sample of agencies visited included both those with small and large monthly collections. The sample was, however, somewhat overweighted with agencies which reported relatively high monthly collections.

as to refunds were in a number of instances incomplete. Furthermore, in some cases, although the reports did not state that refunds had been made, an analysis of the complaints against the agency showed that there had been refunds. It must therefore be recognized that the discussion of the number of refunds is based on material which is an understatement of the facts.

About a fourth of the agencies for whom information was available reported that no fees had been refunded during the year 1937.[24] The remainder in some instances refunded fees to a small proportion and in others to a large proportion of those from whom fees were collected. Although nearly 40 per cent of the agencies returned fees to less than one-sixth of those referred to jobs, it is significant that about 20 per cent reported that from one-half to two-thirds of the applicants sent out returned for refunds, and in one instance fees were returned to three-quarters of those from whom collections were made.

The general agencies usually returned fees to a larger proportion of applicants than did commercial and domestic agencies, and very few refunds were made by agencies operating in the professional fields. Over 50 per cent of the general agencies returned fees to between one-sixth and one-half of those referred to jobs; and 20 per cent, to as many as one-half to two-thirds. None of the commercial agencies returned fees to as many as one-sixth of their applicants; and only a very small number, to as many as 1 in 10. While a few domestic and oriental agencies returned fees to relatively high proportions of their applicants, these and also the professional agencies, in the main, made few refunds.[25]

The fact that refunds are made to a small proportion of those from whom fees are collected may or may not mean a high

---

[24] Apparently this same situation still prevailed in 1939. See California Department of Industrial Relations, *op. cit.*, p. 28.

[25] The sample of agencies visited included agencies making both small and large proportions of refunds and, with respect to refunds, was similar to the larger group for which information was available.

degree of success in making placements. If the policy of the agency was to collect the fee after the placement was made, the proportion of refunds would necessarily be less than in those agencies which collected the fee before the applicant was interviewed by the employer, and it was possible that those agencies which did not collect the fee until after the applicant was employed might actually have made many referrals for every job that was filled.

Information as to the time at which the fee was collected was obtained from the sample of agencies visited. Almost without exception the general agencies collected the fee when the worker was referred to the job. Agencies operating in other fields, on the other hand, with a few exceptions collected the fee after the job was secured, in many cases delaying the payment until the worker had received his first pay check. This difference in policy obviously accounted in part for the generally larger proportions of refunds made by the general agencies. The fact, however, that there were considerable variations in the proportion of refunds within the group of general agencies is evidence that some of these agencies were successful in making a large proportion of referrals in which the worker was presumably employed and thus did not request a refund, whereas others who were perhaps less careful in their referrals had to make refunds to a large proportion.

Complaints.—It is a well-known fact that some fee-charging agencies indulge in a variety of illegal or "sharp" practices. Evidence on this subject was obtained from the records of the complaints lodged with the Labor Commissioner's office. It was obvious that these complaints did not tell the whole story, since many workers might not have known that the Labor Commissioner's office stood ready to protect them, and others might simply not have thought it worth while to go to the trouble of reporting their case. The complaints were, however, the only data available, and they at least gave an idea of the various types of illegal practices.

During the year 1937 the Labor Commissioner's office received complaints involving 67 (44 per cent) of the nontheatrical agencies in San Francisco, Los Angeles, and Sacramento. Of the total of 410 complaints, 382 (over 90 per cent) were referred because of the refusal of the agency to refund the fee. In about a fourth of this group of complaints the worker stated that the job had been misrepresented, usually in such terms as that the hours were longer or the work heavier than the agency had represented, or that the agency had failed to inform the applicant that living accommodations were not provided by the employer, or that a strike was in progress. About another quarter reported that they had been discharged within a period during which the agency is required to refund the fee. Another large group, again about a quarter, stated either that when they arrived there was no job or that the employer, after an interview, refused to employ them. A small number (only about 3 per cent) refused to accept a job offered to them and asked for a refund which the agency did not grant. In about 10 per cent of these cases the complaint merely stated that the refund had been refused and nothing as to the reason for the request.

In a small group of cases (about 4 per cent of the total) the complaint was listed as "violation of the Employment Agency Act." An examination of these complaints showed that they were all complaints against the agencies for reasons other than refusal to refund fees. In one or two instances it was reported that an employment agency had advertised falsely; in others, that the agency was a combination pool hall and employment office, that the agency had failed to renew its license, did not use a uniform receipt or have the fee schedule or Employment Agency Law posted, or had sent a worker to a strike job without informing him of the situation. These complaints were filed in some instances by the applicants for employment and in others by some organization such as the Better Business Bureau or the California State Employment Service.

In only 11 of the 410 complaints was the action brought by the employment agency, and these were in every case attempts to force a worker to pay a fee to the agency.

Nearly 90 per cent of the complaints were against the general agencies. Although over 40 per cent of the agencies in the areas visited were general agencies and the largest number of placements were made by this group of agencies, it is still significant that such a large percentage of the complaints were against agencies operating in this field. Furthermore, it is important that there were complaints against nearly three-quarters of the general agencies, in contrast to only 40 per cent of the commercial agencies. Only very small proportions of the domestic and oriental agencies were involved in complaints, and there was none against the agencies which specialized in the placement of nurses and teachers.

It is of interest to examine the number of complaints in which the various types of agencies were involved. Half of the 32 general agencies against which complaints had been made were involved in less than 5 complaints. For the remainder, the number of complaints varied greatly, with the largest number nearly 50. The largest number of complaints against general agencies occurred in Los Angeles and in Sacramento. In Los Angeles there were from 30 to 40 complaints against 2 agencies, and in Sacramento 3 general agencies were involved in from 30 to 50 complaints. Some light was thrown on the situation in Sacramento by a quotation from a document included in a complaint against the agency which was the worst offender: "The general attitude of the employment agencies here is hostile to the office, hostile to men who return to ask for a refund on their fee. They are told that they will be taken out and kicked in the gutter, and at no time will either of the three . . . refund any fees whatever unless compelled to do so." In the other categories there were seldom more than three complaints against one agency, although in one or two instances the Labor Commissioner had been asked to intercede in eight or nine cases.[26]

It is obvious from the above analysis that the complaints most frequently involved a demand for a refund of fees. The fact that few complaints were submitted to the Labor Commissioner because of violations of other sections of the law may have meant that there were few infringements, although it may have been that other types of violations were not recognized because of lack of understanding of the law or that the worker was more likely to enter a protest when his pocketbook was involved than in other circumstances.

The number and types of complaints against the employment agencies do not tell the whole story. An examination of the disposition of the cases described above is necessary in order to throw light upon the validity of the charges against the agencies. Although the record of the action taken was not always complete, sufficient evidence was available to indicate that in a large proportion there was apparently a justifiable cause for complaint. The Labor Commissioner ordered a refund in nearly 80 per cent (301 of the 382 cases) in which the applicant claimed that the agency refused a refund to which he was entitled. Slightly less than half of these decisions required a full refund, and in about half the agency was ordered to refund a part of the fee. In a few instances the agency was instructed to place the worker with no additional fee, and occasionally the amount of the refund was not specified in the record.[27] In 3 of the 11 cases brought by an agency against workers for nonpayment of fees, the worker was ordered to pay the fee. Slightly

[26] The sample of agencies visited was somewhat overweighted with agencies involved in complaints, and the number of complaints was somewhat larger than for the total group of agencies.

[27] The Employment Agency Law requires a repayment of double the amount of the fee if the fee is not repaid within 48 hours after demand. See Cal. Stats. (1937), ch. 90, pt. 6. In none of the refunds ordered by the Labor Commissioner's office, at the time this study was made, was this clause enforced.

less than 20 per cent of the total claims were dismissed or warned. The dismissed cases were usually those in which claims had been made for refunds which were not justified, although in some of these cases the facts appeared to warrant a refund, but the claimant did not return to the Labor Commissioner's office when requested to do so. The cases which were warned and then apparently dismissed were those which were brought for "violations of the Employment Agency Act," such as false advertising, failure to renew a license, or failure to notify the worker that the job offered was that of a strikebreaker. There were 26 cases (6 per cent of the total) in which the last entry was "deferred" or "pending." Twenty-four of these were in the Los Angeles office and two in Sacramento. All of the Los Angeles cases had been deferred for 6 months or longer (13, for over a year); the Sacramento cases had been pending for 5 months. It appeared that under similar situations these cases would have been dismissed by the San Francisco office, and thus the classifications deferred or pending do not appear to have much significance.[28]

THEATRICAL AGENCIES

Theatrical agencies specialize in the placement of actors, dancers, musicians, and other types of entertainers in the movies and on the radio and stage, and in hotels, restaurants, night clubs, and other organizations that wish to employ entertainers of various sorts. At the time this study was made, there were over 200 theatrical agencies licensed by the Commissioner of Labor in San Francisco, Los Angeles, and Sacramento.[29] As might be

[28] The disposition of complaints in the sample of agencies visited was approximately the same as for the total group of agencies for whom reports were obtained.

[29] Licenses were found in the office of the Labor Commissioner for 214 theatrical agencies. There are, however, undoubtedly a much larger number of such agencies. Many of the agents who place motion-picture stars are not licensed by the state. Since there are literally hundreds of such agents, it was not possible to secure a complete list and to check this against the state licenses. Also, apparently a considerable proportion of the agents licensed by the Musicians Union did not have state licenses. Of a list of 45 such agencies, only 20 were identified as licensed by the Commissioner of Labor.

expected, most of these agencies (203) were in Los Angeles, the center of the motion-picture and radio industry, whereas in San Francisco there were only 10 and in Sacramento only 1.

As has already been stated,[80] it was impossible to visit a sufficient number of theatrical agencies to represent adequately the work of this type of agency. Furthermore, a large number of the theatrical agencies had not sent monthly reports to the Labor Commissioner nor filed a schedule of their fees with this office, and thus little information as to these agencies was available from this source. Another difficulty arose from the fact that in a number of instances the person interviewed was suspicious of the investigator, and therefore the information obtained was unsatisfactory and fragmentary. For the above reasons it will be possible to describe only in very general terms the way in which theatrical agencies functioned.[81] The description will be based on visits to a small number of agencies of various types (4 in San Francisco and 10 in Los Angeles), on interviews with a number of people familiar with the work of these agencies, and on some data made available by the Commissioner of Labor.

Theatrical agencies were of several quite well defined types, although there was some overlapping between types. There were a number, though probably not a very large part of the total, which, in the main, placed actors, singers, dancers, and entertainers of various kinds in variety shows or for hotel, club, lodge, or convention entertainments. A number of these agencies were themselves producers of theatrical acts as well as agents for actors and entertainers who were employed by someone else. Thus these agencies were in some instances in the position of an employer and in others merely an agent. Some in this group reported that when the agency was the employer no employment agency fee was deducted; others apparently deducted

[80] See page 34.

[81] Many important problems, such as a comprehensive study of the number of placements, fees charged, and complaints against these agencies, have been omitted because of lack of time and facilities to gather the necessary data.

a 10 per cent employment agency fee from the salary paid the entertainer and, in addition, received whatever profits might be made as entrepreneur for the show. A second type were those which specialized in placing bands and orchestras, although these agencies also placed some dancers and other entertainers. Some agencies of this sort made most of their placements on the radio, whereas others had their largest business in hotels, ballrooms, and cafes.

At this point it is important to mention the tie-up between certain unions and the types of agencies described above. The American Federation of Actors and the American Federation of Musicians both issued lists of agents who were "licensed" to secure engagements for their members. The Actors Union had ruled that no artist was permitted to book himself directly nor to negotiate for employment without authority from an agent licensed by the American Federation of Actors.[32] The American Federation of Musicians had adopted a similar rule, except that this union permitted its members to seek employment directly with proprietors.[33] The reason for the licensing of booking agents by the union and the mechanism through which this is done can perhaps best be described by quoting a union representative: "The union attempted to sign contracts with employers, but, because our members deal largely with agents and not employers, we were getting nowhere. The licensed agencies are required to sign an agreement with the union whereby the agent promises to represent only union members and to secure engagements only at such standards as have been set up in the contract. Through the licensing of agents, closed-shop conditions prevail." If an agent failed to live up to his agreement with the union, his license was revoked, and union members were instructed not to accept engagements through an agent who

[32] *Flash!* Rulings and Union Prices Adopted by the American Federation of Actors.

[33] *The Musical News,* Official Journal of the Musicians Union, Local No. 6 (San Francisco: Mar. 1938), p. 18.

was not licensed. Since a large proportion of both actors and musicians were union members, the rules regarding licensing had probably resulted in considerable control over the theatrical agencies in these fields, although, at the time this study was made, a number were operating without a license from the union.

In Los Angeles, the center of the movie and radio industries, there were two other important types of agencies. There were a number which secured engagements for actors for small parts in the movies—"extras" and "bit players." In some instances agencies of this sort confined their activities to one racial group. The placements of these agencies were confined to the small, independent producers who did not use Central Casting, the centralized employment agency for this type of talent, which was supported by the large producers.[84] Finally, there was the very large group of agencies which placed high-grade concert artists for personal and radio appearance and stars, feature players, and the higher grades of supporting cast in the movies and radio. Some of the agencies of this sort were operated by the larger broadcasting companies, presumably because they saw that it would be good business to act as an agent and thus receive a fee from the cast rather than to call upon other agents to whom a fee would be paid. These agencies also acted as the artist's agent in personal appearances and in the movies. There were, however, hundreds of agents who were independent of the radio companies and whose clients were chiefly movie stars for whom they arranged appearances in the movies or radio. In the case of the movies, the agency acted as a direct intermediary between the motion-picture company and the actor. In the radio, however, a somewhat different situation existed. Radio programs were put on in part by the radio companies and in part by the advertising companies. Those put on by the radio companies were "sustaining" programs, presumably for the purpose of "building up" a show which would later be in de-

[84] For a description of Central Casting see pages 392–393.

mand for advertising purposes. A considerable number of the people used in the "sustaining" programs were employed directly by the casting department of the radio company, although some—probably those in the higher grades—employed an agent, either the broadcasting company's own agency or some other. By far the largest number of radio programs, however, were produced by the advertising companies. These companies employed the supporting cast and small-part players for the radio shows which they produced from a list of people who applied directly and who thus paid no fee to an employment agency. Stars and musicians, on the other hand, were employed, in general, through a theatrical agency to which the artist had to pay a fee.

The unions of moving-picture actors and radio artists did not license employment agencies as did the unions of musicians and actors. That these unions were concerning themselves with this matter was, however, illustrated by the following quotation from a union official: "The members of this organization are employed through agents who have a general understanding with the union on matters of working conditions. Though the agents are not licensed at present the union expects to bring this about in the near future."

In general, the theatrical agencies apparently charged a basic 10 per cent fee for all engagements secured for their clients. In some instances—it was impossible to determine how frequently—higher fees were charged. Some reported that the fee was increased to 20 per cent for engagements outside the city in which the office was located, and one agency said, "This is a management bureau which maps out an entire career for an artist, possibly part of the year in movies, part in radio, and part in personal appearances. This is more expensive than simply acting as an agent." In cases such as this the fee was probably as high as 20 per cent. There may, of course, have been considerable variations from the fees mentioned above, since only a few theatrical agencies were willing to give information on this subject; furthermore, these agencies seldom had filed copies of their fee schedules with the Labor Commissioner, and thus there could be no verification from this source.

Such evidence as was available indicated that there were wide variations in the number of engagements secured and in the total fees collected by theatrical agencies. Some reported as few as 15 or 20 placements a month; at the other end of the scale, an agency securing engagements for extras and bit players in the movies reported nearly 2,000 placements a month. An agency representing a small number of popular movie stars whose weekly salaries ran to fabulous sums would collect large amounts in fees, whereas the proceeds of agencies placing large numbers of extras and bit players who earn from about $15 to $25 a day would be much smaller. For instance, one of the agencies which had on its list some of the top names in the movie world collected over $200,000 in March of 1937 and averaged over $50,000 a month for the year. This agency made about 200 placements a month. Another agency of this type made an average of only 35 placements a month. The collections of this agency averaged over $20,000 a month, and in January of 1937 over $45,000 in fees were reported. On the other hand, the agency mentioned above, which placed nearly 2,000 extras and bit players a month, collected an average of $1,700 a month in fees. The agencies placing various types of vaudeville and variety performers probably collected considerably smaller sums than those given above, and, again, the sums collected depended to a considerable extent upon the grade of talent. One such agency reported an average of nearly $1,000 a month collected for about 170 engagements, whereas another collected an average of approximately $500 for about 250 engagements.

It must be emphasized that the collections and placements given above are descriptive of only a few of the more prosperous theatrical agencies. There were, of course, a considerable number of agencies in this field which, although collecting more modest sums, were profitable to the owner. However, there were many who had entered this field of business because of the expectation of large gains but who had found it far from profitable. Their clients were few and their collections frequently less than $100 a month. This is a highly competitive business, and theatrical agents go in and out of business almost overnight. One list of such agencies two months old was described by its publisher as of little use because of many changes in the period since publication.

Although it was not possible to estimate the proportion of jobs in the theatrical, movie, musical, and radio world which were secured through fee-charging employment agencies, it is probable that here, more than in any other field of employment, the fee-charging agency had a considerable monopoly over the labor market. The reason for this was perhaps in part because of the nature of the occupation, which required frequent contacts with new employers, in part custom, and in part because artists frequently lack the capacity to manage their own affairs. One of the agents said of movie stars, "They can't even manage their own personal accounts—they ask us to do almost everything for them." It may be that a man earning several thousand dollars a week does need a "manager" and can afford to pay for this service. It is, however, undoubtedly true that a 10 per cent fee to an agent may be a serious burden on those in the ranks of the lower paid, many of whom do not have steady employment. This had been recognized in the motion-picture industry where bit players and extras were employed through Central Casting without expense to themselves. This organization, however, served only the larger companies, and thus many who took small parts in the movies were required to pay 10 per cent to an agent. There was yet no free service equipped to serve the vaudeville actor, dancer, or musician, although an interesting experiment had recently been made by the national headquarters of the American Federation of Actors, which conducted its own employment bureau in New York. "This has been done merely as an experiment in connection with our plan to license all booking agencies dealing with our members. This department has been conducted most successfully. Since its inception, 2,021 members have secured engagements without paying any fee. . . . The success of this department has proved conclusively that wherever the booking agencies fail to coöperate by accepting a code of ethics and establishing a fair minimum wage and equitable contracts, the A.F.A. could easily take over the entire booking interests of its members, which, however, it does not care to do."[35] Apparently the actors and possibly other groups in related fields would not to any extent organize their own placement services unless they failed in their attempt to control to their satisfaction the activities of the existing fee-charging agencies.

CONCLUSIONS

In 1938 there were in California somewhere between 400 and 500 licensed fee-charging employment agencies which were in the business of "selling jobs" to workers. In the large centers, such as San Francisco and Los Angeles, numbers of competing agencies existed in many fields of employment ranging all the way from those in a hole in the wall, which, in the main, attracted unskilled labor, through the more or less elaborate offices placing in clerical and technical pursuits, to the super-luxurious offices of some of the theatrical agencies. Employment agencies could also be found in Sacramento and in other smaller centers of the state, but here the general agency was likely to be the most common type.

The fact that employment agencies are in business for the profit that can be made is, of course, a stimulus to efficiency in the process of bringing together jobs and workers. In some

[35] American Federation of Actors, National Headquarters, *Questions and Answers* (New York), p. 4.

instances they undoubtedly perform an expert service. Not infrequently, however, the profit motive leads these agencies, in their struggle for a none-too-certain existence, to adopt practices which defeat their proper purpose—to serve as a channel between jobs and qualified workers, and not just any job and any worker, as quickly and as economically as possible.[36]

Although some of the California agencies were fair and equitable in their dealings with their clients and made a very real effort to refer workers to jobs for which they were qualified, many collected fees from workers who were obviously unfit for the job and were accused, with justification, of various sharp or illegal practices. In the main, these agencies were charged with refusing to return fees to workers. In some instances refunds were refused to workers who were sent to jobs which did not exist or for which the worker was not qualified. In other cases the worker quit within a short period of time because the agency had misrepresented the job; and sometimes the worker was discharged within a week, and the agency refused the refund required by law. Some agencies were much more frequent offenders than others, and it was reported that certain agencies never returned a fee without a fight. In a few instances employment agencies violated other sections of the Employment Agency Law, such as advertising falsely or sending workers to strike jobs without informing them of the situation.

The fact that hundreds of workers each year bring complaints to the office of the Labor Commissioner, most of which result in action against an employment agency, leads inevitably to the conclusion that there is an incentive for these agencies to collect fees for a service which they do not render and that they erect barriers to the prompt return of fees which may or may not have been collected in good faith.

[36] An analysis of some of these problems in other states will be found in the following publications: Frances R. Whitney, *Employment Agencies in Cincinnati*, Consumers League of Cincinnati (Dec. 1928); Connecticut State Department of Labor, *Private Employment Agencies* (Hartford: 1937). Mimeographed.

It is probable that the nature of the employment agency business is such that there will always be an incentive to certain abusive and illegal practices, and thus the law controlling and restricting the activities of these agencies must be strictly enforced. The California law contains many of the provisions recommended by the United States Department of Labor, Division of Labor Standards,[37] as a protection against the various abuses mentioned above, but, at the time this study was made, there was almost no inspection of the activities of these agencies. Almost the only types of enforcement were the issue of licenses, a none-too-active attempt to secure monthly reports, and consideration of complaints. It was apparent that the deputies gave their chief attention to complaints. In one of the offices of the Department of Industrial Relations the investigator was informed of this fact in the following words: "All the Deputy Labor Commissioner does is to hold hearings." Obviously the consideration of complaints was a matter of first importance, but it should be pointed out that in most instances the complaints were considered as matters for ajudication, and little attention was given to the fact that a series of complaints might indicate that an agency was willfully violating the law, and thus that its license should be revoked. In one or two instances Deputy Labor Commissioners recommended to the Labor Commissioner that "the employment agencies be compelled to obey the law, follow out the instructions of the Labor Commissioner, and comply with the law compelling them to keep proper records." So far as is known, no action was taken on these recommendations, and complaints against gross offenders continued to be filed.

Critics of private employment agencies have agreed that the fees charged by these agencies are sometimes exorbitant and that in the vast majority of cases the sum charged is more than

[37] U. S. Department of Labor, Division of Labor Standards, *Suggested Draft to Regulate Private Employment Agencies* (Washington: Mar. 15, 1937). Mimeographed.

the unemployed worker can afford to pay. The California agencies charged fees ranging from about 10 per cent of a month's salary to 10 per cent or even more of a year's earnings. Clearly, either of these sums may be a serious burden on the unemployed worker. At the time this study was made, there was no legislation as to fees which an employment agency might charge.[38] The California law, however, gives the worker some protection by requiring that the fee schedule shall be posted in a conspicuous place. A member of the staff of the office of the Labor Commissioner said, "Deputies are sent out at the beginning of each year, if we are not too busy, to see that the fee schedules are posted and that other provisions of the law are being obeyed." Since fee schedules were visible in only about a fourth of the offices visited in the course of this study, it seems reasonable to conclude that the deputies were "too busy" to do this job of investigation. Thus in many instances the worker had no opportunity to read carefully the often somewhat complicated fee schedules.

It is impossible to predict the future of private fee-charging employment agencies. If the free State Employment Service is able to develop a strong and efficient organization, and if employers and workers can be convinced that it isn't merely a market for "cheap labor," it may make serious inroads on the business of the fee-charging agency. It is probable that these inroads are most likely to occur in certain fields—domestic service, industrial and agricultural labor, and in some types of commercial employment. It is improbable that the State Employment Service, at least for a long time, will be able to take the place of specialized fee-charging agencies serving professional groups or even to take over the work of the highly selective commercial agency which specializes in a more or less personal service for a few clients, and certainly it is not likely that the theatrical agency will be replaced. Moreover, in every

[38] See footnote 21, page 286.

case there are vested interests involved, and the manager of an employment agency will hold on to his business even though it makes him only a precarious livelihood. For the present, and as long as fee-charging employment agencies exist, strict regulation is essential for the protection of those using these channels between job and worker.

VIII. Labor Contractors

This chapter was written by Mary Gorringe Luck, Research Associate of the Heller Committee for Research in Social Economics.

A PARTICULAR type of intermediary between workers and employers was the labor contractor who supplied labor for farmers.[1] Although it was not possible to define a farm labor contractor precisely, because there were many variations as to the way in which he functioned and the scope of his activities, it could be said, in general, that he was hired primarily because he could produce a crew and that his remuneration for this service was usually paid by the workers rather than by the employer. The type of labor contractor which had received the widest publicity in California, because of abuses of the system revealed in labor disputes, was the man who signed a written contract with the grower to perform a certain operation, usually harvesting, at a fixed price per box or acre. The workers were specified by the terms of the contract to be his employees, not the grower's; he made the wage agreement with them; and he, not the grower, was responsible for the payment of wages. However, there were an infinite variety of other types, ranging from this entrepreneur to the local Mexican who was told to come around next week for the picking and bring six friends. Sometimes the contractor operated a camp for the crew. Sometimes he moved his crew through several states, following crop circuits. Occasionally he was paid directly by the employer for his services in securing labor. Sometimes the workers paid a recognized percentage of their earnings as an employment fee. Sometimes the contractor made his profit in a more dubious fashion. Occasionally his only recompense was the job as fore-

[1] Historically, contractors have been used in California in other occupations than farming, notably in railroad construction, but this investigation found them associated only with agriculture.

man. The distinguishing characteristic of all types was that the contractor acted as an employment agent and furnished the farmer with a crew, just as a fee-charging agency or a free employment service might do.[2]

It was frequently difficult in individual cases to determine whether a man was a contractor of the informal type or a field foreman. Foremen quite often did the hiring of harvest hands with little or no supervision from the grower. Foremen on one-crop ranches with a short harvest season did not work full time the year round. Foremen sometimes "chiseled" the worker out of part of his earnings, but far less frequently than a labor contractor and without the tacit consent of the grower. It was usually impossible to determine what such undercover arrangements were. The basic distinction between labor contractor and foremen appeared to be that the contractor was an irresponsible agent who relieved the employer of the task of finding workers, whereas the foreman was more responsible, by virtue of his closer ties with the employer, and was paid by the employer for his work as a labor agent.

HISTORY OF FARM LABOR CONTRACTORS IN CALIFORNIA

The labor contractor in California came into being as an intermediary between an alien group of workers and the grower who did not speak their language or understand their habits of life. The Chinese who were California's first migratory laborers worked in gangs—mutually protective groups, isolated in a strange country—under a gang boss who appears to have been more of a group spokesman and business agent than an inde-

[2] Since this chapter was written, the hearings of the Tolan Committee of the House of Representatives on interstate migration have been published. Some of the testimony at these hearings describes in detail the history, extent, operation, and abuses of the labor contractor system. The reader is referred especially to the statement of Carey McWilliams, *Hearings before the Select Committee to Investigate the Interstate Migration of Destitute Citizens, House of Representatives*, 76th Cong., 3d sess., Part 6, San Francisco Hearings, pp. 2529–2541.

pendent operator. The Japanese who followed also worked in gangs, but their bosses were true labor contractors, employers of the gang, who divided the territory among themselves and set up an organization of their own to prevent price cutting.[3] However, the Japanese labor contractor at the beginning of the century appears to have been more closely associated with the interests of the group of workers than with those of the employer. He engineered wage increases for the group at the grower's expense and was a part of the group solidarity so often remarked in literature of the period—"If one Japanese quits, they all quit." Hindus and other alien races engaged in California agriculture before the World War also operated under gang bosses, as did some of the Italians. The system was less common among the American-born and North European farm laborers. However, "in nearly all of the cases except among the Japanese the 'boss' is little more than a spokesman and business agent. In some instances where time wages are paid, he receives 25 cents per day extra from the employer for serving in these capacities."[4] The Mexicans and Filipinos who came to constitute the state's chief supply of migratory labor in post-war years largely worked under labor contractors. During the past 20 years the contractor system has lost much of its coöperative and paternalistic character, and the "chiseling" of agricultural workers by contractors has grown to be a widespread source of complaint.[5] The latest influx of migrants, dust-bowl refugees, did not move about in gangs under a boss, and they worked for labor contractors only in crops, such as peas, where the contractors had a practical monopoly.

[3] *Report of the U. S. Immigration Commission,* 61st Cong., 2d sess., S. Doc. 633 (Washington: Government Printing Office, 1911), Vol. 24, p. 27.

[4] *Ibid.,* p. 590.

[5] Cf. pages 325–327.

EXTENT OF THE CONTRACTOR SYSTEM IN 1938

In 1938 the labor contractor, in his infinite ramifications, was still an important factor in the agricultural labor market of California, particularly in crops where alien races were employed. He was one of the media through which the grower found harvest hands and the migratory laborers found work, and one which was subject to very considerable abuses. In the course of the present investigation an attempt was made to find and interview labor contractors, growers were questioned as to whether they hired workers through contractors and the details of their system, and considerable miscellaneous information on the subject was obtained from such sources as county agricultural commissioners and leading men of foreign groups in small towns. However, the resulting data were not a sample adequate to determine for the state as a whole what proportion of agricultural labor was hired through contractors. Two areas where contracting was most prevalent—the Salinas and Imperial valleys—were not visited, and the representation in the sample of fruit and vegetable field crops, largely harvested under contractors, was very small. Contractors and employers who hired them were naturally disinclined to expatiate on abuses of the system, and there was no opportunity within the scope of this study to interview workers who had suffered under such abuses.

Within the limitations described above, the sample indicated the crops and racial groups within which the labor contractor system was most prevalent in 1938 in the areas visited. Filipinos almost invariably worked in gangs of single men under a gang boss who was more the headman of the group than a labor contractor. Many Mexicans were hired independently of gangs, but others worked under contractors, and a very large proportion of the contractors, who might have gangs of various racial composition, were themselves Mexicans. The orientals had almost disappeared from California agriculture as laborers, but there were still some Japanese labor contractors, hiring mostly men of other races. The latest immigrants to California, white families from the "dust bowl," avoided the contractor system where possible.

For all practical purposes the labor contractor system was universal in asparagus and sugar beets in the areas visited. Asparagus was harvested by Filipinos working under their own peculiar gang system, which is described later. In sugar beet operations requiring large numbers of field laborers the established practice for the whole Sacramento area was a system of Mexican contractors who boarded gangs of unattached men, advocated alike by growers and the refineries that financed them.[6] The contractor system was at least widespread in peas. In the areas included in the sample much of the crop was owned by absentee land companies or else sold by the growers to shipping companies while still on the vine, so that the shipping company was responsible for the harvest and delegated the responsibility, as did the absentee companies, to the contractor, who was in immediate touch with the labor supply and skilled at supervising the work. The use of labor contractors was fairly common in the harvesting of prunes, tomatoes, strawberries, and walnuts, especially the latter. Many prune growers in the district west and north of Sacramento hired their pickers directly; many others used some sort of labor contractor system but with no such established pattern as in the beet harvests in the same area. Many types of contractors were used in the tomato harvest around Sacramento. Most strawberries were picked by Filipinos, working in gangs under contractors; Japanese used in

[6] The field agent of a large refining company estimated that only 10 per cent of the sugar beet labor in the area north and west of Sacramento was hired independently of labor contractors. Filipino informants suggested that the local grocer, not a contractor, was the intermediary in small parcel holdings in the Delta. Other informants took the contractor system for granted as an integral part of beet growing.

these operations were hired directly.[7] The pickers who harvested the walnuts in the groves north of Los Angeles in the San Fernando Valley and east around Puente were very largely Mexican families. If the groves were small, the owner hired one or two families for the season; if they were large, a Mexican labor contractor was usually used as intermediary to collect a sufficiently large group of pickers. Some growers of cotton, grapes, hops, and potatoes used labor contractors, although the majority of those visited did not. Less than one-third of the cotton growers visited in Kern County used any system which by the loosest definition could be described as labor contracting, and interviews with well-informed local authorities suggested that the proportion for the area as a whole may have been considerably lower.[8] Of the 45 grape growers interviewed in the Bakersfield and Fresno areas, only one-third used labor contractors, and the pattern of their contracting systems varied widely. The harvesting hands working under labor contractors were chiefly Filipinos and Mexicans, the former principally in the very large vineyards. The Japanese used to be the grape pickers of this area, but only a few groups remained. The Hopgrowers' Association reported that labor contractors disappeared with the orientals, who used to constitute an important element in the labor supply; one of the two growers interviewed reported that some of his labor was supplied by contractors. The great majority of potato growers interviewed in the area around Bakersfield hired their men directly; but there was a parallel system of temporary field bosses who brought their own crews—labor contractors in that they acted as intermediary in the hiring of workers but differing from most contractors in that they appar-

[7] Information about hiring in strawberries and tomatoes came exclusively from growers' associations; no farmers were visited. Therefore it is difficult to determine the proportion of contractors used.

[8] It may be significant that the term "labor contractor" was practically never used in this district, even for obvious examples of the practice, and carried considerable approbrium, whereas around Sacramento the term was used even for year-round foremen.

ently were paid nothing by either employer or worker for their services as employment agent. In deciduous fruits and nuts, other than prunes and walnuts, and in citrus practically no examples of the contractor system were found. It cannot be too strongly emphasized that these conclusions apply only to areas visited, and that other regions of California might use labor contractors to a greater or less extent for identical crops. For example, another investigator reported labor contractors to be universal in cherry picking in the Stockton area.[9] It must also be remembered that there were other crops—notably lettuce and melons—not included in our sample, in which contractors were very widely or exclusively used.

The use of labor contractors was a function not only of the crop but also of the particular operation and of the type of labor employed. In general, the contracting system was economically desirable only when a large number of laborers were to be employed and consequently was primarily used in harvesting. However, it was also used for thinning and hoeing sugar beets, which required a large labor force, and sometimes for pruning deciduous fruits and grapes. In the latter case, the problem was one of obtaining a gang of highly skilled men for a brief period, which was solved by a contractor who moved one or more gangs from ranch to ranch throughout the locality in which he operated. In fruit- and grape-packing operations, whether conducted on the ranch under the grower's direction or in a central plant, little contracting was found, nor was there any use of labor contractors in canning.

The size of ranch might also be a factor in the use of a labor contractor as the employing agent, but investigations produced no conclusive evidence in this respect. The thesis advanced by certain of the better-informed growers was that the smallest farmers could not afford to pay for the supervisory functions usually exercised by a labor contractor but must act as their

[9] Louis Adamic, "Cherries Are Red in the San Joaquin," *The Nation*, CXLII (June 27, 1936), pp. 840–841.

own foremen and hence hired direct. The very large ranches, on the other hand, did not need labor contractors because they had a permanent staff of resident foremen to do both hiring and supervision, and because their prominence in the community and the diversity of their crops ensured a supply of direct applications. It was the growers on moderate-sized ranches who could afford to delegate their responsibilities for assembling a labor force, and who found the temporary services of a contractor economically profitable. Because of the multiplicity of factors involved—locality, crop, operation, race of laborers—in addition to size of farm, it was impossible in this study to obtain a large enough sample to isolate the effect of size of holding on use of labor contractors. Of the farmers visited, the proportion of large and small holdings was much the same among those who used labor contractors and those who did not, but the data were not conclusive. However, it seemed clear that absentee land companies, such as were common in pea growing, and the practice of selling crops to shipping companies before harvesting encouraged the use of an intermediary both to provide a harvest crew and to supervise harvesting operations.

TYPES OF LABOR CONTRACTORS

The diversity of labor contractors and their arrangements has already been mentioned. A description of some of the principal types may indicate their importance as a placement factor in the labor market. It should be noted that the type of contractor tended to vary with the crop and with the race of the farm laborers.

The "Entrepreneur."—Labor contractors of the classic entrepreneur type flourished in the pea harvest in California. The contractor signed a written agreement[10] to harvest specified fields at a specified price per hamper picked and took full re-

[10] For examples of contracts, see *Hearings before the Select Committee to Investigate the Interstate Migration of Destitute Citizens, House of Representatives,* 76th Cong., 3d sess., Part 6, San Francisco Hearings, pp. 2220–2223.

sponsibility for overseeing the harvesting; they set up camps and brought in workers who were, in fact as well as in legal fiction, their own employees, not the grower's. There might be an advance understanding between grower and contractor on the rate of wages to be paid, but the final decision rested with the contractor. In fact, the alleged cause of the 1938 Clarksburg pea strike was that one contractor cut wages. Contractors of this type were not paid directly for their services as intermediary by either the workers or the employers. Their gross income was the difference between the rate per hamper paid to them by the employer under the terms of the harvesting contract and the rate they paid the pickers per hamper. Like most agricultural wages, both these rates were fairly well standardized each season in each community, but there was always room for individual bargaining. In Santa Maria, one of the principal early pea districts of California, the contractors were getting about 30 cents a hamper in 1938 and paying the pickers 25 cents;[11] thus the contractor took one-sixth of the total wage bill. From this he had to pay any expenses incidental to the maintenance of the camp, the salary of the camp boss, and any expenses entailed in harvesting and its supervision. If workmen's compensation insurance was carried, the contractor also paid these premiums. Rumor assigned an additional expense to contractors dealing with representatives of the large farming companies, saying that there was so much competition for the large acreages that the contractor must offer a substantial "kickback" to get the contract. Concrete evidence of this sort of thing is always impossible to obtain. These contractors set up camps for their crews, usually open to all migratory farm laborers, which provided free ground space and water. Many of them were migratory, moving alone or with a skeleton crew through a circuit that followed the progressively ripening pea crops

[11] Pea pickers and often cotton pickers were paid in tickets, punched with the amount earned, which were redeemable weekly in cash. Local grocery stores accepted these tickets—sometimes apparently at a discount.

from the Southwest to the Imperial Valley, north through California to Idaho, and back to New Mexico again. Of the transient contractors, some worked only in peas; some combined summer peas with cotton in the winter in Arizona. There was also a group of resident contractors who worked in the peas during the season, perhaps followed them north a little way, and the rest of the year worked as small farmers, laborers, or foremen in the other local crops.

The foregoing description of the entrepreneur type of contractor applies to those engaged in pea picking, because this was the only crop covered in the sample in which the type was dominant. It appears also to have been the prevalent system in melons, lettuce, and other field crops not included in this survey. The only other example of the entrepreneur contractor appeared in Los Angeles in walnuts. Here some of the Mexican contractors were true entrepreneurs in the sense that they were paid a fixed sum by weight or sack for the whole harvesting operation, gathered a crew, and made the wage bargain with them, paying them from the sums advanced by the grower. In such cases the growers were insistent that the harvest hands, also Mexicans, were employees of the contractor and not of the farmer himself.

The Boarding House Keeper.—Another type of contractor was completely responsible for getting and keeping a crew and for supervising their work, but they were in no sense his employees. His gains were from board and lodging furnished the crews. This system flourished especially in the sugar beet areas around Sacramento. The typical labor contractor in sugar beets was a Mexican, who usually worked for only one employer and frequently lived on his place the year round. The crews were single men,[12] predominantly Mexican, who were boarded by the contractor at a standard rate of $1.10 a day to cover the costs of

[12] The men were not necessarily unmarried but were at least temporarily detached from their families, because family labor was not used in beets in this locality, and families were not permitted in the contractors' camps.

food alone, since the grower provided housing, fuel, and equipment without charge.[13] In addition to operating the cook house, the contractor secured and maintained throughout the season an adequate labor force (the latter an important function in beet harvesting, with its high turnover), exercised the usual supervisory functions of a field foreman, timekeeper, and paymaster, and usually provided transportation.[14] For these services the contractor received 50 cents an acre "bonus" from the grower and whatever profit he could make on boarding the men; estimates of the latter by employers varied from 30 per cent to a net loss. He might also make a profit from the sale of liquor, operation of gambling games, etc., if the grower countenanced it. In former years the men paid the contractor 50 cents an acre—in addition to the grower's bonus—as the price of the job, but under the new Sugar Beet Act the wage rate promulgated by the Secretary of Agriculture must be paid in full to each man individually, obviating or very greatly reducing the possibility of a "kickback" and also making it impossible for the contractor to operate as an entrepreneur, making his own wage bargain with the workers. Nevertheless, half the beet acreage of this area was cultivated and harvested under written labor contracts which implied that the contractor was a wholly independent operator, doing certain jobs for the farmer at a fixed rate per acre[15] and placing no restrictions on the contractor's bargain

[13] Only one contractor was found in the areas visited who owned his own camp on his own land. Local growers paid him, apparently, a camp fee for providing housing.

[14] Transportation to and from the fields if necessary, transportation of new workers from town to the camp, and transportation of the whole crew into Sacramento for week ends. The latter was a picturesque feature of the local system. Traditionally, all labor contractors took their gangs into Sacramento Saturday for a big week-end drunk, returning Sunday night to round them up from saloons and gutters. If their own men could not be found, they loaded into the truck any that were handy, and a worker might sober up on Monday to find himself in a strange camp 50 miles from his last job—or so the story was told. Incidentally, reputable growers quoted this service as one of their prime reasons for employing a contractor.

[15] In 1938 this rate was universally set at the government wage scale plus a bonus of 50 cents per acre.

with the actual laborers. The arrangements to pay workers the full government wage were verbal. In practice, the beet contractor in this region appeared to be changing into a foreman attached to a single farm, paid only when he was working and receiving a large share of his income not from his employer but from the concession for boarding the workers.

This type of contractor appeared only occasionally in other crops. In tomatoes, in the areas visited, a few of the contractors provided camps for the pickers, who were principally Filipinos and Mexicans. A contractor with a camp would work for a number of small growers; he was paid by the box, paying the workers in turn. However, the laborers' piece rate was fixed by the grower. No information was available on whether the contractor charged the workers anything other than board and lodging. Three large vineyards near Bakersfield used Filipino (and, in one case, also Mexican) "camp" or "crew bosses," who did all the hiring of workers of their own nationality.[16]

In addition to procuring, replacing, and boarding the workers, the contractors on these ranches acted as foremen. For these functions one ranch paid the contractor $100 a month plus gasoline; another paid him 5 cents an hour above the workers' wage. It was impossible to determine what, if anything, the camp bosses got from the workers in addition to the profit on boarding them. These were the only examples of this type of contractor among the grape growers visited.

Those Who Charge Fees to Workers.—Certain contractors charged the men a fee for the privilege of working in their gang, a payment for the contractors' activities in finding jobs. This was perhaps most common in grape picking, where certain of the growers expected and assisted the contractors, usually Mexican, to collect a payment from the workers, most commonly 5 per cent. These contractors in grapes provided no housing or

[16] It is notable that on one of these ranches one-third of the pickers were white, and that these whites were hired directly by the ranch foreman and boarded by the ranch, not by the camp bosses.

board and did not always act as foremen on the job. They were usually paid a bonus for getting and keeping a crew. Two Mexican contractors operating in the grape harvest were visited near Fresno. One was a tenant farmer who allowed itinerant Mexican fruit workers to camp on his place, used them himself as needed, and sent them out in gangs to neighbors who applied to him or hunted up jobs for them if necessary. The employers paid this man, who paid the workers and expected them "to pay me something for my trouble and expense in finding them work." Sometimes the employers also paid him a bonus. He insisted, incidentally, that he was not a labor contractor, just a friend to his white neighbors and his itinerant fellow countrymen. The other, frankly a labor contractor, operated in much the same fashion, taking 5 per cent of wages in addition to a cash bonus from the employer. He did not usually act as foreman.

It was extremely difficult to determine the extent to which contractors in other crops charged the workers a fee. In beets, as already described, the system had been abolished. The employers interviewed usually expressed complete ignorance about the financial arrangements between the contractor and his gang or assured the investigators that "Joe doesn't make anything out of the boys." However, it appeared that a fee from the workers was not the dominant pattern outside of the Fresno grape area.

Those Who Charge Fees to Employers.—The grower sometimes paid the contractor directly for his services as a labor agent. The beet contractors got 50 cents an acre. Some of the contractors in grapes received a cash bonus. A few asparagus growers paid a similar bonus. The hop grower who used contractors paid them a percentage of the wage bill. Occasionally strawberry growers paid the contractor for furnishing a crew. More frequently the payment received was for services both as working foreman and as labor agent, and the proportion for each function was indistinguishable.

The "Foreman."—In many cases the labor contractor appeared to receive no payment beyond his wage as foreman. He made up a gang of laborers in exchange for the job of supervising their work. Of course, there may have been a "kickback" from the workers which was not uncovered in some of these arrangements, but in many instances the worker apparently was not required to pay for his job. This was especially true in potatoes and cotton. Each cotton acreage at picking time had a "weigh boss" who acted as field foreman, hiring and supervising pickers, weighing the cotton each worker had picked and issuing him a ticket or keeping a record of his production, and sometimes trucking the cotton to the gin. The weigh boss might be the grower or a member of his family, a permanent foreman on time or piece rates, or a temporary employee. The latter were, on the whole, a type very different from the contractors in asparagus or sugar beets. The majority were permanent residents of the community—small farmers who had some free time in cotton-picking season to work on larger ranches, resident Mexicans or Negroes who worked in other crops or occupations the rest of the year, or "foremen" of neighboring ranches, paid only when they worked, who were at liberty to hire themselves and their crew to other employers between pickings on the home ranch. A very few were regular transients, moving about the country from crop to crop with or without their crew. It was extremely difficult to determine which men who worked in the cotton fields should be considered labor contractors and which should not, because the pickers were not commonly considered in either fact or legal fiction to be the employees of the weigh boss rather than of the grower. The weigh boss was usually paid 10 cents for each 100 pounds weighed. Sometimes he was given a single check from which to pay the workers. Sometimes they were given a "ticket" from an adding machine each time they weighed in a sackful of cotton, tickets which were redeemable either at the ranch headquarters or at local stores. On the larger ranches the timekeeper's office might pay each picker directly. There were no contractors' camps, and only one example of a food-and-drink concession in the field was reported, though there may have been others. All the weigh bosses interviewed denied indignantly that any charge was made to the workers for placing them on their cotton-picking crews, and the growers who were questioned confirmed this. Those growers and gin managers who were opposed to the system said that weigh bosses "chiseled" the workers by short-weighting the cotton picked, but not that they charged fees or split earnings. For the majority of cases it seems safe to say that the weigh boss made little or nothing from acting as employment agent beyond ensuring himself employment at a foreman's wages.

In potato picking there were a few field bosses who made up their own crews. These "contractors" were paid an hourly rate as foremen considerably higher than that paid to the workers, but both rates were fixed by the grower. Such a system was very difficult to distinguish from temporary foremen. Four men of this type were interviewed. One was a Negro who formerly acted as field foreman of crews from the local Negro settlement. Another was the head of a gang of resident Mexicans which stayed together as a unit throughout the year and worked in a number of crops in the locality, including cotton and potatoes. Another was a small farmer who used to get a crew together and contract to harvest other men's potatoes, getting 60 cents an hour himself for "bossing" and providing some of the necessary machinery; the workers were paid 30 cents. He had given up this type of contracting because the 60 cents an hour did not cover his costs. He was genuinely indignant at the thought that he might have made a penny from the workers. The county farm advisor spoke of this type of small-farmer contractor as quite common in potatoes. The fourth field foreman was a member of the staff of a small-town paper except for the two months a year when he made up a crew of about 25 local men, white and Mexican, to harvest potatoes under unwritten contracts with growers under which he acted as foreman and timekeeper but in no sense as entrepreneur. He used to contract for harvesting, planting, pruning, etc., in all the local crops except cotton and kept busy practically the year round; but nowadays, he said, the "farmers" can't afford a foreman, which is what such a contractor amounts to, and the large-scale ranches have their own gangs. One large-scale potato grower had a field boss who was a Russian woman from a nearby town, and who usually brought at least the nucleus of a crew from among her countrymen there; she kept the workers' time and acted as paymaster but made no profit from them.

In tomatoes the most common type of "contractor" was a year-round employee, paid a higher rate than the workers, whose job it was to collect a crew. The difference between these men and an ordinary foreman was not clear from the available information. In walnuts the contractor who was not an "entrepreneur" was paid a fixed sum per sack on the whole picking for exercising the functions of a foreman and for getting together a crew; or for the same work he was paid a higher rate per sack than the other workers; or in other cases he was practically indistinguishable from a working foreman of a different racial group than the grower, who might or might not "chisel" the workers under him. One prune grower described a Japanese "contractor," permanently resident on a large ranch, who was responsible for getting and keeping a crew. This man fulfilled all the supervisory functions of a foreman, for which he was paid 30 cents a ton.

The Headman of a Coöperative Group.—This type of contractor, the original form, had almost completely disappeared except among the Filipinos. There were some discrepancies in accounts of Filipino gangs, but most informants agreed that all gains were shared equally, that their commissaries were run on a communal basis, and that the "foreman" was only the member of the gang who acted as spokesman. This system prevailed in all crops in which Filipinos were employed.[17] It is noteworthy, however, that one large farming corporation growing asparagus, which described the contractor-laborer relationship as a purely coöperative affair in which all shared equally, required all workers to sign a contract specifying that they were employees of the labor contractor and that the owner was therefore released from responsibility for payment of wages. The functions of these Filipino "contractors" were to make the wage contract with the employer, to act as paymaster, to get and keep an adequate supply of workers, and usually to act as straw boss. Reports varied as to what the contractor made. The majority of employers insisted that the contractors received no more than the share of other workers in the group, although some paid him a bonus for his services. Commissary arrangements appeared to be largely coöperative rather than run at a profit by the contractor as in other crops. At least with the large growers, contractors worked for only one employer a season and returned to the same place year after year.

A similar system occasionally appeared among the Mexicans. Some of the prune growers interviewed described a "contracting" system whereby Mexican or white families or "traveling companions" agreed to harvest the whole acreage at a fixed price per ton, dividing the proceeds among themselves.

SOURCE OF THE CONTRACTORS' LABOR SUPPLY

The principal reason for using a labor contractor was his ability to find workers more readily than the farmer could do. As many growers described it, "he just brings along his relatives

[17] Interviews with a leading member of the Filipino community and with storekeepers in a Delta town suggested that some Filipinos might be placed directly with the growers through the intermediary of the local grocers, but this was apparently not customary.

and friends or picks up families that he knows." The migratory contractors sometimes carried a nucleus crew along with them; both migratories and residents could expect a large proportion of the men who had worked for them before to return year after year. When the contractor was of the same racial group as his workers, he had a special knowledge of local individuals who might be seeking work, or the "hang-outs" where Mexican or Filipino laborers congregated. The beet contractors around Sacramento filled up their crews by driving into town and picking up men from the sidewalks and saloons of the "Skidway." The mere existence of a contractor's camp attracted passing job seekers, particularly if, like the pea camps, it was open to all comers. The beet contractors, who remained on one ranch the year round, had a residuum of men who stayed in camp all winter doing odd jobs or being boarded on credit. If these resources failed, the contractor, like the farmer, could fill up his crew from chance applicants who came to the fields seeking work. Only one or two kept a formal list of applications to draw upon. A very few walnut growers said that their contractors occasionally applied to the relief authorities for lists of families and for pressure upon them to take the work. In this connection it should be noted that walnut growers were almost unique in a year of overabundant labor supply in complaining of a labor shortage which they attributed to the relief program. A great deal has been said in public print about handbills and newspaper advertisements for unneeded workers by both contractors and employers. The one authenticated example found in the course of this study was Louis Mort, a state-licensed labor contractor operating in a number of states and crops, who believed himself to have a verbal contract with one of the large companies to pick 700 acres of peas near Santa Maria. He distributed handbills which read, "800 pea pickers wanted about 20 miles west of Santa Maria, California—good camp, good water and store—busy all season—will start about February 25 or March 1," to workers in his winter cotton-picking camp in Arizona and to others in the vicinity and had some people "sign up" in a book. The contract fell through, and large numbers of workers arriving in Santa Maria in response to this solicitation found no work in prospect.[18] Incidentally, some of the other contractors obtained workers indirectly through Mort's advertisements because the families who came in answer to them drifted into the other camps.

The typical labor contractor got his crews together without reference to any type of employment agency. Opponents of the contractor system, particularly among agricultural union organizers, insisted that contractors had a tie-up with fee-charging agencies in town, split fees with them, and so forth. But no evidence to support this allegation was discovered, and the whole picture seen in the course of this investigation suggested that it was untrue, at least within the bounds of the state. This investigation indicated that contractors practically never applied to fee-charging agencies for workers and certainly not often enough to warrant setting up a system of fee splitting. The fee agencies that recruited beet workers in California for other states might possibly have had some reciprocal arrangement with the contractors which was not uncovered. The reciprocal arrangements between contractors and the State Employment Service in Santa Maria have been described.[19] Here the collaboration was purely on paper; the contractor did not actually obtain any applicants from the Employment Service. In Sacramento the agricultural office of the State Employment Service said it was as willing to supply crews to contractors as to farmers, but it was impossible to obtain an estimate of how frequently contractors gave the office orders for men. The S.R.A. office in Los Angeles felt very strongly about abuses practised by labor contractors and would not send men to a job if it was

[18] The proceedings against Mort for misrepresentation of labor opportunities is discussed in a subsequent section. Cf. pages 335–336.

[19] Cf. page 149.

known that they would have to work under a contractor. The Labor Coördinating Bureau of Los Angeles County was the only agency visited which not only would supply workers to farm labor contractors but actually solicited their business. This was in line with their general policy toward agricultural labor, largely Mexican in the districts where the agency operated, which was accepted for placement by the agency only in order to reduce the county relief rolls.

EVALUATION OF THE SYSTEM

Abuses.—The labor contractor system is not only closely tied to the alien races who have traditionally formed a large part of California's migratory labor, but it has also at times brought them the benefits of living and working together as a group under a competent spokesman. There is no doubt that coöperative and paternalistic attitudes still prevail to an indeterminable extent, but it is equally true that exploitation of farm workers by labor contractors of their own nationality has increased in the last 20 years. Complaints from agricultural workers to government authorities of nonpayment of wages and other abuses by contractors have increased,[20] and the grievances of strikers in crops where contractors operate have usually included a demand for the abolition or regulation of contractors. In 1927 the State Commission of Immigration and Housing reported that the number of complaints by Chinese, Japanese, and Filipinos against agricultural labor contractors had notably increased.[21] Testimony before the Committee on Labor, House of Representatives, on agricultural strikes of 1933 was that "at the end of every harvest season the [Deputy Labor Commissioner's] office [in Imperial Valley] is deluged with

[20] Complaints of nonpayment of wages to the Labor Commissioner are not so classified as to indicate which apply to farm labor contractors and which to industry, so that the evidence which can be cited is indicative rather than conclusive.

[21] California State Commission of Immigration and Housing, *Annual Report, January 1927* (Sacramento: California State Printing Office, 1927), p. 11.

complaints by both shed and field workers having to do with the chiseling of bonuses[22] to which they were properly entitled. From May to August 90 per cent of the claims filed in [this] office involved charges of chiseling by labor contractors."[23] The same hearing found that demand for abolition of the contract system was the third most important demand in agricultural strikes in 1933. In 1928 there was a serious strike of Mexican cantaloupe pickers in the Imperial Valley, where the labor contractor system was universally used, which resulted in the adoption of a standard picking agreement drawn up by a committee of growers specifying that "the grower, *not the contractor,* shall assume full responsibility for the payment of all wages."[24] The report of the official investigator of a strike in the same area six years later indicated that the contractor system was still in force and that the proposed remedy had not been widely adopted. Another strike in 1934, of Filipino and Mexican vegetable workers in the Santa Maria Valley, demanded—unsuccessfully—the abolition of the contractor system in certain operations and its regulation in others.

One of the basic flaws of the system, of which employers as well as workers and public authorities had become increasingly conscious, was that it attempted to shift responsibility for wages, workmen's compensation, and housing from the farmer to a financially and socially irresponsible individual, usually a transient with no stake in the community. Although failure to meet these responsibilities might lead to complaints to the Labor Commissioner, the workers usually had no recourse if the contractor had no property and had left the jurisdiction.

[22] This refers to a system of payment whereby part of the wages are retained until the end of the season and then paid as a "bonus" to ensure that the labor force will stay to complete the harvest.

[23] *Labor Disputes Act, Hearings before the Committee on Labor, House of Representatives,* 74th Cong., 1st sess. on H. R. 6288. March 13–Apr. 4, 1935. (Washington: Government Printing Office, 1935), p. 50.

[24] *Mexicans in California,* Report of Governor C. C. Young's Mexican Fact-Finding Committee (San Francisco: California State Printing Office, Oct. 1930), p. 149.

> Lester [the Deputy Commissioner] this week filed a complaint in the Westmorland justice court against S. Tokuda on an NSF check charge. Issuing his field workers a $50 check when he had $25 in the bank was accompanied by the refusal of Tokuda to pay the 13-cent rate for cantaloupe picking for which he contracted, saying, "12 is enough," pickers said.
>
> Lester announced he is investigating another case, involving a Japanese grower who hired a Japanese contractor for packing work and paid only 2½ cents for lidding, rather than the 3 cents agreed in the contract. The grower claims he can waive liability as the labor contractor has left the country, but Lester says he might file proceedings holding him civilly liable for loss suffered by workers if a labor contractor without license or bond is used.
>
> Lester says he has notified one Philibos, a labor contractor operating near Heber, to pay up $50 alleged due by workers by June 16 or face prosecution. In this case the contractor agreed to pay 13 cents a crate, and then made a 2-cent bonus holdout on grounds that the pickers had gathered too many green melons, although the pickers aver that the contractor didn't think of the green melon story until after his contract was complete. If Philibos does not make good, misdemeanor charges as well as civil action on failure to keep his contract will be filed, Lester states.[25]

The older employer-attitude was typified by the head of one growers' organization who declared that the wage rate paid by contractors was of no concern to the grower, and that if the contractor left town with the payroll the grower was not the legal employer and therefore was not responsible. The agricultural sections of the State Chamber of Commerce had come to realize the social undesirability of such a situation and proposed in 1936 and 1937 that "the State Chamber through its Regional Councils arouse public opinion to correct abuses practiced by farm labor contractors who defraud their workers of large sums of money through false promises to pay workers when crops are harvested,"[26] and that "the activities of labor contractors who defraud laborers of their wages should be controlled

[25] *Imperial Valley Democrat* (Brawley, California), June 24, 1934.

[26] "State Chamber Makes Plans," *Pacific Rural Press* (San Francisco), Nov. 28, 1936.

through licensing and bonding."[27] The latter suggestion is typical of plans offered in recent years.

If the workers could be proved to be employees of the contractor and not of the grower, only the former was responsible for carrying workmen's compensation; and again, it was difficult or impossible for the workers to collect from the contractor.

The housing situation was best summarized by a report of the State Commission of Immigration and Housing, which still held good in 1938: "Another problem with which the Commission has had to deal is the method of employment frequently used by operators who are developing large tracts of land for growing intensive crops, such as melons, peas, lettuce, and tomatoes. Many of this class aim to shift the responsibility of operating the labor camps to a contractor. . . . This contractor is usually a Mexican or Filipino . . . whose finances are probably no greater than those of the laborers he employs. . . . This Mexican or Filipino contractor lets the inevitable happen, and that is—the persons he employs must either provide their own housing or take up their residences in any abandoned shack that may be handy. In many instances improvised habitations are built of burlap, boxes, brush, packing cases, tin cans, cartons or whatever may be available on the location. . . . The Commission's agents during the year have encountered many of that class of camp, and it has been necessary to prosecute the contractor to bring about the desired results. By this method of procedure the employer who is using the contractor as a shield has to produce the money to make the improvements or lose his labor supply, because of the contractor's financial inability to do so."[28]

These criticisms applied when the contractor was of the entrepreneur type and might be considered the direct employer.

[27] Statement of Chairman of state-wide agricultural committee of the California State Chamber of Commerce, *San Jose Mercury Herald* (California), Feb. 21, 1937.

[28] California State Commission of Immigration and Housing, *Annual Report, January 1927*, p. 19.

Possibilities of "chiseling" the workers—making them pay for their jobs directly and openly, through concealed taxes, or by fraud—were present in every form of the contracting system.

The contractor sometimes charged the workers a direct fee for their jobs, comparable to the practice of private employment agencies and recognized by common practice, such as the 50 cents an acre paid by beet workers to the contractor before the passage of the Sugar Beet Act or the 5 per cent of earnings commonly turned over to the contractor by grape pickers. In the crops and areas studied, such a uniform recognized fee was the exception rather than the rule.

Charges for board furnished by the contractor, notably in the sugar beet area and on some of the large grape ranches, often furnished the major part of his income. Such charges were usually uniform throughout the district ($1.10 a day in 1938), but there was a wide difference of opinion on the contractor's profit from this undertaking, and probably profits differed widely with the contractor's managerial ability and with the quality of food served. One employer offered fairly conclusive proof that his contractor had been running into debt for the past two years; another estimated that his contractor cleared around 30 per cent of the gross payments for board. Labor organizations, social workers, and some farmers who grew crops other than sugar beets insisted that the board rates for beet workers were far above normal. Possibly an indication of the lack of relation between charges and costs was the widespread opinion that contractors could get around the Sugar Beet Act by raising their board rates to cover the 50 cents per acre formerly paid them by the workers. Whatever the profits, the system obviously was open to abuse because the contractor who furnished board had a monopoly; workers must stay in his camp to get a job instead of camping and cooking with their families or in groups. The extreme view of the evils of this arrangement was presented by a labor paper: "The United Cannery, Agricultural, Packing and Allied Workers of America, Local 33, charges that a state of peonage exists in the majority of the beet camps in the Sacramento Valley. We have found that irresponsible beet contractors are charging board rates that are excessive for food that is of the lowest quality. They are permitted to sell beer and wine in the camps, and are encouraged in this to force the workers to be in direct obligation to the contractor, due to debts. After the work is over, and they must wait a few days until the beets are ready to be gone over again, they are told that, unless they stay in the camp while laid off, they will be fired. This increases their burden of debt. There have been cases where workers have stayed in camp while working on and off, and after eight months have owed the contractor money."[29]

Where the contractor ran not a boarding house but a store or "commissary" in the camp, there were equal accusations of overcharging and probably equal variations according to the ability and disposition of the contractor. In Santa Maria, for example, a lawyer told a contractor client to stop running a commissary when he found that workers "got charged 65 cents for 25 cents' worth of groceries." But the official who investigated another contractor's camp found that he was buying groceries wholesale and selling them for less than the local retail prices.

The situation of the beet worker given credit by the contractor between seasons was somewhat too forcibly described by the United Cannery, Agricultural, Packing and Allied Workers of America as "peonage," but there is no doubt of the opportunities open to an unscrupulous man who makes the loans and keeps the books, when dealing with illiterate workers who can get jobs only through him. In camps with a commissary but no board there were frequent charges of usury on a small scale. In Santa Maria, for example, it was generally believed that one

[29] Quoted in *Oakland Labor Herald* (California), July 7, 1938.

of the large-scale contractors was making loans or extending commissary credit to stranded pea pickers at 5 per cent a week, taking parts of their cars as security. The camp manager, interviewed by a state official, claimed that the interest rate was 25 cents on each $10 for the duration of the loan, which could never be more than a few weeks.

Other alleged types of "chiseling," less common, included gambling games, liquor sales, and prostitutes in the camp, charges for transportation, deductions for timekeepers and leaders, and short-weighting of cotton pickers by the weigh boss. Another loss suffered by workers, although not to the benefit of the contractor, was discounting by local grocery stores of tickets paid them in lieu of wages.

In addition to the disadvantages inherent in shifting the grower's responsibility as an employer to an irresponsible contractor and the possibility of "chiseling" open to unscrupulous contractors, the system involved a further social disadvantage in that it encouraged the importation of an oversupply of labor. Where the contractor had a camp for families in the sense of free camping space, it was generally open to every comer; "The workers just come into camp and light," to quote one grower who was worried by the oversupply of labor in his community. The very existence of the camps encouraged passing migrants or those who heard of them from a distance to come in and settle down in the hope of picking up a few days' work. The most conspicuous recent case of a labor contractor importing an oversupply of labor was that of Louis Mort, already described, who distributed handbills promising work in the peas that proved to be nonexistent and left hundreds of pickers stranded in Santa Maria in the spring of 1938. In 1937 Santa Maria faced a similar situation when a contractor wrote a number of pea pickers whom he knew, promising them jobs on a given date, and also brought along his regular following of families who worked the California-Oregon-Idaho circuit with him. Rain spoiled so much of the crop that only the regular followers could find work, and the others were thrown on the local charities. Two hundred and fifty families gathered in two contractors' camps where living conditions were very bad, and the earnings of most of the "employables" were less than $1 a week. "It was because of the actions of these contractors in bringing in, or encouraging more families to come in, to this county without the assurance that work was available for all that our community agencies became aroused and made a study of camp conditions through a committee appointed by the County Council of Social Agencies. As a result of this investigation, they formulated an ordinance to be presented to our Board of County Supervisors, setting up certain standards and requirements for labor camps in Santa Barbara County."[30] In the preceding examples the labor contractors were guilty of bad judgment or irresponsibility rather than deliberate misconduct, but when the contractor was boarding the men there was a temptation to the unscrupulous to hire more than were needed and to work them on broken time in order to increase the total board bill. At the sugar beet hearings in Sacramento in the summer of 1938 the United Cannery, Agricultural, Packing and Allied Workers of America claimed that many labor contractors engaged twice as many men as were necessary, worked them only half a day, and charged them full board. Another local of the same union, near Bakersfield, reported that the contractors on one of the largest vineyards hired two full Filipino crews and worked each of them only three days a week, charging them 75 cents a day board, so that at the end of the season they had to pool their resources to buy enough gasoline to move on.

At its worst, these were the disadvantages of an unpoliced system of labor contracting to the workers who must find work through contractors and hence, of course, to the community. It

[30] Letter from an official of the State Relief Administration of Santa Barbara County, April 8, 1938. The ordinance mentioned is discussed in a subsequent section.

was, unfortunately, completely impossible to determine the extent of such abuses in the course of this study. The unscrupulous and irresponsible labor contractor might be the common type or he might be the exception. The significant feature of the system was that there was little or no control by employers or governmental agencies over its exploitative possibilities.

Attempts to Regulate the Contractor System.[31]—The only attempt to regulate labor contractors as such by state law in California is their inclusion in the statute requiring licenses for employment agencies.[32] This statute was designed to fit the usual type of employment agency with a fixed office, which takes employers' orders and workers' registrations, dispatches workers to a job, and has no further contact with them or their employers after fees are collected. In 1929 "an amendment to the private employment agency act [was passed] to extend the provisions of the law to farm labor agents in order to safeguard the wages of farm laborers."[33] The law, designed to protect job seekers against extortion, was not a good instrument to protect employed workers against a contractor who absconded with the payroll nor were its provisions applicable to a peripatetic contractor's method of operation. For example, the law[34] provides that the location of an employment agency shall not be changed without the written consent of the Labor Commissioner; that the premises occupied by the agency shall meet certain requirements;

[31] The House Committee investigating the Migration of Destitute Citizens concluded that federal legislation to regulate labor contractors was imperative, because state legislation was necessarily inadequate. *The Need for Federal Regulation of Private Employment Agencies and Labor Contractors Engaged in Interstate Commerce*, Statement by Hon. John H. Tolan, Chairman, Select Committee Investigating National Defense Migration, House of Representatives, 77th Cong., 1st sess., Aug. 11, 1941 (Washington: Government Printing Office, 1941), pp. 1–2.

[32] Insofar as the contractor is legally an employer, he is, of course, subject to the whole state labor code—for example, the laws regulating payment of wages and workmen's compensation.

[33] California Department of Industrial Relations, *First Biennial Report, 1927–1930*, p. 57.

[34] Cal. Stats. (1937), ch. 90, pt. 6. The sections of the Employment Agency Law which relate to labor contractors were amended in 1939. For a brief statement as to the effect of these amendments see footnote 38, pages 335.

that the schedule of fees charged and a copy of the Employment Agency Law shall be posted in a conspicuous place in every room; that each applicant from whom a fees is collected shall be furnished with an elaborate receipt of standard form; that books shall be kept in a specified fashion; and that detailed reports of placements made and fees received shall be made as the Labor Commissioner prescribes. These provisions had not been enforced in recent years for any employment agency. The only action taken by the Labor Commissioner's office, the enforcement agency, had been in response to complaints, usually of refusal to refund fees.[35] In none of the Deputy Commissioners' offices visited was there any record of a complaint against a labor contractor for violation of the Employment Agency Act, although there were numbers of complaints against them for nonpayment of wages under other sections of the Labor Code. The net result of the unsuitability of the law and the absence of enforcement was that only a small fraction of the labor contractors in California were licensed, and that the licensing even of this group was an empty formality. Of all the labor contractors who were interviewed or mentioned by employers, or whose names appeared on the lists furnished by local informants, only four, all operating in Santa Barbara County,[36] were licensed. As one employer put it, "not one in a hundred is bonded." About 60 licenses were issued to labor contractors in 1937–38. With the exception of the four mentioned above, none of them could be located, which was scarcely surprising since the record cards contained usually nothing but a surname, often a common Mexican one such as Garcia, and the name of the small town from which the application was sent in March or

[35] In justice to the Labor Commissioner's office it should be pointed out that the staff of deputies was too small to enforce the body of law under their care.

[36] This county's local licensing ordinance would presumably encourage contractors to obtain state licenses as well. It is interesting to note that the officials interviewed in this county insisted that no contractor operating without a license could escape detection and penalties, in contrast to the situation found elsewhere.

April[37] and to which the itinerant contractor would not return until the next spring. The official then in charge of employment agencies in the Division of Labor Statistics and Law Enforcement pointed out that contractors sent applications from the smallest possible towns because the license fee and bond required varied with size of the town and said that she never required any report from contractors on their activities because they were illiterate, and, besides, the reporting form used for other agencies was not suitable for them. Apparently applications for licenses were never refused and never investigated. In brief, the net result of the state law to license labor contractors as employment agents had been that only an insignificant number applied for licenses and that the licensing authority's contact with the licensees ended when the fee of $10 was paid and the small bond posted.[38]

An example of how existing state legislation may be, but seldom is, used to keep labor contractors in line is the Mort case already referred to. Mort distributed handbills in Arizona urging pea pickers to come to Santa Maria on promise of work, in the belief that he had a verbal contract with one of the large companies to pick 700 acres. The County Agricultural Commissioner complained to the State Labor Commissioner's office, which held a hearing to determine whether Mort, who was licensed under the Employment Agency Act, had violated the terms of his license and whether he had violated that section of the Labor Code which forbids solicitation of employees by mis-

[37] The licensing year begins April 1.

[38] In the 1939 Legislature the employment agency section of the Labor Code was amended to include labor contractors more specifically than before. The new provisions have not yet been tested, but the ambiguity of the wording suggests that, if the contractor is officially the employer rather than the supplier of the workers, he may escape its provisions.

Another bill introduced into the 1939 Legislature, which was not passed, proposed to amend the section of the Labor Code dealing with payment of wages so that no labor contractor, defined in very broad terms to include all but coöperative groups, could operate without a license and a bond large enough to cover the maximum payroll, and any employer knowingly dealing with an unlicensed contractor would be liable for the workers' wages.

representation of work opportunities. His defense was that he had acted in good faith on the assumption that he had arranged a valid verbal agreement with the company representative.[39] The ultimate decision refused to renew Mort's license,[40] which, with the accompanying publicity, made it at least temporarily impossible for him to operate as a labor contractor.

County ordinances are another possibility for regulating labor contractors, but only Santa Barbara County, of those visited in the course of this study, had experimented with this system. The action was taken as a result of the annual drain on relief agencies from the surplus of pea pickers who turned up every spring in a community with no other crops that needed outside labor. Rightly or wrongly, this influx of excess labor was attributed to the contractors.[41] The ordinance passed in April 1937 required a certificate of permission from the County Agricultural Commissioner before causing or inducing agricultural labor to be imported into the county, which should not be issued without evidence from the prospective employers that work existed, that no more than the necessary number of workers would be imported, that they would be financially able to leave again at the close of the season, and that an "importer" other than an employer had a written contract of hire with his prospective employer. In addition, all labor contractors and camp operators had to be licensed by the Commissioner after furnishing proof of "good reputation for honesty, integrity, and fair dealing." This ordinance was apparently enforced in the spring of 1938, but it did not better the conditions it was designed to amend, because it obviously could have no effect upon the excess labor supply that simply drifted into the county

[39] Most local opinion upheld him and felt that the responsibility for the stranded jobless pea pickers who were flooding local relief agencies belonged to the company which had given the contract to another man at the last moment.

[40] The hearing was held just as the new license year opened, so that the problem of revoking his current license did not arise.

[41] See letter from an official of the State Relief Administration of Santa Barbara County, April 8, 1938, quoted on page 332.

on rumors of work nor upon the excess created by unfavorable weather conditions. However, it is interesting as an isolated attempt to rationalize the supply of labor through control of the supplying agencies. Probably it was more effective in improving camp conditions; the Commissioner reported that he coöperated with the County Health Officer in demanding that camps comply with health ordinances before granting a permit to operate.

The employers' attitude on controlling abuses in the labor contractor system might be summarized as "there ought to be a law." In recent years growers' associations and their representatives have frequently urged licensing and bonding of contractors, either by new legislation or by enforcement of existing law. This has been aimed principally at contractors who decamp with payrolls, leaving the employer with the moral if not the legal onus of defrauded workers. It is fairly obvious from past experience that an army of inspectors would be required merely to see that every one of the small-scale, migratory, non-English-speaking contractors had a license and renewed it each year. It is equally obvious that the mere possession of a license and posting of a small bond by a propertyless contractor with no settled place in the community will not obviate abuses without another army of enforcement officers. Nevertheless, it has been the official attitude of organized growers that the responsibility of control rests on state authorities, not on the man who hires the contractor; and it has been only isolated, individual growers who refused to use contractors because they were "racketeers."

When agricultural labor organizes in crops that use contractors, one of their demands is likely to be the abolition or control of the contractor system. It has already been noted that in 1933 the third most important demand in California agricultural strikes was abolition of contractors.[42] Occasionally an agreement after a strike included restriction on the use of contractors

[42] See pages 325–326.

or regulations for their control, as in the 1934 strike in the Santa Maria Valley vegetable fields; but the extent of union control in California agriculture is far too slight to be a significant factor.

Advantages of the Contractor System.—The reverse side of the abuses described above was a group of advantages to the worker inherent in the contracting system, though not great enough in the author's opinion to outweigh its disadvantages. Because in most instances the labor contractor made up his crew primarily from relatives, friends, and acquaintances, it was probably easier for the worker to get a job through a contractor than to hunt for a farmer who was hiring. This was, of course, especially true among the foreign-language groups to whom it was a necessity to make the wage bargain with or through someone who spoke their language and knew their habits. The advantages of the "headman" type of labor contractor, the English-speaking member of a foreign group who acted as spokesman but received only an equal share of group earnings, was obvious. But this type, the original form in California, had largely disappeared except among the Filipinos. The following picture of labor contracting among Filipinos may be too rosy, but it shows the system at its possible best: "This is an interesting and apparently happy and efficient form of labor organization. The laborers are all young fellows, while the contractor is an older man with a definitely paternal attitude towards his 'boys.' In fact, the laborers often come from his home village in the Philippines, and many of them are related to him. This was the case with S., a labor contractor in the interesting group of Filipinos whom the writer interviewed in Salinas in 1933. Mr. S., who is active in the local Methodist-Presbyterian church enterprise, studied three years in the Manila Normal School and was formerly a teacher in the Philippines. He has lived eight years in California, speaks excellent English, has a strong, intelligent, kindly face, and is evidently a wise leader of his men and an active force in local Filipino community affairs."[43]

The so-called "peonage" of debts contracted for food and other necessities, sometimes at usurious rates of interest, during periods of unemployment bled the laborer of much of his wages at the hands of an unscrupulous contractor, but it was the only possible source of credit available to most agricultural workers who had not sufficient funds laid by to see them through the winter or slack periods between different agricultural operations. In the Delta, for example, the Filipino contractors frequently brought in a gang several months before the asparagus season and arranged credit with a grocer for their food until work began. Sugar beet growers and agents of the refineries made the point that contractors who were settled the year round on a grower's property, boarded some of the beet workers on credit during the winter and sometimes lost considerable sums if the workers drifted away in the spring before the work began. Whether or not the interest charged stranded pea pickers at contractors' commissaries was usurious, it was the only way in which these penniless families could get food except through governmental relief agencies. And, in this connection, it is well to remember that the Deputy Labor Commissioner found that prices charged in one of these commissaries were cheaper than those in local stores.

Shifting of housing responsibility to contractors, whose financial resources were generally small, probably resulted, on the whole, in aggravating California's agricultural housing problem; but some of the large-scale contractors were reported to have well-run camps. For example, a county health inspector reported that the largest pea-pickers' camp near Santa Maria, some two hundred tents, cabins, and trailers, was "well equipped, managed, and the people well taken care of. . . . Metal garbage cans are located at frequent intervals, and water

[43] Albert W. Palmer, *Orientals in American Life* (New York: Friendship Press, 1934), pp. 79–80.

has been piped over the small town. . . . Free wood, brought in by rail, is given to all." There was a school, of sorts, with one teacher for 108 pupils.

Similarly, not all contractors ignored their responsibility for providing work for the migratory labor they brought in. Although most authorities of Santa Barbara County held contractors responsible for the annual labor surplus, an official of the State Employment Service there said that it was really the fault of employers who were interested only in getting their crops harvested in a hurry. The contractor, on the other hand, liked to work with as few men as possible because he felt a certain responsibility toward the workers, many of whom worked for him the year round, and liked to keep them employed as long as possible.

The question of why, in the face of opposition to labor contractors and frequent abuses of the system, many agricultural employers continued to obtain their labor supply through contractors may be answered by the advantages to the grower implicit in the foregoing description of the system and the reasons cited by employers who actually used it. The primary reason for employing a contractor was, of course, the same as that for using any other type of employment agency, namely, to delegate the task of supplying workers to someone who had better opportunities for finding them than had the employer. It was especially cogent when the workers did not speak English or when they migrated in groups with the contractor. Another case in which transfer of hiring functions to a contractor was especially advantageous was that of the small absentee grower, the man with a ranch too small to warrant a manager, who spent his own time in town at another job and delegated his farm work. Quite a number of such men who considered the contractor essential were interviewed—cotton gin managers, full-time employees in coöperatives, and men with small businesses in town. Around Santa Maria the large absentee landholders, representatives of California's "industrialized agriculture," were blamed for the presence of labor contractors, on the grounds that they knew nothing either about collecting a crew or about managing harvest operations, so that the contractor took over everything. As one county authority said, "The labor contractor usually knows the people who work for him, knows how to divide them into gangs in order to get the most efficient work out of them, and knows every operation concerned with harvesting a crop." In other areas the large-scale farms either did not use labor contractors or used them under a general manager. But similar testimonials to the contractor's knowledge and ability appeared from growers everywhere. Naturally growers who were explaining why they used labor contractors did not cite the shift of legal responsibility for wages, workmen's compensation, and camps, but critics of the system cited this as one of the prime reasons why employers liked it. Provision of camps by contractors—the fact and not the legal responsibility therefor—was a great advantage, in areas where the harvest season was short, to small growers who felt they could not afford to provide housing. Other reasons, less commonly encountered, were that contractors speeded up the harvest, that labor turnover was so great the farmer could not keep up with the necessary rehiring, that relief had made it too hard to hire workers directly, and that the contractor was needed to discipline the crew. One union official charged that contractors were favored by the employers because they maintained a plentiful and cheap labor supply, which was also the attitude in Santa Barbara County that led to local licensing. But the oversupply of labor throughout California agriculture has been so great in recent years that this can scarcely be one of the major reasons for the use of contractors.

Not all of the employers visited used labor contractors and defended the system. The most common accusation was variations on the theme of "they're all chiselers" or "it's a racket." Other growers refused to use them because, if they skipped with the payroll, neither grower nor worker had any redress. Others saw "no reason why one man should gain from another man's labor"; or the less altruistic pointed out that contractors, unless paid a bonus by the employer, took cuts of varying sizes from the workers' wages, producing inequalities and hence labor troubles, or undercut the locally established wage scales with the same result. The less common objections included a statement that they were not used in the fruit districts to pick fresh fruit for market because they included green fruit and failed to strip the trees, and the solitary statement that the grower "couldn't tell a contractor what to do." Small cotton growers frequently said that a weigh boss "was a nice system" but a luxury they could not afford. Many of the objectors were no more specific than to dismiss all labor contractors as "a bunch of grief."

Can Employers Do Without Labor Contractors?—There has been considerable discussion of the possibility of eliminating labor contractors from California agriculture. In certain crops they are not used at all, and in almost every crop there are some employers who refuse to use labor contractors and feel they are unnecessary. The problem is whether the functions now exercised by the contractor are indispensable and cannot be taken over by the employer, a foreman, or a public agency without inconvenience or loss to the grower. The attitude of beet growers, in an area and crop where the contractor system was universal, was typified by one who said, "Contractors are essential to the beet industry. The grower would be lost without them; they know the amount and kind of help needed and where to get it." The asparagus growers likewise felt that the system was necessary, or, at least, that they would be greatly inconvenienced by its abolition. Both these crops were harvested primarily by foreign-language groups, and it was obviously necessary that the hiring agent should speak their language and know where they were to be found. But in both crops there was a high proportion of the harvest hands who returned to the same ranch year after year, very greatly reducing the necessity for going out to hunt up a crew. And it was difficult to see why a public employment service whose field men spoke Spanish, as is required in Texas, and with which growers were willing to coöperate, could not furnish the new men needed each year by directing the migratory groups to the farms where they were needed. Supervision of the workers on the job could be done as well, if not better, by a man who stood in the relation of foreman to the grower, even if he were only employed for the season. The practicability of the foreman relationship was indicated by an officer of the Associated Farmers who was defending labor contractors as a "necessary evil" and then added that it would be possible to educate the growers to do without them, citing as an example citrus picking around Los Angeles, which used Mexicans and did not use contractors. As a matter of fact, distinct from the legal fiction of the contract which they signed and their function in supplying board, beet contractors in the Sacramento area were becoming indistinguishable from a foreman attached permanently to a single grower. In the entire course of this investigation no one interviewed gave any valid reason why supervision, or even hiring, could not be done as well by a foreman who belonged to the same nationality group as the workers but was directly responsible to the grower as an employee and dealt with the workers as the grower's agent. In fact, a number of farmers in various crops felt that the work was better done this way than through a contractor.

The other reason most commonly cited for needing labor contractors, besides the necessity of having a man who knew where to get workers and how to handle them, was to have them supply camps. Regardless of the convenience to the grower, California's experience with the system whereby financially irresponsible persons with limited resources have been expected to undertake the costs of setting up and maintaining a camp which would not be either a menace to public health or an unjustifiable charge to the workers has indicated that the system is socially most undesirable. Large agricultural companies or large private ranches can maintain their own camps. In areas with many small-scale farms, the community can establish a camp. This has already been tried in crops without contractor's camps, and the F.S.A. camps are a further aid. It is interesting to note that in beets and asparagus the grower provided the housing and equipment, and it is difficult to see why he could not take the further step of responsibility for board when single men were employed. It was being done on some of the large ranches growing other crops.

In brief, the author can see no reason why a system combining foremen, an efficient public farm placement service, and growers' or public camps, cannot replace the labor contractor system to the benefit of workers and the community and with no loss to the growers, aside from a change in established practice, which farmers are notoriously always unwilling to contemplate.

IX. Placement Work of Trade Unions*

THE DISSEMINATION of information as to job openings to members seeking employment is inherently a function of trade unions. The union secretary knows the members who are out of work, and he may have knowledge of job openings through his contacts with employers in the trade. Furthermore, workers of similar skills meet together and naturally pass around the information that certain employers are taking on men. Trade unions have, however, a motive in their placement activities which has its roots in something other than a mere fraternal or friendly interest in seeing that their members are employed. The aim of unionism is to improve the economic position of wage earners; and its cornerstone is collective bargaining, through which the group attains some control over wages, hours, and working conditions. If the employer is free to hire whomever he pleases, nonunion men at lower rates of pay may be employed, and the collective bargain becomes a farce or disappears. All unions are concerned, therefore, with developing some method by which they can prevent the competition of nonunion workers at less than "standard" conditions.

Some unions have assumed the functions of an employment agency, registering workers and jobs and dispatching the worker to the job. Others exercise control over who shall be hired by an agreement with employers that only union men will be hired. The agreement may set up certain rules as to layoffs and hiring. It may provide that employees with the least senior-

* Harold Tipton made available to the writer an unpublished manuscript, "Union Control of Hiring and Hiring Halls." This was a study based on published materials rather than on interviews with unions. In a number of instances Mr. Tipton's manuscript was helpful to the writer in the analysis of the material gathered from the unions.

ity are laid off first and those with the most seniority are reëmployed first. The employers hire workers directly, and the union polices the enforcement of the agreement, but it does not perform the functions of an employment agency.

The purpose of this study of the activities of California trade unions in the placement field was to determine the extent to which these organizations had assumed the functions of an employment agency and something of the mechanics of their work in this field.[1]

A sample of 200 unions were visited in San Francisco, Los Angeles, Sacramento, and Bakersfield.[2] These unions represented the major industrial and occupational groups in these areas. It must, however, be emphasized that since in this study interest was centered on unions which actually performed a placement function, the sample was heavily weighted with unions which assumed some responsibility for dispatching workers to jobs. Interviews with union officials brought to light the fact that 170 of the 200 unions visited operated some sort of a placement service for their members.[3] The remainder of this chapter will therefore be concerned with an analysis of the placement work of this group of 170 unions.

The first step in the analysis of the unions which had assumed the functions of an employment agency was an attempt to classify them in accordance with the degree of control over placements. Since statistics were not available on this subject, the only alternative was to group the unions into two broad

[1] No analysis will be attempted of the various kinds of collective agreements whereby employers agree to employ only union men, but where the union does not act as an intermediary between job and worker.

[2] See pages 37–39 for method of sampling.

[3] Of the 30 unions which did not operate a placement service, 18 were in Los Angeles, 8 in Sacramento, and 4 in San Francisco. Some of these unions, although doing no placement work, exercised some control over who could be employed through agreements, and others were attempting to increase their membership to the point where it would be possible to exert some control over the freedom of employers to hire whomever they wished.

classifications:[4] I. Those in which all placements were made out of the union office. This group includes unions which made all placement in whatever portion of the industry had been organized. All of these unions had organized all, or practically all, of the workers in some part of the trade or industry. With a few exceptions, they had organized at least a major portion of the trade or industry. The employers hired directly no new employees in the unit, craft or industrial, within the union's jurisdiction. This group was further broken down into those which dispatched workers out of the union office in (a) the entire trade or industry, (b) a major part of the industry, and (c) a minor part of the industry. II. Those in which only part of the placements were made out of the union office, regardless of the proportion of the field which was unionized. In this group were some unions which had organized all, or a large proportion of the workers in the trade or industry and some in which only a small proportion of the workers were union members. These unions were again classified in accordance with the strength of their control over placements and the proportion of the trade or industry over which this control was exercised.

DEGREE OF CONTROL OVER PLACEMENTS

Of the 170 unions which offered some kind of an employment service to their members, 58 (a third of the total) stated that all placements in the part of the trade or industry which was organized were made out of the union office. It is important, however, to emphasize that the above figures must not be interpreted to mean that a third of the workers in the trades and

[4] The information upon which this classification was based was obtained from the unions. In some instances it was possible to check the information with persons familiar with the activities of the unions. In a good many cases, however, it was not possible to go behind the original data, and it may be that in some instances other evidence might indicate that a union should have been placed in the class above or below that in which it is found. In most instances the unions were quite willing to discuss their placement work, and it is believed that, in general, sufficient information was obtained to determine their control over placements in general terms.

TABLE 24

UNIONS VISITED WHICH MAKE PLACEMENTS, CLASSIFIED BY EXTENT OF PLACEMENT WORK IN EACH AREA

Extent of Placement Work	Total all cities		San Francisco		Los Angeles		Sacramento		Bakersfield	
	Number	Per cent	Number	Per cent	Number	Per cent	Number	Per cent	Number	Per cent
Total	170	100.0	90	100.0	60	100.0	13	100.0	7	100.0
I. All placements made out of union office	58	34.1	33	36.7	16	26.7	8	61.5	1	14.3
a. Entire trade or industry	30	17.6	20	22.2	5	8.3	5	38.5	—	—
b. Major part of industry	19	11.2	12	13.4	4	6.7	2	15.4	1	14.3
c. Minor part of industry	9	5.3	1	1.1	7	11.7	1	7.7	—	—
II. Some placements made out of union office	112	65.9	57	63.3	44	73.3	5	38.5	6	85.7
A. Relatively dominant position in terms of placements	45	26.5	35	38.9	4	6.7	3	23.1	3	42.9
a. Entire trade or industry	12	7.1	9	10.0	1	1.7	1	7.7	1	14.3
b. Major part of industry	31	18.2	25	27.8	2	3.3	2	15.4	2	28.6
c. Minor part of industry	2	1.2	1	1.1	1	1.7	—	—	—	—
B. Relatively weak position in terms of placements	67	39.4	22	24.4	40	66.6	2	15.4	3	42.9
a. Entire trade or industry	10	5.9	3	3.3	7	11.7	—	—	—	—
b. Major part of industry	27	15.9	13	14.4	13	21.7	1	7.7	—	—
c. Minor part of industry	30	17.6	6	6.7	20	33.3	1	7.7	3	42.9

industries included in this study were required to secure their jobs through a union placement office. This caution is necessary because there were large differences in the number of workers in various occupations and in the degree to which the trade or industry had been organized. Since, however, 49 unions (85 per cent of those in the group described above) controlled placements in the entire or major portion of the trade or industry, it was evident that a large majority of this group of unions had a considerable degree of control over placements. The remaining 9 unions in this group placed all union members, but they had organized only a minor portion of the industry and thus controlled a relatively small proportion of total placements.

Two-thirds of the unions stated that they did not make all placements in any part of the trade or industry. A considerable number (45) of these unions, however, reported that a majority of the workers in the part of the trade which was organized were dispatched from the union office. It therefore appeared reasonable to consider this group along with the 58 which dispatched all workers and to conclude that about 60 per cent of the 170 unions had assumed the function of an employment agency for a large proportion of their members. Although the remaining group of 67 unions considered placement work as one of their functions, at the time this study was made, a majority of their members secured their jobs by other means, most frequently by direct application to an employer.

An attempt was made to secure information as to the membership of the trade unions whose placement activities were studied. It is always difficult to secure accurate statistics as to trade union membership, and those obtained in this investigation can only be considered as rough approximations. The 170 unions reported approximately 250,000 members. About a third of these trade unionists were members of unions which reported that all placements were made by the union. Another 25 per cent were members of organizations which controlled the dispatching of a majority of their members. It is therefore probably reasonable to suggest that somewhere between 50 and 60 per cent of the members of the unions studied placed considerable reliance on their unions to assist them in the job-finding process.

It is of interest to compare the degree of control over placements exercised by unions in San Francisco and in Los Angeles. The proportion of San Francisco unions which had organized the entire trade or industry, and in which all workers were dispatched from the union office, was more than twice as large as in Los Angeles. The study also showed that approximately three-quarters of the San Francisco unions, in contrast with a third of the Los Angeles organizations, dispatched all or a major part of the workers in the part of the industry which was organized.[5] (Classifications I and II A. See table 24.) The stronger control over hiring by San Francisco unions was not surprising, since it is common knowledge that trade union organization is much stronger in San Francisco than in Los Angeles. No comparison between the extent of control over placements in the two metropolitan centers and in Sacramento and Bakersfield will be made, because the sample of unions in these areas was restricted to trades and industries of special importance in the districts and to unions which had organized a considerable proportion of the workers in the trade or industry. The sample of unions in these areas was therefore not inclusive enough to permit comparisons.

Information gathered in the course of this study showed that unions in certain industries had developed an employment service through which they controlled a large proportion of the placements, whereas in other industries this function was less

[5] Caution must be exercised in drawing too fine comparisons between the proportion of unions with a strong degree of control over placements in San Francisco and in Los Angeles, since all of the unions visited in San Francisco were not included in the Los Angeles sample. Unions in the major industries were, however, visited in both cities, and it is believed that the broad differences outlined above show a true difference between trade union control of placements in the two cities.

fully developed.[6] As might be expected, the unions which had a considerable control over placement were those which had been successful in developing a strong trade union organization in other respects. It should, however, be pointed out that some strong trade unions had not developed a strong placement service.

Relatively large proportions of the unions in the maritime, clothing, laundry and dry cleaning, food processing, and transportation and communication[7] industries reported that they exercised a strong control over placements. In all of these industries over 50 per cent, and in two instances from 70 to 80 per cent, of the unions reported that they dispatched all workers in some part of the trade or industry. A much smaller proportion of the unions in the other industrial groups reported a strong position in terms of placements. In only one instance did more than 25 per cent of the unions in these industrial groups report that they dispatched all workers in any part of the trade or industry.

The Maritime Industry

Longshoremen.—The necessity for centralized control of hiring of workers on the docks in the large ports of the world has long been a subject of discussion. Although workers in many occupations are subject to what has been termed casual employment—short engagements and want of selection[8]—this type of demand for labor is peculiarly characteristic of dock workers; thus consideration of this problem has frequently been centered

[6] Because it was necessary to preserve the anonymity of the unions which cooperated in giving information for this study, the specific unions included in each classification have been omitted from the tabulations and from the discussion except when published data are available.

[7] "Transportation and communication" does not include workers in the maritime industry. Because of the size and importance of this group, they have been kept in a separate category. It also does not include workers on railroads, since the unions in these occupations do not perform a placement function, although through seniority provisions they do exercise control over who shall get the jobs.

[8] W. H. Beveridge, *Unemployment, a Problem of Industry* (London: Longmans, Green and Co., 1909), p. 77.

TABLE 25

UNIONS VISITED WHICH MAKE PLACEMENTS, CLASSIFIED BY INDUSTRY AND BY EXTENT OF PLACEMENT WORK IN EACH AREA*

Industry	Total all cities				San Francisco				Los Angeles				Sacramento				Bakersfield			
	Total	I	II A	II B	Total	I	II A	II B	Total	I	II A	II B	Total	I	II A	II B	Total	I	II A	II B
Total	170	58	45	67	90	33	35	22	60	16	4	40	13	8	3	2	7	1	3	3
Agriculture	4	—	2	2	2	—	2	—	—	—	—	—	1	—	—	1	1	—	—	1
Mining and oil	3	—	—	3	—	—	—	—	1	—	—	1	—	—	—	—	2	—	—	2
Building and construction	24	3	9	12	10	—	5	5	9	1	1	7	4	2	2	—	1	—	1	—
Clothing manufacture	6	5	—	1	4	4	—	—	2	1	—	1	—	—	—	—	—	—	—	—
Food processing	25	14	7	4	13	7	6	—	9	5	—	4	2	2	—	—	1	—	1	—
Metal trades	8	2	1	5	5	1	1	3	2	—	—	2	1	1	—	—	—	—	—	—
Printing trades	7	1	2	4	5	1	2	2	2	—	—	2	—	—	—	—	—	—	—	—
Motion-picture production	6	—	1	5	—	—	—	—	6	—	1	5	—	—	—	—	—	—	—	—
Miscellaneous manufacturing	12	5	3	4	6	3	2	1	6	2	1	3	—	—	—	—	—	—	—	—
Maritime transportation	15	8	4	3	11	5	4	2	3	2	—	1	1	1	—	—	—	—	—	—
Transportation and communication (excluding maritime)	12	7	4	1	6	4	2	—	3	2	—	1	2	1	1	—	1	—	1	—
Retail trade and utilities	12	3	—	9	8	3	—	5	4	—	—	4	—	—	—	—	—	—	—	—
Professional service	8	1	1	6	4	1	1	2	4	—	—	4	—	—	—	—	—	—	—	—
Hotels, restaurants, and building service	18	4	9	5	9	1	8	—	6	1	1	4	2	1	—	1	1	1	—	—
Laundry and dry cleaning	7	5	1	1	4	3	1	—	3	2	—	1	—	—	—	—	—	—	—	—
Other domestic and personal service	3	—	1	2	3	—	1	2	—	—	—	—	—	—	—	—	—	—	—	—

* The placement-work classifications used in this table are defined as follows: I. All placements made out of union office; II A. Some placements made out of union office with relatively dominant position in terms of placements; II B. Some placements made out of union office with relatively weak position in terms of placements.

on this occupational group. It is beyond the scope of this study to analyze fully the characteristics of the demand for dock laborers, but the following quotation from a recent study will serve to summarize the conditions which exist in this field of employment: "The demands [for labor on the docks] are sporadic and intermittent, and . . . the industry is subject to variations in activity which are superimposed on the seasonal and cyclical fluctuations and long-time changes common to all industry. . . . Because of the maximum forces required to fulfill the usual necessity of discharging and loading ships in minimum time, and because of the irregularity of sailings, labor is ordinarily engaged for specific jobs only. Such constant dissolution and reconstitution of the labor force of given employers lead inevitably to intense competition for jobs, breed surpluses, and allow easy access into the industry of unemployed men from other industries. . . . The irregularity and unpredictability of demand have led each employer to attempt to attach to himself a maximum reserve."[9] The workers had no knowledge of the particular docks where there might be shortages, and as a consequence there was sometimes a shortage at one dock and surpluses at others and men waiting in line long hours at first one dock and then another hoping, often in vain, that a job would be forthcoming.

Since a fluctuating demand for labor was inherent in this industry, the problem became one of evolving some system of distributing labor by which there would be an orderly transference of workers from job to job, some equalization of employment, and a reduction in the number necessary to perform a given number of tasks; thus the earnings of a smaller group would be increased and regularized. It was recognized that, in order to accomplish the purposes set forth above, there must

[9] Marvel Keller, *Decasualization of Longshore Work in San Francisco*, Works Progress Administration, National Research Project, Report No. L-2 (Philadelphia: Apr. 1939), pp. 1–2. This study had not been published at the time the unions were visited; it has, however, subsequently been used to expand and verify the information obtained from union officials.

be a "port-wide system of registration of the labor supply limited to the normal needs of the port and the drawing upon this labor supply by individual employers from a central registry."[10]

A number of foreign countries had for many years tried out somewhat varied schemes for the decasualization of dock labor which had met with varying degrees of success. In the British ports the system had been controlled, in the main, by joint employer-employee committees, although in some ports it was operated by employers. A few British ports had not adopted a decasualization system because the unions were unwilling to accept a jointly operated scheme, and the employers refused to turn it over to the unions. In other countries the systems were operated by unions, by employers and unions, or by employers, and in some cases there was also government participation.[11]

In the United States systems of centralized hiring of dock workers were set up in the period from 1921–23 in the ports of Seattle, Portland, Los Angeles, and a few small ports in the state of Washington.[12] In a study published in 1932 the following statement appeared: "Seattle, Portland, and Los Angeles adopted their schemes of decasualization only after a long period of serious and violent labor clashes which resulted in the defeat of the local union, members of the international. In none of the three ports is the union now considered an important factor on the waterfront, and the employers refuse to recognize the International Longshoremen's Association as the representative of their men. . . . The plans of decasualization there were originated and are now managed almost exclusively by the employers, with the workers having comparatively very little to say either in the management or in the operations of the respective schemes." The result was that the union regarded decasualization as a union-breaking medium.[13]

[10] *Ibid.*, p. 3. Also see W. H. Beveridge, *op. cit.*, p. 87.

[11] Marvel Keller, *op. cit.*, pp. 2–9. [12] *Ibid.*, p. 9.

[13] Boris Stern, *Cargo Handling and Longshore Labor Conditions*, U. S. Bureau of Labor Statistics, Bulletin No. 550 (Washington: Government Printing Office, Feb. 1932), p. 102.

Prior to 1934 little had been done in the port of San Francisco to decasualize dock labor.[14] Following the general strike of 1934 and the award of the arbitration board, a centralized hiring system was established for longshoremen in San Francisco, Los Angeles, and all of the other major ports of the Pacific Coast. Although the employers recognized the desirability of centralized dispatching and control of the size of the labor supply, they maintained that it was essential that the hiring halls should be controlled by their association. The award as handed down, however, provided for hiring halls operated jointly by the union, the International Longshoreman's Association, and the employers' association, and that those responsible for dispatching men to work must be selected by the union.[15] This latter requirement was very important since it gave to the union a very real control over the hiring hall.

At the time this study was made, there was centralized hiring of all longshoremen in San Francisco and in Los Angeles. Although this hiring hall was under the joint control of the union and the employer, the union, through its control over dispatchers, in fact made all placements. For this reason those unions have been placed in the category of those which make all placements.[16] Both registered and nonregistered men were included in the system. Registered men constituted the basic labor supply, and the number permitted to become members of this group was determined by the joint labor relations committee. Registered men included two groups: those with permanent registration and "permit men," an additional supply of men allowed to attach themselves to the docks in order to insure a more flexible labor supply. At the time this study was made it was reported that all of those with permanent registration were

[14] From 1919 to 1934 membership in the Longshoremen's Association of San Francisco, an employer-sponsored organization, was required in order to get work on the docks. This association, however, apparently did not improve the situation of the dock workers.

[15] Marvel Keller, *op. cit.*, pp. 12–13, 23–26.

[16] *Ibid.*, p. 79.

members of the union. The "permit men" were not union members, but it was reported that "service to the union" was a factor in determining admission to this category. In order to meet the peak demands for longshoremen, nonregistered men could at certain times secure work on the docks.[17] They were also assigned to work from the central hiring hall.

The available evidence appears to indicate that centralized control of placements had to a considerable extent brought order out of chaos in an industry in which in the past there had been almost complete lack of organization in the labor market. The following quotation from a San Francisco study is given in support of the above statement: "The San Francisco work rotation scheme . . . [is] a plan operating within the framework of controls which, in fact, tend to insure adequate employment to the registered labor force. It provides for a labor force which is flexible in size, yet it effectively avoids the usual problem of casual work."[18] Although an exhaustive study was made only in San Francisco, the experience in that city can probably be considered typical of all ports on the Pacific Coast.

Other maritime unions.—In addition to the union of longshoremen, 13 other organizations of maritime workers were visited in the course of this investigation. With a few exceptions these were strong unions with well-developed and strong placement services. Six reported that with the exception of a relatively small group of employees on tankers all of the workers were dispatched from a union hiring hall. Four others reported that, although some workers got their jobs by direct application to the employer, a majority were placed by the union. In all but one case these unions employed a full-time dispatcher. The remaining three unions of maritime workers reported that, although some workers were placed by the union, the bulk of the jobs were secured by direct application. These unions found it necessary to employ only a part-time placement officer.

---

[17] *Ibid.*, p. 32. [18] *Ibid.*, p. 81.

The above analysis indicates that a large proportion of the workers in the maritime trades secured their jobs through centralized hiring halls. In the case of longshoremen the hiring halls were jointly controlled by the union and the employer's association, although actual placements were made by men chosen by the union, whereas in the other maritime trades the hiring halls were entirely union controlled. Centralized hiring systems in the maritime trades had effected a real organization of the labor market and by this means a greater equalization of employment and earnings in an industry in which an intermittent demand for workers was inevitable.[19]

The Clothing Industry.—The garment trades had for many years been strongly organized and had recognized the importance of control over hiring. In 1887 the Journeymen Tailors Union of America passed the following resulotion: "We believe it to be for the best interest of our trade, and do therefore recommend, all local unions to establish employment bureaus as soon as possible."[20] In more recent years the unions' control over hiring has been one of the basic issues in many strikes in the garment trades.[21] In 1937 the New York local of the International Ladies Garment Workers Union published the following statement, which indicated their recognition of the importance of a labor bureau in advancing the cause of progressive unionism: "... we are still faced with the disgraceful situation of workers having to tramp the streets in the market looking for signs in

[19] It has been pointed out that the system of centralized hiring of longshoremen has not operated without difficulties of administration, and in some instances at atmosphere of conflict has interfered with the smooth working of the system. In spite of difficulties, a study of decasualization of longshore work in San Francisco states that the plan has tended to insure adequate employment to the registered labor force. The author of this study is of the opinion that the San Francisco experience is typical of other ports of the Pacific Coast. *Ibid.*, pp. 15, 23, 29, 50, 81.

[20] Charles J. Rowell, *Studies in Trade Unionism in the Custom Tailoring Trade* (Bloomington, Illinois: Journeymen Tailors Union of America, 1913), p. 73.

[21] For evidence upon which this statement is based see Louis Levine, *The Women's Garment Workers* (New York: B. W. Huebsch, Inc., 1924) and James Oneal, *A History of the Amalgamated Ladies' Garment Cutters' Union, Local 10* (New York: Asland Press, 1927).

order to get a job. It is emphatically necessary to establish an employment bureau through which our members will be able to get work, instead of having to wander from building to building and shop to shop in search of signs. So far, we have met with considerable resistance on the part of the employers to this proposal of establishing a labor bureau. We will now have to see to it that the next agreement definitely includes a provision for the creation of such an institution."[22]

It was not surprising to find that five of the six California unions in this industry visited in course of this study made all of the placements throughout most of the industry. Included in this group were all of the San Francisco unions and one of the two visited in Los Angeles. One of the San Francisco unions in this trade reported 100 per cent organization and that all workers were dispatched by a union official. The others reported that they had organized a major portion of the trade, and that the union always acted as an intermediary between job and worker in the organized shops. The Los Angeles union which placed only a small proportion of the workers reported that between 80 and 85 per cent of the shops were organized, but that, although the constitution of the union prohibited union members from soliciting their own jobs, this prohibition was not enforced. Although the unions in the clothing industry operated employment offices for their members, none of those visited employed a full-time dispatcher. The work was done on a part-time basis by the business agent and office secretary.

Although it was not possible within the time available to make a study of the effect of control over hiring on earnings and employment of workers in the clothing industry, there can be little doubt that this group of workers in a seasonal industry benefited when central dispatching was substituted for hit-and-miss, door-to-door job hunting.

[22] International Ladies Garment Workers Union, *Our Union at Work*, A Survey of the Activities of Dressmakers Union, Local 22, ILGWU, from April 1935 to April 1937 (New York: May, 1937), p. 57.

Laundry and Dry Cleaning Industries.—Another group of unions which, at the time this study was made, had developed considerable strength in the field of jobs placements were in the laundry and dry cleaning industries. Five of the seven unions visited in this industry reported that they exercised considerable control over placements. Three of these were strong San Francisco unions which reported that all workers were dispatched by the unions in at least a major portion of the industry. The other two were Los Angeles unions in which the proportion of shops which had been organized was smaller, but the union controlled all placements in the organized shops. One other fairly strong San Francisco union reported that it had not been able to establish a rule whereby all workers in union shops must be employed through the union, although a substantial proportion were dispatched by the union. One organization in this industry reported that only a very small proportion of the workers were dispatched by the union. This was a Los Angeles organization which had as yet been unable to organize any considerable proportion of the workers in the trade and had little control over placements even in the organized shops. An official of this union said, "The union only makes a few placements. Most of the hiring is done directly by the employer." As was true in the clothing industry, all of the dispatching in the laundry and dry cleaning industries was the responsibility of union officials or secretaries, who also had other duties.

The Food Processing Industry.—The unions in the food processing industry covered a wide variety of occupational groups, such as bakers, brewers, and cannery workers.[23] Of the 25 unions visited in these industries, 14 reported that the union

[23] Canning is one of the major industries of California, but unionization in this industry was comparatively recent, and these organizations had not, except in one or two instances, assumed any of the functions of a placement bureau. Some of the unions in the canning industry had agreements which established certain rules and regulations as to the employment of union members. As already pointed out, however, unions in this category were not classified as performing a placement function.

dispatched all workers to organized shops. Furthermore, 10 of this group had completely organized the trade, and two others included in their membership a large proportion of the workers in the trade. The other two unions in this group had organized only a minor part of the industry; and, although they placed all of their members, there were considerable numbers of unorganized workers who solicited their own jobs. Seven other powerful unions reported that most of the placements were made by the union, although they had not been able to establish a rule whereby members were dispatched only through the union office. Only four of the organizations in the food processing business, all in Los Angeles, reported that their control over placements was decidedly weak. One of these unions had organized all of the workers in the industry, but it dispatched "extras" (about 25 per cent of its membership). The other three unions in this group were less strong organizations, and only a small proportion of the jobs were filled by the union.

Only one of the unions in the food processing industry had established a hiring hall with full-time dispatchers. This was a strong union in an industry which was highly seasonal and where jobs varied in length within a season. A somewhat elaborate system of record keeping and dispatching had been developed. The union was concerned with equalizing employment, not necessarily within one season but at least over a period of years. It was not possible to determine in how far equalization was accomplished, but it was at least one of the factors to be considered in dispatching men. The remainder of the unions in these industries were in trades in which, in the main, turnover was not so high and part-time personnel were responsible for the placement work.

Transportation and Communication Industries Other Than Maritime.[24]—Seven of the twelve unions of workers in these

[24] The unions of workers in the railroad industry were not included in this group, since these unions did no placement work, although through seniority rules they exercised considerable control over who should be hired.

industries dispatched all workers in the organized portion of the industry. Of this group, four were strong unions which controlled all placements in all or a major portion of the industry; and three others dispatched all union members, but they had organized only a minor portion of the industry. Four other unions in these industries had succeeded in organizing all or a major portion of the workers, and most of the placements were made by the union, although a rule had not been established that workers must get their jobs through the union. Only one union in these trades, a Los Angeles organization, reported that it had very little control over placements. Although this union claimed that 85 per cent of the workers in the industry were union members, only a very small proportion of the jobs were filled from the union office. Three of the twelve unions, all strong San Francisco organizations, had full-time dispatchers, the remainder depending on part-time personnel to handle the placement work.

Other Industries.—Although the unions in the other industrial groups had to a lesser extent developed strength in the field of placements, a few organizations in the building, printing, metal, retail, hotel and restaurant, miscellaneous manufacturing, and professional categories had assumed control over the dispatching of all or a major portion of the workers in the trade or industry. In every case, however, the proportion of the unions in these categories which controlled a relatively insignificant proportion of the placements was greater than in the categories previously discussed. Only five of the nearly 90 unions in this group employed a full-time dispatcher.

It might have been expected that a large proportion of unions in such strongly organized trades as building and printing would have developed centralized hiring systems controlled by the unions. In a few instances unions in these groups dispatched a considerable proportion of the workers; but half of the unions visited in the building trades and nearly 60 per cent of those in printing dispatched only an occasional worker. The unions in the building trades appeared to be quite satisfied with the system whereby workers tended to "follow a contractor." The union, because of its strength, could require the contractor to employ only union men, and it stood ready to supply the contractor with additional men should the need arise. One union official said, "The union has no particular desire to expand its placement service"; another, "I can see no major function for the union in the placement field." The unions in the printing trades had likewise been successful in organizing practically the entire trade. The fact that relatively few of the unions visited in these trades dispatched a large proportion of the workers from the union office is probably in part related to the fact that these organizations could require the employment of union men; furthermore, these unions had established rules which the employer must follow as to the order in which workers should be employed.

None of the unions visited in agriculture, mining, motion picture, and domestic and personal service controlled all placements in any part of the trade or industry at the time this study was made. A few unions in these categories had reported that they dispatched a considerable proportion of the workers; but, in the main, they had developed their placement work only to an insignificant extent.[25] None of the organizations in these industries employed a full-time dispatcher.

MECHANICS OF TRADE UNION PLACEMENTS

One of the basic causes of labor disputes in many industries has centered around the issue of whether the union or the employer is to control hiring arrangements. This was one of the main

[25] Three-quarters of the unions visited in these fields were in class II B, that is, they made a small proportion of the total placements; 50 per cent of the unions discussed just previously and 15 per cent of those in the maritime, clothing, food processing, laundry and dry cleaning, and other transportation industries were in class II B.

TABLE 26

NUMBER OF HIRING HALLS AND PART-TIME PLACEMENT OFFICERS IN UNIONS VISITED WHICH MAKE PLACEMENTS, CLASSIFIED BY EXTENT OF PLACEMENT WORK IN EACH AREA

Extent of placement work	Total all cities			San Francisco			Los Angeles			Sacramento			Bakersfield		
	Total	Hiring hall	Part-time placement officer	Total	Hiring hall	Part-time placement officer	Total	Hiring hall	Part-time placement officer	Total	Hiring hall	Part-time placement officer	Total	Hiring hall	Part-time placement officer
NUMBER															
Total	170	23	147	90	15	75	60	6	54	13	2	11	7	..	7
I. All placements made out of union office	58	12	46	33	9	24	16	2	14	8	1	7	1	..	1
II. Some placements made out of union office	112	11	101	57	6	51	44	4	40	5	1	4	6	..	6
A. Relatively dominant position in terms of placements	45	5	40	35	4	31	4	..	4	3	1	2	3	..	3
B. Relatively weak position in terms of placements	67	6	61	22	2	20	40	4	36	2	..	2	3	..	3
PER CENT															
Total	100.0	13.5	86.5	100.0	16.7	83.3	100.0	10.0	90.0	100.0	15.4	84.6	100.0	....	100.0
I. All placements made out of union office	100.0	20.7	79.3	100.0	27.3	72.7	100.0	12.5	87.5	100.0	12.5	87.5	100.0	....	100.0
II. Some placements made out of union office	100.0	9.8	90.2	100.0	10.5	89.5	100.0	9.1	90.9	100.0	20.0	80.0	100.0	....	100.0
A. Relatively dominant position in terms of placements	100.0	11.1	88.9	100.0	11.4	88.6	100.0	....	100.0	100.0	33.3	66.7	100.0	....	100.0
B. Relatively weak position in terms of placements	100.0	9.0	91.0	100.0	9.1	90.9	100.0	10.0	90.0	100.0	....	100.0	100.0	....	100.0

issues in the coastwise maritime strike of 1934 and in subsequent waterfront strikes in California ports.

Arguments advanced by trade unions in favor of their control of hiring procedures were largely concerned with pointing out that such control leads to regularization of employment, which works to the advantage of employers and union members alike. If the employer is free to hire as he pleases, grossly unequal opportunities for employment result. If, on the other hand, the work available is distributed by the union, peak demands will be handled advantageously from a known pool of labor, and workers will be assured of a minimum period of unemployment; thus they will have greater economic security, and there will be less drain on unemployment insurance funds and on relief funds. Furthermore, the unions often pointed out that employers can be more certain of a supply of experienced workers, because they are dealing with a specialized placement service whose dispatchers or business agents know the trade thoroughly—both the workers' capabilities and the employers' preferences.[26]

In some instances unions had organized a more or less formal labor exchange or employment service, with one or more full-time dispatchers in charge of a "hiring hall." In this study all unions which employed a full-time dispatcher were classified as having a hiring hall. Twenty-three of the 170 unions had hiring halls as defined above. In the remaining 147, assistance to members seeking employment was the function of a business agent or secretary who performed other duties as well.

Eleven of the 23 unions with hiring halls were in the maritime trades, 5 were in other transportation and communication, and the remaining 7 were unions in a variety of different trades and occupations. Full-time dispatchers were found, in the main, in occupations in which employment was likely to be intermittent, and thus frequent change of job necessary, and in

[26] H. Feldman, *The Regularization of Employment* (New York: Harper and Brothers, 1925), pp. 333–336, 356–359.

unions which had been successful in controlling a considerable proportion of the placements. There were, however, 96 unions which reported a considerable control over placements but which did not have full-time dispatchers. In some instances this was undoubtedly because labor turnover was low, and therefore there was no necessity for a full-time placement officer. In others the lack of funds to pay a full-time salary was probably the reason.

Hiring halls were more common in San Francisco than in the other areas visited. Fifteen of the 90 San Francisco unions, 6 of the 60 in Los Angeles, 2 of the 13 in Sacramento, and no Bakersfield union employed a full-time dispatcher. Again, this was not surprising in view of the greater strength of organized labor in San Francisco.

Techniques of Dispatching in Maritime Unions.—Elaborate procedures and machinery had been developed in the operation of hiring halls, particularly among the maritime unions. The hiring hall of the International Longshoremen and Warehousemen's Union[27] in San Francisco, which was established following the award of the United States National Longshoremen's Board appointed to arbitrate the 1934 strike, had become the pattern with minor variations for other hiring halls established in the maritime industry, not only in San Francisco but also in Los Angeles and Sacramento.

The International Longshoremen and Warehousemen's Union (I.L.W.U.) had as a part of its premises a large hall which served as a waiting room and meeting place for its members. Facing the hall were the offices of the dispatcher, in which a public address system had been installed to announce work assignments and similar details in connection with placements of the waiting men. The hall was advantageously located near the docks and warehouses. In conjunction with the hall and

[27] Formerly known as the International Longshoremen's Association, A. F. of L., until July 1937, when the membership affiliated with the C. I. O.

operated jointly with other maritime unions was a large recreation hall.

Elaborate techniques had been worked out for dispatching longshore workers to jobs. The system was somewhat different for those who worked in gangs and for extra men who were not attached permanently to any gang. The foreman of a gang, which may be "preferred" (attached to a specific employer) or "casual" (not attached to one employer), notified the dispatcher when his gang was ready for an assignment. He was also responsible for notifying the members of the gang when they were assigned to a job. Hours of work were equalized, although the basis of equalization differed for the two types of gangs. Extra men were required to appear at the hiring hall in order to be dispatched to a job. Dispatching of these men was handled by means of the plug-board system.[28] Every man working out of the hiring hall was given a small metal plug on which was stamped his registration number. When he reported daily to the hall to get his work assignment, he inserted the plug in the correspondingly numbered hole in the appropriate section. As each man was sent to a job, his plug was pulled by the dispatcher and returned to him. No one who had worked his full quota of hours during a given week was dispatched again until everyone else in that section of the board had worked the same number of hours. In event that there was not sufficient work for everyone to obtain the maximum (usually 40 hours) amount of work during the week, the dispatcher set a smaller quota which no one was permitted to exceed. Through constant daily checking with employers, the dispatcher was usually able to determine the amount of work available by the middle of the week. Workers were dispatched according to accumulated hours of work, and their working time was equalized continuously.

The plug-board system was ordinarily supplemented by additional information about individual workers. In one organiza-

[28] Marvel Keller, *op. cit.*, pp. 16–50.

tion a registry book in which daily entries were made recorded the individual's name and number, and he was issued a work card before going on a job. Usually a card file was kept to record a brief personal history statement and occupational data for each individual. In one union where the volume of work going out of the hall was very large, a records division had been set up in the dispatcher's office to keep records on the hours of work performed by each worker, so that equalization of hours could be computed at frequent intervals as an aid to the dispatcher.

Techniques of Dispatching in Other Trades.—The plug-board system was feasible and desirable only in circumstances where the frequency of dispatching was high, where a large part of the work was casual, and where individual selection of workers on the basis of special qualifications was not of paramount importance. In an industry employing temporary rather than casual workers, and where the worker's special qualifications were factors in his placement, the union dispatcher used a card-file system. Workers were registered in the hall, and personal and occupational data were recorded on the registrant's card. Cards were filed in order of registration and according to occupational classification. With the exception of this difference between the plug-board and card-file systems, dispatching out of hiring halls was much the same. The main purpose of both was to ensure work rotation and equalization of employment opportunities for the registered labor force.

As indicated previously, only 23 of the 170 unions visited which made placements utilized a hiring hall or full-time dispatcher. In 147 unions visited, placements were made by union officials or office secretaries whose duties were not primarily placement. There were a number of reasons why placement was most frequently in the hands of personnel whose major responsibilities lay elsewhere. Some unions reported that a full-time dispatcher was not necessary, since most of their members kept their jobs for long periods of time, and thus only an occasional worker shifted to a new employer. In others, although employment was not stable, only a few workers or job orders came to the union office because the union had not been able to develop strength in the placement field. Some reported that, at the time this study was made, there was so much unemployment and so few jobs that they could not justify the employment of a full-time placement officer.

In those unions in which placement activity was only a part-time job for one or two employees, the machinery of placement work was very simple. There was no particular necessity for elaborate files of registrants, job vacancies, and placements, because the union placement official in most cases had an intimate knowledge of the employer's needs and of the job to be done. Unless the union membershp was large, he generally knew the personal qualifications of each member. In a majority of the unions visited the employed and unemployed union members were registered in a card file which seldom contained more data than the member's name, address, telephone number, age, marital status, and name of last employer. Few unions were visited which kept detailed records of the member's employment history; many were found which kept only the registrant's name, address, and telephone number. Craft unions, and particularly those whose jurisdictional claims were limited, included a limited number of occupational groups and in many cases the union members had served apprenticeships before being admitted to membership, so that their qualifications were established. In such cases elaborate occupational data were unnecessary.

The union business agent was ordinarily in frequent contact with the employers with whom the union had agreements and was well posted on their requirements. The employer or union members within the plant usually kept the business agent informed of anticipated layoffs or hiring. The usual procedure for handling placements required that the union keep an accurate list of its unemployed members by making it mandatory that they register with the union as soon as they were unemployed. The record was kept in a card file or simply written on a blackboard in the union offices.

RULES IN REGARD TO PLACEMENTS

All of the unions visited which had assumed the functions of a placement agency had certain rules which determined who would be placed by the union, the order of preference in placements, and other matters which pertained to their function as an employment agency. In some instances these rules were embodied in the union's constitution, and in others they had simply been established by custom.

Approximately 40 per cent of the unions restricted their placements to union members. The remaining organizations (nearly 100) stated that they would also place nonunion workers, but their service to this group was restricted to times when there was a shortage of union members in the trade. Some of the unions in this group required that nonunion men who were placed must join the union within a specified time, usually not longer than 30 days. A large group, however, had no such definite rule, and undoubtedly their insistence upon membership depended in part on the strength of the union and in part on whether additions to the union membership might ultimately result in underemployment for all.

Practically all of the unions were willing to place members of other locals of the union within the same city. Less than 40 per cent would accept for placement members of the same union from other cities, and only about a third would place members of other unions.

Although policies as to the union status of those who would be accepted for placement were in many respects liberal, usually members of the local in good standing were given first call when vacancies occurred. If additional jobs were available, members of other locals in the same trade or members of other unions would be placed; and, finally, if any jobs remained unfilled, nonunion men might be referred by the union.

There were a wide variety of regulations governing transfers from union to union. In some of the seafaring unions members could be placed out of any port with no penalty. Some unions, on the other hand, reserved the right to replace a member of another local at any time, and others would accept members of other locals for placement only on an even exchange basis. A considerable number had no definite regulations in regard to the acceptance of transfers, but even this group usually gave preference to their own members.

It was clear that a majority of the unions exercised considerable caution in placing workers who were members of other locals or unions or who were not members of a union. Not unnaturally, labor organizations are primarily concerned with maintaining greater security of employment for their own members and are fearful of an influx of workers who will compete for the available jobs and thus reduce the work available for all and possibly even bring about a breakdown in the standard conditions of work. Except at a time of great industrial activity, when there may be a shortage of labor, trade union placements are probably limited in most instances to members of a particular local.

Any agency which sets up an employment exchange is confronted with the necessity of making decisions as to who, among the applicants for a job, is to be referred. Is it to be the worker with the best qualifications, the one on the spot, who may just be out of a job, or the one who has been longest unemployed? Or are there other factors which are taken into account?

Practically all of the unions visited considered more than one factor in making job referrals, and in most instances the official in charge was either unable or unwilling to state the chief factor taken into account in making referrals.

It was difficult to determine in how far the qualifications of the worker were an important factor in placement preference. Practically all of the union officials stated that ability to do the job was an important consideration. If, as was most frequently the case, the union also took into consideration the length of unemployment, it was impossible to determine which carried more weight. It should, however, be pointed out that all unions had certain basic requirements as to the qualifications of their membership to do the job, and some restricted their membership to those who had had a specified period of training or who had passed an examination. It is probable that in some instances a consideration of qualifications in making placements merely meant that only workers capable of doing the job were accepted as members of the union, whereas in others, particularly in jobs demanding a high degree of skill, the worker of proved capacity was given first choice of the available jobs. Less than 20 of the union officials, however, stated that placements were made entirely on the basis of qualification.

Length of unemployment was a factor in determining the order of placement in all but about 20 of the unions, and it appeared that this was most frequently the major consideration. In most instances the man at the top of the list was the one first placed. About a dozen unions, chiefly in the maritime trades, placed workers in accordance with the amount of unemployment within a given period rather than length of time since the last job. Some stated that they used both methods to equalize employment for their members.

A few organizations considered one or another of a variety of other factors in determining the order of placement. In some instances length of union membership gave preference, although this consideration was usually of secondary importance. Some reported that in certain instances preference was given to members in the older age groups and occasionally to those with large families. In one or two instances unions with members of several racial groups had established quotas for the placement of workers from each group in order to avoid charges of racial discrimination.

Two other questions of importance in the placement procedures of trade unions are: Is the employer required to accept any worker whom the union refers? Must the worker accept the job to which he is referred? Most of the unions reported that it was their policy to refer a worker and, if he was not acceptable to the employer, to send another in his place. Obviously, unless the union was in a very strong position, this was the only possible attitude, since, if the employer could not secure workers from the union who were acceptable to him, he would soon find his workers elsewhere. A few strong unions, about 10 per cent of the total, had been able to come to an agreement with the employers whereby any man whom the union referred would be employed.

About 40 per cent of the unions had adopted a rule that the worker must accept a job to which he was referred. There were a variety of penalties to which the worker was subject if he refused a job. He went to the end of the list, was taken off the unemployed list for a specified time, his unemployment benefits were stopped, a fine was imposed, or he was "simply ignored by the dispatcher." Although a majority had no rule requiring the worker to accept a job, in a good many instances the union official said "a chronic refuser is forgotten."

RELATIONS OF UNIONS WITH OTHER PLACEMENT AGENCIES

California State Employment Service.—Trade unions have been in the past one of the strongest influences in the establishment of public employment agencies in California. The first free agency in Los Angeles, for example, was established in 1893 by labor unions and then taken over by the city and county two years later.[29] A free employment agency sponsored by the state in San Francisco in 1895 was partially supported by financial contributions of trade unions.[30] Sacramento's first free agency, opened in 1902, was established largely as a result of trade union activity in its behalf.[31] Union opposition to the malpractices of the private fee-charging agencies, which were seldom regulated by law, caused the active participation of the unions in movements toward the creation of a free public employment service and the regulation of private agencies.

Paradoxically the trade unions advocated the establishment of public agencies; now that public agencies have been created on a large scale, trade union support is less evident. Most of the unions interviewed in this study had more unfavorable than favorable comments to make about the California State Employment Service, and a large number of the unions visited were either unfamiliar with or indifferent toward the state agency. The reasons for this indifference or unfavorable comment probably may be attributed to the fact that in the early history of public employment agencies trade unions had not themselves developed a system for placements because they were not strongly organized; thus public agencies contained no inherent threat to union control over placements. Furthermore, trade unions believed that every employment agency was a potential strike-breaking institution unless carefully regulated, and this belief had been supported by unfortunate experiences with both private and public agencies.

When the United States Maritime Commission in 1938 proposed the establishment of hiring halls to furnish crews for vessels operated or subsidized by the Commission, the maritime

[29] J. E. Connor, *Free Employment Offices in the United States*, U. S. Department of Commerce and Labor, Bureau of Labor Bulletin No. 68 (Washington: Government Printing Office, 1907), p. 8.

[30] California Bureau of Labor Statistics, *Biennial Report 1895–96* (Sacramento: State Printing Office, 1896), pp. 18–19.

[31] J. E. Connor, *op. cit.*, p. 7.

unions bitterly fought the attempt. In a letter addressed to the Commission, dated April 11, 1938, Harry Lundeberg, secretary-treasurer of the Sailors' Union of the Pacific, made the following comments:

> The U. S. Shipping Board also established shipping offices for seamen during the time the government was experimenting in shipping in the latter part of the War and after the World War. It is a matter of record that these shipping offices established by the U. S. Shipping Board teemed with a system of favoritism and vicious blacklisting of seamen, and were just as bad as any shipowners' private hiring hall when it came to blacklisting seamen, and were hated and feared by the American seamen.
>
> It is common knowledge that the U. S. Shipping Board was a vital factor in breaking the seamen's unions in the 1921 lockout, which drove thousands of bona-fide, trained seamen away from the sea and filled the ships with thousands of nondescript bums, used by the shipowners to break down wages and conditions established by our unions.
>
> The Sailor's Union of the Pacific, as an organization, is on record to fight any and all moves which attempt to take shipping out of our union halls.
>
> As an organization, in 1934, we struck for 82 days; in 1936 for 97 days in order to eliminate the shipping of seamen off the docks; through crimps or other agencies, and we will strike just as long again to keep it where it rightfully belongs—THROUGH THE UNION HALLS![32]

As is clear from Mr. Lundeberg's letter, there was a deep-seated hostility toward and distrust of any agency which interfered with union control of hiring. This feeling, of course, was not common to all unions or even a majority of them, but most of the unions visited which exercised any considerable control over placements felt that any agency which was a definite competitor of the union was to be viewed with some distrust. This view was summarized by one of the union representatives visited, who, when asked for his opinion on the strength and weaknesses of the State Employment Service, remarked that agents of the California State Employment Service were consciously competing with the union in a field which the union could handle

[32] *West Coast Sailors* (San Francisco), Apr. 15, 1938.

by itself, and that the California State Employment Service competed on a basis which called for "sales talks" and derogatory remarks by its agents pointed at the union's service.

Approximately one-third of all the unions visited had no comments to make about the California State Employment Service or were indifferent. They were either unfamiliar with the agency's work, had not heard of it, or had so little relationship with the California State Employment Service that they would not or could not express an opinion. Of 219 opinions expressed,[33] 156 could be classified as unfavorable and 63 favorable toward the California State Employment Service. The favorable opinions were largely to the effect that the California State Employment Service was a good agency for placing unskilled and unorganized labor or those unable to pay fees, or that it was good as a means of increasing general employment. A few believed that the California State Employment Service was tolerable as long as it did not interfere with the union; that it performed valuable statistical work; that it helped to employ relief workers; that it coöperated with the union in time of strikes; and that it was useful in placing domestic and agricultural workers. Very few unions were found which could be termed enthusiastic about the California State Employment Service or which enjoyed close and coöperative relationships with it.

The chief criticism expressed—other than the fear that it might undermine union control—was that the California State Employment Service was not as well acquainted with the industry and personnel as the union and therefore could not perform as satisfactory a placement service. Frequently voiced criticisms were that the California State Employment Service placed too many workers in substandard jobs; that it was inefficient in making placements; that there was corruption and

[33] The total number of opinions is more than the total number of unions visited because frequently one union representative voiced several comments.

discrimination in giving jobs; and that it was unnecessary. There were numerous criticisms that the California State Employment Service was staffed with personnel who did not know how to classify workers properly. A few commented that the California State Employment Service sent workers to jobs where strike conditions prevailed; that nonunion workers were sent to jobs where a union shop agreement existed; that its work should be limited to nonunion fields; and that too much red tape was involved in the registration and placement of workers. A few unions affiliated with the C.I.O. accused the California State Employment Service of favoritism toward members of unions affiliated with the A.F.L.

Whether or not the unfavorable criticisms were fancied or real, it was significant that their expression indicated lack of coöperation between unions and the California State Employment Service and also implied that there were serious shortcomings in the public relations policies of the California State Employment Service. The fact that nearly one-third of the unions visited were indifferent to or not aware of the activities of the California State Employment Service gives point to this. Unquestionably many of the criticisms expressed had no basis in fact, but the failure of the California State Employment Service to acquaint the unions with the real nature of its work indicated the need for an improved public relations policy.

Undoubtedly a considerable period of time will elapse before trade unions will be able to overcome their suspicions of any competitor in the placement field. These fears will probably not be conquered until such time as labor relations between unions and employers are established on a more peaceful basis than they have been up to the present time. As long as there is organized opposition to trade unionism per se on the part of employers, trade unions will not readily relinquish their control over placements which they have struggled to win. European experience indicates that close coöperation between trade unions and public employment services can be achieved, but it has been attained more readily when trade unionism was accepted as a fundamental and necessary institution in the economic life of the nation.

Fee-charging Employment Agencies.—The union officials interviewed in the course of this investigation were asked questions as to their relationships with private employment agencies and their opinion of these agencies. It is believed that the opinions were significant because they represented the attitude not only of organized labor but also of workers in crafts that were only partially organized who were likely to be familiar with the problems of the unorganized as well as the organized worker in securing employment.

Only about 10 of the unions reported that they had any relations with private employment agencies, and only in the case of unions in the amusement field was there any real dependence on fee-charging agencies in the placement of union members.[34] The other unions in this group reported no formal coöperation with fee-charging agencies but stated that these agencies were occasionally called if there was a labor shortage, and under similar circumstances a fee-charging agency might call the union.

A dozen unions reported that their members sometimes registered with fee-charging agencies, a practice which the union frequently tried to discourage. Some penalized members using private employment agencies by means of a fine or a reprimand at union meetings, and two strong unions paid the employment agency fee for their members and then requested the employer to pay the charge.

The attitude of the unions visited in the course of this study was one of hostility toward fee-charging employment agencies. Some had no comments to make, which perhaps indicated that these agencies were not important competitors or that they had

[34] See pages 296–298 for a description of these arrangements.

no strong animosity toward them. A large majority, however, expressed strong disapproval. The objections were, in the main, related to the fee practices, the type of job filled, union discrimination, and type of worker placed. Some said that no worker should have to pay for a job; others, that the fees charged were exorbitant, that the agency split fees with employers, foremen, and stores, and that the agency frequently refused to refund the fee if the worker quit. Many claimed that the fee-charging agencies placed workers in substandard and temporary jobs, and that they attempted to destroy wage standards and tried to increase labor turnover. A number were of the opinion that fee agencies were primarily a source of supply of strikebreakers. A C.I.O. union official stated that a C.I.O. union had called a strike; a fee-charging agency recruited strikebreakers and sent them to an A.F.L. union for a union card, from which office they were sent out to break the strike. Another frequent statement was that the fee agencies furnished inferior workers. In some instances it was suggested that this was the result of the lack of qualified personnel to pass satisfactorily on the ability of applicants. Others said that men didn't go to these agencies until they were down and out, and some charged that the fee agencies deliberately sent out inefficient men in order to make another placement and collect another fee.

The attitude of trade union officials toward fee-charging agencies had not changed over a period of years. Shelby M. Harrison, in his book on public employment offices, stated: "Organized labor has long been opposed to the private bureaus, charging that they are used as strike-breaking agencies, that they favor the employer, and that their sole purpose is to exploit the worker."[35] In 1938 one of the locals of the International Brotherhood of Electrical Workers passed a resolution urging various labor organizations to coöperate in introducing

[35] Shelby M. Harrison, *Public Employment Offices* (New York: Russell Sage Foundation, 1924), p. 85.

legislation at the next session of the California Legislature to abolish all private agencies, and in 1939, at a meeting of labor representatives and officials of the public employment service, a prominent labor leader urged further activity in "driving out the private agencies who take the blood and marrow from workers."

Other Employment Agencies.—The unions had few comments to make on other types of employment agencies. In a special category, however, were the technical schools which endeavored to find employment for their graduates. In only one industry (aircraft in Los Angeles) were these schools considered by the unions to be a particular menace to the union's control of placement activity. The unions' objections to these schools were that high tuition rates were charged and students were encouraged to take courses which they would never utilize as workers in the industry; that they misrepresented employment opportunities, and, as a result of widespread advertising to this effect in trade journals with national circulation, the local market was flooded with an influx of workers from all parts of the country; and that the aircraft industry used these schools to attract a large labor supply in order to depress wages and defeat union organizational efforts. The unions complained that, while hundreds of their members were unemployed, advertisements like the following appeared in trade journals and newspapers:

> Years of steady employment ahead for you, if you are a —— graduate. Help wanted at every factory. Indorsed by the industry. Aviation pays better wages. Crying need in the industry for more trained workers.

SUMMARY AND CONCLUSIONS

This study of the activities of California trade unions in bringing workers and jobs together has shown that labor organizations in a wide variety of trades and industries had recognized the importance of a union-controlled, centralized employment service. There were wide variations in the degree to which unions had organized the labor market for a particular trade or industry. Some unions (about a third of those visited[36]) had been able to secure an agreement whereby employers agreed to hire all workers through the union office. Most of these unions had organized at least a major portion of the industry; thus most of the workers in the trade or industry secured their jobs via the union employment office. Although two-thirds of the unions had not been able to establish a rule whereby all workers in any part of the trade or industry must be dispatched by the union, a considerable number in this group had developed strong placement services and dispatched a large proportion of the workers. About 40 per cent of the unions visited, while recognizing the importance of a union employment service, did not dispatch more than a small proportion of the workers at the time this study was made.

It appeared that the development of employment exchanges by trade unions has been part of their program to increase the strength of their organizations. In part it has been an outgrowth of a desire to provide for the worker a central source of information as to job openings, thus saving him the time and energy often expended in hit-and-miss job hunting; and in part it was a means of insuring that agreed rules and regulations in regard to hiring of union members would be maintained. Most of the unions concerned themselves not only with getting jobs for their members but also made some attempt to equalize employment and thus give greater security to all. Union placement offices, like other types of labor exchanges, cannot make jobs where none exist. They have, however, at least in some instances, been an important factor in bringing some order out of chaos in the marketing of labor.

[36] See pages 347, 349 for the characteristics of the sample of unions visited. It does not follow that one-third of all unions in the cities visited controlled the placements of their members.

X. Employers' Associations

A WIDE VARIETY of associations have been organized by groups of employers. Although these associations are always for the purpose of furthering the mutual interests of the employing group, there are considerable differences in the lines of activity they pursue.

Such organizations as Chambers of Commerce have been set up with the very broad purpose of representing the interests of the employing class as a group, rather than of a particular trade or industry. They concern themselves in part with interpreting the business man's point of view to the community and to the law-making bodies, frequently in civic as well as in business matters. Chambers of Commerce also furnish various sorts of technical and administrative services to their membership, such as information on traffic routes, credit ratings, and methods of packing for foreign shipping, and occasionally they engage in activities in the field of labor problems.

Another type of employers' association is the trade association, an organization of employers in the same trade or industry. The purpose of such an association may be similar to that of a Chamber of Commerce, and it may thus concern itself largely with legislation, public relations, and meetings of members to discuss problems of mutual interest. These associations are, however, likely to perform a number of technical services for their membership, such as setting up standard accounting procedures and a statistical information service. Not infrequently the work of these association has culminated in the establishment of uniform price and production policies. Another and often an important function of these associations is united action in dealing with labor questions. In some instances this consists of negotiating agreements with trade unions, but more frequently the purpose is to combat trade union organization.

There are also some associations which cut across a number of industries, such as a general industrial association or an organization of merchants and manufacturers. These associations may include within their scope a number of the activities mentioned above, although frequently they concentrate their attention chiefly on labor problems.

Although employers' associations are most commonly thought of as an industrial phenomenon, agricultural employers have also formed organizations to consider problems of special interest to this group of employers. Many of these organizations are coöperative marketing associations, others are special sections of Chambers of Commerce, and some are general farmers' associations, of which the Associated Farmers is the best-known example.

Since employers' associations often include labor problems within the scope of their activities, it was important to attempt to determine to what extent organizations of this sort had established employment bureaus or in other ways assisted in bringing together jobs and workers in the areas visited in this study.

ASSOCIATIONS IN INDUSTRY

Number of Associations Doing Placement Work.—In San Francisco informed sources agreed that there was only one employers' organization in the city that ran a regular employment office.[1] Investigation disclosed another that acted as a casual clearing house for a few jobs and applicants that happened to drift in; others of this type would probably have been found if the trade associations of the city had been thoroughly sampled, but such effort seemed unprofitable. In Los Angeles employers' associations were more active in this field. Of the 18 industrial associations visited, 6 operated regular employment bureaus,

[1] This office was subsequently closed in a reorganization of the association.

4 did some informal placement work,[2] and there were probably numerous other organizations in the field which were not covered by the sample. An officer of the Personnel Managers Association ventured the prophecy that "sooner or later every major industrial group will have its own employment bureau." Nevertheless, the progress toward such a goal was still in its infancy, as may be gauged by the relation between the 10 associations which did at least some placement work, with possibly a few others of less importance not visited, and the hundreds of trade and business associations in Los Angeles. In Sacramento and in Bakersfield apparently none of the industrial employers' associations engaged in any sort of placement work.

Reasons for Entering the Placement Field.—Employers' associations had, in the main, organized placement bureaus either to forestall union control of hiring or to keep union members or "agitators" out of the plants in the community. At the time this study was made, a second factor was also of some importance in the development of this field of activity. Several Los Angeles associations mentioned the importance of a central employment bureau through which workers could be transferred expeditiously from plant to plant as a method of reducing the cost of unemployment compensation.[3]

Although it was common knowledge that employment offices of employers' associations in California had frequently been organized and maintained to combat union activity—to supply workers for "open shop" firms, to supply strikebreakers, and blacklist union organizers—it was practically impossible to secure definite answers to questions on these points from the officers of the associations. However, a number of statements made by officials of the employment bureaus of all the large

[2] This did not at all represent the proportion of employers' associations in Los Angeles that did placement work, because only those organizations were visited where there was reason to expect an employment office of some type.

[3] These employers were looking to the future when, under California's merit rating plan, contributions might be reduced for employers who maintained a given reserve in their unemployment insurance account.

employers' associations in San Francisco and Los Angeles, with the exception of the motion-picture industry, indicated quite clearly antiunion activity. They were "open-shop organizations"; they had been established at the time of a threatened strike; they were set up to "give employer and employee freedom under the 'American plan' when unionism was becoming strong." "Workers who believe in industrial freedom patronize us." "If a strike exists and the reason is not that the employer has failed to pay the rates agreed to by the association, men will be sent to the job." "You may have heard that this is a strikebreaking organization. This is not true. If one of our members is having labor trouble and if his workers walk out, we instruct the employer to notify his workers that the plant will be open on a certain day and that the conditions of work will be as stated. If the workers refuse to return to work, the bureau calls men from its files for interview. They are told the wages and hours and that there is a strike in progress. They can accept the work or not, as they like. On their card of introduction to the employer is stamped 'strike,' which is required by law." The difference between this and any other form of strikebreaking was hard to see. Blacklisting was the most common of all allegations against employers' associations and the most difficult to prove. The same organization just quoted cited a recent example of an employer who asked that two specific men be sent to him by the placement bureau; the office manager checked their cards, found them to be active union members, and sent two other men instead. Other organizations were more reticent about this phase of their activities, but the universal emphasis on checking references of all referrals may have been significant.

As further indication of the importance of "open shop" policies in establishing employment bureaus, quotations from the investigations of the Senate Civil Liberties Committee in Los Angeles in January 1940 may be cited, particularly since the organization investigated was also included in our sample.[4] Moreover, it was the archetype of a number of large employers' associations in California cities. "The day's hearing . . . was devoted to activities of the Merchants and Manufacturers' Association in its admitted campaign on behalf of the open shop in Los Angeles industrial plants. Fred R. Fysch, general manager of the association and the second witness called, defined its objective as the open shop, and La Follette read from its own files a record of the disbursement of $598,000 during the last six years. . . . Stuart Neary . . . told of its efforts to rally industrialists to the support of the association. 'The purpose of the reorganization [in March 1936, because of the National Labor Relations Act] was to enable the Merchants and Manufacurers' Association to maintain somewhat of an equality with labor and prevent the domination of labor by the closed shop,' he said. As to the definition of the closed shop, Neary said heads of the association had found themselves unable to agree. 'The Merchants and Manufacturers' Association makes a fight for the principles of the open shop and the members didn't agree what it is?' Senator La Follette asked. The reorganization, Neary said, was impelled by criticisms that the association acted only on behalf of its own members. . . . La Follette read an affidavit from Perry . . . in which he declared he resigned as association manager in 1936 when 'reactionary interests on the board of directors reasserted themselves' and he believed their plans 'to be in violation of the national recovery act.' Neary denied that was the case. . . . The agency, said an association pamphlet . . . 'has placed thousands of open-shop workers.' 'Many of them,' it said, 'formerly carried union cards.' Len O. Gunn, manager of the employment office, declared the union affiliation of a job applicant never was a matter of inquiry. . . . He denied nonunion men were given preference as to jobs and

[4] Associated Press dispatches from the *San Francisco Chronicle* (California), Jan. 11 and 12, 1940.

when Senator La Follette called attention to check marks on the face of some registration cards, Gunn reiterated they 'didn't mean a thing.' He persisted in that stand even when the chairman read from the reverse of one of the cards so marked that the applicant 'joined the Truck Drivers' Union' and from another that the subject 'said he would not take a strike job. Joined the union.' La Follette then put into the record a report of the committee's investigators on their check of 798 cards from the agency's files, half those of persons who had taken strike jobs and half who had not. The investigators reported that two and one-fourth times as many persons who had accepted strike jobs were sent to other jobs later as those who had not taken strike work. 'A strikebreaker was more than twice as likely to get a job, compared to nonstrikebreakers,' their report said. Fred R. Fysch . . . testified the association furnished 5,081 maritime workers during the 1934 Los Angeles waterfront strike, 1,281 longshoremen, and the rest crewmen on ships. La Follette put into the record a digest made by committee staff members from records of the association, showing a total of 896 persons had been furnished to employers by the replacement bureau under strike conditions in the last three years. It stated that strike replacements in 1937 constituted 19 per cent of all the bureau's placements; that in 1938 they made up 12 per cent and last year 9.5 per cent."

A few of the employment bureaus in these employer groups had been organized for quite different reasons. Central Casting Corporation, which supplied all the extras used by the eight major motion-picture companies, was organized in 1925 to eradicate the evils of the previous, uncontrolled hiring system.[5] Under earlier conditions all hiring was done at the door, forcing the extras to make the rounds daily at great expense of time and carfare, or through commercial agencies, which charged fees and chiseled the extras in a variety of ways. The new setup

[5] This development occurred following a survey of the situation by the Russell Sage Foundation.

made hiring through Central Casting obligatory, it was financed by the studios so that its services to extras were entirely free, and it had made various efforts to solve the problem of a very grave oversupply of labor either by spreading work or by tacitly limiting calls to a small group of registrants, who thereby received more nearly full employment. It was worthy of note that no registrant would be accepted unless he was a union member.

Another organization which was not in the union-breaking category was the Stock Exchange Institute in Los Angeles, which acted as a "central personnel office" for member firms, keeping records of applicants and doing the preliminary selection and interviewing in a highly specialized, very limited field, where the average firm had a relatively small number of employees and could not therefore afford its own personnel offices. It was closely tied up with the Institute's educational work. There were no unions nor immediate threat of union activity in the field.

Some further comment should perhaps be made as to the effect of unemployment compensation on the development of employment bureaus by employers' associations. As has already been stated, a number of these associations in Los Angeles mentioned the reduction of the costs of unemployment insurance as one of their primary aims. A model system for this purpose implied: (1) that members report all layoffs and send the men to register at the bureau; (2) that members agree to hire only through the bureau; (3) that preference in placing men be given to those who are at the end of their waiting period but who have not received any benefits. Only one organization visited claimed to have such a system in operation, and outside skeptics suggested that it was far from functioning perfectly. The chief difficulty apparently lay in securing members' full coöperation. The reason for this, suggested by one officer of an association, may be applicable to others. This man said that employers were afraid of losing permanently some of their good workers who were laid off during the slack season, and therefore they would not send them to register for other jobs. Moreover, to judge from the employers visited, few were willing to relinquish their right to select their own workers even to their own trade association. Another very significant reason for failure in attempts to shift laid-off workers to another employer in the industry before they began to collect unemployment insurance benefits was that in most industries the slack season was the same for all firms. In slack periods there were no openings for the workers referred to the bureau; in busy seasons the bureau could not fill its members' orders. This was especially true in the clothing trade, one of whose branches had been attempting unsuccessfully to help members to qualify for merit rating.

Method of Financing.—All of these employment bureaus were wholly financed by the parent trade association and offered their services free to the job seeker. Consequently the bureaus and their activities were outside the jurisdiction of the State Labor Commissioner's office, because the California Employment Agency Law applies only to agencies which charge fees.

Field of Activity.—The field in which these employers' association placement offices operated covered a wide variety of industries and jobs. The most important in terms of numbers placed were moving pictures, metal trades, building and construction, printing, and "manufacturing and construction," as specified by one Los Angeles organization which purported to cover everything from aircraft mechanics to cooks. It is difficult to generalize from the data which were obtainable; but apparently the emphasis was on supplying skilled and semiskilled operators in the industries covered, as might be expected if one of the purposes of these bureaus was to combat unionization. The smaller offices supplied office workers for stock exchange firms, for Italian commercial firms, and for retail lumber dealers, electrical salesmen, operators for the cotton garment trade, and crews for oil tankers.

Nearly half the associations visited would fill orders only for member firms. A notable example was Central Casting, which supplied extras only to the eight companies supporting it. The definitely antiunion organizations, in which category all the large placement offices except Central Casting must be included, were willing to supply workers to any firm, whether a member of the parent association or not; and the Merchants and Manufacturers Association, the most openly antiunion of them all, was actively soliciting business from a wide variety of Los Angeles firms, offering possible reductions in payroll taxes as one of the inducements.

Almost all of these associations limited their operations to the immediate vicinity, but a few said that they filled jobs throughout the state or all up the west coast.

Scale of Operation.—Seven of the employers' associations visited had a separate department for placement work with at least one full-time person in charge. All of these except Central Casting had a staff of less than six—typically, a manager, assistant, and secretary—even though they were doing a very large business. Central Casting reported a staff of 35, many of them telephone and teletype operators. In four other associations there was no regular placement officer, and the employment bureau was operated by the secretary or his stenographer. In one the only placement work was extremely informal, casual referrals of jobs or applicants which happened to come to the manager's attention.

The number of placements in 1937 ranged from less than 25 in one bureau to a quarter of million in another. The latter figure, representing 294,000 jobs for 16,000 different people, was for Central Casting. Four offices reported between 2,000 and 4,000 placements; two, between 300 and 400. Two made probably less than two placements a month; one had just started operations; one had formerly been very busy, but the depression had so reduced the turnover in the industry that the bureau was doing little or no work.

The number of placements made by any given employment office should, of course, be qualified by the proportion which were temporary, but this information was surprisingly difficult to obtain. Perhaps the answer lay in one manager's suggestion that many supposedly temporary jobs proved permanent. The very large number of jobs filled by Central Casting was explained by the fact that all motion-picture extras' jobs were temporary, frequently for no longer than a single day. Building and construction jobs were also essentially temporary. Of the other large bureaus that reported on this matter, one said that most of the jobs it furnished were permanent; the other, that the great majority were temporary—a difference not explained by the industries they respectively served. The bureau reporting a great reduction of turnover in its industry was now making permanent placements. Some of the small bureaus reported most of their jobs to be permanent; one had filled only three or four permanent jobs in its whole history; others could not furnish the information.

Placements.—The techniques of bringing together jobs reported and the applicants who had registered in these bureaus presented no points of interest significantly different from the procedures common to any employment agency, except for the telephone system installed by Central Casting, which is described below. However, the methods of obtaining job openings and applicants were necessarily different in organizations whose membership consisted of employers than in agencies with less close affiliations with the men who had jobs to be filled. Naturally the chief source of openings for all these bureaus was the member firms which supported the bureau for their own use and convenience. As has been mentioned, about half of the employment offices visited served only their own membership.

Two of the large ones that welcomed orders from outside firms sent field men to solicit orders, and one of them did extensive and frequent direct mail advertising. Two others occasionally reminded their membership of the existence of the employment bureau. The remainder made no attempt of any sort to solicit patronage. The majority of the employers' association placement offices visited were not even listed as employment agencies in the classified section of the telephone book. In a few cases the members' inducement to use the employment bureau which they supported was implemented by an agreement not to hire from any other source.[6] This was true of the organization already mentioned which was attempting to qualify its members for merit rating on unemployment compensation taxes by finding jobs for employees laid off before they became eligible for compensation. These firms agreed to rehire first from their own list of layoffs and subsequently to call only their own association; infractions of this rule were disciplined. The producers belonging to Central Casting hired all their extras through that organization, none directly. One other organization said it did all the hiring for the parent companies; another did all the temporary hiring and was the only agency used, although much permanent hiring was done by the firms from direct application or friends' recommendations. The other organizations obtained only part of the business of the parent firms. One, which had been set up in an attempt to qualify for merit rating, but which was proving a failure, supplied only a very small fraction of the new employees, both because its scale of operations was too small and because the seasonal factor made all the firms' labor needs rise and fall simultaneously.

The association membership was also the chief source of workers seeking jobs. One employer interviewed referred all layoffs to the employment bureau to register. Several others sometimes referred layoffs as part of the program to obtain

[6] For a check on how fully this agreement was being kept, see below.

merit rating. Many offices reported that member firms referred likely looking workers who applied at the door, and that this was an important source. All of them relied to a large extent upon their reputation and word-of-mouth advertising. Only three reported occasional newspaper advertisements when men of special skills were needed. The large offices all said they had long lists of applicants, built up over a period of years, on which to draw.

In this respect, as in most others, the Central Casting Corporation was unique, and its method of operation warrants special mention. Organized to remedy a situation of planless direct application or exploitation by commercial agencies, it took over the registration lists of these agencies when it started operation. The determining factor in its situation was not to find jobs, since all the coöperating companies turned over to it the hiring of their extras, nor to find applicants, since its registration covered some 12,000 persons, with an average of only 600 to 800 jobs available per day, but to distribute the available work among an immense surplus of job seekers, to select the suitable type for each studio call from this mass of registrations, and to handle efficiently an immense volume of business. The solution found was to install an elaborate private telephone exchange. Orders were received from the studios by teletypewriter, specifying number and type of extras needed and sometimes apparently calling for individuals by name. The casting men selected individuals to fill the orders from their personal knowledge of the extra list, from a file, from a directory-board system, or from the elaborate Hollerith cards prepared for all registered extras giving their qualifications in detail. Extras who wanted work were told to call Central Casting several times a day; their calls were switched to the casting room through a loud speaker and picked up by any casting man who had selected them for an assignment; if not picked up, they were told to call again. Individuals needed for a particular assignment were reached by telephone if they failed to call. This system handled an average of 12,500 calls per working day with a staff of 35 people and reduced the extra's job hunting to a couple of telephone calls a day.

Relations to Other Employment Services and Importance in the Labor Market.—All of these employers' association placement bureaus were convinced that no other agency could handle their particular job, and those which were not openly opposed to the State Employment Service were convinced that it was of little use in their field. Oddly, perhaps, the men interviewed in these organizations had little love for fee-charging agencies, in comparison with the widespread praise they received from individual employers.

The principal reasons alleged for their own indispensability were that they knew both the industrial processes and the individual employers and workers in the industry as no outsider could, and that in many cases, they combined with their placement work the functions of a central personnel and labor relations department. It was their contention that men familiar with a single field could discover from an interview the specific skills and experience of an applicant, catalogue him correctly, and, when an opening offered, select from their files the persons with precisely the skills needed to fit the job. This the State Employment Service was failing to do. One man in the needle trades, as an example of other similar complaints, described calling the Employment Service for workers when his own lists were exhausted and said that "the young girls there didn't know one operation from another" and sent him operators who could not do the job he had specified. Sometimes this failure to classify workers properly and fit them to job requirements was blamed on untrained interviewers, sometimes on "politics," sometimes on the absence of desire to do good work, etc. But even the most thoughtful and least prejudiced of the men in these organizations were doubtful whether intimate technological knowledge of many fields was possible for interviewers in a large-scale, centralized placement system. Most of the bureau managers made a point of their personal acquaintance with the idiosyncrasies, abilities, and tastes of employers, foremen, and workmen in their industry—for instance, which company liked middle-aged workers, which preferred "live wires," and which man was always "talking himself out of a job"—and could therefore take into account the personal element in fitting a man to a job. Most of them stressed the fact that they always checked applicants' references, which the State Employment Service could not or would not do. Other criticisms of the State Employment Service were that it would not take into consideration a worker's status in relation to unemployment compensation and thereby promote attempts to establish merit rating for payroll taxes, that a man with a long and good work history had no better chance of being placed than a man on the margin of employability, and that its officials were "crude and discourteous."

Several organizations were running a sort of personnel or labor relations service along with the employment bureau, enforcing their own minimum standards of wages and "employment practices" in open-shop industries to prevent "unfair competition," investigating such problems as that of a foreman who fired too many men, and doing much of the interviewing and selecting of new employees for employers who trusted their judgment.

Contacts and coöperation with the State Employment Service, even in the organizations not openly hostile, were very limited. Sometimes the Employment Service referred workers to these agencies to register; occasionally it called one of them for an applicant to fill a job. Several of the organizations referred to the Employment Service unskilled or handicapped applicants whom they would not themselves accept. One of the large bureaus had a unique arrangement whereby the local Employment

Service office would send out for a man whom the bureau wanted in a hurry for a job, and in exchange all the bureau's very considerable number of placements were reported by the Employment Service as part of its monthly placement record, although there was no official connection between them. None of the employers' associations anticipated any closer collaboration or any taking over of their work by the state in the future. There was even less contact with other community placement agencies, although two of the offices had applicants referred to them by some of the philanthropic organizations for placement.

Use of These Associations by Employers Interviewed.—Only a small fraction of the firms interviewed in San Francisco and Los Angeles reported using trade associations as a source of new workers. However, several factors in the sampling process may have contributed to the apparent discrepancy between this and the reports of large placements by some of the trade associations visited. The sample of employers consisted chiefly of large firms, and it is possible that small firms without personnel departments of their own and with fewer unsolicited applicants for work might have made more use of a central agency. Moreover, the questions about source of new workers presumed normal conditions, ruling out applications to trade associations during strikes. In addition, the industries served by some of the trade associations visited were represented very lightly or not at all in the sample of employers. The most notable examples of this were the construction and metal trades in San Francisco.

Of the 76 firms visited in San Francisco, only two ever called on a trade association to supply labor, one commonly, one very seldom; neither association was visited for this study. In Los Angeles 11 of 74 firms reported making use of trade associations for workers. The claims of the association which was attempting to reduce the cost of unemployment insurance through a compulsory use of the centralized employment bureau was partly confirmed. Four of the six firms visited supposedly covered by the association agreement[7] mentioned the association as at least their chief source of new workers, though one refused to refer its layoffs there for fear of blacklisting. They spoke of the central employment bureau as a great boon to small firms. The claim of one large Los Angeles trade association that it placed workers in many fields was not entirely substantiated by the employers visited. Although airplane mechanics were listed among the fields it covered, none of the aircraft manufacturing concerns ever called on them for workers. The same was true of automobile and a number of less important industries.[8]

ASSOCIATIONS OF AGRICULTURAL EMPLOYERS[9]

As has already been stated, there were a number of different types of associations of agricultural employers. Many were coöperative marketing associations with highly organized central offices serving members through local associations. These organizations performed functions similar to those of an industrial trade association. Others were for the more general purpose of interpreting the farmer's point of view to the community.

Very few of these associations in 1938 had extended their functions to serve the grower's interest as an employer by operating an employment bureau. One of the factors which must not be ignored in the situation, although it was impossible to weigh and nicely judge its total effect, was the very large oversupply of agricultural labor in California in recent years, which tended to make such efforts superfluous. Some indication

[7] One large firm visited had been mentioned by the association as not included in their membership.

[8] Here, again, it should be noted that none of the manufacturing or commercial firms visited were questioned about the sources they might call upon for strikebreakers.

[9] Certain agricultural enterprises—cotton gins and packing sheds—which were run by private companies and not by a coöperative association were included here, because their activities as distributors of labor paralleled those of their coöperative competitors.

may be found from the fact that certain of the associations, especially the Chamber of Commerce, either scouted for agricultural workers in earlier years when there was a shortage or actually imported them in large numbers from other states or countries, notably from Mexico, and that the only organized agricultural employment service run by the employing groups was set up in 1926 to meet a shortage and had done progressively less work in recent years.

San Joaquin Valley Labor Bureau.—Only one of the agricultural employers' associations visited—and they covered most of the crops included in this study—was actually set up as an employment office. The San Joaquin Valley Labor Bureau was inaugurated in 1926 to take over the business of a defunct organization serving fruit growers but soon branched out into cotton and other crops. It had a board of directors, representing various farm interests and Chambers of Commerce and a staff of three established in an employment office of the usual type beside the railroad tracks in Fresno. It was financed by growers, processors, Chambers of Commerce, sugar companies, and other agricultural interests.[10] The chief aim of the organization was to be a "labor insurance policy for the farmers." Secondarily, it was to act as a public relations representative for farm interests in dealing with such government agencies as the immigration authorities or the Industrial Accident Commission and to sponsor meetings of certain farm interests in the lower San Joaquin Valley to set up wage rates each year in certain crops. During the earlier years workers were obtained from direct applications to the Fresno office, from the manager's wide acquaint-

[10] Total subscriptions to the San Joaquin Valley Labor Bureau were from approximately $6,000 to about $8,500 in the years 1932 to 1936. For the year ending January 31, 1937, subscriptions amounted to nearly $11,000, and in 1938 approximately $6,000 was subscribed. For a list of subscribers to the San Joaquin Valley Labor Bureau in 1938 see *Hearings before a Subcommittee of the Committee on Education and Labor, United States Senate,* 76th Cong., 2d sess., Part 51, California Agricultural Background, Dec. 20 and 21, 1939 (Washington: Government Printing Office, 1940), pp. 18822–18823.

ance among the Mexicans who were at that time the chief source of agricultural labor, by distribution of leaflets in Spanish,[11] by scouts sent out to locate migratory workers and tell them where to go, and by establishment of a temporary branch office during the cotton picking season at the southern entrance of the Valley to direct incoming migrants to the areas where they were needed. An estimate of the number of workers needed and the localities in which a shortage might occur was obtained in advance of the season by questionnaires to growers. It was noteworthy that the greater part of the work of this office was apparently directing the flow of migratory workers to localities rather than filling specific orders. Two large growers in Bakersfield, closely connected with the San Joaquin Valley Labor Bureau, described the system as one in which the Bureau merely routed laborers to a district and left it up to the individual grower to choose his workers.

Under such a system it was obviously difficult to estimate the amount of work done by the office. A total of 18,000 placements was claimed in 1927, with no figures available for subsequent years. Obviously the volume had fallen off greatly, both because of the huge surplus of agricultural labor in almost all districts of the state and because Mexicans, who were accustomed to make contacts through this office, had become a small fraction of the labor force. According to the manager, the Bureau had been attempting to work through the State Employment Service almost exclusively in recent years. Growers' orders had been transmitted directly to the State Service, or, when the growers objected to this procedure, workers were obtained from the State Service and forwarded through the San Joaquin Valley Labor Bureau. This system was reported to have worked fairly well until July 1938, when unemployment compensation became so important in the California State Employment Service offices that the Employment Service per se was swamped.

[11] Printed in red to simulate announcements of bullfights.

Probably a more accurate picture of the true status of the Bureau is given by the fact that of the group of nearly 150 farmers visited from Sacramento to Los Angeles—two-thirds of them in the Bakersfield and Fresno areas, where the Bureau purported chiefly to operate—not a single one reported obtaining any workers from the Bureau in recent years. Only one grower of all those visited in Sacramento mentioned it as a potential source of labor if a shortage should occur; none, in Los Angeles. Of the 65 growers visited near Bakersfield, the vast majority had either never heard of the San Joaquin Valley Labor Bureau or had no occasion to use it; man after man assured the investigators that no one in his locality used it. Less than a half-dozen growers spoke favorably of the Bureau as having been useful in the past and a possible resource for the future. Obviously the temporary branch office was a matter of ancient history. In Fresno, its home district, the Bureau was better known; but a greater proportion of growers spoke of it with disfavor, either because of its policies or because of their experience with the labor it furnished in past years. As in Bakersfield, the majority had no occasion to use it. It was noteworthy that the praises of the San Joaquin Valley Labor Bureau came almost entirely from men who represented the big-scale, industrialized farmer, officials of the Associated Farmers, and representatives of these interests. They were couched in the general terms that it was the only organization that gave any satisfaction and that the manager knew more about agricultural labor than anyone else in the state, but they gave no indication that these men obtained workers there when, as in 1938, they could be hired at the gate. The small grower continued, sometimes unknowingly, to support the Bureau through his annual contribution to his local farm bureau or Chamber of Commerce, but he knew it principally, and by no means always favorably, for its sponsorship of the annual wage-fixing meetings for cotton, grapes, and other crops.

Other Agricultural Employers' Associations.—The other farmers' organizations that did any employment work in the areas visited in 1938 made no attempt to recruit labor or even to estimate the labor needs of their membership. They acted purely as informal distributing points for the migratory workers who dropped into the office asking, "Where are they picking today?" and sent them out either to growers who had called or to men who, from the officials' general knowledge, were likely to be in the market for harvest hands. All but one of these were coöperative packing sheds in small towns. The exception was the local Chamber of Commerce in a small town south of Fresno, situated directly on the highway, which, as an accommodation to its farmer members, posted on an outside blackboard notices of job openings for the benefit of the transients who, apparently, frequently stopped in. It also directed transients to likely places off the main stream of migratory traffic along the highway. The packing sheds and coöperative cotton gins were variations on much the same pattern, without the blackboard. Transients who dropped in were directed to the farmers who had called to say that they needed some extra hands. On the whole, there was little or no solicitation of either workers or jobs. One plant would call former employers to see if they had an opening when their last year's hand turned up or would telephone a fee-charging agency in Sacramento if there were no workers available to fill a call. Another noted the location of crew bosses' camps and referred prospective employers there. In every case, of course, the motive was service to the employer membership. It was noteworthy that only transients were dealt with; presumably the local residents knew as much about local job opportunities as did the packing-house officials.

Commercial cotton gins were not employers' associations and perhaps should really be classified with businesses that gave service to their customers. But their method of distributing labor informally among the growers who sent word that they needed pickers was indistinguishable from that of a coöperative fruit packing shed or the rare coöperative cotton gin. The gin was a focal point for transients entering the community and for farmers who were seeking labor, but in no case was there any registration, solicitation, or any type of formal placement activity.

It was completely impossible to estimate the number of agricultural placements through these employers' associations, because only two kept any record of actually directing specific individuals to specific jobs. The Chamber of Commerce mentioned above sent out 400 in 1936 but less than 100 in 1937 as the custom of applying directly to the farm became more widespread. A packing house in the foothills above Sacramento, by far the best organized of these services, sent out individuals only on order and had furnished 384 men during 1937—according to their estimate, about 75 per cent of all nonresidents employed in the harvest in that locality. When the workers were merely directed to localities, or when the employers came to pick them up from the shed platform, it was not only impossible to estimate the number "placed," but such estimates of numbers of applicants handled would be meaningless.

Reason for Entering the Placement Field.—Probably the chief reason why the placement services which the farmers' associations offered to their members were so haphazard was the great surplus of agricultural labor in California in recent years, which made it unnecessary for growers in most crops to look further than the crowd of applicants at their own gates. In earlier years at periods of labor shortage efforts had been made by various employer organizations to supply the deficiency. The Los Angeles Chamber of Commerce said it imported 5,000 Mexicans during the World War and had been recommending since 1926 a clearing house plan for importing Mexican laborers under contract to be registered, guarded, and subsequently repatriated. It is notable that one of its representatives had also been urging child labor in California agriculture. "California has one great economic labor reservoir which has been permitted to become stagnant. I mean the children of the state."[12] The earlier efforts of the San Joaquin Valley Labor Bureau have already been described. When there was an agricultural strike in 1937 at Winters, a small town in the Sacramento area, a citizens' committee with headquarters in the city hall advertised for workers, registered transients, assigned them to local camps, shifted crews from grower to grower, and organized the labor market quite successfully, according to local residents. These were examples of the sort of effort that was made by employers' organizations to obtain workers for their membership when the supply was short or when strikes had cut off the normal supply.[13] But these efforts were uncoördinated and temporary. It is perhaps surprising that the militantly antiunion organizations, notably the Associated Farmers, had made no attempt to set up some control over the agricultural labor supply through a centralized placement system. The chief weapons used were propaganda and attempted legislation. "If the 'closed shop' and the 'union hiring hall' are to be forced on agriculture, with the result that farm workers are made subject to the whims and prejudices of hiring hall bosses, and farmers are denied the right to employ the men best suited to work on their farms, then even the best-equipped farmers of tomorrow are foredoomed to failure."[14] There was no indication of any developments to be expected that would parallel the employment offices of some of

[12] George P. Clements, *Talk before the Annual Conference of "Friends of the Mexicans,"* Claremont, California, Nov. 13, 1926.

[13] Commercial companies giving service to their customers have also made special efforts at such times to supply field labor. According to one source, the sugar companies used to import Mexicans on a considerable scale. One gin manager described his attempts to scout for labor in an adjacent community during a local shortage.

[14] ". . . a recent news release . . . by Ralph Taylor, executive secretary of the Agricultural Council of California . . . ," Bulletin of the Associated Farmers of California, Inc., *From Apathy to Action* (San Francisco: May 9, 1938).

the nonagricultural employers' associations, such as the Merchants and Manufacturers Association.

The characteristic feature of placement work done by agricultural employers' associations was that it was completely decentralized and more or less random. Only local offices did any of the directional work, to which placement activities were limited, and the distinction between the packing sheds which did and those which did not seemed largely a matter of historical accident. According to what information was available, most of the local deciduous fruit associations around Sacramento were informal clearing houses for fruit pickers, but it was not invariably true, and the scale of these operations varied greatly. In the grape area around Fresno labor was apparently more likely to go directly to the farmer than to the shed. The central office of the walnut association in Los Angeles indicated that the local associations tried to help their members find pickers, but there was no sign of such activity in those visited, although walnuts were one of the few crops in which there was no surplus of labor. In one major crop (citrus) the packing houses sent out their own crews to harvest, so the farmer had no labor problem except for occasional activities, such as smudging; one of the many packing houses visited reported that it assisted its members in finding such crews as were needed. The strawberry association in Sacramento reported that in times of shortage it tried to help its membership find crews but was usually no more successful than the farmers had been.

The only indication of increased future activity in the placement field by agricultural employers' associations was a plan being worked out by a committee of citrus marketing associations. As has already been pointed out, these associations operated packing houses which employed not only workers to pack the fruit but also the labor for picking, and all of these workers were covered by unemployment insurance. In order to take advantage of the merit rating provisions of the unemployment insurance law and thus to reduce the costs of this insurance, a committee was considering the possibility of establishing a pool of labor for the citrus industry and a system whereby workers could be transferred quickly from place to place and steadier employment provided for a given group. According to the official interviewed, the plan also included a system of rating in accordance with the worker's unemployment insurance status. "If 10 men are equally well qualified for a job, preference will be given to the man who would draw the largest unemployment insurance benefits. Furthermore, the work will be spread so as to keep as many off unemployment insurance as possible." Although the above statement includes the words "qualified for a job," it was clear that the proposal was primarily to reduce unemployment insurance payments rather than to place workers who were most qualified for the job.

At the time this study was made, the above description applied merely to a paper plan. It is possible, however, that in the future similar plans may be developed and put into action by a number of employers' associations whose workers are covered by unemployment insurance. Such a development would appear to be an unnecessary duplication, since there exists a state-wide public employment service. In order to avoid this, however, employers must be convinced that the California State Employment Service will give them good service and not send "any floating bum." While it could hardly be expected that the California State Employment Service would make placements on the basis of the unemployment insurance status of the worker, if workers formerly employed in a certain industry were given preference in placements in that industry, it would probably be unnecessary to work out a complicated and perhaps unfair "unemployment insurance rating" in order to meet the needs of the industry.

SUMMARY

Only in a few instances had employers' associations organized employment bureaus on an elaborate and extensive scale. Although there were undoubtedly a considerable number of these associations which did a little informal placement work, in the main, the scope of their activities was limited to other fields—interpreting the employer to the community or various forms of technical service.

Employers' associations employment bureaus in industry had most frequently developed as a bulwark to the employer's "freedom"—freedom to employ nonunion workers. They have therefore been found most often when trade unions were gaining a strong foothold. The motion-picture industry must, of course, be mentioned as an exception. In this industry the employment bureau was organized to bring some order into the labor market for "extras." All those who registered must be members of the union, and thus the purpose of this bureau was in no sense to break the union.

Agricultural employers' associations had entered the placement field to an even less extent. There appeared to be only one such association in California which operated an employment bureau at the time this study was made, and this agency merely directed workers to areas where jobs might be available rather than referred specific workers to jobs. A few other associations of agricultural employers occasionally acted as an intermediary between workers and farmers, but these organizations had not set up anything which resembled organized placement services.

It is not possible to prognosticate the future of employers' associations in the placement field, but it is likely that they will become more active when labor shortages develop. It is important to recognize that there are certain dangers which are to a considerable extent inherent in employment bureaus of this sort. While employers' associations may organize placement services for the sole purpose of facilitating quick transference of workers from job to job, other motives may also be present. There is always the possibility of discrimination against union members and of blacklisting former employees for union activities or for other reasons not related to the capacity of the worker. It would be far better in most instances for the pool of labor to be centralized in a free employment service whose aim should be to place qualified workers, and in which it could be expected that there would be no ulterior motives in choosing Jones instead of Smith for a job.

XI. The California Labor Market

THUS FAR in this study the agencies operating in the placement field have been classified in accordance with the institution or group which organized and administered the service. The preceding chapters have described numerous free placement services organized by various units of the government, by social service organizations, trade and professional schools, businesses as a service to customers, trade unions, employers' associations, and occupational and fraternal associations. Also included in the analysis were large numbers of agencies which charged a fee, and which had been organized by individual entrepreneurs, and labor contractors operating in agriculture. Although there was some specialization on the part of certain of the institutions in the placement field, almost any worker in search of a job was confronted by so many choices that he might easily find it more economical of time and money to tramp from factory gate to factory gate rather than from the door of one employment agency to another. Employers similarly might choose one of many agencies or just count on workers to turn up when they were needed. An attempt will now be made to view the employment services from the point of view of the occupations which they served and to point out wherein there were differences in job-getting techniques in the various occupational groups.

PROFESSIONAL WORKERS

Certain professions, such as physicians and lawyers, are largely self-employed and their placement problems were not considered to come within the scope of this study. Other professional persons such as teachers, nurses, engineers and social workers, except in occasional instances do not set up in business for themselves, but rather seek an employer in need of their services. This study yielded certain information as to how persons in professional employments were placed. It was somewhat surprising to find that the professions which have so frequently organized for educational or social purposes have given little attention to the marketing of their services. The labor markets for teachers and nurses and for motion-picture extras were examples of some considerable degree of organization.

It is probable that a very large proportion of the teachers in the primary, secondary, and high schools of the state were placed either through the California Teachers Association, which had offices in San Francisco and in Los Angeles, or through the placement bureaus of the universities or state teachers colleges. There were also a few fee-charging employment agencies which operated in this field, but their importance was probably quite insignificant. Although the placement of teachers in California was largely through placement bureaus rather than by hit-and-miss canvassing of the labor and job markets, it should be pointed out that there was undoubtedly considerable duplication of work and competition between the several nonprofit organizations. It was frequently stated that both teachers and principals shopped around among the various agencies. Not all of the agencies in this field operated an employment service which was free to teachers. The California Teachers Association charged only 2½ per cent of a year's salary, but even this sum might be a considerable burden to the low-paid beginner. For those who were placed through a private fee-charging agency, the sum paid was much higher.

A number of agencies had been organized to place persons in the nursing profession. The California Nurses' Association was undoubtedly the agency which made the largest number of placements of nurses in the 13 cities in which it operated offices. A flat charge of $10 a year was made by these Registries. It was customary for certain hospitals in Los Angeles and in San Francisco to use the placement services of the California Nurses' Association exclusively for private-duty nurses, and in San Francisco the Registry also made large numbers of placements in private homes. In each of these cities this association reported that in 1938 they were making from 2,000 to 2,400 placements a month. There were also in this field in Los Angeles a number of private fee-charging agencies which charged nurses from 20 to 50 per cent of a month's salary for a permanent position and 10 per cent of total earnings for every temporary job. Of eight fee-charging nurses agencies which reported the number of their placements, six made from 100 to 200 placements a month, and two placed smaller numbers. This was in sharp contrast to more than 2,000 placed by the Nurses' Association. A few persons in this profession—probably, in the main, practical nurses—were placed by the California State Employment Service.

The most complete organization of the labor market for professional workers was found in the field of motion-picture extras. The eight major motion-picture companies in Los Angeles had organized Central Casting Corporation, and they employed all extras through this employment bureau. The purpose of this organization was to eradicate the abuses of fee-charging agencies and to provide a central pool of information and thus avoid the necessity for daily rounds of all the motion-picture companies. Central Casting, although an employers' organization, was unique in that it registered only union members. In the year this study was made, it was reported that 16,000 different people were placed and that nearly 300,000 jobs were filled. This agency was not only doing an enormous volume of business but a highly specialized job of placing persons suitable for a wide variety of studio calls. Although extras employed by the smaller companies were still hired directly, Central Casting was undoubtedly serving the vast majority of workers in this occupational group. Actors—both motion picture and those on the legitimate stage—and musicians depended almost entirely on fee-charging agencies for placement.

A careful survey brought to light practically no attempt at organization of the labor markets in professions other than those described above. The California State Employment Service was, of course, available to professional persons as well as to all job seekers, but it had not taken a very important place in these fields, as is indicated by the fact that in 1937 and in 1938 less than 600 placements in professional pursuits were made by the California State Employment Service throughout the state. Mention should also be made of one fee-charging agency operated by a group of engineering societies to place persons in these professions. This organization reported that about 300 placements were made in the year prior to this study. Some persons in engineering and in other professions were placed through the university employment bureaus, and certain professional schools in universities, such as engineering, law, medicine, and social service, made it their business to try to place their graduates. These professional schools did not operate employment bureaus, but, through their contacts with prospective employers, they were probably able in quite an informal way to place a considerable proportion of their graduates. It was impossible to estimate even roughly the proportion of recent graduates who were placed by the university employment bureaus and by the professional schools, but probably the latter had the highest record of placements. Other resources open to the professional person included meetings of professional societies where a job might turn up as the result of a casual conversation, the interest of a former teacher in an individual student, or information passed along by relatives or friends.

Large numbers of those in professional pursuits applied directly to prospective employers. Some made the rounds of companies likely to employ people with their type of training; others read in the newspapers that a company was about to undertake a new job or heard of openings through friends or relatives already employed in a plant. It was impossible to secure an estimate of the relative importance of direct application in contrast with the other methods of securing jobs in professional pursuits, but it was obvious that in almost every instance the employers visited relied to a very large extent on direct application.

SALESPERSONS

A large number of persons in every community are employed as sales workers. Almost the only way salespeople secured permanent employment was by direct application to a firm, either just on the chance that there might be a job or at the suggestion of a friend already employed by the establishment. The California State Employment Service operated in this field and reported in 1938 that nearly 1,800 salespersons were placed in San Francisco and over 5,000 in Los Angeles. It is probable that most of these placements were in temporary jobs. Among the employers visited there was consistent evidence that the State Employment Service was used only to a very limited extent and, in the main, on occasions when extra employees were needed. There can be little doubt that the State Employment Service placements of salespeople were an insignificant part of the total. There were apparently no fee-charging or other employment agencies which operated to any extent in this field.

The custom of hiring employees who applied directly seemed to be strongly entrenched in this occupational group. The reason for this is probably in part related to the fact that so many women without any specialized training are drawn into sales work for part of the year, and thus even in a prosperous year there is likely to be a surplus of direct applications. It may also in part be due to the fact that many establishments, particularly in retail trade, have set up quite elaborate employment or personnel departments, and thus there is a sort of vested interest in the situation as it now exists.

CLERICAL EMPLOYMENTS

A somewhat different situation existed in the field of clerical employment. For this group of job seekers, which included office clerks, typists, stenographers, bookkeepers, operators of business machines, and private secretaries, there existed literally dozens of competing agencies operating employment bureaus. The offices of the California State Employment Service were, of course, available to this group of workers, but in the large cities at least there were many other types of employment bureaus operating in this field. In the two cities of San Francisco and Los Angeles, there were 34 licensed fee-charging employment agencies which reported that they specialized in placements in commercial employments. Some of these placed office workers of all kinds and degrees of skill, whereas others specialized in placing workers for a particular type of business or in the placement of highly skilled office workers. There were also in these two cities about 75 private business and secretarial schools. Only a small sample of these schools was visited, but since each of these considered placement as one of its functions, and since the possibility of securing a job was one of their drawing cards, it is probably fair to assume that each of the 75 schools was operating some sort of a placement service. Another type of employment agency operated for this group of workers was the typewriter or business machine company which ran a placement service, primarily to supply its customers with operators for the machine it sold. Fourteen establishments of this kind were visited in San Francisco and in Los Angeles, and, since only two of this group did no placement work, it can probably be concluded that it was a customary activity for businesses of this sort.

A number of other agencies which had entered the placement field for commercial employments should also be mentioned. In San Francisco a guidance and placement bureau had been organized by a group of business and professional women's clubs. This organization was specially designed to serve the woman over 40 in the business field. In Los Angeles a bureau of vocational service concerned itself with the placement of women between 25 and 35. The Y.W.C.A.'s, in connection with their vocational counseling, placed a few women in the business field.

The next question is the extent to which the various types of agencies had assumed a position of importance in the marketing of labor in commercial employments. In 1938 the office of the State Employment Service in San Francisco reported about 2,500 placements in clerical occupations; the Los Angeles office, about 4,000. Although the above figures are of a size not to be ignored, the employers visited did not indicate that they considered the State Employment Service a very good or important source of workers in clerical occupations. Only a very small number had called the Employment Service for this type of worker, and in almost every case the order was for a temporary employee. Although the sample of employers visited was small, the fact that the evidence was usually the same probably warrants the assumption that a large proportion of the State Employment Service placements in clerical employments were temporary.

The fee-charging agency was of considerable importance in the marketing of labor in clerical employments. Although it was not possible, at the time that this study was made, to secure placement statistics for the fee-charging agencies specializing in commercial employments, a recent publication of the Department of Industrial Relations gives these figures for the year 1939. In that year the commercial fee-charging agencies reported nearly 25,000 placements throughout the state. Of this total, 10,000 were made by agencies in San Francisco and 14,000 in Los Angeles. The fee-charging agencies made more than twice as many placements in clerical employments as did the State Employment Service in 1939, and the difference was even more striking in San Francisco and Los Angeles. Fee-charging agencies in San Francisco made nearly four times, and in Los Angeles more than three times, as many placements as did the offices of the State Employment Service in those cities. Although only about 40 per cent of the employers in industry and commerce who were visited in the course of this study reported that they used fee-charging agencies, it was evident that this type of agency held a position of greater importance in clerical than in other fields of employment. Approximately 70 per cent of the employers who used fee-charging agencies for any type of worker limited their calls to office help.

It was not possible to secure statistics as to the total number of placements made by business and secretarial schools. That they occupied a position of some importance is indicated by the fact that, for those visited, annual placements varied from about 200 to 2,000. In every interview there appeared a statement to the effect that "we can place all graduates who want to be placed." It is probable that these schools were most concerned with finding first jobs for their graduates, although some claimed that graduates were placed in job after job until one became permanent. This latter statement is probably particularly true of the small, "select" secretarial school. Of the employers interviewed, only about 20 per cent reported that they had called upon business schools to supply workers.

Although a few of the typewriter and business machine companies which did placement work had organized fee-charging agencies which did a considerable volume of work, in the main they operated more or less informal placement services and seldom made more than 10 or 12 placements a month. Although the volume of placement work of these companies was apparently not large, almost a third of the employers visited reported that they occasionally called a business machine company for an operator.

The other agencies mentioned as available to workers in commercial employments were performing a specialized service for a restricted group of workers, and their total placements could not have been large.

Although most of the San Francisco and Los Angeles employers visited in the course of this study reported that a large proportion of their clerical employees were hired directly, a considerable number used one or another of the various types of employment agencies for some of their office workers. It was quite evident that the use of an intermediate agency was much more widespread in clerical than in most other occupational groups. There was, however, no evidence that employers recognized the wastefulness of haphazard, door-to-door canvassing and large numbers of competing agencies.

DOMESTIC AND SERVICE WORKERS

Another large group of workers includes those who work as domestic servants in private homes, or who do similar work in hotels and restaurants, and such service occupations as beauty parlor operators.

Because of the nature of the work and the lack of standardization of working conditions, the turnover of domestic workers in private homes is extremely high. Moreover, it is important to recognize that, for this occupational group, there is practically no chance of door-to-door application for employment, and thus there existed a wide variety of agencies where this type of labor was exchanged. Although the possibility of direct application was not so limited for cooks and waiters in restaurants, there were also a number of agencies available to this group of workers. In the course of this study it was found that workers in domestic and hotel employments might register with the State Employment Service, with fee-charging agencies, or with various types of public and private social service agencies. In the case of hotel and restaurant workers the union was sometimes a placement resource. The only other service trade for which any considerable amount of information was gathered was that of beauty parlor operator. The State Employment Service claimed to place some workers in this occupation, but much more important were the schools of beauty culture. This was not surprising, since workers in this field must have a certain number of hours of training in order to secure a license. A large number of schools offered this type of training, and a placement service was important in their competition for students. Unions in this field were attempting to set up placement offices, but, at the time that this study was made, they had not become an important factor.

The two chief sources of placements for those engaged in domestic and hotel employments appeared to be the State Employment Service and the fee-charging agencies. In the year 1939 nearly 82,000 placements were made by the Employment Service in domestic and service employments throughout the state. Although it was not possible to break down this figure by domestic, hotel, and other service employments, evidence from previous years permits the assumption that by far the largest proportion were placed in domestic or hotel employments.

The Department of Industrial Relations reported that there were approximately 100 fee-charging agencies which specialized in the placement of domestic and hotel workers in 1939, and that these agencies made about 84,000 placements.[1] A direct comparison cannot be made between this figure and the 82,000 State Employment Service placements because the Employment Service figures include service workers as well as those in domestic and hotel employments. It is, however, probably justifiable to conclude that the State Service was at least holding its own in competition with fee-charging agencies in domestic employments. The fee-charging agencies were, how-

[1] California Department of Industrial Relations, *Fees Charged by Private Employment Agencies in California*, p. 33.

ever, relatively stronger in these fields of employment in San Francisco and in Los Angeles than in the remainder of the state. In 1939 the fee-charging agencies reported approximately 13,000 placements in hotel and domestic employments in San Francisco, in contrast with slightly less than 8,000 by the State Employment Service, and in Los Angeles the fee-charging agencies reported nearly 45,000 in contrast with not quite 30,000 by the State Employment Service.[2] Throughout the remainder of the state, the Employment Service made over 40,000 placements in domestic and service employments in contrast with about 25,000 by the fee-charging agencies.

Competing with the agencies mentioned above, in San Francisco and in Los Angeles were a large group of private social service organizations—about 14 in San Francisco and 18 in Los Angeles—and the Indian Bureau and the S.R.A. placement office in Los Angeles. It was impossible to determine the magnitude of the work done by these agencies, but it is probable that their placements did not mount to any significant proportion of the total.

Although no employers of domestic workers in private homes were interviewed, it is obvious that housewives must ordinarily call an agency when in need of domestic service. The statistics clearly indicated that housewives did use the State Employment Service. It may, however, be true that a good many of the better jobs were listed with the fee-charging agencies on the theory that the more highly skilled workers were more likely to be found there than at the State Employment Service.

Although only a small number of hotels and restaurants were visited in San Francisco and in Los Angeles, the evidence seemed to point to the conclusion that the fee-charging agencies were not as important in these cities as the figures given above

[2] The reader is cautioned to recognize that the State Employment Service figures include other service employments as well as those in domestic and hotel work. It is also probable that a good many of the fee-charging agencies' placements were outside the cities in which the offices were situated.

would indicate. This was probably due to the fact that a large proportion of the fee-charging agencies' placements were in jobs outside the cities in which these offices were located. Only one San Francisco restaurant reported any use of fee-charging agencies for kitchen and dining-room employees, and in Los Angeles direct application seemed to be the rule—one manager said, "I know a thousand people in the trade." In San Francisco, on the other hand, the unions had assumed a relatively strong position, and with one exception the hotels and restaurants visited reported that the union was a placement resource. However, some workers were usually employed from among those who applied directly. In no instance did a hotel or restaurant report any use of the State Employment Service.

It was impossible to determine the relative importance of the various types of agencies in the placement of beauty parlor operators, but it is probable that the schools of beauty culture placed the largest numbers. One of these schools reported that the State Employment Service was making a considerable number of placements in this field. The statistics of the State Employment service were not published in a form which would permit checking of this statement. Unions were trying to enter this field of placement, but their placements were insignificant at the time that this study was made. No employers of beauty parlor operators were visited, but it is probable that here as elsewhere many jobs were obtained by direct application.

MANUAL WORKERS

The largest group of workers in California, as in any other locality, are, of course, those in manual employments. The marketing of this type of labor is obviously of great importance, not only because of the numbers concerned, but also because the turnover in employment is probably greater in these employments than in many other occupational groups. Since the methods and problems of placement are to a considerable extent different for manual workers in industry and in agriculture, the following discussion will be divided into two sections.

Manual Workers in Industry.—Although, at the time that this study was made, the vast majority of workers in manual employments secured their jobs by door-to-door application, there were numerous agencies which were attempting to act as an intermediary between this group of workers and their employers. These workers might secure jobs through fee-charging agencies, the California State Employment Service, trade unions, employers' associations, and, in Los Angeles, the county Labor Coördinating Bureau and the S.R.A. employment bureau.

In San Francisco, Los Angeles, and Sacramento there were numerous fee-charging agencies which placed workers in manual employments. These agencies were located along a street in the poorer section of the city which was frequented by job hunters, usually members of the lower-skilled groups. It was not possible to secure any statistics as to the number of industrial placements by these agencies, since they all made placements in both industry and agriculture and there was no breakdown of figures by these occupational groups. Information secured from the fee-charging agencies visited indicated that most of their industrial placements were in construction, mining, and logging, usually at some distance from the city in which the office was located. It is probable that, at the time that this study was made, few industrial workers were placed by fee-charging agencies in San Francisco, Los Angeles, and Sacramento. Evidence in support of this conclusion was obtained from nearly 200 employers visited in the course of this study. Less than 1 in 10 of these employers reported that they used fee-charging agencies as a source for manual workers, and it is further significant that practically without exception the use of such agencies was limited to an occasional call, as a last resort, for extra help. Clearly, in the areas visited, the fee-charging agency was of little importance in the marketing of manual labor.

The California State Employment Service reported that in 1938 nearly 130,000 placements were made in manual employments. The proportion of these placements in industry as distinct from agriculture can only be estimated. If it is assumed that most of the placements in agriculture were in manual employments, and, if the total agricultural placements, which are not broken down by occupation, are subtracted from the total placements in manual employments, it can be estimated that about 100,000 industrial placements were made in 1938. Probably about two-thirds of these placements were in unskilled, about 20 per cent in semiskilled, and about 15 per cent in skilled occupations.[8]

Although it was impossible to estimate the importance of 100,000 placements in the total labor market for industrial workers in California, interviews with employers in San Francisco, Los Angeles, Sacramento, and Bakersfield furnished conclusive evidence that at least in these areas the State Employment Service was functioning only on the fringes of this job market. Whether the plant was one which manufactured clothing, food products, iron and steel, machinery, automobiles, or airplanes, there was practically no employer among those visited who reported any considerable use of the State Employment Service. A few occasionally called the State Service if a rush order came in. Among this group, there were a few who were satisfied with the workers referred, but many were of the opinion expressed by two manufacturers of oil machinery who said, "We have occasionally called the State Employment Service, but the men they send are never any good," or, "They sent only haphazard mechanics." The opinion of the large

[8] These figures are for all manual employments. The percentages of semiskilled and skilled workers were probably greater in industrial than in agricultural employments.

group who did not use the California Employment Service can be illustrated by an employer of loggers who said, "We would be taking a chance on men from the State Employment Service," and a clothing manufacturer who said, "We have only experienced workers, and the experienced people won't register at the State Employment Service." An occasional employer was making some attempt to coöperate with the State Employment Service, but such arrangements were apparently not very successful at the time this study was made. The State Employment Service had made an effort to convince airplane manufacturers of the advantage of using this agency and had attempted to set up a sort of central clearance system for this industry. Several airplane companies were visited, but only one reported any considerable use of the State Employment Service. The others said, "We don't want to give the State Employment Service the necessary information," or, "The system will help only if all companies coöperate, which isn't yet true." A steel company was making a pretense at coöperation but said, "We put the State Employment Service off by putting in a standing order for an operator who is almost impossible to find, and thus we are relieved of further annoyance." Although it is perhaps not fair to generalize on the basis of information obtained at a time of an overcrowded labor market, there was certainly no evidence that employers of industrial workers, even in theory, looked upon the State Employment Service with any degree of favor. They not only lacked confidence in the efficiency of this organization but were also suspicious of its "political" entanglements, and, furthermore, they were strongly of the opinion that the best man seeks his own job.

Two other governmental agencies in Los Angeles, the Labor Coördinating Bureau and the S.R.A. employment bureau, claimed that they placed manual workers in industrial employments. Although these agencies undoubtedly did place some industrial workers, it appears significant that, among the employers visited, not a single one reported any use of either of these services.

Another marketing place for manual workers was the employers' association which operated an employment bureau, usually set up to combat union activity. Associations of this sort were not important in San Francisco at the time this study was made. In Los Angeles, on the other hand, a number of such associations reported considerable activity, and their reports were confirmed by several of the firms visited. One steel manufacturer reported exclusive use of the Metal Trades Manufacturers Association. One oil machinery company said, "If we have no one on our own list we call the Association"; another in the same industry said, "Our chief source of labor supply is the Trade Association"; and a third, "We call the Metal Trades Manufacturers Association for skilled workers and the Merchants and Manufacturers' Association for less-skilled workers. We seldom employ anyone at the gate. Why should we, when the associations have lists of workers whom they know?" That these associations had nothing like a monopoly of the labor market was indicated by the fact that three steel manufacturers denied emphatically that they ever used the employers' association employment bureaus. It appeared that the chief strength of the employers' association employment bureaus in Los Angeles was among employers in the metal trades, although one employers' association claimed that it made placements in a wide variety of industries. The placements of these associations were probably an insignificant part of total placements in manual employments. With the few exceptions mentioned above, Los Angeles employers of manual workers almost universally preferred to replenish their labor force from among those who applied directly rather than to call an employment bureau conducted by a trade association.

To workers in organized trades, the trade union frequently offered a placement service. The best-known example, and probably the most complete union control over hiring, was in the maritime trades. A considerable number of workers, however, in other transportation and communication industries and in the clothing, laundry and dry cleaning, and food processing industries secured their jobs through the union offices. There was also a scattering of unions in a number of other trades which placed all or a majority of the workers. Interviews with union officials indicated that, in general, the San Francisco trade unions had been able to establish a stronger degree of control over placements than had those in Los Angeles. Further verification of this was found in the interviews with employers. Approximately two-thirds of the San Francisco employers in the manufacturing and mechanical, transportation, and fishing industries reported that a considerable proportion of their workers, at least in certain occupational groups, were secured through the union office. In Los Angeles, on the other hand, less than 20 per cent of the employers interviewed in the above industries and in the extraction of minerals reported that they called the office of a trade union for workers. In Sacramento only one employer, in the woodworking industry, and in the Bakersfield district only three employers, all in mining, reported that any placements were made by the union.

With the exception of employers who, because of an agreement with a union, were required to use the union placement office and a single firm in the metal trades which employed all its workers through a trade association, every employer visited reported that the vast majority of his manual workers were picked from those who applied at the factory gate or at the personnel department. Some of these men came on their own initiative, just on a chance that there might be a job; others came at the suggestion of a friend who had a job in the plant. It must again be emphasized that this study was made in a depression year, when applicants for jobs were plentiful, and that undoubtedly in a time of labor shortage there would be an incentive to make more frequent use of various types of employment agencies. There was, however, strong evidence that, although in times of labor shortage employers might be forced to look to an employment agency for assistance, they would, even at such times, prefer to employ the man who sought his own job. The opinion was not infrequently expressed that the better man doesn't depend upon someone else to hunt his job. Not a single employer recognized the advantages inherent in a better organization of the labor market through the use of a labor exchange. As has already been pointed out, they disliked the State Employment Service and had little sympathy for other types of employment services.

Manual Workers in Agriculture.—Large numbers of agricultural laborers in California are employed each year in planting, hoeing, weeding, cultivating, pruning, picking, and processing of crops which are highly specialized as to area, and which require vastly different numbers of workers from one season to another. While the handyman, the milker, and certain other employees may stay the year round on one farm, by far the largest group of agricultural workers must shift from crop to crop and from place to place many times during a year. Here, more than in almost any other type of labor, continuity of employment is a practical impossibility unless there is some system of orderly shifting of workers from crop to crop. This study furnished bountiful evidence that agricultural laborers depended on the most elementary and wasteful methods in their inevitable frequent transfers from job to job. Most often the news as to available jobs just came via the "grapevine," which might originate in the casual remark of a fellow camper by the roadside who had heard that "help wanted" signs were plentiful along a road many miles away; again, it might originate in a sign in a local office of the State Employment Service stating that 100 or 1,000 pickers were needed in a distant spot; or a labor contractor might pass along the word that the picking season in beets, cotton, or peas was about to open. Job information travels fast, and a few casual words might result in hundreds arriving where dozens were needed.

There were several agencies which purported to make placements of agricultural labor at the time this study was made. Operating in this field were the State Employment Service, the Labor Coördinating Bureau and the S.R.A. employment bureau in Los Angeles, some associations of employers, fee-charging employment agencies, and labor contractors.

In 1936 the California State Employment Service reported nearly 60,000 placements in agriculture; in 1937, 65,000; and in 1938 the number declined to slightly over 30,000. This decline was perhaps in part due to the general economic recession of 1938, but there can be no doubt that in neither year was the State Employment Service making more than an infinitesimal part of the total agricultural placements in California. It has been estimated that three-quarters of a million jobs must be filled each year in California agriculture.[4] Although this figure is only an estimate, it certainly indicates that the State Employment Service had made practically no impression on the organization of the agricultural labor market in California. In 1938 the California State Employment Service was not set up in such a way as to do an effective job in agriculture. The offices were located in cities and towns, often many miles from the center of agricultural activity, and no attempt had been made to open temporary offices at the times and places where jobs were available and workers congregated.[5] Although there existed a farm placement service under the supervision of two men appointed by the United States Employment Service, these two men alone could do little to develop a strong agricultural placement service. Placements in agricul-

[4] See page 161 for source and method of this estimate.

[5] In 1940 a number of temporary offices were opened in the farming districts.

ture, as in other occupations, must be the responsibility of the local office, and it was reported that limitations of staff and "too much red tape" hindered the expansion of placements on farms. It was probably true, however, that long-established prejudices and preferences on the part of farmers were the most serious obstacles to development in this field.

Only about 25 of the 162 farmers interviewed reported that they had ever used the State Employment Service. Only a half-dozen had employed workers referred by the State Employment Service in the year in which this study was made, and only two reported the employment of any considerable number of workers from this source. Most of the farmers interviewed could see no reason for an employment service. This was perhaps in part due to the fact that, at the time that this study was made, there were in most places "two men for every job." However, running through many of the interviews there was a quite definite prejudice against the State Employment Service expressed in such terms as: "When there is a plentiful supply of labor we don't need it, and when there isn't we won't use it because we don't believe that we can get qualified workers."

Two other government agencies, the Los Angeles Labor Coördinating Bureau and the S.R.A. placement bureau, claimed that they placed agricultural workers. Although adequate statistical evidence was not available, the number of placements on farms by these two agencies was undoubtedly small. Over a three-year period the Labor Coördinating Bureau reported only about 4,000 agricultural placements, and in 1937–38 the total placements of this agency, including both agricultural and industrial workers, were slightly less than 7,000. Not a single farmer interviewed in the vicinity of Los Angeles reported any use of either of these agencies.

In certain areas another government agency, the Farm Security Administration, had opened camps to house agricultural labor, and it might have been expected that camp managers would concern themselves with the placements of residents. The camp managers had been instructed to urge the camp residents to register at an office of the State Employment Service. This was, however, a farce, since usually a visit to an office of the State Employment Service would have required a round trip of from 40 to 60 miles—far too expensive in time and in money for the average camp resident. The camp managers in various other ways attempted to give some assistance in the job-hunting process. They publicized whatever information was available as where jobs might be opening up or where there was an oversupply of labor, and they attempted to convince neighboring farmers that the camps were a good resource for labor. In this latter activity they met with little success, since farmers were often of the opinion that they did not want to employ men from the F.S.A. camps because these camps were "centers of radical activity."

Several associations of farmers assisted in one way or another in the process of bringing together workers and jobs. The best known of these, and the only one which was organized for the specific purpose of operating an employment bureau, was the San Joaquin Valley Labor Bureau. It is probable that the Bureau in the early years of its existence placed large numbers of Mexicans in agriculture. No recent statistics as to placements were available, but no evidence could be found that in 1938 this agency was making any considerable number of placements. Of the 150 farmers visited, of whom two-thirds were in the Bakersfield and Fresno areas, not a single one had used the Bureau in recent years. The vast majority of the farmers around Bakersfield reported that they had never had occasion to use the Bureau, and in its home territory, Fresno, it was looked upon with definite disfavor.

A few other farmers' organizations acted in an informal way as distributing points for agricultural labor. A Chamber of Commerce in a small town posted job notices for the benefit of those who stopped as they drove down the highway. Packing sheds and cotton gins in some instances directed workers who dropped in to see if there was any work in the community to farmers in need of workers. Only in one instance, that of a packing shed in the foothills above Sacramento, was there any real organization of the placement service offered. The farmers in this locality had become accustomed to calling the packing shed for workers, and referrals were made only when an order had been received from a farmer. It was impossible to estimate the number of placements made by these organizations, but there was no indication that the numbers were large enough to be significant except in the one community just described.

The fee-charging employment agencies in San Francisco, Los Angeles, and Sacramento claimed that they placed large numbers of workers on farms. It is possible that these agencies made a considerable number of placements of permanent farm hands, milkers, and camp cooks; but, at the time this study was made, it was evident that few farmers depended on these agencies for seasonal workers. Of more than 150 farmers interviewed, only about a dozen used fee agencies, and almost without exception these farmers indicated that fee-charging agencies were called only upon rare occasions. It is, of course, possible that in a time of labor shortage fee-charging agencies would assume a position of greater importance in agriculture, but there was no indication that farmers had found fee-charging agencies a satisfactory source for labor. Their attitude may be illustrated by the statement of a raisin grower who said, "When there was a shortage of labor a few years ago we used to send trucks to the Los Angeles agencies, but the workers from any agency are not satisfactory—people who really want to work apply directly."

A special type of labor agent in the field of agriculture was the labor contractor who assumed responsibility for securing labor crews for the farmer. It was impossible within the scope of this study to determine the extent to which the labor contracting system was prevalent throughout all of California's agriculture. Certain conclusions can, however, be drawn as to the importance of this type of labor agent in the crops and areas visited. The labor contractor system was almost universal in asparagus and in sugar beets. It was widely used in peas and important, though probably less extensive, in prunes, tomatoes, and walnuts. In cotton, grapes, hops, and potatoes only a few of the farmers visited used labor contractors and practically not at all in other deciduous fruits and in citrus. Since the labor contractor system originated among groups of foreign-born workers, it was not surprising to find it still important among Filipinos, Mexicans, and Japanese. In recent years, however, large numbers of dust-bowl migrants had been working in such crops as peas where the labor contractor controlled much of the employment. In some instances these workers were employed by labor contractors, but not infrequently, when both native and foreign workers were employed on the same crop, the foreign workers were employed by a labor contractor and the native workers directly by the farmer. The fact that foreign workers had more frequently than natives been dependent for jobs on a labor contractor was probably to a considerable extent related to the fact that these workers, because of language difficulties, needed an intermediary. It might, however, in part be related to the types of crops in which they were employed and in part to historical accident.

Although the labor contractor system was in no sense universal in agriculture, wherever it existed it was subject to abuses. In spite, however, of abuses and a considerable amount of unfavorable public opinion it continued to exist. It permitted the farmer to shift his responsibility for getting a crew together and for finding replacements for the man or whole crew who failed to turn up after a Saturday-night spree in town. In addition, there was the possibility of shifting the responsibility for wages, workmen's compensation, and for adequate housing.

Slightly over half of the 162 farmers interviewed reported that "when the season opens, workers flock in" or "there is no need for any organized employment service." These farmers depended solely on chance applications for work and used no organized employment service, labor contractor, or pool of labor of any sort. In the main, those farmers who did not "just wait for workers to turn up" secured their labor through a labor contractor. As has already been pointed out, the labor contracting system was used in many of California's crops, although it was much more prevalent in asparagus, sugar beets, and peas than in other crops. It was thus not surprising to find that the labor contractor was used by about 40 to 50 per cent of the farmers interviewed in the areas around Sacramento, Bakersfield, and Fresno and by only about a fifth of the growers in the vicinity of Los Angeles. The very small group of farmers who secured workers from any kind of an organized placement service reported that these calls were limited to "once in a while for a skilled operator" or to "help in a peak season when there was a labor shortage." A few reported that they occasionally employed workers from certain informal pools of labor such as a packing house, an F.S.A. camp, or congregations of workers on a neighbor's farm. The number in this group was, however, insignificant.

SPECIAL GROUPS

In addition to the occupational groups mentioned above, there are certain categories of the population for whom various special types of employment arrangements have been developed, or who present special problems. These groups include young people just entering the job market, members of veterans and fraternal organizations, certain foreign, religious, or racial groups, organized workers, and relief clients.

Juniors.—The boy or girl just out of school or junior college is to a large extent unfamiliar with the methods of marketing labor. In some instances a young person may follow his father, brother, or sister into a store or workshop; in others he may have to make his own contacts. He may have a definite vocational interest or training, but frequently he is uncertain as to where his particular aptitudes may best fit into industry. In each of the cities visited the schools were making some efforts to assist young people to secure an entrance to industry. Only in Los Angeles, however, was there a more or less coördinated effort to organize placement work for this group of job seekers. In Los Angeles the Central Placement Bureau of the high schools was the Junior Department of the California State Employment Service, and both the Frank Wiggins trade school and the junior colleges had well-organized placement services. Although these organizations by no means had a monopoly of the placement work for their students, they had apparently achieved considerable success in bridging the gap between school and job for large numbers of young people. In San Francisco the schools and the California State Employment Service were conducting overlapping services, and it was generally recognized that no agency was offering a proper service to juniors. In Bakersfield and Taft the State Service was doing practically nothing for young people, and the schools were chiefly concerned with finding part-time jobs for youngsters in school. In other areas visited, the State Employment Service had not set up any special service for juniors; and, although the schools were not visited, it is doubtful that they had taken a very important place in securing jobs for their graduates.

Veterans.—Organizations of veterans have sometimes attempted to assist those who have served in the army in their efforts to secure employment. Only in Los Angeles was there an organized veterans employment service. This agency reported that, in the main, the jobs filled were for unskilled work, and that a majority were for temporary employment. In the other areas visited, a veterans organization might occasionally attempt to assist an unemployed member to find work, but, on the whole, these organizations relied upon the State Employment Service. By agreement with the United States Employment Service there was someone designated in each office of the California State Employment Service to give special attention to the placement of veterans. Apparently these men were chiefly concerned with seeing that veterans were given their legal rights to preferences in certain jobs, such as public works. Occasionally some special attention was given to including a few veterans when an order was filled for which veterans who were registered could qualify. On the whole, it appeared that veterans were referred in accordance with the same general principles as were applied to other registrants. If the State Employment Service is to build up an efficient organization, it must refer the best-qualified worker to the job. This necessarily precludes special preference to veterans except in those cases in which they have been granted legal preference.

Members of Fraternal Orders.—In some instances members of fraternal organizations were given assistance in securing jobs by the fraternal order. However, only one such organization, the Masons, had actually organized employment offices. Two offices maintained by the Masons were visited. These were active and apparently efficient bureaus, and they had developed a sense of responsibility on the part of members who had jobs to offer. At the time that this study was made, the San Francisco office was making about 100 placements a month and the one in Los Angeles, nearly 500 a month. While this service was only available to members of the Masonic order and their families, very real assistance was offered to members of this group. While such organizations as those described above overlap with the State Employment Service, it is likely that they will continue to exist and give a special service to a membership which possesses a sense of mutual responsibility.

Foreign, Religious, and Racial Groups.—Since there are a number of foreign, religious, and racial groups in California, it appeared likely that there might be certain special placement services available to these groups. A wide variety of associations of foreign, religious, and racial groups were visited, but only a few reported that they assisted their members in finding jobs. In the main, the agencies which had developed any sort of placement work were social welfare organizations. In Los Angeles several assisted the Negro population in finding employment. One Mexican agency and one Jewish welfare agency also did placement work. The Japanese branch of the Y.M.C.A. in Los Angeles did a little informal placement work for young people of this race, and the Indian Bureau had established a placement office whose work was almost entirely confined to Indian women in domestic service. In San Francisco there appeared to be little development of placement work for these special groups. Although organizations of all of the major foreign, religious, and racial groups were visited, the only ones which did any placement work were the Chinese and Japanese branches of the Y.M.C.A., and their work in this field was of the most informal sort. It should perhaps also be mentioned that there were one or two other types of agencies which offered special services to certain racial groups. In both San Francisco and Los Angeles there were a number of fee-charging agencies which limited their placements to Japanese, Chinese, and Filipinos, and in San Francisco the State Employment Service had a Chinese department which was headed by a man of that race.

Most of the placement bureaus which limited their services to persons of certain foreign, religious, or racial groups specialized in the placement of persons in domestic employment. There were, however, one or two exceptions to this. The employment service of the Jewish Social Service Bureau in Los Angeles made no domestic placements because people of this group seldom enter theis field of employment. A Negro agency was making special efforts to place Negroes in shops where persons of this race made their purchases.

Although with a few exceptions the general community resources were available to persons of all races, it was evident that in many instances few persons in the groups mentioned above were placed. Occasionally the specialized agencies were performing a service of very real importance, but, by and large, their placements were in low-skilled, low-paid jobs, and the numbers placed were insignificant. Agencies of the sort mentioned above were able, through concentrated efforts, to assist small numbers of certain groups in securing employment. Few had been able, however, to afford the expense of a highly developed employment service; and, furthermore, such a separation of the population seeking employment is probably undesirable from the point of view of bringing all workers into contact with the labor market.

Organized Workers.—As mentioned in an earlier section of this chapter, certain groups of workers in professions and in trade unions had developed placement services for their members. The members of these organizations were particularly fortunate in that a central pool of information was substituted for door-to-door job hunting. Although only a small number of these placement services had a monopoly of the labor market, in some instances they made a large proportion of the placements of a given occupational group, and in every case they facilitated job hunting for certain workers. The success of occupational associations in organizing their respective labor markets depends to a considerable extent on the attitudes of employers seeking workers. There is every reason to suppose that employers will have confidence in employment bureaus operated by professional associations. Employers are, however, likely to be distrustful if not actively opposed to the use of employment bureaus operated by trade unions. The union is concerned with control over placements, not only for the purpose of improving job-getting techniques for its members, but also to increase its bargaining strength. This the employer opposes, and except in cases where the unions are very strong they are not likely to succeed in bringing about a complete organization of the labor market even for their own members.

The Relief Population.—During periods of wholesale unemployment when large numbers of employable persons are thrown on the relief rolls, this group of persons creates a special placement problem. The community must concern itself with the problem of getting these people back to work, not only for reasons of economy, but also to protect them against the disintegration of work habits and of morale which results from long periods of unemployment. Although few jobs are available during a severe depression, it was obviously necessary during the 1930's to keep those on relief in as close contact with the labor market as possible. From almost the beginning of the various programs for the relief of the unemployed, the Federal Reëmployment Offices or the State Employment Offices were designated as the registration agency for all who applied for work relief, and in many instances registration was also required of those who applied for direct relief. The public employment offices were given the responsibility for placing this group of the population in such private employment as was available, and until 1936 these offices were also responsible for placements on W.P.A. projects.

In California, as elsewhere throughout the country, the attempt to keep the unemployed on relief in contact with the labor market resulted in a chaos of incomplete and often inaccurate registrations, resulting not infrequently in referrals of people who were not qualified for the job. There appeared to be little if any tendency for the California State Employment Service to give relief clients preference in referrals. Although such preference has sometimes been advocated, it clearly should not be an accepted policy. An efficient employment service which can secure the confidence of employers and employees alike must make placements in accordance with qualifications and not in accordance with relief or nonrelief status. There was, however, some evidence of the opposite tendency—that is, not to give relief clients an equal chance with others in making job referrals. Although jobs were scarce, it was without doubt unfortunate that the personnel of the California State Employment Service seemed to class a large proportion of those on relief as marginal workers. Some, perhaps even many, were on the margin of employability, but this did not justify placing all who were the unfortunate victims of unemployment in this category.

In a few instances special agencies had been set up to assist relief applicants to secure jobs. A number of private social service agencies, sometimes through a separate department, and sometimes in a much more informal way, attempted to place their clients. The services of these agencies were usually limited to a particular group who were considered to be at a particular disadvantage in the labor market. Seldom did they make any considerable number of placements.

In Los Angeles there were two governmental agencies, the Labor Coördinating Bureau and the S.R.A., which were particularly concerned with the placement of those on relief. The Labor Coördinating Bureau limited its services to registered voters, and insofar as relief clients were registered voters it may have assisted considerable numbers in getting jobs. It was, however, looked upon with considerable disfavor and frequently described as a political racket to get jobs for people in order to get votes. The S.R.A. employment office was set up specifically because of the conviction that the State Employment Service was not doing an effective job in placing relief clients. It reported several thousand placements in 1938. Clearly this office overlapped the functions of the State Employment Service. If the State Service was discriminating against relief clients, the situation should have been corrected within the State Service rather than by setting up a competing governmental employment bureau. In none of the other areas visited had the S.R.A. or other relief agencies set up independent placement offices, but rather they depended on the State Employment Service. It was generally admitted, however, that few relief clients were placed, and that they were discriminated against. Furthermore, it should be mentioned that most of the other agencies engaged in placement work were reluctant to place relief clients.

POSSIBILITY OF FUTURE ORGANIZATION OF THE LABOR MARKET

Preferences based on custom and prejudice cannot be considered a justification of the present wasteful system of bringing together jobs and workers. There is an obvious need for centers from which labor may be marketed. Labor is not unlike a commodity in that there must be an exchange between buyer and seller; and, unless there is some orderly arrangement through which employers and workers are brought together, there is economic waste and human suffering.

There appears to be no good reason for the existence of numerous employment agencies serving the same group of workers, and it certainly does not appear desirable that workers should have to pay for their jobs. There is need for a coördinating agency, and the State Employment Service is the agency best suited to perform this function. It is not suggested that the State Employment Service should assume responsibility for all types of placements. It should, without doubt, operate in those fields in which there are no efficient free employment agencies operating over a wide area. Where existing facilities have brought about a fairly complete organization of the labor market, the State Employment Service should work out some sort of a coöperative arrangement rather than attempt to compete with these organizations.

This study has shown that the State Employment Service had accomplished little in terms of any real organization of the labor market. Two questions may be asked: What were the obstacles which prevented this agency from doing an effective job? What can be expected of the future? The obstacles were many. The most important were probably the lack of any general realization of the value of substituting centers for the exchange of labor for the custom of personal application, a very definite prejudice against employment exchanges in general and the State Employment Service in particular, the very magnitude of the job of setting up a new institution to serve vast numbers of employers and workers at a time when the market was flooded with workers and jobs were scarce, and the existence of vested interests in large numbers of competing agencies.

The future will undoubtedly bring changes in the place of the State Employment Service in the organization of the labor market. It is to be expected that the lapse of time will make it possible to develop more efficient procedures, and that a job well done will break down some of the prejudice against this government agency. When labor shortages develop, employers will have a strong incentive to use this Employment Service, and if it rises to the occasion and provides workers where they are needed, a new habit may be developed which will carry over to a time when the employer's need of assistance is less urgent.

The State Employment Service should be able to establish distributing points for persons in sales and clerical occupations, for domestic workers, and for manual workers in industry and in agriculture. There is plentiful evidence that there is need for some sort of organized labor market for these groups of workers—not a labor agency which sells jobs, which exists as an appendage to a trade school, or which has been organized to serve the special interests of employers or workers in any particular trade or industry, but rather a public free employment service organized for the sole purpose of bringing together jobs and workers as rapidly as possible and which gives no special privilege to any person or group.

Although there are certain special skills required in the placement of the above-mentioned groups, there is no reason to suppose that the State Employment Service could not be staffed by personnel equipped with the training necessary to select persons with the qualifications required of a salesperson, stenographer, cook, factory operative, or farm laborer. The problem of the placement of agricultural workers requires special comment. This is undoubtedly the occupational group which has the greatest need for a state-wide system of public employment offices, and yet, at the time this study was made, the State Employment Service had had little success in placing workers on farms. Farm workers were, in the main, employed by direct application or through labor contractors. The State Employment Service should be able to establish a placement service which would to a large extent replace the present hit-and-miss job hunting and eliminate the labor contracting system, which is subject to so many abuses. Labor contractors would not be necessary if the State Employment Service took over the responsibility for getting crews on the job, if foremen were employed to supervise, and if large farmers or government agencies provided housing. It is essential, however, for the State Employment Service to organize an agricultural placement service which can be relied on to provide workers when and where they are needed. It is suggested that California might well adopt some variation of the system used by the Texas State Employment Service. The Texas program includes the working out of seasonal calendars of work, offices at strategic points within a reasonable distance from the work to be performed, and a program to educate growers and workers as to the advantage of an employment service. If such a program were adopted, it might be possible, at least in part, to protect the workers from the abuses of the labor contracting system and to accomplish the objectives of an organized labor market—the orderly movement of workers from one operation to another with the consequent provision of year-round employment for a larger group of workers.

There are certain occupational groups—motion-picture extras, actors, musicians, teachers, and nurses—which can perhaps be served better by specialized employment bureaus than by the State Employment Service. The elaborate and highly organized Central Casting Bureau for motion-picture extras was undoubtedly performing a service for these workers which could not be equaled by the State Employment Service, and there appeared to be no reason for the State Service to attempt to compete with the specialized agency which served this occupational group. It is also doubtful whether the State Employment Service will be able to develop the specialized service necessary for the placement of actors and musicians. It is probable that, if these professional groups are to be placed without the large sums now paid to fee-charging agencies, a special service will have to be set up. An illustration of an employment service for actors is found in a plan in use in Germany which was reported in a study published in 1934: "A special office (Bühnen Nachweis) for the placement of actors has been created outside the Federal Institution [for Placement and Unemployment Insurance] but under its control and with its financial assistance. This office is administered by employers and employees of the profession."[6] Fee-charging agencies were, however, still active in the placement of vaudeville actors and musicians at the time that the study of the German employment service was made.[7]

[6] Oscar Weigert, *Administration of Placement and Unemployment Insurance in Germany* (New York: Industrial Relations Counselors, Inc., 1934), p. 108.

[7] Fee-charging agencies were legislated out of existence in Germany as of June 1931, but agencies serving the two groups mentioned above were exempted from this law. *Ibid.*, p. 164.

It is probable that the schools and colleges are the logical agencies to handle the placement of teachers, although the California Teachers Association and a few fee-charging agencies also operated in this field. The placement of teachers requires accurate and elaborate records for each candidate, and this information is most readily available at the teacher-training institutions. The State Employment Service might take some part in this program in areas distant from the educational institutions, but this should be in close coöperation with the educational institutions rather than an independent venture.

The California Nurses' Association and a number of fee-charging agencies were operating in the field of nursing, an occupational group in which most placements were made through an intermediary. The Nurses' Association appeared to operate an efficient service in the areas in which it had set up offices. It would seem reasonable to suggest that the State Employment Service might through some sort of a coöperative arrangement make use of the facilities of this organization in the cities in which it offered a placement service, and in areas not served by the Nurses' Association it should provide a center at which nurses and their employers could register.

In a few other instances organizations of professional persons had set up placement services, but the most important organizations in the professional fields, other than those mentioned above, were the employment bureaus of universities and certain professional schools which in an informal fashion attempted to place their graduates. It is suggested that there should be some sort of central organization where persons in the professions could register, and where employers could expect to find records of training and of work experience.[8] This might be accomplished through a coöperative arrangement between the university employment bureaus and professional

[8] In Germany interregional clearance has been organized in the local office of Central Berlin to handle placements of the members of scientific, social work, and artistic professions in the whole country. *Ibid.*, p. 108.

schools. In order for this to be done, it would, however, be necessary for the university bureaus to accept for placement any professional person, thus doing away with the customary rule that only students of the parent institution are accepted for placement. It is unlikely that the university employment bureaus could accept such a responsibility without financial assistance, and it is therefore suggested that the State Employment Service might provide funds for additional personnel and turn over the placement of professional persons to such an organization.

In certain instances special arrangements have been set up for other groups. The most important of these groups were young people, organized workers, and relief clients. There can be no argument as to the importance of assisting young people in taking the step from school to job. There has been, however, some difference of opinion as to who should administer an employment service for juniors. Some maintain that the school department should assume this function; others, that the State Employment Service should set up a special department for this group. Certainly there should not be two overlapping government agencies. It appears that the Los Angeles system, whereby the Central Employment Service of the school system through a coöperative arrangement with the State Employment Service has assumed responsibility for registration and placement of juniors, has worked well. In areas in which the school system has not established a strong placement service, it might be preferable for the State Employment Service to take the responsibility; but always there should be coöperation between the employment service and the school system, which has special knowledge of the qualifications of the young people.

Trade unions have frequently been of great assistance in organizing the labor market for certain groups of workers. The question may well be raised as to the function of the State Employment Service and of the unions in the placement of organized workers. It cannot be overlooked that employers in most trades are not likely to have complete confidence in employment bureaus conducted by trade unions, nor that unions will hesitate to relinquish their placement function, since their development of this activity has been not only to assist their members in finding work but also to act as a bulwark to the maintenance of certain established standards of employment. Furthermore, it should be pointed out that frequently the trade union employment office, since it specializes in certain occupational groups, has knowledge of the occupational qualifications of its members, which could hardly be matched by the staff of a state employment service.

In certain trades, such as longshoremen, where employers have accepted union management of hiring halls, it is suggested that the State Employment Service should not set up a competing and probably less efficient service, but rather, through some sort of a coöperative arrangement, permit these placements to be made through the hiring hall. Where mutually satisfactory agreements as to hiring arrangements have not been worked out between employers and organized workers, the State Employment Service cannot relinquish placements to the union hiring hall. Even in these cases, however, the State Service should coordinate its work with that of the trade union so that information as to jobs and workers available will be reported both to the union office and to the State Service. Coördination of the work of the State Employment Service and trade unions will be difficult; unions are fearful lest nonunion workers be placed in union plants, thus undermining the strength of the union, and rules in regard to placements may differ in these two types of placement organization. The State Employment Service must place the man best fitted to fill the job, whereas trade unions frequently, in an effort to equalize employment, take into account length of time unemployed in making placements. It could be argued that a state employment service could employ personnel with the necessary knowledge of the various trades, and that it could provide a service both more neutral and more economical than can a trade union. The fact of the case is, however, that trade unions have a strong foothold which they will not easily give up. Little can be accomplished by the State Employment Service if it ignores the existence of trade union placement systems or tries to fight them, even in the name of economy. Until such time as unions can be convinced that it is to their advantage to place their confidence in the State Employment Service, this agency should attempt to work with the unions in bringing workers and employers into contact with each other. It is interesting to note that in Great Britain a coöperative arrangement has been worked out whereby certain trade unions are permitted to register and place their members and also to pay unemployment insurance benefits, for which they are reimbursed.[9]

A number of organizations have offered a special placement service to relief clients. This certainly cannot be recommended. There is always likely to be prejudice against persons who have been on relief on the part of employers, and a separate placement service for this group could hardly fail to increase this prejudice. The State Employment Service should assume this function. If there is to be confidence in a placement agency, referrals must be based on occupational fitness, a principle which is far more likely to be adopted by a public employment service than by a relief agency. If there is any violation of this principle or of the principle of equal treatment to all regardless of relief status, the proper procedure is to discipline the State Employment Service, not to set up a competing agency.

This study has shown that, although many organizations existed for the purpose of assisting in the process of bringing together jobs and workers, there was no real organization of the market for labor in California. Furthermore, for this statement

[9] Chegwidden and Myrddin-Evans, *The Employment Exchange Service of Great Britain*, pp. 105–106.

to be true it is not necessary to adopt a narrow definition of organization of the labor market. There was no center at which even a considerable proportion of workers and jobs in most occupational groups were brought together. Some centralization in the marketing of labor had been developed for a few occupational groups, but the broad picture was one of competing and overlapping services, operating in a field in which more or less haphazard methods were widely accepted as inevitable and, in the main, as preferable to a coördinated system of labor exchanges. While perfect organization of the labor market is an ideal which will probably never be attained, the State Employment Service should be able through coöperation with other agencies and through independent action to extend the scope of its activities to the point to which organized markets for labor will to a large extent take the place of the present uneconomic and haphazard methods of buying and selling of labor.

APPENDIX

California State Employment Service Statistics

IT IS GENERALLY agreed that a public employment service should be a source of valuable information concerning those who are seeking employment. Unless all unemployed workers register at the public employment offices, the statistics from this source will not give a figure of total unemployment, nor will there be any certainty that the characteristics of the group who are registered will be representative of the entire unemployed population. Nevertheless information as to the number and characteristics of those who are registered is essential both for the proper administration of the Employment Service and as a source of information for those who use the Service.

With the inauguration of a system of unemployment insurance, under which all insured persons who are unemployed are required to register at the public employment offices, statistics will become available as to the entire insured population who are unemployed. It thus should become possible to publish data as to the number and characteristics of a known group of the unemployed, and, furthermore, to compute the per cent of unemployment among insured working people by geographic area, occupation, industry, and such other categories as appear to be significant. This would be a valuable addition to other indices of industrial activity, and it might serve as an indication of declining and growing industries and occupations which could be used as a guide to those about to enter new fields of endeavor.

Statistics should also be available as to the placement activities of the Employment Service. Such statistics would provide evidence as to how far the Employment Service is fulfilling its ultimate function of bringing together workers and jobs. Mere numbers alone are not, however, sufficient. Placement statistics must be available in terms of industries, occupations, geographic areas, and in terms of permanence of the employment.

Since, in the last analysis, employers' orders limit the placements which can be made, statistics relating to this field of activity should also be available. Placement statistics are an index of employers' orders filled, but they furnish no evidence as to orders received and not filled. Employers' orders broken down by industries, occupations, and reasons for orders not filled are essential as a basis for judging the effectiveness of the Employment Service in meeting the specifications set up by employers in various industries. It would also serve as a check on the availability of workers with various qualifications in the active file of the Employment Service.

The analysis of statistical data included in this study was, of necessity, based on available series,[1] and no attempt could be made to check the accuracy of the statistics except where discrepancies were found in material from various sources.

From 1935 to 1938 the following general types of statistics were available for the state as a whole and for the offices in the counties included in this study:

1. Registrants in the active file
2. New applications
3. Placements

Registrants in the Active File.—Monthly statistics of the total active file are available from 1935 through 1938. At intervals during this period, inventories of the active file were

[1] The California State Department of Employment issued the following publications for varying periods of time: *Operations of Offices*, May 1935–June 1938; *Classified Reports of Applications and Placements*, May 1935–March 1938; *Analysis of Placements by Occupation and Industry*, March 1937–October 1940; *Employment Service Placements by Age Groups*, July 1939–October 1940; *Field Office Activities*, September 1938–March 1940. In August 1940 a new publication was issued: *California Employment Security Survey*.

made and the registrants were classified in terms of industry, occupation, and age. These breakdowns were published only for the country as a whole, but through the courtesy of the U.S.E.S. in Washington figures for the State of California and for certain offices were secured.

Some discrepancies were found between the total active file figures published by the California State Department of Employment in *Operations of Offices* and those secured as a result of the U.S.E.S. inventories of the active file. These discrepancies were, at least in part, due to differences in dates within the month at which the active file was counted by the C.S.E.S. and by the U.S.E.S. for the inventories. In a number of instances, however, the discrepancies were too great to be accounted for by the difference in dates. In some months the divergence between the two sets of figures amounted to more than 10,000, and sometimes the inventory figure was larger and sometimes smaller than that found in *Operations of Offices.* Both the state and the federal offices of the Employment Service were asked for information which would clear up the discrepancies. Their answers can best be given in their own words. The following quotation is from a letter written by W. H. Stead, Associate Director for Standards and Research of the U.S.E.S., February 1, 1939:

> Certain minor discrepancies arose from the differences between preliminary totals first issued in the general summary reports and the final totals secured by machine tabulation of the actual individual records. Still other discrepancies of a relatively minor extent are due to operating conditions in the mechanical tabulating unit, where in a few instances punch cards were omitted or inadvertently duplicated.

An interoffice letter from S. T. Russell, Statistical Supervisor, to H. M. Huff, Research and Statistics Officer, California State Department of Employment, January 24, 1939, stated:

> The one specific case for which I have requested an explanation . . . was for the inventory of July 1937. On this particular inventory 12,000 more registrations were shown in the Hollerith tabulations than we

had shown in our inventory list. As this amounted to a little better than a 6 per cent error of the total active file, I requested an explanation from Washington and was advised by them that, as they were in a hurry to have the results of the inventory, they had added to the file all new applications taken during the elapsed interval from the last inventory and had removed the cards for all regular placements . . . without waiting for the submission of our inventory and making a check of the numbers submitted. They included in their analysis all cancellations, that is, cards for applicants who had been removed from the active file for any reason other than complete placement of regular duration. As I do not know any means by which we could correctly ascertain what the actual should have been, their explanation was accepted and no attempt was made to reconcile.

Another statement in this letter also throws some light on the problem:

A list of numbers would be received from Washington stating that they were unable to locate punched cards for the numbers shown and . . . in quite a few cases when the lists were cleared with the local field office involved, they advised that certain numbers should not have appeared in the inventory.

The State Department of Employment in California also pointed out that in some instances the differences were due to clerical inaccuracies in Washington, a fact which was also mentioned by Dr. Stead.

It was obviously impossible, on the basis of the above statements, to determine the relative degree of accuracy of the two sets of active file figures. Both will of necessity be used in the analysis of the active file, since the C.S.E.S. monthly figures give only the total active file, whereas the U.S.E.S. inventories furnish, at certain times, breakdowns by industry, occupation, and age. As a result of the discrepancies mentioned above, the discussion of the total active file will be based on figures which differ from the totals in the tables which characterize the active file in terms of industry, occupation, and age. Clearly either one or both of these totals is incorrect, and thus both the totals and the distributions by industry, occupation, and age must be interpreted as approximations.

New Applications.—Figures as to the number of new applications each month were published by the C.S.E.S. in *Operations of Offices* and in *Classified Reports.* There were only a small number of discrepancies in these two sets of figures, the largest being about 300 in September 1935. An explanation of this and other discrepancies was given in an interoffice letter from S. T. Russell to H. M. Huff, March 30, 1939. This letter stated that the figures published in *Operations of Offices* were compiled in California, and those in *Classified Reports* were the result of Hollerith tabulations made in Washington. In one instance a check was made in Sacramento, and it was found that the Hollerith tabulations had failed to count 301 new applications in the Berkeley office. Since the discrepancies between these two sets of figures were small, they are perhaps unimportant.

Placements.—Placement statistics for the period from May 1935 through 1938 were available in several sources and in a number of forms. The two monthly publications of the C.S.E.S., *Operations of Offices* and *Classified Reports,* contain placement statistics—the former, merely total placements; the latter, various breakdowns such as relief status, age, and industry. In addition, placement statistics are published in *Monthly Labor Review* and in *Employment Service News,* a publication of the U.S.E.S., and occasionally in special surveys such as *Filling Nine Million Jobs.*[3]

It seemed reasonable to assume that identical monthly statistics of placements of the public free employment service could be drawn from any of the above sources. This, however, did not prove to be the case, and very large divergences were found in the first year of the period under discussion.

The series taken from *Operations of Offices* and from *Classified Reports* from May 1935 to April 1936 sometimes differed by as much as 25,000. From May to October 1935 the figures

[3] United States Employment Service, Division of Standards and Research, *Filling Nine Million Jobs.*

from *Operations of Offices, Monthly Labor Review,* and *Employment Service News* were identical, and in this period there was agreement between *Classified Reports* and *Filling Nine Million Jobs.* From November through April 1936 *Monthly Labor Review* and *Employment Service News* again agreed, but they differed from both *Operations of Offices* and *Classified Reports,* although they approximated those appearing in the latter publication. From May 1936 to the end of 1938 all of the published placement statistics, with minor exceptions, agreed.

It was essential to attempt to account for the discrepancies between the various series of placement statistics and to secure a series which would most closely represent the placement activities of the C.S.E.S.

In the comparison of the placements reported in *Classified Reports* and in *Operations of Offices* for the early part of the period, it appeared probable that some large group had been omitted from the latter publication. Investigation proved that placements on relief work projects had been omitted from the series published in *Operations of Offices.* The Sacramento office explained this by the fact that the U.S.E.S. form for reporting a summary of activities, from which *Operations of Offices* statistics were compiled, was set up in such a way as to exclude this part of the work of the office, whereas the report form from which *Classified Reports* were compiled required a report of all placements, both relief and nonrelief. From April 1936 relief work placements were included in both *Operations of Offices* and in *Classified Reports* as long as these placements remained a responsibility of the C.S.E.S.

On the basis of the above information, it appeared reasonable to expect that if relief placements were added to total placements as given in *Operations of Offices* and also to the placement figures published in *Monthly Labor Review* and in *Employment Service News,* identical series would be obtained. These additions did not, however, produce identical figures, and letters were written to the California Department of Research and Statistics in Sacramento and to the U.S.E.S. in an effort to determine the reasons for the discrepancies. The state office accounted for the differences, in some instances, by failure to include C.C.C. placements in relief placements and, in others, by errors in tabulations from Hollerith cards in Washington. The U.S.E.S. stated that they were due to differences in counting by the C.S.E.S. and the machine tabulation in Washington.[3] The state office attempted to reconcile the figures as found in *Operations of Offices* and *Classified Reports* and furnished the writer with a corrected series which will be used in this study since it appears to be the most accurate information available.[4] A breakdown of placements by industry, occupation, and age for the years 1936 to 1938 was also obtained from the State Department of Employment. There are slight discrepancies between the totals shown in these tables and the corrected figures for total placements. The differences were, however, so small as not to warrant a complete recount of placements by industry, occupation, and age. One further comment should be made in regard to the industrial and occupational statistics. The industrial classification included two categories of relief work placements, and, since these are not properly industrial categories, they were excluded from the tables showing industries represented by placements. Workers on relief projects, on the other hand, were given an occupational classification, and thus they are included in the tables showing occupations in which placements were made.

Evaluation of Statistics.—It must be obvious to the reader that, although a mass of statistical data is available as to the activities of the C.S.E.S., compilation of statistical series was rendered difficult because of discrepancies between the various published figures. As has already been pointed out, some of the

[3] Letter from W. H. Stead, February 1, 1939.

[4] These figures are not found in any published report.

differences could be accounted for and corrections made, but in other cases divergences remained which were apparently due to errors in counting in one or the other of the series. It must be remembered that the C.S.E.S. was under great pressure in the period 1935 to 1938, and that it is not surprising that difficulties arose in statistical reporting as in other activities of the Employment Service. It is, however, significant that there appeared to be little realization of the importance of accurate reporting and analysis of statistics for the purpose of guiding the administrator. The offices in the metropolitan centers had statistical departments with a statistician in charge, whereas in the smaller communities the statistical work was frequently the responsibility of a junior clerk or junior interviewer, who in some instances was reported to be entirely uninterested in keeping any records. In all of the offices visited, it appeared that the statistical reporting was looked upon as just so much paper work. There was little concern with accuracy or with discrepancies between various reports from one department. For instance, in one office reports were available as to orders filled and placements by department. The two did not agree, and yet there was no interest in correcting what must have been an error. One statistician, on the other hand, said, "There is too much emphasis on accuracy of individual items; slight errors are unimportant and, furthermore, will be compensating." This appears to be a dangerous point of view unless evidence were available that errors would not be cumulative instead of compensating.

There was an impression on the part of some of the people interviewed that the pressure for a good record of placements led to a padding of figures. It was impossible to investigate placements and thus check the validity of such statements. However, there appeared to be considerable evidence that a variety of arrangements existed through which placements that were not strictly Employment Service placements were included in the statistics of this organization (see pages 149–150).

All the available evidence seems to point to the conclusion that there were deficiencies of various kinds in the Employment Service statistics. In part, these deficiencies were in terms of failure to compile, within a reasonable time, information on such subjects as employers' orders or to furnish individual offices with statistics as to the industrial and occupational characteristics of the registrants in the active files and of workers placed, so that the information would be useful for administrative purposes. It should also be pointed out that the statistics were usually published without any analysis or interpretation, which in many instances made them useless in the hands of administrators, who either lacked the time or the ability to interpret statistical tables.

It has been pointed out that there were certain inaccuracies in the Employment Service statistics. How great these inaccuracies were it is impossible to determine. Minor inaccuracies may be unimportant in terms of analysis, but unless the Employment Service personnel is made aware of the importance of accurate statistics to be analyzed for administrative purposes, and unless accuracy is tested from time to time, it is likely that reporting will be considered merely as paper work possibly with a view to making a good showing with little relation to the facts of the case. If this is the case, the result will be statistics which are so inaccurate as to be useless.

www.ingramcontent.com/pod-product-compliance
Ingram Content Group UK Ltd.
Pitfield, Milton Keynes, MK11 3LW, UK
UKHW040234290926
15471UKWH00002B/181

9 780520 351929